Capital in the Mirror

SUNY series in New Political Science

Bradley J. Macdonald, editor

Capital in the Mirror

CRITICAL SOCIAL THEORY AND
THE AESTHETIC DIMENSION

Edited by

Dan Krier and Mark P. Worrell

SUNY
PRESS

Published by State University of New York Press, Albany

For information, contact State University of New York Press, Albany, NY
www.sunypress.edu

Library of Congress Cataloging-in-Publication Data

Names: Krier, Dan, 1965– editor. | Worrell, Mark P., editor.
Title: Capital in the mirror : critical social theory and the aesthetic
    dimension / editors, Dan Krier, Mark Worrell.
Description: Albany : State University of New York Press, 2020. | Series:
    SUNY series in new political science | Includes bibliographical references
    and index.
Identifiers: LCCN 2019016748 | ISBN 9781438477756 (hardcover : alk. paper) |
    ISBN 9781438477763 (pbk. : alk. paper) | ISBN 9781438477770 (ebook)
Subjects: LCSH: Critical theory. | Capitalism—Social aspects. | Capitalism
    in literature.
Classification: LCC HM480 .C37 2020 | DDC 142—dc23
LC record available at https://lccn.loc.gov/2019016748

10 9 8 7 6 5 4 3 2 1

Contents

Acknowledgments

The editors thank Bradley J. Macdonald, series editor for the SUNY Series in New Political Science, and Michael A. Rinella, senior editor at SUNY Press, for their support and guidance. We wish to thank colleagues at Iowa State University who supported the 2016 Symposium on New Directions in Critical Social Theory, especially Chester Britt, Chair of the Department of Sociology; Beate Schmittmann, Dean of the College of Arts and Sciences; Arne Hallam, Associate Dean of the College of Liberal Arts and Sciences; Chad Gasta, Chair of World Languages and Cultures; Heimir Geirsson, Chair of Philosophy and Religious Studies: and Christopher Hopkins, Director of the Center for Excellence in Arts and Humanities. We thank Kevin Amidon and Giles Fowler for their thoughtful comments on several chapters. We also extend our gratitude to faculty, students, and staff in ISU's Department of Sociology who assisted with the symposium or with the preparation of this manuscript, including Leanna Bouffard, Rachel Burlingame, Sydney Dighton, Deb McKay, Nick Van Berkum, and Danqing Yu.

The Mirror of Capital

An Introduction to Critical *Poiesis*

DAN KRIER AND MARK P. WORRELL

Critical theorists periodically anticipate the demise of capitalism like presumptive heirs in detective fiction; they hover around the sickbed of a despised aunt straining to hear the rattle of death in each phlegm-filled hack. The last such scene began a decade ago, when localized financial crises spread globally, leading to severe recession, septicemia, and a terminal diagnosis by critical theorists. In fiction, the dying testatrix often rallies to an inconvenient recovery that disappoints her heirs, embarrassed in their desire for premature burial. Similarly, capitalism perpetually rebounds from crises, evading the grave prepared for it by dismayed critical theorists. Of course, Marx dispelled all doubt about the dynamics of capital and its ultimate fate over 150 years ago: one fine day, in the fullness of time, it *will* die. Eventually, in the midst of some future crisis, one sickbed prognostication will turn out to be correct, and capital will go the way of all flesh. Critical theorists have always been right about capitalism's impending doom, but the manner and timing of its inevitable passing remains in question.

To comprehend capitalism's resilience, critical theorists have been led beyond the field of political economy onto the wider plain of aesthetics. Critical theory first ventured into the aesthetic dimension when Eduard Fuchs completed his pioneering historical-materialist analyses of Western popular culture (Amidon & Krier, 2017). This foray continued

1

in Lukács's wide-ranging cultural criticism (1966), in the writings of
Adorno, Horkheimer, Benjamin, Kracauer, and others associated with
the Frankfurt School (Worrell, 2008), and in Bakhtin's sociological poetics developed through readings of Rabelais and Dostoevsky (Bakhtin &
Medvedev, 1985). In the late 20th century, Marxist literature studies pro-
liferated outside of social science (Eagleton, 1976; Swingewood, 1977),
perhaps most prominently by Frederic Jameson (e.g., 1981). Cultural
sociologists also wrote about film, music, and other aesthetic products
(Inglis & Almiri, 2016; Williams, 1995), including those that indexed
and helped promote movements for progressive change (Eyerman &
Jamison,1998). Though approaching culture from a dizzying array of theoretical positions within sociology, few maintained contact with Marx or
critical theory. We face then a double problem: Cultural sociology has
failed to be critical, and critical theories have failed to be sociological,
occupying a niche position in the humanist fields of literary and film
studies.

The approach taken by literary studies to human praxis is twofold.
On the one hand it involves the subjection of texts to hermeneutical
interrogation with an eye toward the creation of an array of emergent,
relative, and playful readings. On the other hand, it is concerned with
the dynamics of an intertextual web unfolding across time and space. In
such approaches, texts are not so much the work of particular authors
(who "died" sometime after modernism, but no one knew it before Der-
rida), but autonomous creations of history carrying contingent authorial
attributions. Zizek's (1999) assorted self-referential works are typical of
critical theory as practiced in literary and film studies in that Marx is
refracted through psychoanalytic theory to focus upon ideology to the
exclusion of political economic dynamics.

What cultural studies, hermeneutics, and *Zizekianism* have in
common is what we might call an ontology problem that fails to rise
above subjectivism or goes off the rails into transcendentalism. Zizek,
for example, combines both "sins" whereby his work relies on the paradoxical fusion of psychological reductionism (there is no big Other,
merely individual psyches trying to "get off" as best as they can) and a
structural transcendentalism of the unconscious. Zizek's designation for
his ontological position is one of "transcendental materialism," but this
would presuppose a countervailing *empirical idealism* as its mirror opposite,
both of which are alien to the social realism we find in Hegel as well
as Marx and Durkheim, the founders of modern sociology.

The chapters in this volume were originally written for the Symposium for New Directions in Critical Social Theory at Iowa State University in June 2016. This biennial gathering of sociologists, philosophers, political scientists, and cultural theorists has grown from modest beginnings into an ongoing, formally structured workshop aimed at the reinvention of critical social theory and critical sociology. In this book, critical social theorists reexamine cultural reflections of capitalism in iconic prose, poetry, and photography to locate decisive contradictions and emancipatory possibilities concealed within our historical past and contemporary moment.

A catalyst for this book was Thomas Piketty's (2014) *Capital in the 21st Century*, an academic blockbuster that energized debates on capitalism and inequality. Piketty's book charted unequal income distributions with detailed time-series data and was most compelling when Piketty looked up from the gray plain of statistics to find capitalism's dynamics already theorized in full color by 19th-century novelists Honore de Balzac and Jane Austen. These writers depicted fictional characters whose intimate decisions about love were conditioned by calculations of expected returns: leisurely marriage to wealthy partners versus earnings from professional work. Piketty found that his statistically labored argument had been prefigured a century earlier in the ethical calculus of fictional strivers for patrimony through matrimony. By looking in the mirror of literature, Piketty's view of capital sharpened to reveal social distortions that arise when returns to wealth exceed rewards from work. The connection between inequality and aesthetics is decisive because when a population becomes radically unequal a gulf opens between individuals and groups and, where there are separations and divisions of this nature (alienation), they undergo moral inversions and transformations: Where there were once individuals and citizens, the good in other words, there now appears to be an opposition between the good and a morally impure remainder. Radical inequality, in other words, always already entails an aesthetics of evil—a distortion in the collective moral optics nestled in the heart of neoliberal social reorganization and institutional dissolution. These distortions appear to us as aestheticized objects, things, and weird reflections in politics, economic transactions, religious devotion, and culture. Along with cinema, literature and poetics contain the potential for social critique.

Aesthetic objects, crafted as poetic reflections of the contradictory world that they inhabit, are simultaneously theorized and theorizing. Like

Piketty, this book follows Karl Marx, Max Weber, Emile Durkheim, and Sigmund Freud (among others) into the fields of aesthetic culture to locate condensed imagery and fresh insight into the workings of capitalist modernity. This book begins at the point where Piketty's brief cultural turn ended by systematically exploring the aesthetic dimension for reflective visions of capital that would be difficult, if not impossible, to obtain through even the most rigorous statistical analyses and the juggle of lifeless variables. While Piketty focused on wealth inequality, this book is addressed to a much wider range of problems at the frontiers of critical social theory, including alienation, anomie, accumulation crisis, ecological collapse, empire, financialization, ideology, state power, and warfare, as well as emancipation, human flourishing, and social regeneration.

The chapters in *Capital in the Mirror: Critical Social Theory and the Aesthetic Dimension* work closely together to analyze contemporary capitalism through the prism of classic works of fiction and film renowned for their aesthetic artistry. Each chapter generates clarifying syntheses of acclaimed imagery and cutting-edge critical social theory. Famous narrative elements—Ahab's pursuit of the white whale in Melville's *Moby-Dick*; demonic summonings, perverse desires and productive frenzy in Mann's *Doctor Faustus*; the socially electrified bodies of Whitman's *Leaves*; dystopian projections of current sci-fi cinema—appear here as stylized but distorted reflections of social life within capital.

Theoria beyond Praxis: Critical *Poiesis*

This book is grounded in a reconsideration of Aristotle's (see also Arendt 1958) ancient distinction between *praxis* (theoretically informed political activity as an ethical end-in-itself) and *poiesis* (creative production as means to sustain an ethical *oikos*). *Poiesis* as creative production points to emancipatory activity beyond and distinct from the political horizon. In Plato's *Symposium*, discussed at length in Lacan's seminar on transference (2015), Diotama provides a profound definition of the poetic realm: "all creation or passage of non-being into being is poetry or making, and the processes of all art are creative; and the masters of arts are all poets. . . . they are not called poets, but have other names" (Plato, 1902, pp. 497–498). Agamben (2016), like most critical theorists, privileged *praxis* as a superior and honorific arena of human *energia* precisely because it is addressed to politico-ethical ends, while *poiesis* (labor, work, or *ergon*) is disprivileged since aimed at *oiko-nomic* production. The cultural privileging of praxis over *poiesis* is central to Veblen's (1899) critical analysis of leisure class activity (political, military, destructive, honorific, status-seeking) as superior to but dependent on working-class production (economic, productive, technical, craftsmanship). In contrast, Fromm (1973) distinguishes between *productive-biophilic* cultural action that emphasizes potency, the capacity for loving production in the furtherance of life, and *destructive-necrophilic* cultural activities, impotent, unproductive, focus on power over others that thwarts life.

Most Marxists and critical social theorists think of themselves as engaged in politically charged *praxis*, working toward capital's collapse in unrecoverable crisis or searching for openings that lead to fantasized revolutionary situations. Society after-capital is often imagined as either automated production by robots or as a society composed only of labor. Work either vanishes entirely into the unethical shadow of robot producers (repressed into the social real) or is projected into the sublime (the surreal) under a regime of Lukacs-esque labor-fetishism populated by the heroic Workers. Marx himself imagined a future where humans acquire freedom from *poiesis* (permanently turned over to the robotic general intellect) so that they can dedicate themselves full time, without cessation, and without limit to politico-ethical praxis. Worrell and Krier (2015) note that Marx's utopian postrevolutionary imaginary continues the Aristotelian privileging of politico-ethical praxis over economic-productive *poiesis*. Following Weber, we view *poiesis* as more than mere labor (Arendt's *animal laborans*) or pure "use of bodies" (Agamben 2016) but as an ethically significant realm of activity in its own right: intellectually engaged, cooperative, and life-furthering.

To avoid falling into the trap set by revolutionary, praxis-oriented, "Beautiful Souls," the chapters in this book suggest that after-capitalism must result from the negation (*aufhebung*) of capital, not just tearing down, but "cancelling upward" while preserving what is productive and biophilic. While others theorize revolutionary praxis, we theorize the *poiesis* of after-capital, comprehending what must already be there, inside of capitalism, such that the negation of domination results in a worthwhile, democratic, life-furthering society. While many Marxists fantasize automated/robotic production technologies as important foundations of after-capital, we suggest that subversive subjectivity (widespread democratic social character rather than reactionary/necro-philic/authoritarian social character), and a deeply ingrained, enduring cultural commitment to productive "callings" are much more important.[1]

What does the distinction between praxis and *poiesis* mean for crit-ical social theory? While waiting to deliver the *coup de grace* to capital, what can be done to build subjects capable of enduring the freedoms and possibilities of after-capitalism? What can be done to build a firewall to limit reaction and re-barbarization? Critical *poiesis* as important adjunct to praxis and theory, with goal of building culture of self-chosen, coop-erative *creative work in callings*—moving toward others (Horney) to work together in creative production. Rather than draining *poiesis* away while filling the world with *praxis*, perhaps better to reconstruct subjects/cul-ture so that *poiesis* is a way of life and *praxis* (political struggle/factional discord/ power-over others) kept to a minimum, an intervention of the Big Other that "comes and goes."

Outline of the Book

The book is divided into two sections: the first devoted to shadowy images of domination and alienation (Twilight), the second to prophetic visions of transformation (Dawn). Twilight opens with Tony Smith's chapter, "An Insane Book, an Insane Country, an Insane System: *Moby-Dick*, U.S. Hegemony, and the Catastrophe of Capital." U.S. capital seized a dominant position in the capitalist world market first in whale oil and other by-products of the whale's carcass. Melville's detailed depiction of the various phases of the particular capital circuit of a particular unit of capital in this sector illuminates the general direction world history would take in the century to come: U.S. capitals would come to dominate most of the important sectors in the global mar-kets. Ample investment capital would be available, along with a racially and ethnically diverse labor force of diverse skills and a high level of collective energy, intelligence, and creativity. The most technologically advanced means of production would be put in place. A competent supervisory apparatus capable of overseeing complex and sophisticated labor processes would be found. Persons with the highest level of tech-nical skills, immense energy, and unremitting dedication would be found to manage the production process as a whole. And in crucial sectors U.S. capitals would face few demand constraints, producing commodities for expanding markets. While the demise of the whaling industry would soon follow *Moby-Dick*'s publication, the book is a poetical prophecy of coming U.S. hegemony in the world market. The novel, however, is also a poetic sibling of the theoretical critique of "the American century" in specific and the reign of capital in general. A series of unresolvable (and irresolvable, within the confines of a capitalist order) antinomies haunt Melville's text. The workforce must be skilled and engaged, but its voice cannot be heard. Technologies serving capital's end can support some forms of human flourishing, but it will be partial and precarious at best, with a risk of catastrophe never far away. And these technologies can be diverted to other ends; the technical rationality meant to be subordinate to capitalist rationality can be distorted by the substantive irrationality of those supposed to be capital's agents. Last but certainly not least, the insane drive to accumulate as much capital as possible, as fast as possible, will invariably deplete resources at a faster rate than they can be replenished and generate wastes at a faster rate than they can be processed. Natural organisms must pay a high price if they fail to establish and maintain an appropriately symbiotic relationship with their environment. The destruction one particular whale inflicts on the particular ship called the Pequod prefigures the fate of our species if it fails to overthrow the yoke of capital.

Christian Lotz authors the second chapter, "Marxist Aesthetics, Realism, and Photography: On Brecht's *War Primer*." In this chapter, Lotz conceptualizes critical aesthetics in connection with a theory of society that problematizes the distinction between the socially visible and invisible. By reconsidering Marx's method in *Capital*, Lotz argues that the modern problem of rendering the invisible visible, especially representing capital from an artistic point of view, originates in Marx's philosophy and in Marxist methodology. Lotz argues that one could read the entire problem of Marx's genetic concept of social categories as an aesthetic problem. Lotz tests this thesis in reflections upon a case study, Brecht's *Kriegsfibel* (*War Primer*), first published in 1955 in the GDR. In this work, which takes the form of "photo-epigrams," Brecht presents a history of World War II as captured in 81 photographic plates (taken from magazines) that display main figures and atrocities from the second world war. These images are accompanied by their original caption along with brief four-line poems by Brecht. The principle of montage, in Brecht a proper *realist* practice, is central to this book, and was developed by Brecht from the 1930s forward, as one can see from his *Journals*. Brecht highlights the problem of how to represent abstract social structures such as war that is bound up with the problem of *remembering*. Put differently, the problem of (in)visibility can be found on virtually all levels of critical aesthetics: theory-capital-war-memory.

Patrick Murray and Jeanne Schuler author the third chapter, "The Poetics of Nihilism: Representing Capital's Indifference in Dickens' *Hard Times*." This chapter focuses on how Charles Dickens' novel *Hard Times* (1854) critically represented mid-19th-century industrial capitalism while uncritically adopting much of its mindset. Murray and Schuler argue that *Hard Times* is primarily about capital's shadow forms—indifference, egoism, utility, the calculative mentality—and only secondarily about its constitutive forms—value, money, wage labor, capital. They also argue that Dickens accepts key bifurcations involved in modern conceptions of reason and society and seeks only to harmonize them or ameliorate their ill effects. The chapter opens with thoughts from Hegel on art and philosophy as a counterpoint to Dickens' false split between reason and imagination. Dickens is disturbed to see the utilitarian mentality spread across the whole social order and wants to shield the political and the domestic spheres, especially education. At the root of Dickens' indifference to particularity is the reduction of the qualitative to the quantitative such that all life's issues become calculations. The novel centers on shadow forms of capitalism, above all, indifference: What does it matter? Shadow forms are easier to grasp; they disclose a world but not the mainspring of its dynamism. At the core of capitalist society is the emptiness of value, which shows itself in money. Not surprisingly, emptiness reverberates throughout the shadow forms and fosters a nihilistic mindset. Some shadow forms negate the reality of self and world more completely than the constitutive forms. By seeming to lack historical grounding, shadow forms appear irreversible. Constitutive forms, by contrast, are grounded in history. Tracing shadow forms to constitutive forms, then, keeps time from standing still.

The darkness continues with Dan Krier's chapter, "The Repressed Returns: Mann's *Doctor Faustus* and the Fugue of Capital." Krier interprets Thomas Mann's *Doctor Faustus* as critical *poiesis* about *poiesis*, a creative production about the work of creative production. Mann's *Doctor Faustus* is a cultural product of the highest caliber that highlights the centrality of ethically infused callings in capitalist modernity. Those with a calling produce high-quality creative work as the central realm of freedom, meaning, and ethical action. As in other of Mann's works, the vicissitudes of callings—the trauma of separation from primary ties and the equally traumatic installation in professional work—determines the life trajectory of characters. Adrian Leverkuhn, the symphonic composer at the center of the novel, wagers his soul with the devil, but unlike previous incarnations of the Faust story, he does not seek universal knowledge, unlimited pleasures, or unceasing experience. Instead, he seeks nothing more than creative potency in his calling. Leverkuhn lives an almost entirely sinless life while devoting himself ascetically to the most intensive creative work. Leverkuhn's fate is a strange sort of tragedy because he gets what he bargained for, a life without "cow warmth" but thoroughly infused with creative productivity and ethical achievement. Mann depicts a particularized calling as a magic circle of masterly productivity inscribed in the symbolic order, marked by desire, fantasy, and *jouissance*. Leverkuhn plays in and between three symbolic orders—philology, mathematics, and theology—before finding his calling as a master of a fourth symbolic order, musical composition. Mann's ability to "write music," to detail the immanent (rather than transcendent) structure of tonality, harmonics, polyphony is unparalleled. The book details symbolic effects of the calling, shaping organic responses and imaginary projections at the coordinates of the vocational order. Finally, and most important, *Doctor Faustus* depicts history's dialectic as a fugue-like "insistence of structure" in which motifs, even when repressed, return in variant form. This should give pause to critical theorists who desire after-capital: We need to be careful lest the thing we destroy returns in even darker form.

Dawn breaks with a second chapter by Tony Smith, "'Shakespearean Politics' and World History." While contemporary literary criticism remains fascinated with Shakespeare's personal political views, Smith views his plays as extended thought experiments on the vicissitudes of political rule. The first part of his chapter explores three main political themes that Smith isolates in the Shakespeare's plays. These themes, repeated across the history plays, present political authority as (1) determined by power struggles between competing elites rather than by a natural order, (2) maintained by normatively questionable means (e.g., deceit, subterfuge, brute force), and (3) "normally" oppressive of subordinates and failed contenders to power. Smith then speculates on conclusions that reasonably follow from these themes regarding the essential nature of the political sphere. Since we cannot claim anything about Shakespeare's own political views, Smith refers to these theses and

conclusion as a form of "Shakespearean politics." Shakespearean politics
are grounded in a worldview that is neither a conservative endorsement
of traditional political authority nor an endorsement of a radical political
alternative. Instead, it centers on the fundamental ethical irrationality of the political realm, and the idea that the normative satisfaction
that cannot be found in politics must be sought instead in the private
domestic sphere, where the great dramas of reconciliation of husband
and wife, parents and children, birth and death, are played out. From
this standpoint the greatest political dramas in world literature endorse
an apolitical mode of being in the world, a combination of critique
and acceptance. Smith ends his chapter by returning to the plays to
construct and defend an alternative, critical version of "Shakespearean
politics." Smith asserts that underneath Shakespeare's deep pessimism
is an affirmation of the reality status of normative advances. He argues
that the mirror function of cultural products like Shakespeare's plays
conditionally contributed to normative advances in the past and might
again contribute, under the right conditions, to normative advances in
our time. This alternative Shakespearean politics underscores the possibilities for normative advances that makes critical social theory and
praxis worth pursuing.

The sixth chapter is authored by Michael J. Thompson, "The Radical Implications of Hölderlin's Aesthetic Rationalism." Thomas Mann
wrote that "all would be well in Germany . . . the day that Karl Marx
reads Friedrich Hölderlin." Thompson's chapter tests Mann's proposition,
noting that Hölderlin's is not well known to critical theorists and, what
is known, has been overshaded by Heidegger's existentialist reading of his
work, resulting in the image of an impractical Romantic without political relevance. Thompson returns to Hölderlin's aesthetic-philosophical
project that engaged the dilemmas of modern reason that forced us to
make a choice between one-dimensional life of domination and unrealized potential and a new multilayered way of living, thinking, and
feeling encompassing the full potentialities contained within nature.
Thompson reveals Hölderlin's aesthetic theory as a more holistic and
ambitious conception of rationality than the predominant *Aufklärung*
ideas prevalent in his time. Hölderlin's conception of aesthetic reason
provides a deeply anti-reificatory conception of rationality and human
reflection that provides the framework for a theory of the "good" and
truth that can help expand the concept of critical agency and contribute to a critical theory of human reflection and judgment. Hölderlin's

problematic was similar to Horkheimer and Adorno's *Dialectic of Enlight-enment*. It is man's separation from nature—and hence his separation from himself—and his domination of nature—and hence his system-atic domination of himself—that Enlightenment reason has spawned. For Hölderlin, the Enlightenment is therefore a necessary but deficient development in human culture. It requires that we expand the circle of reason—expand it to the extent that is encompasses beauty as well as truth. That our ability to know truth is only possible once we can experience the absolute, the "unconditioned," and overcome the radical separation between the subject and the object. Once this is done, a new man will emerge: a new form of subjectivity, of agency, of culture, society and a true kind of freedom. In the end, Hölderlin's critique of modernity is not a regressive, Romantic movement to the past, but an aesthetic-philosophical vision far wider than the narrow Enlightenment conception of the rational subject.

Chapter 7, authored by James Block, is entitled "From Mirror to Catalyst: Whitman and the Literature of Re-Creation." The forces of social transformation are in need of a vision that integrates the great achievements of the modernist age and dialectically locates them within a greater vision of human possibility. Progressive social theory has mis-understood its project as rejecting every category of liberal discourse and lexicon. For liberalism as a modernizing movement first generated the categories of liberation and then turned them in ways that undercut their emancipatory potential. Its goal became to insulate modern pop-ular society from their full unveiling and expression in order to protect the new post-theological common Author in a popular body politic—Society—from the full dynamic and dislocations of an individualizing modernity. Progressive theory, in order to renew and further advance this liberating dynamic begun by liberalism, must once again offer a vision of emancipation, truly evolved conceptions of individual and individu-alism, autonomy and freedom, development and self-development and self-realization, consent and genuine democratic citizenship, recognition and self-recognition. This chapter contends that the fulcrum through which to lift us into the age of emancipation lies in the poetry of Walt Whitman. Whitman knew the power of literature advocating in Dem-ocratic Vistas for poets of the new to lead the way as only literature could (once religion was gone) to create the characters, selves, and identities that would help Americans and others shape themselves for full democratic life. Poetry could as no other form of expression as well call each to the journey in a popular age where all were to be included by forging new selves. Poetry (as literature), in other words, was a form of activism and an agent of transformation.

The immense significance of Whitman for understanding the relationship between critical social theory and critical *poiesis* is underscored in a chapter by Mark P. Worrell and Dan Krier entitled "The City of Brothers." Whitman was not "merely" a poet but, as others have noted, also a social philosopher working in the Hegelian vein and even a 'social scientist' of sorts, juxtaposed to Marx and Durkheim. At the level of social ontology Walt Whitman solves a number of problems that plagues naive realism as well as the intersubjective hyper-fluidity at the heart of pragmatism that rebels against anything like a social absolute. The "Cosmic Walt" (objectified in *Leaves of Grass*) represents a kind of Hegelian vision of the absolute spirit that resists reification while also rooting individuals in a universal moral matrix that persists beyond fleeting interactions that, as Marx would say in reference to the accidental value form, come and go with each transaction.

Harry F. Dahms takes us out of the world of literature and into contemporary cinema in the ninth chapter, entitled "Critical Theory, Sociology, and Science-Fiction Films: Love, Radical Transformation, and the Socio-Logic of Capital." As a distinctive tradition, the critical theory of the Frankfurt School emerged for the stated purpose of tackling a confounding challenge: to scrutinize the logic of capital as it manifests itself in politics, culture, and society, in order to discern and delineate the gravity concrete sociohistorical circumstances exert on efforts to illuminate the constitutional logic underlying modern societies. While the original program of critical theory stressed the need to scrutinize how, in modern societies, economic logic and social logic are interlinked in specific and seemingly unfathomable ways, the commitment of critical theorists to confront these challenges has been weakening with each subsequent generation. As a genre located in the field of tensions between politics, culture, society, and the capitalist economics-economy nexus, science-fiction films have been playing a most paradoxical role in perpetuating, amplifying and concealing the logic of capital, while also drawing attention to and criticizing the centrality of those tensions to modern life. Especially since the late 1990s, through their importance to the film industry, science-fiction films have been fulfilling a key role in supporting the logic of capital. On the other hand, by relaying a type of subversive and largely overlooked message relating to the link between love and radical transformation, science-fiction films also have been broadcasting, as it were, the social, political, cultural, and ecological destructiveness of the logic of capital. By both recognizing explicitly and explicating the peculiar message about "love" that is built into and at work in the narrative structure of most acclaimed science-fiction films, the opportunity opens up to access an aspect of modern societies that has been neglected in social, political, and philosophical thought (including critical theory), and in both Marxist and Marxian discourse: the entwinement of the system of modern social relations and the logic of capital. This neglect has been detrimental to both theoretical probity—to think is supposed to be "unthinkable" to members of modern societies, and to practical relevance—to conceive of practical and political strategies that are "unimaginable" as long the link between the logic of capital and the system of modern social relations implicitly is taken for granted in all efforts at critical reflection. Appreciating explicitly the message about love and radical transformation in science-fiction films reveals a powerful aesthetic vision of the modern age and opens up perspectives on the future that have been—and are supposed to be, from the vantage point of the existing social economic structures—too audacious for social scientists and social theorists to entertain with any measure of seriousness.

Mark P. Worrell's chapter "Magical Marx: Objective Method and Aesthetics" examines the dialectical method that Marx uses to accomplish three important things from the standpoint of our problem: first, the subversion of the reified and alien nature of the commodity; second, the dialectic moves the thing, discursively, into the arena of contested objects that have to legitimate their existence with reasons; and finally, the dialectic weaves together a third, irreducible and objective perspective (constellation of judgments) from the sublation of its shuttling back and forth between the twin dead ends of materialism (the concrete) and idealism (the abstract). *Capital* is a masterpiece of analysis whereby the bourgeois sacred (money, commodities, and capital) is exposed via analytical inversion to be not holy but an *unholy* nightmare resting on the brutalization and exploitation of the laboring classes. Marx theoretically "kills off" the new god of modernity and appears to restore workers to a place of honor. However, a few things muddle this accomplishment. First, postcapitalist relations are nowhere in Marx's writings made coherent or even plausible. Analytical dissection cannot be separated from the larger problem of distinctions and setting things aside—anything set aside or excluded (Marx and Durkheim) are either reduced to profanity (devaluation) or undergo moral inversions of one kind or another and only the magician of cultural anthropology can control these doublings. The "magical" moment of dialectics is necessary but insufficient on its own as a critical sociological method because, on one hand, it leads to total disenchantment and possibly diabolical reenchantment when pursued to the end and, on the other, it fails to realize that magical negation already presupposes a "positive" but conceptually irrational moment. Without a conscious and conceptually plausible counter-dialectics that engages in an absolute reconstruction and, crucially, a synthetic reconstruction that does not function merely as a fatalistic restoration, the best we can hope for is social anarchy. Durkheim's sociology is presented as a way to sublate Marxist theory in such a way that society is still possible. For Durkheim, the program of sociology is not one of destroying the absolute (reducing the world to a "happy go lucky" world of pragmatic fluidity and hyper-constructionism) but rendering the collective representation, the substantial phantom known as the big Other, luminous and nonterrifying where it was once an opaque Thing of awesome and uncanny powers. We can have the absolute, a Big Mirage, without it being a big, nasty Thing casting unbearably long shadows.

∾

Since staring directly at gorgons turns the viewer to stone, the sound policy when approaching monsters is to view them in a mirror. Like Piketty, Marx, and many others, the theorists in this book know that approaching capital directly through quantitative data analysis generates lifeless statistical reports rather than living theory. Just as Perseus slayed the gorgon by looking at its reflection in his shield, our critique of monstrosity proceeds with a vision of capital in the mirror of culture. The great cultural products of the 19th and 20th centuries, from Brecht, Dickens, Goethe, Holderlin, Mann, Melville, Shakespeare, and Whitman, speak to us profoundly and advance our projects. Good cultural productions anticipate theory by generating apt representations of great imaginary power, images that are already distilled, with accidentals removed, and essentials placed in proportion. The most theoretical useful cultural products are imperfect mirrors that distort reality, enlarging some elements while shrinking others. The best *poiesis* theorizes with images and the best critical social theorists—from Marx to Piketty—have relied on literary and artistic creations to complete their work. We aim to reorient critical theory so that *poiesis* supplements praxis in the ongoing project to negate capital.

Note

1. On the subversive subject, see Zizek, 1999: 247–260; on the reconstruction of social character as a crucial project of critical theory, see Fromm, 1973; Reich, 1946, 1949; Adorno et al., 1950; Worrell, 2003; Krier and Feldmann, 2016; Worrell and Krier, 2015.

References

Adorno, T. W., Frenkel-Brunswik, E., Levinson, D. J., & Sanford, R. N. (1950). *The Authoritarian Personality*. Oxford, UK: Harper.

Agamben, G. (2016). *The Use of Bodies: Homo Sacer*. Translated by A. Kotsko. Stanford, CA: Stanford Meridian.

Amidon, K. S., & Krier, D. (2017). The constellation of social ontology: Walter Benjamin, Eduard Fuchs, and the body of history. In D. Krier & M. P. Worrell (Eds.), *The Social Ontology of Capitalism* (pp. 235–262). New York, NY: Palgrave Macmillan.

Arendt, H. (1958). *The Human Condition*. Chicago, IL: University of Chicago Press.

Bakhtin, M., & Medvedev, P. N. (1985). *The Formal Method in Literary Scholarship: A Critical Introduction to Sociological Poetics*.Cambridge, MA: Harvard University Press.

Eagleton, T. (1976). *Marx and Literary Criticism*. Oakland: University of California Press.

Eyerman, R., & Jamison, A. (1998). *Music and Social Movements: Mobilizing Traditions in the Twentieth Century*. Cambridge, UK: Cambridge University Press.

Fromm, E. (1973). *The Anatomy of Human Destructiveness*. New York: Holt, Rinehart and Winston.

Horkheimer, M., & Adorno, T. (2007). *Dialectic of Enlightenment*. Stanford, CA: Stanford University Press.

Inglis, D., & Almiri, A.-M. (eds.). (2016). *The Sage Handbook of Cultural Sociology*. London, UK: Sage.

Jameson, F. (1981). *The Political Unconscious: Narrative as a Socially Symbolic Act*. Ithaca, NY: Cornell University Press.

Krier, D., & Feldmann, T. (2016). Social character in Western pre-modernity: Lacanian psychosis in Wladyslaw Reymont's *The Peasants*. In D. Krier &

M. P. Worrell (Eds.). *Capitalism's Future: Alienation, Emancipation, Critique* (pp. 175–216). Leiden, UK: Brill.

Lacan, J. (2015). *Transference: The Seminar of Jacques Lacan, Book VIII.* Cambridge, UK: Polity.

Lukacs, G. (1966). *History and Class Consciousness: Studies in Marxist Dialectics.* Cambridge, MA: MIT.

Piketty, T. (2014). *Capital in the 21st Century.* Cambridge, MA: Harvard University Press.

Plato. (1902). *The Dialogues of Plato, Vol. 1.* Translated by B. Jowett. New York, NY: Scribner's.

Reich, W. (1949). *Character Analysis.* New York, NY: Farrar, Straus and Giroux.

Reich, W. (1946). *The Mass Psychology of Fascism.* Oxford, UK: Orgone Institute Press.

Swingewood, A. (1977). Marxist approaches to the study of literature. *The Sociological Review, 25,* 131–149.

Veblen, T. (1899). *The Theory of the Leisure Class: An Economic Study of Institutions.* New York, NY: Macmillan.

Williams, R. (1995). *The Sociology of Culture.* Chicago, IL: University of Chicago Press.

Worrell, M. P., & Krier, D. (2018). Atopia awaits! A critical sociological analysis of Marx's political imaginary. *Critical Sociology, 44*(2), 213–239.

Worrell, M. P. (2008). *Dialectic of Solidarity: Labor, Antisemitism, and the Frankfurt School.* Chicago, IL: Haymarket Press.

Zizek, S. (1999). *The Ticklish Subject: The Absent Centre of Political Ontology.* London, UK: Verso.

PART I

TWILIGHT

Chapter 1

An Insane Book, an Insane Country, an Insane System

Moby-Dick, U.S. Hegemony, and the Catastrophe of Capital

Tony Smith

Introduction

All art is social. But art can be social in countless ways. A realist novel depicting modern capitalist society must place its characters in relationship to circuits of money, if only briefly or implicitly. As Thomas Piketty has brought to our attention, in Jane Austen's works the government bonds, rent extracted from tenants, and investments in slave plantations that generate the income of the gentry are usually left in the background, despite their crucial role in determining who can marry well and who cannot. Similarly, in Balzac's novels "the fact that land (like government bonds) yields roughly 5 percent of the amount of capital invested is so taken for granted that it often goes unmentioned. Contemporary readers were well aware that it took capital on the order of 1 million francs to produce an annual rent of 50,000 francs" (Piketty, *Capital in the Twenty-First Century*, p. 53). A main theme of *Middlemarch* is the contrast between indebted heirs of the landed aristocracy, doomed by the expropriating power of financial capital, and the ambitious sons of

19

lower orders—whose adaptation of the latest scientific and technological improvements to agriculture proves they are deserving of true love.

Aesthetic quality cannot be measured by the accuracy of a work's reflection of the social world. Nonetheless, no artistic achievement of the highest order fails to say something profound about the world beyond the covers of a book, the frame of a painting, the marks on a stave. When Marx returned throughout his life to Shakespeare and Balzac, his love of literature and his powers of critical social analysis were simultaneously enriched.

Melville's *Moby-Dick* deserves a place on the shelves of critical theorists alongside Shakespeare and Balzac. I cannot hope to convey here its astonishing exuberance of language, profound mixture of tragedy and comedy, multileveled symbolism, or any of its other striking aesthetic features. I shall instead simply mention some themes in the work that resonate with the concerns of critical social theorists, aware that this is but one dimension of a multidimensional novel (and not adequate to that one dimension). As we shall see, these themes go far beyond the income streams to the wealthy that Piketty focuses on.

Whaling was just one among many sectors of the U.S. economy in the mid–19th century, its demise fated to begin not all that long after the 1851 publication of *Moby-Dick*.[1] Melville, however, discerns the universal in the particular. His detailed depiction of specific features of the whaling industry illuminates general factors of the U.S. economy at that historical moment. Writing in a period when the U.S. had barely entered the world stage, his creative shaping of setting, characters, plot, and dialogue, within Ishmael's vast interior monologue vividly depicts the strengths that would enable the United States to become the hegemonic power in the century to follow. This claim is defended in the first part of this chapter.

We also find in *Moby-Dick* a close attention to the unresolved (and unresolvable) tensions and shortcomings at the core of the U.S. capitalist project. Melville's work prophetically anticipates the horrors these tensions and shortcomings will inflict. Readers receptive to this dimension of the work may find themselves forced to ask whether the project of U.S. capitalism and, ultimately, the reign of capital, must be abandoned. These themes are explored in the second part of the chapter.

In a very obvious sense, Melville was no critical social theorist. In another sense, however, he may well be the greatest social theorist the United States has produced. He is surely the author who best conveys the full insanity of the U.S. project of constructing an empire of capital (Wood, 2003).

A preliminary remark on the writing style of *Moby-Dick* is in order. The book is shot through with an energy, an exuberance, a rushing forward that echoes the energy, exuberance, and drive to rush forward characterizing United States capitalism in its ascendency. This quality sets it apart from works like *Remembrance of Things Past* and *Ulysses*, which are similar to *Moby-Dick* in important respects. They too have a vastness of scale, seamlessly combining biological, psychological, sociological, economic, political, religious, and cultural themes in one immense stew. They too examine the invisible bonds tying surface events of the present to long-forgotten past moments. And, like *Moby-Dick*, they too obliterate the supposed division between "high" and "low" culture. But neither France nor Ireland was about to seize the center stage of world history when they were written, and that social fact lurks within the prose. In both cases, the writing is somehow detached while engaged, abstract while concrete, introspective while depicting actions. Melville's masterpiece, in contrast, is somehow engaged even when detached, concrete at its most abstract, and pointing to action even when most introspective. There is a sense in which for Proust or Joyce the least interesting thing about an action is the action itself. For Melville, in contrast, the thoughts of characters matter because of what they do or don't do.

To some extent these differences can be explained on elementary biographical grounds. It is simply impossible to imagine Proust or Joyce signing on to serve as a sailor on a whale ship as Melville did, let alone jump ship and live with a Polynesian tribe. But even a reader who knew nothing of Melville's life would surely notice how every sentence of his text, even those describing repose, has a restlessness, a dynamism, that works of comparable genius lack. For works of similar stylistic energy we must turn to the epics of Homer or the plays of Shakespeare. Perhaps it is no coincidence that they too were written on the cusp of a new historical period, when their authors' societies were also about to begin a mad rush to claim a central place in the world order of the time.[2]

Moby-Dick:
A Prophetic Anticipation of U.S. Hegemony

The world order of Melville's time was a capitalist world order. The circuit of capital discussed by Marx in *Capital 1* provides a useful framework for organizing the following discussion (see Figure 1.1).

$$\text{Capital} \longleftarrow$$
$$\longrightarrow \text{M} - \text{C} - \text{P} - \text{C}' - \text{M}'$$

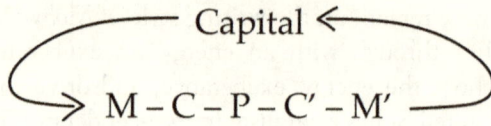

Figure 1.1. Marx's circuit of capital.

The circuit begins with capital in the form of investment money (M), used to purchase commodity capital (C), the commodity inputs required for commodity production. These inputs fall under two headings: means of production—machines, tools, building, etc.—and the very special commodity, labor power. The production process (P) follows, where laborers transform some means of production (raw materials, partially finished goods) with the aid of others (tools, machinery). A new set of commodities (C') then emerges as the output. Finally, for capital to be accumulated, the produced commodities must be sold for a greater sum of money (M') than the initial amount invested. Marx terms the entire circuit a *valorization* process, since it is essentially a process of producing and appropriating *surplus value* (the difference between M' and M). The main circuit of capital is located on the macro (aggregate) level of total social capital (Moseley, 2015). Its constitutive elements are the circuits of individual units of capital.

Regions that seize hegemonic positions in the world market have competitive advantages over other regions in the various phases of the capital circuit (Arrighi, 1994). Reading *Moby-Dick* with this in mind brings to the fore Melville's powerful sense of the factors underlying the United States' rise to the center of the global economy.

M (Investment Capital)

The novel is set at the supreme height of U.S. whaling, the first non-agricultural sector of the U.S. economy to win a dominant position in the world market.[3] Few other forms of investment promised investors higher profits.

The two leading investors in the *Pequod*, Peleg and Bildad, are both retired captains who worked their way up from the lowest positions on whaling ships over the course of many years. The captains represent a historical moment when investment funds were much more closely tied to their sector of origin than would soon be the case. The fortune they left for their heirs—assuming the tragedy of the *Pequod* did not ruin them—would likely not have been so tied to this particular sector, and so better reflect the intrinsic mobility of money capital—the inherent universality—of capital. (Their heirs will probably also be freed from the need to spend their lives working in such an onerous vocation.).

No specific figures are ever given regarding the capital required to purchase and equip a ship like the *Pequod*. A considerable amount was clearly necessary, since it exceeded the reach of the two main investors, men of substantial wealth.[4] The former captains, however, have made a large enough proportion of the total investment to obtain complete control over its allocation. In years to come, a much lower proportion of the total investment will often suffice to obtain substantial control over a unit of capital.

In the book we also do not learn about the specific financial practices that enabled the investment capital of the two retired captains, the trust funds of widows and orphans, and the idle money capital of other investors to be aggregated into the M that begins the individual circuit of capital involving the *Pequod*. We do not need to. The important point is that a framework was in place allowing a plurality of distinct monetary sums to be aggregated together to take advantage of opportunities when promising high returns.

The general lives in the particular. The first beachhead in the U.S. project of establishing a global empire of capital under its hegemony was won by ships like the *Pequod*. Melville depicts how small towns on the New England coast were able to mobilize the relatively high level of investment capital required to outfit a fleet of whaling boats scattered across all the oceans of the planet, and thereby dominate one of the most profitable sectors of the world market for decades.[5] In this respect *Moby-Dick* presages how U.S. capitals in the period to follow proved able to amass the investment capital required to fund activities with the greatest profit potential as they emerged.[6]

Commodity Capital$_1$: Inputs (C)

The initial investment capital (M) is value in the form of a particular concrete thing with the strikingly universal and abstract property of "generalized exchangeability." Determinacy is introduced into the circuit of capital when there is a metamorphosis from capital in the form of money, able in principle to purchase any commodity whatever, into commodity capital (C) with the purchase of the specific commodities necessary for a specific production process. In the case at hand, these were the commodities necessary at that point in time to produce whale oil and other by-products of a whale carcass.

Besides the ship itself and all its parts (riggings, etc.), the tools used to hunt whales and to forge and repair implements, the vast vat for boiling blubber to transform it into oil, containers to store the oil over the course of a multiyear voyage, and so on, all needed to be purchased. In so far as these commodities could be reused in subsequent expeditions, they counted as fixed capital. The provisions of food and drink, along with all the parts of the ship and tools that needed to be replaced either during or at the conclusion of a voyage (worn-out sails, hurled harpoons, etc.) fell under the heading of circulating capital. They too represented a major capital investment.

As already noted, the ability of the U.S. economy to mobilize the capital investment required to outfit a vast fleet of whaleboats, each undertaking multiyear voyages, can be taken to illustrate the general capacity of U.S. capitals to mobilize the investment required to power a long period of economic growth, eventually culminating in usurping a position at the center of the world market. A national economy, however, does not grab a position of hegemony in the world market simply because it can access a critical mass of investment capital. (If that were all that were required, Britain would have maintained its hegemonic position far longer than it did.) The investment capital must in addition purchase means of production enabling levels of productivity higher than the social average in the world market to maintained for an extended period.

Melville makes it clear that the means of production employed in the U.S. whaling industry were second to none. The *Pequod* itself was not new. But it was customized for maximum effectiveness, technologically unsurpassed by any other floating fixed capital encountered in the book. We can assume that this judgment is meant to be extended to other relevant forms of commodity capital as well. The smith's forging of Ahab's harpoon (Chapter 113) is as symbolically overdetermined as everything else in this symbol-drenched work. Whatever else it might signify, Ahab's technological advantage over other whale hunters prefigures the technological advantage in means of production U.S. capitals proved able to claim in crucial sectors of the world market.

Of course, without a toolmaker there would be no tool. The smith is not presented as someone with theoretical training or even a significant degree of intellectual capacity. But he does possess the embodied ("tacit") knowledge that is such a crucial element in the effective use of technologies. This he has in abundance. The point can be generalized. For units of capital in a region to claim a hegemonic position in the world market, an abundance of labor power with an abundance of high capabilities must be available for hire. In their rise to global preeminence U.S. capitals were able to mobilize the labor force it needed for rapid capital accumulation. The *Pequod* can be seen as an aesthetic representation of this historical dynamic.

The past training of the labor force on the *Pequod* is as striking as its level of expertise, and played a noteworthy role in developing that expertise. Ishmael is a paradigmatic representation of a flexible worker, tied down neither by place nor previous occupation, restlessly moving from one opportunity to another, adding to his general skill set from job to job. The pattern asserted to hold in the whaling industry—rural agriculture laborers left to work on the great northern canals, where they received training and experience making them attractive hires for the whaling industry—can be seen as a particular variant of a general pattern of skill development holding in the U.S. economy as a whole to the great benefit of U.S. capitals.

Moby-Dick also depicts how U.S. enterprises could call on international recruits whenever native-born Americans were either not available in sufficient numbers or lacked the requisite specialized skills. The crew of the *Pequod* reflected the massive waves of immigrant labor (including, of course, involuntary slave labor) that U.S. capitals were able to take advantage of, another crucial factor in their rise to global hegemony.[7] Not one of the harpooners, whose skills are obviously essential to the success of the voyage, is a white citizen. Two come from outside the capitalist core, Queequeg from the Peloponnesian islands and Daggoo from Africa. The third, Tashtegot, is from the "internal periphery," a tribe of native Americans almost entirely displaced from Martha's Vineyard. Each of these truly exceptional persons would have been leaders in their own communities, had they remained and their communities remained viable. We are reminded that hegemony in the world market can be established and maintained in other ways besides direct imperialist force (although that is the backstory of Daggoo, the descendent of slaves). A "brain drain" where energetic and highly talented individuals leave their home societies for the sake of the opportunities available to them in the center can also further the interests of "the all-grasping western world" (87/414).

The officers on the *Pequod* hold a "contradictory class location" in the ship's hierarchy. They are charged with organizing and disciplining the crew, and enjoy the (supposed) privilege of eating with the Captain.[8] They are to receive a larger share of the proceeds of the voyage as well. And yet in another sense they too are workers. They generally work alongside regular sailors, with their supervisory activity mostly limited to providing the coordination necessary in any complicated labor process.

In the course of the book we get to know two officers, Starbuck and Stubbs, very well. They are both flawed human beings, the one trapped by a conformism making him incapable of resisting Ahab's command, the other defined by a cynicism that is no less acquiescent to power. Dispositions to conformism and cynicism in those holding supervisory positions proved extremely useful to the complex organizations established by U.S. capital in its period of ascendency. Melville rightly intuits that there will be no shortage of candidates for these positions willing to accommodate hierarchical power in return for a few perks. No less importantly, Starbuck and Stubbs are highly competent, possessing extensive formal and informal technological knowledge and embodied tacit skills. A broad stratum of supervisors with these capabilities was a necessary precondition for the "American system of manufacturing" that soon enabled the United States to become an industrial global power. *Moby-Dick* suggests that it will be there when needed.

Capital in Production Process (P)

The production process in the whaling industry can be understood in a broader and a narrower sense. In the broader sense of the term, the entire voyage made up the process of producing whale oil and associated commodities. Sailing the ship to the regions where the whales were hunted was obviously as necessary to produce whale oil as hunting and processing the whales; so too the time spent transporting oil back to harbor. Whale oil stored in the hold of a ship in the middle of the ocean is not yet a commodity in the full sense; it only truly becomes a commodity when available for sale. However, it is also possible to define the production process more narrowly, proceeding from the first sighting of the prey and the lowering of whale boats, through the hunting and killing, towing of the carcass back to the ship, dismembering it, burning blubber to extract oil, storing of the oil, and, perhaps, cleaning of the ship in preparation for the next round of activity.

The entire book unfolds in the course of a single production process in the broader sense of the term, while the longest section of the book is devoted to the production process in the narrower sense. Four dimensions of the latter will be discussed here: the complex combination of coercion and consensus in the workplace, the allocation of risks there, its temporality, and the relationship between collective social labor undertaking the production process and the social wealth it generates. All concern matters of great import to the valorization process of capital.

Consent and Coercion. In the first pages of the book, Ishmael discusses the disciplinary authority exercised over seamen, and explains his own justifications for submitting to it. He believes, first, that he can retain his equal dignity by maintaining an active internal subjectivity, treating his subordinate status in the production process as a merely external matter. Ishmael also naturalizes and universalizes this subordination, insisting that everyone is equally subject to external coercion in one form or other. ("Who ain't a slave?" he asks.) Since this is as true of people at the top of the workplace hierarchy as it is for those in the lowest positions, a fundamental equality is maintained despite status differences.[9]

U.S. capitals could not have been as successful as they were during their period of ascendency in the world market without a certain degree of consent to their control over the production process. Defining autonomy as a matter of internal subjective life, while confusing social and historical forms of domination with ahistorical and natural ("metaphysical") constants of the human condition ("the universal thump") was crucial to the generation of this consent in the United States (and elsewhere).[10]

Of course, in hierarchical workplaces, coercion is never far away. On sea, as on land, the danger of the bounds of legitimate authority (as understood by those consenting to it) being overstepped was always present. Melville reminds us of this in the long digression—no mere digression—on the tale of the *Town Ho*, relaying both the ease with which authority can be abused on a ship and the support abusers were given by the law (Chapter 54). The *Pequod* itself is hardly a workers' paradise, even if the physical abuses we see on the ship are relatively trivial and comic.[11] When Ahab's personal authority does not evoke immediate compliance, his threats are compelling enough that no resort to actual violence is necessary. This too counts as coercion.

The Allocation of Risks

Physical violence was hardly the only threat faced by sailors in the production process in the broader sense. Ishmael notes that the slightest inattention while on watch can cause someone to plummet from the mast (35/173). (This fate later befalls an unnamed sailor on his first day of watching for Moby-Dick.) Typhoons and other extreme weather events, near-certainties in the course of a multi-ocean voyage, also warrant mentioned here.

Other risks are specific to the hunt. The only named character to suffer serious harm prior to the final catastrophe is Pip, a young African American boy on his first voyage. Pip jumped off the whaleboat in terror after his first face-to-face encounter with a whale's immensity. Although the beast had already been harpooned, Stubb, the officer in charge of the whaleboat, called off the chase to rescue Pip. Stubb angrily informed Pip this would not happen again. When uncontrollable fear led the adolescent to jump overboard a second time, Stubb was true to his word. Pip was left floating in the ocean as the *Pequod* and its whaleboats raced out of his field of vision in pursuit of their prey. While he was eventually rescued, Melville stresses how contingent this rescue was. No abandoned sailor could ever be assured he would be saved.[12] And it came too late; Pip went mad from suffering the invisible terrors of the ocean in solitude.[13]

It hardly needs to be said that the danger facing those who remained in whaleboats, engaging in intense battles with gigantic animals enraged by wounds, was enormous as the animal they fought. The dangers did not cease after the whale had been killed and returned to the boat. The vivid depiction of Tashtego dangling from a rope off the side of the ship, the rope held with one hand as he carves into the dead whale's head with the other, would have conveyed horrific risk even if he had not slipped and fallen into the dead whale's endless throat, condemned to a sure death had it not been for Queequeg's heroic rescue. No less striking is the image of Queequeg being lowered by rope off the side of the boat so that he can attach a hook to a dead whale, allowing its blubber to be peeled off and lifted to the boat for processing. As he does this, a small army of sharks voraciously feasts on the carcass. If Queequeg slips just a bit, the sharks will feast on him as well.

To this we can add the severe health risks from the toxic smoke emitted from burning blubber, and the danger from burning oil spilling from its pots as the ship is battered by waves.[14]

As readers, we can only marvel at the exceptional bravery and humor of a workforce faced with such a variety of truly monstrous threats.[15] The text asks more of us than this, however. We are invited to reflect on capital's general willingness to climb to the top of the world market on the bodies of those sacrificed in production processes. The risks imposed on whalers were more different in kind than in magnitude from those imposed on the builders of railways, bridges, or skyscrapers, or those working in the infernos of steel mills, the dungeons of mines, or in the midst of breakneck dismemberments in packing plants. The human sacrifices required for the triumph of U.S. capital were incalculable; capital floated on a sea of workers' blood.[16]

Political economists and their contemporary descendants defend returns on capital investment as a reward for risks undertaken. Marx's critique of political economy explains theoretically why this is a truly ludicrous idea. Melville shows the ludicrousness. Those with the "right" to appropriate any resulting profits from the *Pequod's* trip are safe in their New England mansions. Those facing horrors beyond the imagination of Dante receive a fraction of a fraction of a fraction of the wealth generated in the course of confronting horrific risks—if they survive at all.

The Politics of Time

Less dramatic—but in terms of costs to human flourishing, no less profound—dimensions of the production process are on display on the decks of the *Pequod* as well. The production process occurs in time: the time of the hunt, the time required to dismember the dead whale, the time required to extract oil from boiling the blubber, the time it takes to transport barrels of oil to storage, the time necessary to clean the deck in preparation for the next round. This time is capital's time, so to speak. The more it expands, the more the time humans require for sleep, recovery from extreme stress and exertion, personal projects, companionship, and so on, is restricted. If a new whale is sighted as processing a previous victim concludes, human time could be eliminated altogether for an indefinite period.[17] Few could physically endure such labor processes as they aged. Elderly seamen were discarded like whale carcasses when no more value could be extracted from their activities.

If we count the time of production as the entire time at sea, not all of it was the regimented, disciplined time of capital. There were long intervals where sailors were free to engage in pursuits of their own choosing. Ishmael is obviously a voracious reader. We do not know which of the vast number of works he refers to in the course of his narration were read while on the *Pequod*, and which were read before or after. But it is easy to imagine a huge heap of books from a vast and quite idiosyncratic range of genres piled disorganized around his bunk. Others engaged in scrimshaw engraving, carving astoundingly elaborate designs on whales' teeth. Melville's text suggests that a commitment to a complex labor process requiring the highest degree of concentration and skill is not incompatible with pursuing other endeavors with comparable seriousness. The more time to develop a range of capabilities, the less a worker is reduced to a mere cog in the machinery of production.

In retrospect, we can see that capital refrained from appropriating this time only because in the given historical circumstances it had no other option. Whenever the representatives of capital feel they can eliminate time that does not augment capital accumulation by filling in the pores of the production process, so to speak, they will attempt to do.[18]

Collective Social Labor. The production process on the *Pequod*, no less than the funds invested and the commodity inputs purchased with that money, is a phase in capital's circuit. Nonetheless, it is striking how much of the production process on the ship is self-organized by workers themselves rather than imposed by capital's representatives. Explicit commands are rarely uttered by officers. For the most part the shipmates appear to already know that they must do, how to do it, and how to coordinate their activities together to when they need to attain results that can only be attained collectively.[19] We see the power of this "commonalty" in hunts of the leviathans, where crew members would be lost without sufficient trust in each other. We see it in quotidian scenes when life and death are not at stake, such as the collective work of squeezing the lumps out of spermaceti extracted from the whale's head (Chapter 94).[20]

The role of cooperation in the production process is illustrated especially starkly in the rope attached to Queequeg as he cuts up a carcass that sharks are feasting upon inches below. Queequeg's fate depends on Ishmael, who must adjust the rope attached to Queequeg, depending on where he must slice next and where he is in relation to the sharks. The other end of the rope is attached to Ishmael himself; if he loses control and Queequeg slips off the slippery skin into the sea, Ishmael too will plunge into the shark-infested waters. Ishmael informs us that this arrangement was an idiosyncrasy of the *Pequod*, and not a common practice in the whaling industry. No matter. It is no mere picturesque detail added to increase the drama of the scene. As Ishmael's notes, it graphically depicts the general co-dependence of those engaged in the production process and, pushing the point even further, how co-dependence is "the precise situation of every mortal that breathes."[21] Marx theoretically established the ludicrousness of the claim that capitalist markets reward individual agents for individual contributions; there are no individual contributions that can be considered separately from collective social action. Once again, Melville shows poetically what Marx proved in theory. Every phase of the processing of the whale depicted in chapters 66 through 70 reinforces the point that the production process is undertaken collectively and characterized by mutual interdependence.

On first reading Queequeg's rescue of Tashtego after he slips and falls down a dead whale's throat (Chapter 78), it seems like a comic book superhero tale. Queequeg dives from the ship and descends deep into the ocean. On reaching the place where he calculates Tashtego has fallen, he cuts a hole in the corpse, reaches in, feels Tashtego's feet, turns him around, and pulls him out head first from the opening.[22] He then carries the limp but living body safely to the surface. We are surely meant to take Queequeg's extraordinary courage (along with his poised and generous character in more normal circumstances) as a pointed critique of white supremacy (Braune 2014; Rogin, 1979). But his actions here also provide an extraordinary illustration of ordinary life today: The production processes of complex modern industries involve a high degree of mutual interdependence. Melville here anticipates the Hart and Negri thesis that the multitude is the truly constituting power of modern society, as opposed to the constituted sovereign power of empire (Hardt and Negri, 2009).

Melville's text also shows how participating in shared labor need not force workers in the production process to lose their individual sense of self. Ishmael certainly hasn't. His curiosity and self-reflective nature, expressed in almost every sentence of the book, is not eroded as his friendship with Queequeg deepens, and as the experience of comradeship on the boat helps him transcend the narcissistic self-absorption and alienation from others expressed at the beginning of his narration.[23] The other characters we come to know in the course of the book—the officers, the harpooners, the carpenter, the blacksmith—all have their distinct personalities, their unique backstories. Their personalities remain distinct through the final moment of catastrophe, when Starbuck and Stubb face certain death in quite different ways, true to who they are.

Melville's extensive discussion of the production process on whale ships in the mid–19th century anticipates the period to come, when U.S. capitals were able to mobilize a collective workforce fully capable of undertaking production processes contributing to valorization (the transformation of M into a greater M') on an unsurpassed level. If we push this dimension of the novel just a bit further, we arrive in the vicinity of Marx's core idea that valorization is in fact nothing but the process of collective social labor producing wealth in an alien form.[24] And if we push matters just one further step, we approach the idea of self-managed workplaces as an alternative to the reign of capital. That, of course, remains unsaid in the novel. But as C.L.R. James first showed, it is there implicitly (James, 2001).[25]

As stated previously, the transportation of stored oil to market counts as part of the process of producing oil as a commodity. Once this process has concluded, the next phase in the circuit of capital can commence.

Commodity Capital$_2$: Output (C')

Melville could not have foreseen that whale oil was to give way to fossil fuels relatively soon after the publication of *Moby-Dick*, let alone the central role petroleum would play in the coming period. Nonetheless, Melville's portrayal of U.S. dominance of the whale industry foreshadows how (direct or indirect) control over flows of oil across the planet would become the heart of its geopolitical project.

Whale oil was a special commodity. Its biggest use was for lighting, in effect extending the day for households, businesses, and communities.[26] Like petroleum, however, the whale carcass was a commodity of commodities. The products that could be produced from the raw material provided by a dead whale included perfume, machine lubrication, scrimshaw, umbrellas, canes, handles, and even food (74/362).[27] Melville's references to this wide range of goods remind us just how crucial discovering the full range of petrochemicals and other petroleum-derived products was to the U.S. economy in the "long twentieth century."[28]

The range of products produced in the capital circuits of the whaling industry is a use-value consideration. But having use-values is only a necessary condition for a product to play a role in capital accumulation, not a sufficient one. For the circuit of capital to reach its imminent end the produced commodities must be successfully—that is, profitably—sold.

Valorized Money Capital (M')

The final stage completing the capital circuit is C'-M', when the produced commodity outputs are sold for more money than the initial amount invested. Ultimately the C'-M' phase is played out on the stage of the world market, a higher-order unity incorporating national economies within it. *Moby-Dick* presents two dimensions of this phase in the U.S. whaling industry of the mid–19th century. Both can be generalized to U.S. capitals in ensuing decades.

The first dimension can be introduced by noting that the world market has not generally been favorable to national economies specializing in the export of raw materials. Until very recently the greatest "value added" portion of the production chain has been located in regions where raw materials have been processed into products for final sale.[29] In its first decades the main export of the United States economy to the world market was cotton produced in slave plantations, destined to be exported to the British textile industry. The greater share of "value added" was appropriated in the latter, rather than the former.

For many readers, the chapters at the center of *Moby-Dick* devoted to the transformation of whale blubber to usable whale oil are the most tedious parts of the book. For the social theorist, however, these chapters are a bold assertion that a new power was arising in the world market, one that would refuse to merely provide raw materials (blubber) for others to process, but would instead process those materials itself, and thereby keep for itself the most profitable parts of the production chain.[30]

The importance of this point is reinforced when we note a second striking aspect of the C'-M' phase of the capital circuit in the whale industry. The gulf between production and sale—so troubling to units of capital in almost all other contexts—plays no role whatsoever in Melville's story. No one ever expresses any concern that the oil the *Pequod* returns with might not be sold for high profits. The only worries are that some of the vast number of barrels they have brought might not be filled, and that leaks in barrels might not be corrected in time to prevent significant losses.

We know now that Melville composed his book at the height of the whaling industry, and that demand for whale oil was soon to decline drastically with the shift to fossil fuels. Nonetheless, the book anticipates how the coming hegemony of the United States in the global economy will rest in good part on its advantages in the C'-M' phase of capital circuits. It is a tautology to assert that the economic growth of the country will tend to not be constrained if it efficiently produces the commodities most in demand in the world economy. The longer this state of affairs persists, the more likely it is that this region will become the hegemonic power in the world market. Whale oil and its associated commodities prefigure the manner in which control of fossil fuels and development of petrochemical-based industries allowed U.S. capitals to leap over the gulf between C' and M' easier than their main competitors.

The first part of this chapter has shown that Melville's work reflects the moment of world history when U.S. capitals ascended to dominance of the world market, a process that had just begun in his own day. His particular tale of a particular unit of capital in a particular and soon to be outdated sector poetically conveys the dynamic energy of a national economy with ample investment capital, access to technologically advanced means of production, a labor force of diverse skills, high collective intelligence, creativity, and initiative, and a committed and technically proficient supervisory apparatus, all of which made it capable of producing commodity products in high demand in the world market efficiently and profitably. From this standpoint, *Moby-Dick* is more than a work of tremendous poetical power. It is also a great work of social and historical analysis. As the second part of this chapter will show, it is a profound exercise in social critique as well.

The Antinomies of the Period, The Antinomies of Capital

The project of U.S. capitals in the mid–19th century and beyond, and of capitalism in general, is beset with irresolvable tensions and antinomies. These tensions and antinomies haunt Melville's text. They continue to haunt us today.

Ahab and the "Principal/Agent" Problem

It may be surprising that Ahab has not yet been discussed at length, given his stature as one of the most striking characters in world literature. Aspects of his story could have fit in the previous section. His life illustrates how those holding the most privileged positions in a corpo-rate hierarchy also pay a serious cost for the colonization of their time by capital. When his leg is destroyed during a first confrontation with Moby-Dick prior to the opening of the novel, there is no other "Ahab" apart from the whale hunter, no other self capable of finding solace in human relationships or challenge in other pursuits. There is only Ahab the Defeated Hunter, who must now become Ahab the Avenger to make good his humiliating maiming. Ahab's personal failure to avoid being consumed by his obsession is simultaneously the social failure to prevent an industry from colonizing so completely the time and subjectivity of those working within it. The formation of a complex person with Whitmanian multitudes has been ruled out. Those needed by capital will be incorporated within capital's circuits with a ruthlessness that Ahab's monomaniacal drive to kill Moby-Dick but palely reflects.

Ahab, of course, is not subsumed within capital circuits in the same way ordinary sailors or ship officers are. Bildad and Peleg granted him close to absolute authority on the ship. He is their agent, and they (and the other investors) are the principals in a principal/agent relationship. Melville writes at a time when most owners of units of capital were them-selves managers. In the whaling industry, however, those wealthy enough to be main owners were either not disposed to undertake—or no longer able to withstand—the rigors of a multiyear voyage. It would be decades before this split between ownership and control became entrenched in most leading industries. When units of capital in other sectors eventually institutionalized principal/agent relationships of this sort, an essentially a new type of social agent entered center stage, whatever parallels the agents of capital might have with those appointed to authority positions in previous social formations.

U.S. capital's rise to a position of hegemony in the world market required a qualified and dedicated managerial stratum, capable of run-ning complex and highly technical enterprises. Ahab spent much of his adolescence and almost all of his adult life in the industry, developing expertise in every dimension of the production process. His extremely high level of competence is never in question. He has sacrificed family life to develop this broad and deep expertise.[31] The technical expertise, dedication, and leadership skills that form the basis of Ahab's stellar reputation among the elite investors of Nantucket presage the success of U.S. capitals will enjoy in obtaining the services of highly trained and dedicated managers in their period of ascendency in the world market.

To accomplish the tasks assigned by the principals, agents must either share the same ends, or at least pursue ends that are broadly compatible with those of the principals. In the case at hand, the end that matters is capital's end, valorization. In a world where products needed for subsistence and a decent life generally take the form of commodities that must be purchased with money, the latter condition is usually met less spontaneously. The need to obtain monetary resources will tend to spontaneously make many ends agents pursue—including individual self-preservation, the fulfillment of my responsibilities to their dependents and so on—"naturally" coincide with capital's end, the self-valorization of value, since these ends of agents can generally only be obtained through participating in a circuit of capital aiming at valorization. Other sorts of ends—the desire of agents to develop their capacities and win the respect of family, friends, acquaintances, and the community at large—also "naturally" fit with the end of capital, since in a capitalist society contributing to circuits of capital is the primary way capacities are developed and respect of peers won in adult life.

Despite these tendencies, there is always a risk of agents developing ends conflicting with capital's. A ship captain must have delegated authority over the collective resources mobilized by capital, but at the end of the day there are no guarantees that this power will be used in a manner consistent with the role of an agent of capital. Technologies and workforces meant to serve capital's end can be diverted to other ends. No one would say that the principal/agent relationship in capitalism is necessarily more fraught than it was in, say, the feudalism depicted in Shakespeare's plays, where a king's aristocratic agents do not always grant the interests of the monarch primacy. But capital's abstractness tends to make the principal/agent relationship between those who allocate capital, and those who lead organizations dedicated to the pursuit of capital, more impersonal than they were in previous periods, leading agents to be less constrained by custom, traditional roles, or religious values.

This concern brings us to the heart of *Moby-Dick*'s plot, revolving around the dynamic set off when Ahab's end no longer coheres with capital's. Despite Starbuck's pleas, the extremely concrete and particular goal of the destruction of a particular beast has usurped the place where capital's abstract and general end of valorization should be.[32] As the agent of capital Ahab has at his disposal the natural and social forces that have been mobilized in the *Pequod* by capital investment. But he directs them toward an end that can be foreseen to be incompatible with capital's. Immense damage was done to the interests of the principals in the principal/agent relationship, the *Pequod*'s investors.

In capitalism, there are selection mechanisms to reward individuals (communities, nations, continents) that further or are at least compatible with capital accumulation, and to weed out those that aren't. Suppose Ahab successfully slaughtered Moby-Dick and returned to Nantucket. Once the story of the voyage became known, he would never have been given control of another ship by investors again, never given another chance to use resources put in place by capital to pursue ends conflicting with capital's.[33] Starbuck, whose devotion to family and contractual obligations fits perfectly with capital's end of valorization, would likely be promoted to Captain status to replace Ahab. But capital's selection mechanisms need time to work. The *Pequod* never returned to Nantucket; the selection mechanisms never came into play

The ship's captain is an early variant of the same social type as today's Chief Executive Officer of a multinational corporation, also charged with representing the interest of investors. Mythological resonances aside, there is an obvious parallel between a CEO who destroys the corporation in his or her charge out of megalomania and Ahab. The CEO driven to build an empire through mergers and acquisitions no matter how much the long-term interests of the corporation must be mortgaged to do it is a staple of the business press today. This too is a concrete goal that may effectively rule out the attainment of capital's abstract end. In hierarchical capitalist organizations, "value" (in the nontechnical, non-Marxist sense) can be created only under the leadership of managers. This gives them the power to dissipate "value" into thin air on a massive scale through hubris and mad projects.

If the immense concentration of power capital places in the hands of its main agents cannot be reliably checked by the investors who delegated that power, it is not likely to be adequately checked by those subjected to it. From this standpoint, the destruction of the *Pequod* and all its crew represents the destruction that unchecked managerial power can inflict on the social world in general when freed from effective oversight.

The point can be pushed a step further. The state does not play any direct role in *Moby-Dick*, although its law remains operating in the background. Whatever other tasks the capitalist state takes on, it must provide the preconditions for capital accumulation that are not provided by capital itself for one reason or another.[34] In this sense state officials are agents of capital every bit as much as the captains of a capitalistically owned ship, or the managers of capitalist firms. Reflecting on the destructive figure of Ahab from this perspective therefore raises disturbing questions about state officials as well. The success of capital requires that its agents have the concentrated power needed to fulfill their function, whether it is overseeing the production and distribution process, or providing the preconditions for accumulation capital cannot provide for itself. In both cases selection mechanisms can be established that systematically select for those who use this power effectively for capital's end, and systematically select against those who do not.[35] But in both cases these mechanisms take time to operate. In the meantime, considerable harm can be inflicted upon capital by state officials who, like Ahab, do not operate appropriately as agents in a principal/agent relationship. And here too, finally, the harms that can be inflicted on ordinary citizens subject to the authority of political elites can be catastrophic.

In the Cold War period, it was common to interpret Ahab as prefiguring fascist or Stalinist despotism.[36] These analogies are not implausible. But the straightforward facts are that he was appointed to his position by investors, and the hierarchical power he possesses was delegated to him to serve as their agent. The figure of Ahab can be directly read as a poetic depiction of the horrors those living in a capitalist society may suffer when capital's agents "go rogue," so to speak, and how few safeguards there are in place to prevent this from happening. A mad captain of a whaling ship can contravene the interests of capital and bring about the destruction of the ship and crew before the priority of "shareholder value" over the captain's personal agenda can be reaffirmed. A mad leader of a capitalist state with nuclear weapons can bring about the destruction of human society as we know it. That too would be against capital's interest. That too would nonetheless result from a power that had to be in place for capital to be accumulated, but which capital itself cannot fully control.

There is one final point to be made here. If the figure of Ahab serves as a warning to capital, it also serves as a warning to capitalism's critics. A charismatic authority refusing to be leashed to capital's end does not necessarily offer an acceptable alternative to the reign of capital. There is a long history of those engaged in struggle against capital supporting charismatic rulers who have resisted capital's imperatives. This history is often tragic.

Ahab's charismatic authority over the crew raises other issues as well of central import to critical social theory.

The Crew and the Limits of Democracy in "Democratic" Capitalism

Ahab is an extreme case. His authority explicitly disavows the legitimacy he would otherwise be able to claim as the agent of the *Pequod's* owners. But an abnormal case can bring out the abnormality of the normal. Ahab's despotism over the crew would be no less despotic if he had kept within the accepted confines of the principal/agent relationship.

From this standpoint, *Moby-Dick* can be read as a parable about the fundamental category mistake at the heart of modern society. Capitalism emerged from a historical process differentiating an apparently depoliticized sphere of free agreements among private individuals, on the one hand, and a political sphere where public power is exercised, on the other. In the "democratic" variant of capitalism exercises of public power are supposedly subject to public control through elections based on universal suffrage, competing political parties, and so on. Underlying the formally free agreements of labor markets, however, there is a form of social coercion. Those who do not own or control society's nonhuman productive assets are forced to sell their capacities to labor to those who do own them in order to gain access to the means of subsistence they and their dependents require. The terms of this sale force them to cede all claims to the social surplus to those with the money capital to purchase their labor power. How could a macrolevel social power enabling one class to control both the living labor of another and the surplus produced in the society be accurately described as "private" and "nonpolitical" in any truly meaningful sense of those terms? It cannot be. To think otherwise is to commit a category mistake. The democratic principle that all exercises of public power must be subject to public control simply cannot be adequately institutionalized in any variant of capitalism. Ahab's (abnormal) authority over the *Pequod* is a poetic illustration of "normal" capitalism, where those exercising authority in capital's name are not accountable to those over whom the authority is exercised.

Ahab's pursuit of the leviathan is not in the shipmates' objective material interest, even if we put aside the tragic end they all hoped to avoid. If the time spent hunting the object of Ahab's obsession meant they would return with less oil than they would have otherwise, their income from the voyage would be less than it could have been. If it meant they would be forced to spend a more extended time at sea to fill the available barrels, this additional work would not have brought additional pay. Ahab has no reason to care about such things.[37] They do. But these various risks "normally" imposed on seamen, and the various ways their time is colonized at great cost to their flourishing, would have all remained in place even if Ahab had been a perfect agent for Bildad and Peleg. The risks and cost were not lessened when Ahab ignored the dictates of the valorization imperative to further his own agenda. Other categories of threat were simply added.

Nonetheless, the crew acceded to Ahab's agenda.

Ahab dismissed the sailors as mere cogs in his machine. At crucial points in the narrative, that is exactly what they are (e.g., 37/182–83). Ishmael no less than others is swayed by Ahab's charisma, swept along by his furious demand to obliterate the thing he has come to hate.

I noted in the first part of the chapter that for U.S. capital to rise to hegemony in the world market, workers had to grant a sufficient measure of consent to the exercise of authority in the production process. *Moby-Dick* surveys a number of the most important forms this consent can take, and so anticipates how this crucial presupposition would be met.[38] The consent granted to charismatic authority when a leader's dictates directly conflict with working men and women's fundamental interests belongs on this list.

Moby-Dick does not provide readers with any reason to believe that either charismatic authority or the irrationality it injects into a modern world can be eliminated. The work shows how inordinate pride in the rationality of this world is misguided in other respects as well.

Technical rationality, the use of efficient means to pursue a given goal, can be found in abundance on the *Pequod*, from the embodied (tacit) skills of the carpenter, the blacksmith, the harpooners, and officers, to the formal and scientific knowledge of navigation and the behavior of ocean-dwelling mammals possessed by Ahab. It is found in abundance in modern capitalist society generally. Technical reason, however, is not self-contained. It requires an end that is not itself a mere technical means.

Capitalist rationality is a matter of selecting effective means to attain the end of capital accumulation. Important human ends can be furthered in the course of furthering capital's end. But Melville's masterpiece shows how the furthering of human ends in capitalist enterprises necessarily tends to be partial and provisional, due to impersonal coercion, the class bias in the allocation of risks, and the profound constraints on human flourishing imposed by capital's systematic colonization of time. It is hardly rational for those suffering these social costs to consent to the system of practices imposing them. The irrationality of charismatic authority is even more striking when a rogue agent like Ahab replaces the abstract, formal, and quantitative goal of valorization with a concrete, substantive, and qualitative goal that is clearly mad. And yet such consent is given nonetheless.

Melville forces us to confront questions most would rather avoid. Is there a general tendency in our society to submit to charismatic authority? Is it possible that our consent to such authority could bring us to a catastrophe analogous to the *Pequod*'s? It would be difficult to deny how strongly the novel suggests a "yes" answer to both questions, opening a path to apolitical pessimism Melville himself took after *Moby-Dick*.

But perhaps the book offers a glimpse of another path as well.

Moby-Dick powerfully depicts the limits of merely technical rationality, the too often invisible irrationality underlying capitalist rationality, and the blatant irrationality that charismatic authority can inflict on the social world. Ahab stands as one of the greatest exemplars of substantive irrationality in the history of literature. Is it possible to comprehend the limits of technical rationality and capitalist rationality, and the outright irrationality of charismatic authority, without having some implicit notion of *substantive rationality* as a point of comparison? Perhaps *Moby-Dick* can be read as a *via negativa* toward an understanding of substantive rationality. Just as medieval thinkers hoped to approach a better understanding of their God by comprehending more deeply what The Divine was not, we can reach a better understanding of what our society requires to avoid catastrophe by comprehending more deeply what is absent on the *Pequod*.

Consider the doubloon scene, perhaps the most graphic depiction in literature of consent to a charismatic authority leading the consenters to their doom. Before Ahab utters his first word, a key feature of the background social context has already shaped the discussion to come, making the culminating moment of acclamation far more likely than it might otherwise have been: Ahab captain completely controls the situation. Only Ahab's proposal to replace the ship's primary mission with another is discussed. Only arguments in its favor are spoken. How many on the ship, socialized into its hierarchical status order, could even imagine challenging him with a counter-discourse? Of those that could imagine this, how many of them could imagine withstanding the repercussions such an affront to the chain of command would evoke?

Starbuck recognized the folly of Ahab's agenda from the beginning. However, the status of the captain's authority in the given institutional setting did not leave any institutionalized space to publicly question Ahab's project, let alone revoke his authority. Starbuck mentions his concerns to Ahab in private. Unsurprisingly, they are immediately and scornfully dismissed. The paths for protecting himself and others from Ahab's irrational quest (Ahab must either be shot or put in chains) do not appear either viable or acceptable.

Now imagine a different social setting. Suppose Starbuck had been given a fair opportunity to express his position. Imagine he laid out the ways Ahab's agenda broke the contractual agreement with the ship's owners, and explained how Ahab's agenda would either risk lowering the crew's pay or else extend the period they would have to work to gain the same return. Suppose there had then been a chance for everyone to share reasons for and against the diversion to hunt the white whale. It is fully possible that Ahab's charisma would have still have carried the way, whatever anyone said. But it is also possible that the tragedy would not have proceeded on its course. Institutional frameworks matter. The same people with the same complex and contradictory dispositions and beliefs do not necessarily act in the same manner in different institutional settings.

Later, the crew as a whole comes to share Starbuck's worries, as the veneer of romantic heroism with which Ahab painted the pursuit faded. But an institutionalized social space for articulating these worries, or for revoking their previous acclamation of Ahab's project, or for removing him from his position of authority over them, was absent.[39] Unable to reconfigure the social space in the radical manner that would be required for these things to be possible, they instead withdraw into despondent silence as the catastrophe unfolds. At that point they are indeed what Ahab takes them to be, mere cogs in the machine he has set in motion.

What is lacking here is a social space enabling those who have acquiesced to a particular policy at a particular point in time to revoke that acquiescence at a later point, after a critical mass of them have come to believe that that the policy in question does not in fact further their legitimate interests. Such a space is lacking on the *Pequod*, as it is in other capitalist workplaces. The more gripping the consequences of its absence are depicted, the stronger the implicit defense of it. From this perspective, *Moby-Dick* may be considered one of the greatest defenses of deliberative democracy in workplaces and communities ever written.[40]

Ahab knows that while his means are rational, his end is not. He knows his project would not be considered reasonable by reasonable people, fair by fair people.[41] He cannot state his reasons publicly, but must rather disguise his insanely misplaced hatred behind the rhetoric of chivalrous quests. He knows he has no plausible response to obvious counterarguments, and so he must employ a variety of strategies to ensure they are not posed, including call and response engagement with the audience, promises of economic gain (the doubloon), theatrical spectacle (nailing doubloon to the mast, the grabbing of the lighting rod line in an electrical storm, creating a compass), and the ritual sealing of an oath with alcohol (Chapter 36). The measure of his awareness of how fleeting consent won by such tricks can be is the vehemence with which he proclaims the oath nonrevocable.

What does Melville's depiction of substantive irrationality suggest regarding what substantive rationality might look like? If a substantively irrational end is one that cannot be stated publicly, but rather depends exclusively on rhetorical subterfuge, spectacle, or ritual for its acceptance, this suggests that a substantively rational end *can* be stated publicly. It can be accepted as reasonable by reasonable people, as fair by fair people. This does not imply that substantive rationality is incompatible with rhetoric, spectacle, or ritual. It is fully compatible with the claim that rhetoric, spectacle, and ritual are necessary elements of social life. But if we hope to minimize our vulnerability to future Ahabs they must complement deliberative democracy; not replace it.

By giving us a glimpse of something close to the highest possible degree of substantive irrationality, *Moby-Dick* provides strong hints of what it would take to lessen its occurrence: (1) All matters of general concern must be subject to open deliberation. (2) It must be possible to revoke decisions when experience and further reflection reveal that they do not in fact further ends that reasonable and fair people would regard as reasonable and fair. (3) It must be possible to remove leaders who have shown themselves to be pathologically committed to their own private agendas whatever the social costs inflicted on those subject to their authority. (4) The reasons behind public policies must be capable of being stated and defended publicly. However much rhetoric, spectacle, and ritual shape political life, they cannot be the only determining matters.

The substantive irrationality of the *Pequod* was not solely due to Ahab's notable idiosyncrasies. The normal institutionalization of authority in capitalist workplaces came into play as well. This dimension of the novel suggests that the concentrated power exercised in the course of producing social wealth needs to be subjected to deliberative democracy no less than the concentrated power exercised in civic administration. Both are exercises of *political* authority in the only sense of the term that ultimately matters. Both must therefore be equally subject to the consent of those over whom the authority is exercised.[42]

Once this conclusion has been reached, the question whether there might someday be agents capable of establishing deliberative democracy in all realms where political authority is exercised becomes inescapable. Given the profound tension between capitalist social relations and deliberative democracy in the workplace we cannot expect those who are in effect personifications of capital to support this transformation. This group includes owners like Peleg and Bildad as well as agents, like Ahab, who are granted authority on the supposition that their voice will be the voice of capital. In contrast, it would seem that ordinary seamen, harpooners, and even the officers have a higher-order interest in bringing bring about a world where their first-order interests in flourishing could be taken into account far better than they are under the reign of capital. But here, as elsewhere, the implications of Melville's text are deeply ambiguous.

Moby-Dick does not give us any reason to think differences among members of the workforce can always be spontaneously resolved in a spirit of mutual respect. The book, written shortly before irresolvable conflicts over slavery led to the Civil War, continually reminds us how deep the racial divide within the collective workforce has been in the United States both economically and culturally.[43] The work depicts as well how religious, ethnic, and nationality differences can generate stark divisions among the workforce. As a result, a tendency for violence lurks just a little below the surface, ready to erupt on the slightest provocation. The racially driven knife fight about to occur between Daggoo and a Spanish sailor, halted only by the threat of imminent destruction by a typhoon, provides the clearest illustration (40/192). Agents of capital, rogue or otherwise, can be trusted to know how to manipulate those divisions for their advantage. We may assume that Ahab refrained from such manipulation only because his charismatic appeals made them unnecessary.

Moby-Dick, however, does not merely point toward divisions and conflicts among those subject to capital. Ishmael's lived experience points beyond them. When he first meets Queequeg, he reflects, "Ignorance is the parent of fear, and being completely nonplussed and confounded about the stranger, I confess I was now as much afraid of him as if it was the devil himself . . ." (3/24). He immediately comes to realize that "It's only his outside; a man can be honest in any sort of skin" (3/23). As ignorance is overcome through companionship with Queequeg, so too is the fear that underlies racism.

The Spanish sailor who hoped to knife Daggoo points to a possible future where working men and women remain divided by mutual fears. If we focus on Ishmael and Queequeg's relationship, however, a path opens up in the opposite direction. As far as future history is concerned, Melville leaves the alternative unresolved. From the standpoint of social ontology, however, the latter path has the greater claim. It is the collective social labor of shipbuilders, sailmakers, carpenters, blacksmiths, sailors, harpooners, and officers (among others) that creates social wealth. The fact that their activity is only allowed to occur when subsumed within a circuit of capital does not change this state of affairs. The capital that mobilizes their collective powers appears as the dominant subject of the society, imposing its ends on the social world. But it is a pseudo-subject, the alien form in which the powers of collective social labor appear. The day a critical mass of social agents institutionalize the priority of human ends will be the last day of capital's reign. *Moby-Dick* provides no reason to think this will happen automatically, or even that it will ever happen. But it provides every reason to think that another world is possible.[44]

The Revenge of Moby-Dick, the Revenge of Nature

For all its attention to human concerns, the title of the book is not *Ahab* or *Ishmael*. The main protagonist is a nonhuman animal, part of the natural world humans so often consider themselves separate from. Ahab is a paradigmatic instance of that attitude.

Ahab has no special nostalgia for his lost leg, and is not fundamentally motivated by revenging its loss.[45] What he cannot abide is the reversal whereby he, Moby-Dick's attacker, was himself attacked. Ahab's quest is as much metaphysical as it is an expression of personal pathology. His aim is to restore a cosmic order where human subjectivity and calculations define reality. Moby-Dick's resistance to the role Ahab assigned makes the white whale a surd, beyond the only framework for comprehending the world Ahab possesses.

This framework centers on *the* founding principle of modern Western political philosophy, the "natural" liberty of subjects to claim unowned objects. Ahab's mania is a particularly extreme and perverse form of the possessive individualism that capital "normally" generates and reproduces, projecting onto the world a crude ontology of subject and object. Every object in the world from the lowliest bit of inorganic matter to the most majestic animal is taken to be a thing capable of being possessed by the acquisitive subject, who then has the radical freedom to do with it whatever he (and we do primarily think of males here) chooses.

From this perspective, Melville's discussion of the distinction between "fast fish" and "loose fish" is no mere digression. The rules for distinguishing the two categories are the starkest possible expression of the notion of "justice in acquisition" found in Locke, Hegel, Nozick, and many other modern social theorists, reduced to its pure core:

> Yes; these laws might be engraven on a Queen Anne's farthing, or the barb of a harpoon, and worn round the neck, so small are they.
>
> I. A Fast-Fish belongs to the party fast to it.
>
> II. A Loose-Fish is fair game for anybody who can soonest catch it.
>
> . . . [P]loughed up to the primary rock of the matter, the two great principles laid down in the twin whaling laws . . . will, on reflection, be found the fundamentals of all human jurisprudence; For notwithstanding its complicated tracery of sculpture, the Temple of the Law, like the Temple of the Philistines, has but two props to stand on

(89/432–434).

Moby-Dick's continued existence is an affront to the radical freedom of subjects to take what we find in nature and transform it into as many commodities as human ingenuity can devise. Ahab's mad thirst for vengeance is simultaneously a mad insistence that the subject/object dualism capitalism projects onto the world must not be challenged.

Marx made three main points regarding the theoretical framework underlying Ahab's actions. First, it fundamentally misrepresents human being in the world. Humans are unlike other animals in their capacity to imagine a world different from what it is at a given moment, and to act in ways that bring about what had only been imagined before.[46] Nonetheless, in his early manuscripts Marx insisted that humans are part of nature, not "outside" it, reaffirming this view later in his discussion of the metabolic relationship between human activity and natural processes (Marx, 1981, pp. 958–959). The subject/object dualism at the heart of generalized commodity exchange is an ideological delusion. However much we confront nature as if it were a heap of objects "outside" us to be dominated, owned, transformed, traded, used, and thrown away, nature is not an alien realm external to us. We are ourselves physical organisms, and like all species must necessarily live out our lives within an environmental niche.[47]

Second, Marx noted that capitalist market societies ironically operate in a manner that inverts the very framework those within it are conditioned to accept as "natural." In capitalism, human subjects, defined in terms of the "natural" freedom to possess and use objects, are themselves treated as objectified means to further the ends of the true "dominant subject," capital (Marx, 1976a, p. 255). Melville (Ishmael) generalizes the point in a passage worth quoting at length:

> What are the sinews and souls of Russian serfs and Republican slaves but Fast-Fish, whereof possession is the whole of the law? What to the rapacious landlord is the widow's last mite but a Fast-Fish? What is yonder undetected villain's marble mansion with a door-plate for a waif; what is that but a Fast-Fish? What is the ruinous discount which Mordecai, the broker, gets from poor Woebegone, the bankrupt, on a loan to keep Woebegone's family from starvation; what is that ruinous discount but a Fast-Fish? What is the archbishop of Savesoul's income of £100,000 seized from the scant bread and cheese of hundreds of thousands of broken-backed laborers (all sure of heaven without any of Savesoul's help) what is that globular 100,000 but a Fast-Fish? What are the Duke of Dunder's hereditary towns and hamlets but Fast-Fish? What

to that redoubted harpooneer, John Bull, is poor Ireland, but a Fast-Fish? What to that apostolic lancer, Brother Jonathan, is Texas but a Fast-Fish? And concerning all these, is not Possession the whole of the law?

But if the doctrine of Fast-Fish be pretty generally applicable, the kindred doctrine of Loose-Fish is still more widely so. That is internationally and universally applicable.

What was America in 1492 but a loose-fish, in which Columbus struck the Spanish standard by way of waifing it for his royal master and mistress? What was Poland to the Czar? What Greece to the Turk? What India to England? What at last will Mexico be to the United States? All Loose-Fish.

What are the Rights of Man and the Liberties of the World but Loose-Fish? What all men's minds and opinions but Loose-Fish? What is the principle of religious belief in them but a Loose-Fish? What to the ostentatious smuggling verbalists are the thoughts of thinkers but Loose-Fish? What is the great globe itself but a Loose-Fish? And what are you, reader, but a Loose-Fish and a Fast-Fish, too? (89/434–435)

Marx never put it better.

Ahab senses that some sort of inversion has occurred that fundamentally threatens his own claim to be the "dominant subject" of his world. He even comes close to naming the force behind the inversion:

Forty years of continual whaling! forty years of privation, and peril, and storm-time! forty years on the pitiless sea! for forty years has Ahab forsaken the peaceful land, for forty years to make war on the horrors of the deep! . . . When I think of this life I have led; the desolation of solitude it has been; the masoned, walled-town of a Captain's exclusiveness, which admits but small entrance to any sympathy from the green country without—oh, weariness! heaviness! Guinea-coast slavery of solitary command!—when I think of all this; only half-suspected, not so keenly known to me before—and how for forty years I have fed upon dry salted fare—fit emblem of the dry nourishment of my soul—when the poorest landsman has had fresh fruit to his daily hand, and broken the world's fresh bread to my mouldy crusts—away, whole oceans away, from that young girl-wife I wedded past fifty, and sailed for Cape Horn the next day, leaving but one dent in my marriage pillow . . . and then, the madness, the frenzy, the boiling blood and the smoking brow, with which, for a thousand lowerings old Ahab has furiously, foamingly chased his prey—more a demon than a man!—aye, aye! what a forty years' fool—fool—old fool, has old Ahab been! Why this strife of the chase? why weary, and palsy the arm at the oar, and the iron, and the lance? how the richer or better is Ahab now? (132/590–591)

But others have gotten richer. Capital has been accumulated through the all but complete appropriation of Ahab's life energies. Capital, however, remains invisible to him to the end.

On this last voyage Ahab has refused to be capital's agent. But he does not recognize that the power with which he defies capital was delegated to him by capital. He does not recognize that it is capital's relentless and ruthless drive for valorization that has colonized his life to the point of meaninglessness. He instead reifies exponentially. He first reifies the (reified) power of capital, projecting it onto to unseen malignant spiritual forces. He then reifies this reification of a reified power by proclaiming a white whale to be the physical embodiment of those invisible malignant forces.[48] Destroying the whale becomes his way of attacking the malignant spirits that inverted his (supposed) position as a sovereign free subject. The object that is the (supposed) embodiment of those spirits asserted independent agency over him and his (supposed) "natural" right to claim ownership of unowned things. It must be destroyed to reaffirm the primacy of his subjective personality. But this leaves in place the forces that have in fact subsumed that personality over the course of his life, transforming it into an objectified means of capital accumulation. Unsurprisingly, Ahab utterly fails to comprehend that his own reduction of the crew to mere mechanical implements of his will parallels exactly capital's subsumption of Ahab's own activities within its circuit of valorization.[49] *That* objectification is not the affront to human dignity he refuses to accept, unaware that leaving it in place leaves his own objectification in place as well.

A third point made by Marx regarding the relationship between humanity and nature is captured in the following passage:

> [A]ll progress in capitalistic agriculture is a progress in the
> art, not only of robbing the worker, but of robbing the soil;
> all progress in increasing the fertility of the soil for a given
> time is a progress towards ruining the more long-lasting sources
> of that fertility . . . Capitalist production, therefore, only
> develops the techniques and the degree of combination of the
> social process of production by simultaneously undermining
> the original sources of all wealth—the soil and the worker.
> (Marx 1976a, p. 638)

Ahab's catastrophic relationship with Moby-Dick merely exaggerates the "normal" relationship of the human species to its environment in modern capitalism.

Every organism, no matter the species, lives by absorbing resources from its environment and generating wastes back into its surrounding ecosystem. The evolutionary success of a species is measured in good part by its success in establishing a symbiotic relationship with this ecosystem. This is essentially a matter of establishing and maintaining complementary temporalities: The rate at which resources are depleted and wastes are generated must roughly correspond to the rate the surrounding environment replenishes those resources and processes those wastes.

In modern capitalism, the evolutionary niche of the human species has become the planet as a whole, and the temporality of human society has been accelerated into hyperdrive. Each unit of production must attempt to appropriate as much capital as possible, as fast as possible, or risk being destroyed in market competition by its competitors. The valorization imperative, in other words, impose on each unit of capital the corresponding imperative "grow or die!" (R. Smith, 2013). Accumulating as much capital as possible, as fast as possible, implies producing and selling as many commodities as possible, as fast as possible. When capitalist social relations were in place in only a relatively few regions for a short time, the full consequences of this dynamic could be ignored. But capitalism has now been in place for centuries, operating on a global scale. Over time it has become increasingly clear that the temporality of modern capitalism is fundamentally discordant with the temporality of the natural world. As long as capitalism is in place—as long as the commodification imperative and the valorization imperative reign on the level of society as a whole—resources needed by the natural beings called "humans" will necessarily tend to be exhausted at a faster rate than they can be replenished, and wastes will necessarily tend to be generated at a faster rate than they can be processed.[50] As long as capitalism is in place, humans do not fit within their ecosystem in a sustainable way, threatening the evolutionary prospects of the species.

In Chapter 105, Ishmael asks whether the whale is bound to become extinct, as the buffalo seemed to be becoming when Melville wrote. He answers no. Unlike the buffalo, the whale has all the oceans of the world to hide from its human pursuers, including under the Artic ices, which Ishmael thought would provide impenetrable protection. This was a failure of imagination on his part; the technological means for hunting whales to extinction have been developed and may yet be used. (Even if they are not, changes to ocean chemistry and flows of ocean current at least partially brought about by human activity may cause the extinction of the largest mammals on the planet, as they are now causing the extinction of so many other species.) But the fate of the whale in particular is less Melville's concern than the "blowback" to human society from planetary processes set off by the commodification of the natural world.[51] Moby-Dick's attack is the most powerful image of that blowback in world literature. The destruction of the *Pequod* with which the book concludes is a prophecy of humanity's fate if the valorization imperative of capital ("grow or die!") continues to reign. Like other prophecies, it is a call to change our behavior before it is too late. It is, in brief, a call for social agents to

> [G]overn the human metabolism with nature in a rational way, bringing it under their collective control instead of being dominated by it as a blind power; accomplishing it with the least expenditure of energy and in conditions most worthy and appropriate for their human nature. (Marx, 1981, pp. 958–959)

Conclusion

Critical social theory is not exhausted by the critique of the despotic powers bestowed upon capital's agents, the critique of substantive irrationality (and by implication, the defense of the substantive rationality requiring deliberative democracy), and the critique of the distortions to the "human metabolism with nature" imposed by capital's insane hypertemporality. But no social theory excluding these critiques could possibly be adequate to the theoretical and practical challenges of the twenty-first century. In so far as *Moby-Dick* explores these themes with unparalleled poetic power, its contribution to critical social theory is hardly less than its contribution to world literature. Few works offer stronger confirmation of Piketty's insight that literature and social theory are intertwined.

Notes

1. The death knell of the whaling industry can be traced to 1859, when a steam-driven drill and boring process were first used to extract oil by drilling into the earth's crust (Wagner, 2010, p. 121). See Casarino, 2002, pp. 79–82.

2. The later Melville is a different story. Personally disappointed by the failure of *Moby-Dick* to find an audience, and disillusioned with social and political developments in the United States, his later writings are far more restrained in general.

3. "And thus have these naked Nantucketers, these sea hermits, issuing from their ant-hill in the sea, overrun and conquered the watery world like so many Alexanders; parcelling out among them the Atlantic, Pacific, and Indian oceans, as the three pirate powers did Poland. Let America add Mexico to Texas, and pile Cuba upon Canada; let the English overswarm all India, and hang out their blazing banner from the sun; two thirds of this terraqueous globe are the Nantucketer's. For the sea is his; he owns it, as Emperors own empires; other seamen having but a right of way through it" (14/70; here and elsewhere citations refer to the chapters and pages, respectively, of the Penguin edition cited in the bibliography: Melville, 1992).

4. "Seated on the transom was . . . Captain Bildad, who along with Captain Peleg was one of the largest owners of the vessel; the other shares, as is sometimes the case in these ports, being held by a crowd of old annuitants; widows, fatherless children, and chancery wards; each owning about the value of a timber head, or a foot of plank, or a nail or two in the ship. People in Nantucket invest their money in whaling vessels, the same way that you do yours in approved state stocks bringing in good interest" (16/81–82).

5. "New Bedford rose in terraces of streets, their ice-covered trees all glittering in the clear, cold air. Huge hills and mountains of casks on casks were piled upon her wharves, and side by side the world-wandering whale ships lay silent and safely moored at last; while from others came a sound of carpenters and coopers, with blended noises of fires and forges to melt the pitch, all betokening that new cruises were on the start; that one most perilous and long voyage ended, only begins a second; and a second ended, only begins a third,

and so on, for ever and for aye. Such is the endlessness, yea, the intolerableness of all earthly effort" (13/66).

6. Melville's brilliant satire of the Protestant Ethic in the beginning chapters is worth noting in passing. The good Quaker captain Bildad continually pores over the Bible whenever he is not otherwise occupied. Few of his utterances fail to include a pious reference to the sacred text. Yet his life has been spent inflicting carnage: "Though refusing, from conscientious scruples, to bear arms against land invaders, yet himself had illimitably invaded the Atlantic and Pacific; and though a sworn foe to human bloodshed, yet had he in his straight-bodied coat, spilled tuns upon tuns of leviathan gore. How now in the contemplative evening of his days, the pious Bildad reconciled these things in the reminiscence, I do not know; but it did not seem to concern him much, and very probably he had long since come to the sage and sensible conclusion that a man's religion is one thing, and this practical world quite another. This world pays dividends" (16/83). Bildad's Biblical allusions invariably are designed to further his self-interest as a principle investor in a profit-driven venture, as in his efforts to talk Ishmael into accepting a lower share of the returns from the voyage than his skills as an experienced hand on merchant ships warranted. He religiosity also proved compatible with notoriously overworking his crews in his captain days ("For a pious man, especially for a Quaker, he was certainly rather hard-hearted to say the least. He never used to swear, though, at his men, they said; but somehow he got an inordinate quantity of cruel, unmitigated hard work out of them" (16/83). Perhaps Protestants of an earlier century and a different place suffered an internal doubt of their personal salvation, alleviated only by the worldly prosperity they took as evidence of God's Plan. By the mid-19th-century United States, however, the rhetoric of the Protestant Ethic has become a weapon used by those who own and control investment capital to restructure social relationships to their benefit, a pious cover to hide transgressions against established notions of fairness and a discourse allowing them to change the subject whenever these transgressions are questioned. Perhaps it has been always thus.

7. "As for the residue of the *Pequod*'s company, be it said, that at the present day not one in two of the many thousand men before the mast employed in the American whale fishery, are Americans born, though pretty nearly all the officers are. Herein it is the same with the American whale fishery as with the American army and military and merchant navies, and the engineering forces employed in the construction of the American Canals and Railroads. The same, I say, because in all these cases the native American liberally provides the brains, the rest of the world as generously supplying the muscles" (27/131).

8. They must cease eating when abstentious Ahab leaves the table, causing the lowest ranking officer—who can only enter the cabin after all the other

officers have entered, and must first depart—to be perpetually hungry. Officers must also eat in silence, while the harpooners and other crewmen eat convivially.

9. "What of it, if some old hunks of a sea-captain orders me to get a broom and sweep down the decks? What does that indignity amount to, weighed, I mean, in the scales of the New Testament? Do you think the archangel Gabriel thinks anything the less of me, because I promptly and respectfully obey that old hunks in that particular instance? Who ain't a slave? Tell me that. Well, then, however the old sea-captains may order me about—however they may thump and punch me about, I have the satisfaction of knowing that it is all right; that everybody else is one way or other served in much the same way—either in a physical or metaphysical point of view, that is; and so the universal thump is passed round, and all hands should rub each other's shoulder-blades, and be content" (1/6).

10. To this we can add the consent Ishmael and other crew members grant to Ahab's command due to his charismatic authority (discussed further below). This form of consent has also characterized many workplaces.

11. On the way out of the harbor, Ishmael is kicked in the rear by Peleg for not working hard enough (Peleg and Bildad remain on board until the ship leaves the harbor). Stubb later kicks the cook for bringing nonalcoholic drinks to the harpooners, despite the fact the cook merely followed the instructions of Bildad's pious sister, Aunt Charity. In Melville's other writings set at sea, the physical and psychological abuse of shipmates is much more frequent and severe.

12. *Moby-Dick* concludes with Ishmael's own rescue by the *Rachel*, an accidental by-product of the doomed attempt to rescue its captain's lost son, himself abandoned so that a boat with more sailors could be saved instead (Melville discussed the tragic dimension of "trolley car" cases, and the tension between partiality and impartiality, long before they became stable themes of analytic ethics.)

13. "Now, in calm weather, to swim in the open ocean is as easy to the practised swimmer as to ride in a spring- carriage ashore. But the awful lonesomeness is intolerable. The intense concentration of self in the middle of such a heartless immensity, my God! who can tell it?" (93/453).

14. "To every pitch of the ship there was a pitch of the boiling oil, which seemed all eagerness to leap into their faces" (96/463).

15. Stubb's exhortations to the crew of his whaleboat as they row inches away from a cornered prey orders of magnitude bigger than their boat shows he would have made a brilliant standup comic.

16. "For God's sake, be economical with your lamps and candles! not a gallon you burn, but at least one drop of man's blood was spilled for it" (45/224). Blood for oil, we see, hardly began with Bush the Junior's wars.

17. "[M]any is the time, when, after the severest uninterrupted labors, which know no night; continuing straight through for ninety-six hours; when

from the boat, where they have swelled their wrists with all day rowing on the Line,—they only step to the deck to carry vast chains, and heave the heavy windlass, and cut and slash, yea, and in their very sweatings to be smoked and burned anew by the combined fires of the equatorial sun and the equatorial try-works; when, on the heel of all this, they have finally bestirred themselves to cleanse the ship, and make a spotless dairy room of it; many is the time the poor fellows, just buttoning the necks of their clean frocks, are startled by the cry of "There she blows!" and away they fly to fight another whale, and go through the whole weary thing again. Oh! my friends, but this is man-killing!" (98/469).

18. We should not think this theme is no longer relevant to us, having 19th-century capitalism far behind. The factories of Foxconn, where a predominantly female and migrant workforce is forced to work 80-hour weeks so Apple can meet its arbitrary and unreasonable deadlines, shows this to not be the case, as does the overwork of knowledge workers (Crary, 2014).

19. This theme is introduced early in the book: "[F]or the most part the Commodore on the quarter-deck gets his atmosphere at second hand from the sailors on the forecastle. He thinks he breathes it first; but not so. In much the same way do the commonalty lead their leaders in many other things, at the same time that the leaders little suspect it" (1/7).

20. Ishmael takes a step—or two—beyond merely fraternal feelings toward his co-workers in this chapter. The political dimension of these beyond merely fraternal feelings is explored at length in Casarino, 2002, pp. 156–179.

21. "[T]his situation of mine was the precise situation of every mortal that breathes; only, in most cases he, one way or other, has this Siamese connexion with a plurality of other mortals. If your banker breaks, you snap; if your apothecary by mistake sends you poison in your pills, you die" (72/349).

22. And yes, Melville goes out of his way to draw the parallel with an obstetrician helping a woman give birth by correcting a breach. There is more than a little in this book of interest to critical gender studies.

23. I cannot accept James's reading of Ishmael as a representative of an intellectual stratum alienated from the working class, or McWilliams's claim that Ishmael (along with every other person on the boat), is an "isolatoe" cut off from society. (James 2001; McWilliams 2013). That may have been the case at one point in his life. But his deep friendship with Queequeg, and his often-expressed respect and admiration for Tashtego and Dagoo, rule out thinking that it continues to hold. Much has been made of the alienation from the harpooners Ishmael supposedly expresses as he looks down on their respite from laboring on pots burning "hissing masses of blubber":

> As they narrated to each other their unholy adventures, their tales
> of terror told in words of mirth; as their uncivilized laughter forked
> upwards out of them, like the flames from the furnace; as to and

fro, in their front, the harpooneers wildly gesticulated with their huge pronged forks and dippers; as the wind howled on, and the sea leaped, and the ship groaned and dived, and yet steadfastly shot her red hell further and further into the blackness of the sea and the night, and scornfully champed the white bone in her mouth, and viciously spat round her on all sides; then the rushing *Pequod*, freighted with savages, and laden with fire, and burning a corpse, and plunging into that blackness of darkness, seemed the material counterpart of her monomaniac commander's soul. (96/463)

There is indeed alienation here. But as Ishmael clearly tells us, it is an alienation from the *Pequod*'s "monomaniac commander's soul." Ishmael is alienated from the harpooners only insofar as they, like himself, have been incorporated within Ahab's project. In other words, the Ishmael writing the narrative is no more alienated from the harpooners than he is alienated as the narrator from his previous self, part of the story he is narrating. For he too has been incorporated within Ahab's project. All his subsequent references to these fellow workers (the harpooners) are highly sympathetic, and so this statement cannot be taken as Ishmael's views regarding who they are in other relationships, apart from the relationship to Ahab.

24. "[C]apital . . . valorises itself through the *appropriation of alien labour*" (Marx, 1986, p. 233.) "All the powers of labour project themselves as powers of capital" (Marx, 1976a, pp. 755–756). "The development of the *social* productive forces of labour and the conditions of that development come to appear as the *achievement of capital*" (Marx, 1976b, p. 1055).

25. It is implicitly asserted most rapturously in this oft-quoted passage:

[T]his august dignity I treat of, is not the dignity of kings and robes, but that abounding dignity which has no robed investiture. Thou shalt see it shining in the arm that wields a pick or drives a spike; that democratic dignity which, on all hands, radiates without end from God; Himself! The great God absolute! The centre and circumference of all democracy! His omnipresence, our divine equality!

If, then, to meanest mariners, and renegades and castaways, I shall hereafter ascribe high qualities, though dark; weave round them tragic graces; if even the most mournful, perchance the most abased, among them all, shall at times lift himself to the exalted mounts; if I shall touch that workman's arm with some ethereal light; if I shall spread a rainbow over his disastrous set of sun; then against all mortal critics bear me out in it, thou just spirit of equality, which hast spread one royal mantle of humanity over all my kind! Bear me out in it, thou great democratic God! (26/126)

26. "But, though the world scouts at us whale hunters, yet does it unwittingly pay us the profoundest homage; yea, an all-abounding adoration! for almost all the tapers, lamps, and candles that burn round the globe, burn, as before so many shrines, to our glory!" (24/119).

27. A humorous illustration of the latter comes when Stubb insists on immediately consuming a whale steak from the animal he has just killed. Stubb consumed whale steaks; capitalist agriculture today produces "petrofood."

28. The importance of petrochemicals in the U.S. economy is a central theme in Pynchon's *Gravity's Rainbow*, a work in direct line of descent from *Moby-Dick*.

29. This has changed since communication and transportation technologies allowed cross-border production chains to be established. Now the greatest "value" is appropriated by owners of brands and intellectual property rights, with subcontracted manufacturers incorporated as junior partners.

30. Northeastern manufacturing, protected by high tariff barriers, affirmed the same project. This path was confirmed by the Civil War defeat of states based on the plantation economy.

31. Melville reminds us in passing of the social costs of devoting so much of one's life to profit-driven growth paid by wives, left alone to do the care labor society depends upon, and by children, left in a condition indistinguishable from fatherlessness.

32. After Ahab reveals his true goal, Starbuck complains in private: "I am game for his crooked jaw, and for the jaws of Death too, Captain Ahab, if it fairly comes in the way of the business we follow; but I came here to hunt whales, not my commander's vengeance. How many barrels will thy vengeance yield thee even if thou gettest it, Captain Ahab? It will not fetch thee much in our Nantucket market." Ahab replies: "Nantucket market! Hoot! But come closer, Starbuck; thou requirest a little lower layer. If money's to be the measurer, man, and the accountants have computed their great counting-house the globe, by girdling it with guineas, one to every three parts of an inch; then, let me tell thee, that my vengeance will fetch a great premium here!" "He smites his chest," whispered Stubb, what's that for? methinks it rings most vast, but hollow" (36/177–8).

33. "Had any one of his old acquaintances on shore but half dreamed of what was lurking in him then, how soon would their aghast and righteous souls have wrenched the ship from such a fiendish man! They were bent on profitable cruises, the profit to be counted down in dollars from the mint" (41/202).

34. The provision of law, money, basic research, and crisis management, are some examples.

35. Some of these mechanisms include campaign contributions, the revolving door offering lucrative employment to favored state officials after leaving "public service," the dissemination of ideology through privately owned media,

support of educational institutions that socialize future state officials into the dominant ideology, the need for state deficits to be financed through the purchase of government bonds on a massive scale, the need to make investment in the domestic economy attractive enough to avoid capital flight, and the ever-present threat of social chaos created by a capital strike, with the mobilization of death squads a final option when all else fails.

36. Relevant literature is surveyed in Spanos, 1995.

37. Ahab does not in fact care about returning to Nantucket with all barrels filled. When a leak in the barrels stored below deck is discovered, Starbuck insists it must be investigated and corrected:

> "What will the owners say, Sir?"
>
> "Let the owners stand on Nantucket beach and outyell the Typhoons. What cares Ahab? Owners, owners? Thou art always prating to me, Starbuck, about those miserly owners, as if the owners were my conscience. But look ye, the only real owner of anything is its commander; and hark ye, my conscience is in this ship's keel." (109/517)

Ahab later relents, the sole point in the novel where he eventually agrees to do something he did not originally want to do. In a way, this reveals an intuitive understanding of the collective power over him the crew potentially possesses; he does not want to risk that power being mobilized in response to the crew's discovery of his indifference to their supposedly shared interests or, rather, the fundamental incompatibility of his agenda and their interests. As Melville writes, "To accomplish his object Ahab must use tools; and of all tools used in the shadow of the moon, men are most apt to get out of order" (46/230).

38. Consent to external social authority can be given because freedom is thought to be a purely internal matter (Ishmael), or because it is (mis)identified with the unavoidable "natural" ("metaphysical") constraints that are part of the human condition (Ishmael again), or because religion demands it (Starbuck), or because it is no more senseless than anything else in this senseless world (Stubb).

39. Ahab unilaterally declines the intensely heartfelt plea of the captain of the *Rachel* to join a search for his son. That would have temporarily delayed the hunt for Moby-Dick, and he accepts no delay. The crew is shocked by this refusal to do what elementary decency requires. But there is no institutionalized space where the case for a more sympathetic response could be weighed against Ahab's agenda.

40. This thesis is anticipated in Goldner, 2006. Goldner sees *Moby-Dick* calling for a world historical break from the long historical period that began when collective social power first took alien form with the rise of the state in the ancient near east, and the concomitant rise of a theological politics sanctifying this alien power.

41. "Now, in his heart, Ahab had some glimpse of this, namely: all my means are sane, my motive and my object mad. Yet without power to kill, or change, or shun the fact; he likewise knew that to mankind he did now long dissemble; in some sort, did still" (41/202). As Ishmael notes, "There is a wisdom that is woe, but there is a woe that is madness" (96/465).

42. The themes of this subsection are explored at length in T. Smith, 2017.

43. After abandoning a harpooned whale to rescue Pip, an African American boy, Stubb instructs him to not need rescuing again: " 'Stick to the boat, Pip, or by the Lord, I wont pick you up if you jump; mind that. We can't afford to lose whales by the likes of you; a whale would sell for thirty times what you would, Pip, in Alabama. Bear that in mind, and don't jump any more." Hereby perhaps Stubb indirectly hinted, that though man loved his fellow, yet man is a money-making animal, which propensity too often interferes with his benevolence (93/452).

44. Ishmael is a compulsive analogizer. As he and Queequeg weave a mat on the deck he compares their activity to the work of the Fates of ancient mythology, weaving necessity, freedom, and chance together in the Loom of Time:

> There lay the fixed threads of the warp subject to but one single, ever returning, unchanging vibration, and that vibration merely enough to admit of the crosswise interblending of other threads with its own. This warp seemed necessity; and here, thought I, with my own hand I ply my own shuttle and weave my own destiny into these unalterable threads. Meantime, Queequeg's impulsive, indifferent sword, sometimes hitting the woof slantingly, or crookedly, or strongly, or weakly, as the case might be; and by this difference in the concluding blow producing a corresponding contrast in the final aspect of the completed fabric; this savage's sword, thought I, which thus finally shapes and fashions both warp and woof; this easy, indifferent sword must be chance—aye, chance, free will, and necessity—no wise incompatible—all interweavingly working together. (47/232)

At first the analogy seems a bit strained and hyperbolic. But it resonates. Perhaps we are meant to reflect on the extent collective social labor, itself incorporating necessity, freedom, and chance, can take responsibility for the course of the world upon itself, and not leave it in the hands of alien gods . . . or that alien thing that is not a thing, capital, and its agents. But then a whale is sighted, and possibilities momentarily opened up by the poetic comparison are closed off once again.

45. His replacement leg is a paradigmatic technological fix, requiring (as is so often the case) a further series of technological fixes (special holes for the tip of the artificial leg must be drilled into the deck of the ship, and special

resting places must be constructed in the whale boat). Like many technological fixes, one problem is solved only to cause another; at some point prior to the start of the novel Ahab has been maimed (perhaps castrated?) by his (and yet not his) replacement leg in a horrific accident. Having previously failed to note the irony of a whale hunter's body being literally fused with the body of a whale, he now fails to discern his own role in the chain of events leading to this maiming. He takes it as yet another reason to hate the whale that left him needing to restore a completeness that is forever incompletely his.

46. "A spider conducts operations which resemble those of the weaver, and a bee would put many a human architect to shame by the construction of its honeycomb cells. But what distinguishes the worst architect from the best of bees is that the architect builds the cell in his mind before he constructs it in wax" (Marx, 1976a, p. 284).

47. The person known to us as Ishmael understands and accepts that the boundary line between the self and not-self is porous, fated one day to dissolve altogether. While on the mast the vastness of the ocean appears all encompassing. He finds it easy to imagine yielding to it, falling into it, being absorbed by it. Natural dialectician that he is, Ishmael turns away from this dissolution of the self. The many may be one, but it is no less true that the one must be many: "[T]here is no quality in this world that is not what it is merely by contrast. Nothing exists in itself" (11/59). He intuitively recognizes that the substance of the world and his own self-conscious subjectivity are somehow united while remaining distinct. Ahab possesses a quite different subjectivity; Ahab cannot accept that he himself is not the ultimate substance of the world, with the ontological status of everything else reduced to a mere instrument of his will.

48. "The White Whale swam before him as the monomaniac incarnation of all those malicious agencies which some deep men feel eating in them, till they are left living on with half a heart and half a lung. That intangible malignity which has been from the beginning; to whose dominion even the modern Christians ascribe one-half of the worlds; which the ancient Ophites of the east reverenced in their statue devil;—Ahab did not fall down and worship it like them; but deliriously transferring its idea to the abhorred White Whale, he pitted himself, all mutilated, against it. All that most maddens and torments; all that stirs up the lees of things; all truth with malice in it; all that cracks the sinews and cakes the brain; all the subtle demonisms of life and thought; all evil, to crazy Ahab, were visibly personified, and made practically assailable in Moby-Dick. He piled upon the whale's white hump the sum of all the general rage and hate felt by his whole race from Adam down; and then, as if his chest had been a mortar, he burst his hot heart's shell upon it" (41/200).

49. "They were one man, not thirty. For as the one ship that held them all; though it was put together of all contrasting things—oak, and maple, and pine wood; iron, and pitch, and hemp—yet all these ran into each other in the

one concrete hull, which shot on its way, both balanced and directed by the long central keel; even so, all the individualities of the crew, this man's valor, that man's fear; guilt and guiltiness, all varieties were welded into oneness, and were all directed to that fatal goal which Ahab their one lord and keel did point to" (134/606).

50. Substitutes have sometimes been found for depleted resources, as well as ways to reduce the generation of wastes, or to use them and thereby transform them into resources. But these are contingent developments, unable to negate a necessary tendency as powerful as the one discussed in the main text. We also cannot expect this tendency to be put out of play by the rise of a "dematerialized" economy. The Jevons paradox is relevant here. Jevons, one of the founders of neoclassical economics, saw that each generation of machinery in the course of the first industrial revolution was more "dematerialized" than the generation before in the sense that less coal was required per unit output than the in generation before. (Today we would emphasize that each generation of machinery involved lower CO_2 emission than the generation before, and hence counted as an advance to a more "sustainable technology.") Nonetheless, the total use of coal (and total carbon dioxide emissions) continued to grow over this period. The paradox is easy enough to explain. However much a more "dematerialized" and "sustainable" technology reduces the use of resources and generation of wastes per unit output, if the total units of outputs produced is increasing at a sufficiently fast rate, any positive effects will be overwhelmed.

51. "However baby man may brag of his science and skill, and however much, in a flattering future, that science and skill may augment; yet for ever and for ever, to the crack of doom, the sea will insult and murder him, and pulverize the stateliest, stiffest frigate he can make" (58/298).

References

Arrighi, G. (1994). *The Long Twentieth Century*. New York, NY: Verso.

Braune, L. (2014). *Herman Melville and Richard Wright: Camaraderie and Revolt*. Master of Arts Thesis (Unpublished), University of Texas-Pan American.

Crary, J. (2013). *24/7: Capitalism and the End of Sleep*. New York, NY: Verso.

Goldner, L. (2006). *Herman Melville: Between Charlemagne and the Antemosaic Cosmic Man: Race, Class and the Crisis of Bourgeois Ideology in an American Renaissance Writer*. New York, NY: Queequeg Publications.

Hardt, M., & Negri, A. (2009). *Commonwealth*. Cambridge, MA.: Belknap Press.

James, C. L. R. (2001). *Mariners, Renegades and Castaways: The Story of Herman Melville and the World We Live In*. Hanover, NH: Dartmouth University Press. (Original work published 1953)

Marx, K. (1976a). *Capital, Volume I*. Translated by Ben Fowkes. New York, NY: Penguin Books. (Original work published 1867)

Marx, K. (1976b). Results of the Immediate Process of Production., appendix to *Capital, Volume I*, translated by Ben Fowkes. New York, NY: Penguin Books. (Original work published 1933)

Marx, K. [1939] 1986. Outlines of the Critique of Political Economy' [*Grundrisse*, beginning], in *Marx and Engels Collected Works*, Vol. 28. New York, NY: International Publishers. (Original work published 1939)

McWilliams, S. (2013). Ahab, American in *A Political Companion to Herman Melville*, Edited by Jason Frank. Lexington: University of Kentucky Press.

Melville, H. (1992). *Moby-Dick, or The Whale*. New York, NY: Penguin. (Original work published 1851)

Moseley, F. (2015). *Money and Totality: A Macro-Monetary Interpretation of Marx's Logic in* Capital *and the End of the "Transformation Problem."* Leiden, UK: Brill.

Piketty, T. (2014). *Capital in the Twenty-First Century*. Translated by Arthur Goldhammer. Cambridge, MA: Belknap Press.

Rogin, M. (1979). *Subversive Genealogy: The Politics and Art of Herman Melville*. Berkeley: University of California Press.

Smith, R. (2013). Capitalism and the destruction of life on Earth: Six theses on saving the humans. *Real-World Economics Review*, 64, 125–150.

Smith, T. (2017). *Beyond Liberal Egalitarianism*. Leiden, UK: Brill.

Spanos, W. *The Errant Art of Moby-Dick: The Canon, The Cold War, and the Struggle for American Studies*. Durham, NC: Duke University Press.

Wagner, R. D. (2010). *Moby-Dick and the Mythology of Oil*. Charleston, SC: CreateSpace.

Wood, E. M. (2003). *Empire of Capital*. London, UK: Verso.

Chapter 2

Marxist Aesthetics, Realism, and Photography

On Brecht's *War Primer*

Christian Lotz

Those at the top say:
It leads to glory.
Those down below say:
It leads to the grave.

—Bertolt Brecht

Introduction: Iconophobia in Critical Theory?

Critical aesthetics in the tradition of the Frankfurt School has often been accused of being elitist, in distance to popular culture, and overtly hostile to pictorial art traditions. The accusation of iconophobia intensified in recent decades during which photography has emancipated itself from painting and established itself as one of the major forces in contemporary art. Most recently, this critique has been forcefully put forward by Susie Linfield in her popular and well-received book *The Cruel Radiance: Photography and Political Violence*, within which she opens her reflections on the sociopolitical dimension of contemporary photography and photo-journalism with a harsh critique not only of photography criticism from Sontag through Barthes, but also of the Frankfurt School aesthetics, such as Adorno, Benjamin, Kracauer, and Brecht. She writes: "Benjamin was highly suspicious of the passive, aestheticized society that he feared photography was helping to create" (Linfield, 2010, p. 18). In relation to Kracauer and Brecht, she writes:

> it was Kracauer's mandarin, often censorious tone that would flourish among successor generations of cultural critics who write about photography. Most of all, though, it is Brecht whose shadow hangs over photography criticism and whose sensibility continues to define it. Brecht, I think it's fair to say, really loathe photographs. (Linfield, 2010, p. 20)

These statements are not only factually wrong,[1] but more importantly also display a deep misunderstanding of Brecht's overall aesthetic positions and philosophic ideas. It is factually wrong that Brecht despised photographs, which can easily be seen in his use of them in his decades-long journal, in which he collected ideas and daily notes in connection with press photographs. It is true, however, that both Brecht and Benjamin did not think of photographs as isolated things; instead, they thought about them as being embedded in social and political practices that were based on specific uses and developments of the modern media. Accordingly, photographs for Benjamin and Brecht do not exist as isolated entities; instead, they are analyzed as parts of social relations. Linfield underestimates the *critical* aspects of the type of aesthetics that she attacks, insofar as she does not understand that the critical aspect in thinkers such as Brecht, Benjamin, and Adorno is not based in their critical attitude toward images; rather, being critical toward any kind of social praxis is derived from a larger theory of society. Accordingly, Brecht and Benjamin do not take on a critical position toward images or photographs in general; rather, they criticize specific artistic and nonartistic practices in which images are used and, as a consequence, are related to capitalist society as a whole. Both were interested in developing different practices in which diverse media would be produced and apprehended in a better—that is, emancipatory—way, and, hence, would, via cultural changes, foreshadow a different, postcapitalist, world.

Moreover, Linfield distorts almost all of Brecht's famous quotes on photography, which are presented in an isolated fashion, without reflecting on the proper context of these quotes. This proper context is Brecht's Marxist aesthetics and his work as a whole. One of these famous quotes reads as follows:

> The tremendous development of photojournalism [*Bildreport-age*] has scarcely yielded any *truth* about the world's current conditions: in the hands of the bourgeoisie, photography has become a terrible weapon *against* the truth. The enormous amount of pictorial material that is spat out daily from the printing press and that appears to bear the character of reality actually serves just the obfuscation [*Verdunkelung*—literally: darkening] of facts. *The camera can lie just as the typewriter.* The task of the AIZ is to serve the truth and to reconstruct the true matters of fact. (Brecht, 1993/21, p. 515)

As we will see in what follows, what Brecht had in mind is not that photographs could not be used for non-bourgeois purposes, such as the labor movement or for revolutionary goals. On the contrary, he envisioned a photographic practice that could be used in a critical fashion and function even within a critical artistic practice. He saw this foreshadowed in how the *Arbeiter Illustrierte Zeitung* (AIZ), which was a news magazine for the labor class and based on photo montage, worked with images. As I will argue in the following, Brecht's *War Primer* is such a critical project in which photographs are embedded in a different practice that imply a different relation to war, to the past, and to society, and therefore function within a critical and realist art practice. Consequently, though it is true that for a long time the left tradition was skeptical about the mass media, iconophobia is not *per se* the consequence of Marxist aesthetics. What is at stake is not a rejection of images and photography, but the social practice and the social relations in which they are embedded.

This task of developing different critical perspectives in both artistic and theoretical practices has reached a new urgency in our neoliberal times, and we can observe that questions related to the concept of realism have reemerged in contemporary art, film and photography. As I have argued elsewhere (Lotz, 2017a), a critical and realist concept of art is confronted with the problem of how to make that which (invisibly) rules and dominates us, such as the market and capital, visible. As Anita Chari in her *The Political Economy of the Senses* has it:

> I suggest that artistic representations of capital emerging now in response to the political antinomies of neoliberalism are themselves signs of an alternative critique of political economy, one that is better able to negotiate between political experience and economic form. The key for me is that new ways of representing and inhabiting the economy, what I call *econopoesis*, are crucial for challenging dominant representations of the economy by mainstream economics, which is both undialectical and in service to financial capital, feeding off the incomprehensibility and unalterability of finance to citizens and political theorists alike. (2015, p. 169)

The problematic relation between the socially visible and the socially invisible has been reflected in Marxist inspired art and aesthetics before the arrival of neoliberalism throughout the 20th century, which includes theorists such as Brecht, Eisenstein, Kluge, Beuys, Benjamin, and Adorno, as well as artists such as Rosler, Farocki, Schlingensief, Sekula, Burtynsky, the Center for Political Beauty, and Pagen. Brecht's *Kriegsfibel* stands in this tradition that runs from Eisenstein's idea to make a film about *Capital* to Pagen's photo series of night photographs of NSA facilities and security companies that spy on all of us. All of these projects, especially since they are defined as "critical realism," are confronted with the problem of visibility and invisibility because artworks cannot remain within the conceptual and theoretical realm alone, insofar as they are in need of the sensual presence of meaning. Representing the socially invisible becomes here a sensible task. The problem becomes more difficult, however, when artists either explicitly work from a critical and Marxist standpoint or implicitly want to address capital, capitalism, globalization, economic issues, and the like in their work. The question, then, is very simple: How can something socially and actually abstract, such as money, capital, exchange, global structures, trade flows, banks, and financial speculations, be made perceptible? Put plainly, how can that which is invisible be rendered visible? The problem of the photograph, at least as long as it is not embedded in a *critical* media praxis, falls into the same category, insofar as isolated photographs have a meaning and can, as Barthes argued, be read on some level internally; however, being placed in media practices, such as newspapers, magazines or blogs, implies that these photographs are representing "invisibly" certain social relations.

As we will see, in the *War Primer* Brecht encounters a similar problem, which in his work is treated in relation to war, insofar as those who, according to Brecht, wage wars *on the people* in the name of power and capital remain as invisible as capital as a dominating principle. In the *War Primer*, the problem of visibility and invisibility is "echoed" by modern warfare, since the war from the air (air planes, long distance missiles, drones, satellites, virtual warfare) is itself fought as one in which the aggressors and their deadly tools remain as "invisible" as the millions of victims who died during World War I and World War II. As a famous line from the *Threepenny Opera* has it, "There are some who are in darkness / And the others are in light / And you see the ones in brightness / Those in darkness drop from sight." It is precisely this problem of the visible in regard to photography, memory, war, class, and war that Brecht tackles in his *War Primer*.

The Visible and the Invisible in Marxist Methodology and Aesthetics

Let me start with a reminder that the problem of the visible and the invisible not only runs through the Marxist tradition, but also through the entire main body of modern philosophy, which is especially visible in the genetic conceptions of philosophy developed post-Hegel. As I have dealt elsewhere with this issue in more detail and in regard to Lukacs's concept of realism (Lotz, 2017), here I only sketch the most important aspects. As Foucault demonstrates in his *Order of Things*, with the downfall of Hegelian metaphysics, the transparency of being and essence, of word and meaning, as well as of knowledge and concept, falls apart. Instead, conceptions of reality, meaning, and knowledge move to the forefront that are largely characterized by their emphasis on genesis and genetic reconstruction. For example, Nietzsche tries to trace morality back to embodied practices, Freud traces the surface of consciousness back to earlier developments and psychic functions, Husserl offers an account of how abstract knowledge of nature goes back to the lifeworld, and, finally, Marx most famously develops a genetic method of how to conceive of the categories of political economy in *Capital*. He thereby sets up the entire problem of the visible and the invisible for the Frankfurt School tradition. In fact, one could argue that the aesthetic problem of how to depict something that, as totality, is inaccessible, such as the totality of capitalist social organization, is already implied in Marx's method, which the work of early critical theorists, such as Adorno and Benjamin, extend. For example, Benjamin's *Passagenwerk* and Adorno's early attempt to appropriate Benjamin's concept of dialectical images explicitly take on the problem of how to render the invisible visible in the realm of theory.

The view of photography in early critical theory is just the consequence of the larger problem in Marxist methodology, which is not very clearly understood in the noncritical contemporary discourse on these issues. What is particularly missed is that all of this goes back to Marx. Here is what Marx says in *Grundrisse*:

> In present bourgeois society as a whole, this positing of prices and their circulation etc. appears as the surface process, beneath which, however, in the depths, entirely different processes go on, in which this apparent individual equality and liberty disappear. It is forgotten, on one side, that the presupposition of exchange value, as the objective basis of the whole of the system of production, already in itself implies compulsion over the individual, since his immediate product is not a product for him, but only becomes such in the social process, and since it must take on this general but nevertheless external form; and that the individual has an existence only as a producer of exchange value, hence that the whole negation of his natural existence is already implied; that he is therefore entirely determined by society; that this further presupposes a division of labor etc., in which the individual is already posited in relations other than that of mere exchanger, etc. (Marx, 1993, p. 247)

What Marx has in mind here are two things: It remains hidden at the surface of market transactions and the simple commodity circulation that not only the entire production and distribution process is *contained* in the surface, but also that the individual market agent who appears at the surface of these transactions as an isolated contractor and exchanger is already determined by the entire process of social (re)production (by which Marx means the structural determination of *what* an agent is). Accordingly, the genetic method of Marx's thinking is supposed to reveal the social relations that make up what *appears* to be isolated entities. Similarly, Marx conceives of the categories presented and developed in *Capital* as a process throughout which the origin of the categories and their relational genesis disappears after each step. For example, the money mystery is based on the structural problem that the genesis contained in money (and which *Capital* is supposed to reconstruct) disappears in its results and "leaves no trace behind." As Marx puts this,

> What appears to happen is not that gold becomes money, in consequence of all other commodities expressing their values in it, but, on the contrary, that all other commodities universally express their values in gold, because it is money. The intermediate steps of the process vanish in the result and leave no trace behind. Commodities find their own value already completely represented, without any initiative on their part, in another commodity existing in company with them. These objects, gold and silver, just as they come out of the bowels of the earth, are forthwith the direct incarnation of all human labor. Hence the magic of money. (Marx, 1990, p. 187)

Accordingly, even without going into the details of Marx's method and the problem of research and presentation of the economic categories, we can see that the problem of visibility and invisibility not only is deeply embedded in the genetic method of Marx's thinking, but also that the problem can easily be transferred to an *aesthetic* problem, namely, how the conceptual reconstruction of the capitalist social organization as a whole can be transferred into the problem of how in given artistic practices this capitalist social organization can be "presented" [*darstellen*].

Brecht's Critical Aesthetics

It is clear that Brecht's entire program is based on this problem of presentation. More specifically, he is concerned with the problem of how to deal with the break between the visible and the invisible and the attempt to "bridge" it via a genetic method. This is most prominently visible in the problem of how photographic images hide or reveal the social reality that they are supposed to depict. As Brecht has it in a famous statement (of which unfortunately usually only the first two sentences are quoted)[2]:

The situation [in capitalist society as a whole] is now becoming
so complex that a simple "reproduction of reality" says less
than ever about reality itself. A photograph of a Krupp factory
or the AEG says practically nothing about these institutions.
Reality itself has shifted into the realm of the functional.
The reification of human relationships, such as the factory,
no longer betrays anything about these relationships. And so
what we actually need is to "construct something," something
"artificial," "posed." What we therefore equally need is art.
But the old concept of art based on experience is invalid.
For whoever reproduces those aspects of reality that can be
experienced does not reproduce reality. For some time reality
has no longer been experienceable as a totality. But speaking
in this way, we speak about an art with a completely different function in social life—that of depicting reality. (Brecht,
1993/21, p. 469)

Accordingly, Brecht does not talk only about photographs here; in
addition, he tasks art, at least in the critical fashion in which Brecht
envisions it, with what theory is supposed to do in Marxist philosophy.
Instead of revealing the reality in what only appears as surface through
theory, art has to "deal" with the reality in its own forms of existence,
which, for Brecht (and Benjamin), are *social practices of media uses.*
Conceiving art as dealing with media practices is the proper materialist
approach to what, in traditional aesthetics, was conceived as a problem
of art "genres." As we need critical theory in a society that as a whole is
intangible, not given, and not directly present (although its abstractions
are real),[3] we are in need of critical art and media practices. If Adorno's
claim that critical theory is "society's consciousness of itself" (Adorno
in Demirovic, 1999, p. 465) is true, then, from Brecht's perspective,
the highest possibility of critical aesthetics and art practices should be
conceived in a similar fashion. Art, in Brecht's case mainly poetry and
theater, is society's consciousness of itself. Since we are living in a social
reality characterized by the capitalist mode of production and capitalist
social form, critical media practices need to reflect and express this fact,
too. Hence, Marxist theory and Marxist aesthetics are based on the
attempt to reverse the process of forgetting and to reverse the misconception of society of itself. The *War Primer* can therefore be understood
as a contribution to this project, now developed in the form of critical

mimesis and memory of World War II and its underlying social system of production and power.

Brecht's concept of realism is, accordingly, the coherent consequence of what determines the overall framework of Marxist aesthetics. As he puts it:

> The problem is the following: It is only one goal of true realism that the reality is recognized [*wiedererkennen*] on the theater stage. However, the reality has to be understood [*durchschauen*], too. The laws that govern the developments of the life processes should become visible. These laws are not visible in photographs. (Brecht, 1993/22.2, p. 792)

Accordingly, the Marxist concept of mimesis (for this, see Lotz 2017) as the *recognition* of reality cannot be understood as a simple naturalism, insofar as the *presentation* [*Darstellung*] of the reality is supposed to be, at the same time, a consideration and rational reflection *of* this reality. Again, given that the social reality is determined by capitalist society, critical realism is based on the presentation and, *in and through* this presentation, a consideration of this reality. As a consequence, the audience must be kept in a critical distance to the presentation in order to allow for judgments about what is considered in these critical art practices.

This, however, *does not* mean, as Linfield argues (2010, p. 22) that the sole focus of Brecht's aesthetics is based on rationality alone. The opposite is the case: Brecht tries to find the proper balance between the emotional and rational relation of the audience to the work of art. As Didi-Huberman puts it, Brecht's work is based on the assumption that works of art transmit "emotions, *in order to think*, and even to call for action instead of dreaming on" (Didi-Huberman, 2011, p.219). Emotions, we might say, *become* critical throughout the confrontation with the poetic, dramatic, or image work. This is even more true for photographs. As Benjamin puts it:

> . . . photography is unable to convey anything about a power station or a cable factory other than, 'What a beautiful world!' The World Is Beautiful—this is the title of the well-known picture anthology by Renger-Patzsch, in which we see New Objective photography at its peak. For it has succeeded in transforming even abject poverty—by apprehending it in a

fashionably perfected manner—into an object of enjoyment.
(Benjamin, 2005, p. 775)

This statement by Benjamin has often been interpreted as hostile to
popular culture and "enjoyment." Though this interpretation is not false,
we should read it in the larger context of how to rethink the relation
between emotion and rationality through the lens of a critical concept
of mimesis and realism. Being against enjoyment does *not* mean that the
work remains at the rational level alone; instead, what is desirable is an
enjoyment that is not based on good "feelings" alone; instead, it is based
on the *transparency* of the emotional relation between work and audience
or readership. The emotions must be liberated from being dominated,
too. According to Brecht, what we need is a *different type* of enjoyment,
namely, an enjoyment that is not based on art as a means of *consumer*
enjoyment, insofar as consumer enjoyment is *passive*, whereas Marxist
aesthetics operates with an audience that is emotionally *and* rationally
active throughout its reception. This structure underlies the *War Primer*
project, at least insofar as the reader is forced to actively engage with
the images that Brecht put together for the publication. Consequently,
enjoyment *per se* is not a problem for critical aesthetics; instead, it is
only the *immediacy* of enjoyment, which does not allow the revelation
of the underlying structures and social determinations of what each
specific work is about.

What emerges here and elsewhere in Brecht's (and Benjamin's)
writings is an expanded understanding of cultural production. It is no
longer a question of supplying the market with attractive artifacts or
Genußmittel. It is, rather, a question of developing new cultural forms
that encourage active involvement in the production of political consciousness rather than passive consumption of artistic commodities. Long
argues, in my view correctly, that Brechtian aesthetics, which makes
both author and audience into a producer, "shifts the whole emphasis
of literary epistemology from a reflected 'content of knowledge' to an
active, 'critical' reorganization of experience." (Long, 2008, p. 205)

The Arbeiter-Illustrierte Zeitung

Finally, decisive for a proper understanding of Brecht's *War Primer* is also
the principle of montage. I will come back to the principle of montage
in connection with memory in the next section of this chapter. I will

here just briefly point to the background of how Brecht appropriates montage in the *War Primer* and how this underlies the work. Brecht was very fond of the *Arbeiter Illustrierte Zeitung* (AIZ), a daily newspaper targeting the German working class that contained collages produced by avant-garde artists. The *AIZ* tried to break through the official suspicion of the Communist and Social Democrats during the Weimar republic. As one scholar puts it:

> The *AIZ*'s inventive practice may have arisen, therefore, when this near iconoclastic distrust for the surface of appearance met photography, the medium most attentive to precisely that same surface. Again, this would form the origin of what I wish to describe as photo ambivalence—a simultaneous suspicion for and attraction to the medium's documentary capacity. (Zervigón, 2010, p. 151)

Brecht's practice of combining poems with photographs from World War II in the *War Primer* should therefore not be seen as an invention; instead, in this work Brecht transforms a given social practice of combining text with photographs into his own art by carefully selecting images and poetic "commentaries" that reflect the problem of visible surface and invisible social determinations, such as the relation between the power of Nazi leaders and the suffering population and the relation between war ideologies and the underlying weapon production by the German military industry.

Accordingly, the methodological problem of invisibility, the representation of capital, as well as the Marxist attempt to reverse the process of social forgetting, has a political side, insofar as one of the goals of right-wing conservatism, especially in the form of the fascist bourgeoisie and industrial capital, tried to do everything in order to make their own class position, the domination of the population, as well as surplus value production, invisible. Hence, invisibility is not only a socioeconomic concept, but also, if not primarily, a political *concept*. As the AIZ was based on revealing that which the German ruling classes tried to hide, the *War Primer* tries to deal with the same structure through memory and mimesis.

Accordingly, critical aesthetics here means that the *real* process behind the appearances and behind the societal and economic surface should be rendered visible and, at the same time, critically challenged and interrogated. Since the *War Primer* was published after World War II, it should be conceived of as an attempt to push the critical project into the critical mimesis and memory *of* the Second World War. This problem of memory is of course also deeply embedded within the critical practice of appropriating and dealing with photography.

Photography and Mimesis as Memory

Siegfried Kracauer made a distinction between photographs and what he calls "memory image" in his widely read essay on photography. Whereas the photograph remains on the level of facts that are serially organized, the memory image is based on a different temporal logic mainly characterized by *synthesis* and filling in what can never be simply taken as a linear series of events. As he argues, the photograph remains on the level of historicism, which does not really grasp the *meaning* of history. History, according to Kracauer, can emerge only through the destruction of historicism and the linear ordering of photographs. What he has in mind—and this is important for Brecht's montage practice—is that photographs should be taken out of their isolation and re-integrated into a *different*, higher, unity. Krakauer writes:

> On the whole the advocates of such historicist thinking believe that they can explain any phenomenon purely in terms of its genesis. That is, they believe at the very least that they can grasp historical reality by reconstructing the series of events in their temporal succession without any gaps. Photography presents a spatial continuum; historicism seeks to provide the temporal continuum. According to historicism the complete mirroring of a temporal sequence simultaneously contains the meaning of all that occurred within that time. (1993, p. 424)

What Kracauer has in mind here is the assumption that the meaning of events is internal to the linear ordering of events, but, as he argues, this is an illusion because the mere reconstruction of facts, which are not *united* through meaning, remain mere positivistic repetitions. Historicism assumes that historical events are meaningful through simply *repeating* them. Similarly, the photograph remains on this level of repetition, since it cannot go *beyond* the past. History, as opposed to historicism, however, is on a different level. This level can be achieved only through a different (art) practice of dealing with photographs in a different temporal fashion. As Kracauer has it:

> In order for history to present itself the mere surface coherence offered by photography must be destroyed. For in the artwork the meaning of the object takes on spatial appearance, whereas in photography the spatial appearance of an object is its meaning. The two spatial appearances—the "natural" one and that of the object permeated by cognition—are not identical. By sacrificing the former for the sake of the latter the artwork also negates the likeness achieved by photography. This likeness refers to the look of the object, which does not immediately divulge how it reveals itself to cognition; the artwork, however, conveys nothing but the transparency of the object. (Kracauer, 1993, p. 427)

What Kracauer calls here the "transparency of the object" is precisely what I have elsewhere described as "bracketing" the underlying photograph and as opening it up for a new temporal synthesis in which the image does not remain tied to the past; instead, the past *as* past is opened up to the full synthesis of the entire dimensions of temporality, that is, to the synthesis of past, present, and future.[4] As he argues, the photograph, especially the everyday photograph and magazine illustration, are not really seen. For we see too many of these every day and we do not really look most of the time (unless we see them in special places, such as the museum, but then they are on the verge of being conceived in a different mode). As Kracauer argues:

> [. . .] the flood of photos sweeps away the dams of memory. The assault of this mass of images is so powerful that it threatens to destroy the potentially existing awareness of crucial traits. [. . .] In the illustrated magazines people see the very world that the illustrated magazines prevent them from perceiving. The spatial continuum from the camera's perspective predominates the spatial appearance of the perceived object; the likeness that the image bears to it effaces the contours of the object's "history." Never before has a period known so little about itself. (1993, p. 432)

We should see the *War Primer* in this tradition of how to conceive the relation between photography and history. As I have argued elsewhere (Lotz, 2015, 2017), mimesis is not simply a process of imitation; rather, it is a process through which we gain insight into something. Mimesis can thus be viewed as a form of recognition. Mimesis is a material process throughout which the image is mimetically and empathetically developed out of the material. The material process in Brecht is the principle of montage, which allows him to reach unity through and via dispersion, rupture, and reordering of the material. Mimesis should then be conceived as a process because Brecht develops his material into an image *of* the war through the forming principle of montage; he thereby also presents a new appropriation of the "means of artistic production" that Benjamin called for. Let me now move on to the *War Primer* itself.

The Visible and the Invisible in the *Kriegsfibel*

The *War Primer* has a politically interesting publication history. After Brecht had sporadically worked since the 1920s on his working journals, this work on the combination of text and press photographs intensified during Brecht's exile. He sent a first version of the *War Primer* to Karl Korsch in 1945, and Korsch reacted enthusiastically; Brecht's epigrams were "the very best we have about this war up to this day" (see Meyer in Kebir & Hörnigk, 2005, p. 80). In 1948, his Munich publisher did not want to print the book and, ironically, even the publication committee of the *Sozialistische Einheitspartei Deutschlands* that ruled over the GDR rejected the publication of the book in 1950 because it was "too pacifist" (!). This rejection was based not only on the aesthetical preferences of the GDR authorities that were conservative and based on petty bourgeois taste, but also because it did not fit the official party propaganda rhetoric of the central committee. The committee was also seemingly suspicious of Brecht's American background and the attempts of the West Allies to "re-educate" the German people (see Meyer in Kebir & Hörnigk, 2005, p. 82). For East German authorities this was just another attack on the "anti-imperialist" stance of the SED. Brecht, as someone who was suspicious of any kind of state bureaucracy, reacted furiously about the authoritarian attempt to eradicate his autonomy as an artist by the party committee (Wizisla in Kebir & Hörnigk, 2005, p. 160), but he could not change the committee's mind. The rejection of the publication of the *War Primer* goes along with the suppression of the artistic Weimar avant-garde in Germany. For example, earlier books based on critical photomontage (such as Tucholsky, Heartfield, and Russian constructivism) had disappeared behind the veil of East European and Soviet propaganda machineries. However, finally, the *Kriegsfibel* was published in 1955 since the GDR authorities could no longer dismiss Brecht after he received the Stalin Peace Prize in 1954 nor after Brecht reestablished himself internationally as a leading artist of the 20th century. The book was over-dimensional in its size, contained large black-and-white press photographs with short press commentaries and Brecht's own four line poems, which he called "photo-epigrams."[5] The cover features an image of four returning and visibly suffering soldiers, one of whom appears to have lost his eyesight.[6] Though they do not directly look into the camera, their "look" and the framing and perspective of the photograph produces a tense closeness to the viewer. Brecht wanted the book to be distributed in high numbers to the entire population. As such, the book would have functioned as what is called in the United States a "coffee table book." It is safe to assume, though, that the book would not have ended up in middle-class bourgeois households, given that it is based on a deep contempt of propaganda and the rejection of heroic appropriations of World War II à la the History Channel.

The (In)Visible I: Memory

Leaving the concrete political context and the publication history of the 1950s aside, the *War Primer* was published at a time when most Germans had not yet started to mourn their past and instead busied themselves with rebuilding the country. The *War Primer* is produced from the perspective of a *poetic and memorial practice*, which, following Brecht's overall vision, was not only moral and poetic, but also based on his avant-garde artistic appropriation of the modern mix of media. As Benjamin, Brecht thought about art through the new media developed at the beginning of 20th century and, as such, he remained in distance to Adorno's focus on classical music, as well as Lukacs's rather conservative taste for bourgeois literature. We should not underestimate this fact, since otherwise we miss the point that the *War Primer* is not just "any" work on World War II, but, instead, is based on a *precisely* defined artistic task of appropriating modern media for the purpose of the arts, as Kracauer called for (see last section). Whereas Adorno, at least for some time, took Schönberg's *Survivor from Warsaw* (Op. 46, composed in 1947) as the only (!) work that deals properly with the atrocities of the Second World War, Brecht's aesthetics never lost sight of the "normal" people and of critically dealing with the fascist reality in Germany. Accordingly, Brecht's book, as Berlau reminds us in her foreword, functions as a critical reminder and critical form of *working through* the past that the Germans at that point of their history tried to suppress. Consequently, the concept of realism that underlies the book, is transformed into the attempt to mimetically appropriate the past via the explicit act of remembering the war and to practice memory. The book demonstrates how to confront news media practices with poetic praxis in order to achieve a higher unity of enlightened reflection of the past. To some extent, one could even argue that Brecht was well ahead of what then became the explicit political and cultural appropriation of the German past in the 1960s and '70s. In Brecht's *War Primer*, art becomes a critical counter-strategy to hiding the reality. Given what I have said in the first part of this chapter, we might say that the book is based on the concept of a *realism of the invisible*. As Brecht underlines in his essays on realism and in response to Lukacs's critique of avant-garde modernism, realism for him means that a work of art is more realistic when it is able to master the reality within and with the means of the artistic process. Applied to the *War Primer*, this means that we are not supposed to simply remember the past; rather, we are supposed to *work through* it and thereby "repeat" the working through of the work itself in our mimetic and critical appropriation. Overcoming "historicism" in Kracauer's sense could then be achieved by art as a critical praxis. The result of this conception is a de-fetishization of the reality that the images in their original function as propaganda are hiding and covering up. As a consequence, the process of forgetting, as philosophically done in Marx, is matched by the work of Marxist art, that is, with the means of art and its material. When Brecht published the *Kriegsfibel* in 1955, he speaks of the suppression of the past [*tolle Verdrängung*] in a letter (Brecht, 1993/30, p. 472). I do not need to point out that the word *Verdrängung* stems from Freud's vocabulary.[7] However, as Freud, Brecht is not interested in an exclusive mimetic process based on rationality; rather, he fully understands that this process must contain both rational judgment and emotional "working through." As such, the *War Primer* reacts to the *silence* of the Germans about their horrific past, although it should be noted that Brecht neither thematizes the murdering of the European Jews in general, nor the concentration camps as such.

Critical art is here directly opposed to war. We can easily see that Linfield's criticism, to which I referred in the first part of this chapter, is misguided, insofar as Brecht's memorial practice is based on a deep compassion with what he deals with in his works. Although Brecht knew that Hitler was supported by many Germans, he never shows any harsh judgments on the "normal" people, as long as they do not become exploiters, torturers, class oppressors, or the like. His solidarity with "the" people remains intact. In this vein, we should also remember that in her famous essay on Brecht, Arendt makes the point that Brecht's work is based on gesture of compassion (Arendt, 2013, p. 292), which is expressed in his closeness to normal people, his appropriation of the everyday German language and its tradition in some parts of the German literature, his love for the world, and, as Arendt says, his thankfulness for heaven and earth (Arendt, 2013, p. 286). All of this is prominently featured in the *War Primer*, although it is a deeply critical work. As Didi-Huberman has argued, Brecht's concept of "alienation effect" [*Verfremdungseffekt*] is a dialectical concept that contains both pathos and compassion (Didi-Huberman, 2011). It is astonishing that so many commentators dismiss the concept as being too rationalistic; however, for Brecht all writing emerges from a deep sympathy with those who suffer. In the *War Primer* this is most visible in the distinction between above and below, that is, the power interests that drive the war and those who suffer from it. Brecht maps the social distinction between poor and rich onto the structure above/below in two regards: (1) the *War Primer* shows leading Nazis in relation to "normal" people, and (2) it shows special attention to the centrality of warfare from the air in contrast to the destruction on the ground. The distinction between the interests of the people and its suffering is contrasted with the interests and artificial behavior and rhetoric of the dominating group in power. All of this is translated in a reversal of the emotional relation between work and viewer, insofar as the emotional quality of the work turns into one that is based on judgment and reflection. For Brecht, emotions and, in turn, the empathy and "feeling in" (*Einfühlung*) that audiences develop in their reception of works is a concrete social relation determined on social factors, such as class and politics. They are not timeless. In order to achieve this, however, the relation between audience and work needs to be unsettled. This is achieved in the *War Primer* primarily through breaking through news photographs as displaying "facts" by confronting them with the epigrammatic function of the commenting poems.[8] Following Kracauer in this regard, Brecht tries to turn pictures that are equal to a loss of history into *images of history*. The poetic four-liners transcend the positivistic quality of the picture, unsettle the referent of the photograph, and turn the picture into an image.[9]

The (In)Visible II: Montage

The working through the *War Primer* is most visible in the principle of montage that underlies the work. Given the long debate on the principle of montage in Marxist aesthetics, I will only briefly mention its aspect of relevance to the *War Primer*, namely, the assembly character of the work in relation to the problem of mimesis and memory. One commentator describes the assembly character of Brecht's works in the following way: "The practice of real-life remembering emphasizes the finished product and pays little attention as possible to the assembly stage. The work of art, on the contrary, concentrates on the process of establishing images" (Mueller 1989, p. 69). In my view, Mueller nicely describes the core of the "montage" process since she points out that the montage principle leads to seeing the reality as a *process* (in this case the reality as remembered). This conception of reality as a process is central for Brecht and underlies his conception of realism. Let me briefly develop this point.

We often forget that montage is a practice done by *hands* and involves manual activities, such as sticking, moving, cutting, and ordering. Montage is therefore not, as Lukacs once thought, a helpless attitude toward a no longer understood social totality; rather, its material activity is the *concrete* reconstruction of a totality with other means that are, in opposition to abstract concepts, based on "handy" work, which was essential for Brecht's idea of what it means to be an artist (see Geyer in Kebir & Hörnigk, 2005, p. 78). The journals on which the *War Primer* is based are an ongoing reflection *on* the material by organizing and shaping the material itself. Montage is the opposite of a mindless potpourri of anything goes. The fact that Brecht adds to the image material textual strategies is of course based on the assumption that images, if they want to be understood, need some kind of distance by the viewer, which in Brecht's case is established through the commenting function of the text as well as by isolating the press photographs from their original propaganda context. The act of isolation is itself the result of a practical task of cutting out and preparing the photographs for their new "neutral" black paper background (which is how the images are presented in the book).

This distance through process, however, does not simply equal the distrust of "iconophobic" Marxist intellectuals; rather, it is itself an aesthetic praxis that is more complex than simply adding controlling text to images. For example, the relation between text and image is here characterized by an entire arsenal of techniques such as poetic alienation, contrast, surprise, (un)familiarity, irony, newness, break, shock, attention to aspects, contradictions, analogies, and metaphorical relations. *Contradiction* is by far the most important aesthetic principle for Brecht, insofar as both the aesthetical praxis *and* the reality are for him characterized by contradiction. A contradictory reality, as, we might say, one in which "nothing hangs together," can only be appropriated by an aesthetical praxis that is *in its form* based on contradiction. As Brecht aptly puts it, "reality not only is everything that is; rather, it is everything that becomes. It is a process. This process is contradictory. If one does not acknowledge its contradictory character, one does not know it at all" (Brecht, 1993/22.1, p. 459). And further: "Flat, shallow, are poems if they take away the contradictions from their material and if the things with which they deal do not appear in their living and all-sidedness, and if they are not formulated in their finite, and non-finalized form" (Brecht, 1993/22.2, p. 129). Consequently, Brechtian montage

> carries with it an emphatic break between units, leaving the audience free to "confabulate." It interrupts the continuity of space and time and in this way prevents the equivocation between reality and its representation. Brechtian realism is not based on a direct correspondence between sign and referent. (Mueller, 1989, p. 89)

Brecht follows this idea of montage as a systematic juxtaposition of opposites and the structural determination through contradictions in many of his works, including the arrangements of scenes and characters in his plays. Opposing Lukacs on this point, Brecht argues that true realism is not based on what he takes to be a bourgeois idea of "totality," but rather on the inner reflection of the breaks and incoherences of that totality. Consequently, he comes to the conclusion that true realism is the artistic realization and *recognition* of the reality as contradictory. The mimetic process of art is the logical consequence of the reality itself, the point of which is also recognized by Benjamin in his reflections on Brecht. In relation to poems written in the context of the *War Primer*, Benjamin writes:

> The first line of this poem could be placed at the head of each of the *War Primer* poems. These inscriptions are not, like those of the Romans, intended for stone but, like those of underground fighters, for fences. Accordingly, the character of the *War Primer* may be seen in a unique contradiction: these words, whose poetic form implies that they are meant to survive the forthcoming end of the world, contain the gesture of a slogan scrawled in haste on a plank fence by a man being pursued. In this contradiction lies the extraordinary artistic achievement of these sentences constructed out of primitive words. (Benjamin, 1998, p. 66)

The (In)Visible III: War

Brecht's work is in important respects related to war. This fact is not only the result of his biography and the times during which he wrote; rather, with his firm footing in the Marxist tradition, Brecht always remained interested in critically analyzing the relationship between capitalism and war. As we know, the main line of thinking about the relation between war and capital has its origin in Luxemburg's and Lenin's theories about the necessary expansion of the capitalist system through colonialism, imperialism, and expanded commodification of areas that have not yet been subsumed under capital. Whenever the accumulation process comes to an exhaustion, capital must either expand its reach through an ongoing primitive accumulation, that is, war and violence, or destroy capital in order to get the process of surplus value generation flowing again. In addition, wars themselves can be very profitable for capital. As Herfried Münkler has argued (in Kebir & Hörnigk, 2005, pp. 16–33), Brecht's take on the 17th-century peasants war in Europe, which Brecht deals with in his play *Mother Courage*, is a very contemporary play, insofar as the peasant war was not structured by the confrontation between nation-states. Additionally, Brecht shows how individuals, once they are part of the war, can live and profit from war in many ways. Economy and war, according to the Marxist tradition, do not necessarily exclude each other, but instead, feed on each other.[10] Brecht is an astute observer of these relations during World War II, and his journal entries, which ultimately lead to the *War Primer*, are full of observations related to the relations between power, the dominating class, industry, and war. Among others, themes are the industrialization of war, the reduction of the individual to a functioning cog in the machine, and the destruction of individual characters and virtues (which, in turn, must be reflected in a theater proper to its times).

According to Brecht (following Marx), capitalism, and here we are returning to the problem of the relation between visibility and invisibility, is a social system that *suppresses* its own crimes and is based on making its own past invisible. As Berlau writes in her foreword to the *War Primer:*

> Why do our workers of state-owned industry, our communal farmers, our progressive intellectuals, why does our youth, who already enjoys the rations of happiness, why must they all at this moment hold in front of them these grim images of history? He who forgets his past does not escape it. This book [*Kriegsfibel*] wishes to teach the art of reading images. It is as difficult for the novice to read images as it is to read hieroglyphics. The great ignorance about societal relations, which the forces of capitalism carefully and brutally perpetuate, turns the thousands of photographs in the media into true panels of hieroglyphics, indecipherable to the unsuspecting reader. (Brecht, 1993/12, p. 129)

Images and photographs are used within a propaganda machinery that distorts the truth for the purpose of those who have an interest in prolonging the war. Brecht's strategy in the *War Primer* is to counter this *production* of images for the purpose of distorting the reality through a production of images that is truth oriented. In order to establish this different goal, a break and distancing from the pictures is necessary; the four-line poems that Brecht wrote in connection with the images are supposed to establish the critical distance to the referents of the pictures in order to enable the viewer to come to her own judgment about the images. "The thinking human," as Brecht writes, "tries to correct everything that he reads or hears. With each sentence, he replaces untrue assertions with true assertions. This exercise lasts as long as he is no longer able to read or hear otherwise" (Brecht, 1993/22.1, p. 90).

Conclusion

In conclusion, we might say that Brecht's *War Primer* is the best example of an artistic practice that proves *in actu* that some of the skeptical suspicions the Frankfurt School's handling of the modern mass media are unwarranted, insofar as Brecht does find a way of dealing with this material critically. The *War Primer* introduces mimesis as a process of emotional cognition and emotional remembering; it thereby "translates" the problem of Marxist methodology, as outlined by Marx himself in *Capital*, in artistic categories and as *aesthetic form*. As such, it turns the photographic picture and abstractions from being a tool of forgetting into the process of critical remembering and re-appropriation of the past on a reflective level. As Berlau points out in her foreword to the work,

> The great ignorance concerning social relations, an ignorance nursed carefully and brutally by capitalism, reduces thousands of photos in illustrated journals to hieroglyphs which are undecipherable for the unsuspecting reader. Like an ancient hieroglyph, the press photograph is "undecipherable" for anyone who lacks the appropriate training. Brecht's book is offered, therefore, as a practical manual, demonstrating how to "read" or "translate" press photographs. At the same time, it seeks to provide some basic lessons about the nature of modern warfare. (Brecht, 2008, n.p.)

The accompanying poems function as a mimetic recognition of what is forgotten in the images. The goal of this work is not the elimination of emotional responses; rather, it is supposed to lead to proper compassion in order to open up venues toward a different future.[11] To be certain, Brecht is a poet in the best tradition of the enlightenment and therefore differs from much a-political and uncritical art that has, with important exceptions, flooded many Western art markets after World War II. As one commentator has it:

> The *Kriegsfibel* activates historical awareness; it instructs the reader/viewer to critically engage with and question the many images of war; it also offers a practical example for the claim that history is conceived as images corresponding to the metaphorical language of photography—a claim made famous

by Brecht's fellow exile and collaborator Walter Benjamin. (Imbrigotta, 2010, p. 29)

Notes

1. Brecht engaged with different image media throughout his work life; his decade-long journals show a deep interest in photographs, and he also worked early on with film. Moreover, images were included early on in his practical theater work. For example, he considered his *Modelbücher*, which contained series of photographs of his theater production, as essential for his work. As Mueller has it, "Brecht considered this kind of visual instruction indispensable and not to be replaced by conceptual formulas" (Mueller, 1989, p. 78).

2. The shortening of the quote is one reason some contemporary commentators do not understand what critical aesthetics and Marxist aesthetics is struggling with. For example, Linfield (2010) in her attack on Brecht quotes only the first two lines and, as a consequence, misses the entire problem of what is behind Brecht's critical media practice.

3. For this, see Lotz (2014).

4. I have called this process *essentialization* (for this, see Lotz 2015, pp. 130–133).

5. The oversize of the book might go back to the *AIZ*. As Zervigón writes: "Less noticeable in this reproduction yet key to the impact of its furiously unveiled history is the picture's size, splashed across a centerfold surface nearly double the dimension of today's American tabloids. This aggressive lurching forward of repressed history, therefore, operates as a photographic revelation taking place only inches in front of the reader's face" (2010, p. 153).

6. On a side note, *Verso Books* has just recently (2017) republished the *War Primer*; unfortunately, the entire black-and-white aesthetics as well as the cover image has been changed. The removal of the soldier image distorts the role of empathy in Brecht's aesthetics. One could argue that this is, ironically, based on some kind of censorship, too, since Verso apparently did not take seriously that for Brecht *how* the material is presented is essential for *what* is presented and how it is to be understood.

7. See my remarks on Marx's method in relation to Freud (Lotz, 2017b).

8. There is controversy over the origin of Brecht's "photo-epigrams;" insofar as some argue that Brecht goes back to the Baroque epigram tradition and others argue that this Brecht invented it for Marxist aesthetics (for this, see Knopf 1986, 213).

9. For a detailed conception of this process of turning photographs into images as a hermeneutical process, see Lotz (2015).

10. The Marxist tradition is opposed to the Kantian tradition that argues that capital cannot be interested in expansive wars, as this hinders the further development of exchange and the establishment of stable structures needed for capital and investment.

11. In this vein, the musical appropriations of the *Kriegsfibel* by composer Hans Eisler and singer and actress Kathrin Angerer even more intensively reveal the dialectic between the rational and compassionate nature of the *War Primer*. For the sake of the main topic of this chapter, I left these complex interpretations of Brecht's work aside.

References

Arendt, H. (2013). *Menschen in finsteren Zeiten.* München, Germany: Piper.

Benjamin, W. (1998). *Understanding Brecht.* Translated by Anna Bostock. London, UK: Verso.

Benjamin, W. (2005). *Walter Benjamin: Selected Writings, Volume 2, Part 2: 1931–1934.* Edited by M.W. Jennings. Translated by R. Livingstone et al. Cambridge, MA: Harvard University Press.

Brecht B. (1993). *Große kommentierte Frankfurter und Berliner Ausgabe.* 30 Volumes. Edited by Werner Hecht. Frankfurt am Main, Germany: Suhrkamp Verlag.

Brecht, B. (2008). *Kriegsfibel.* Berlin, Germany: Eulenspiegel. (First published in 1955)

Chari, A. (2015). *A Political Economy of the Senses: Neoliberalism, Reification, Critique.* New York, NY: Columbia University Press.

Demirovic, A. (1999). *Der nonkonformistische Intellektuelle: Die Entwicklung der Kritischen Theorie zur Frankfurter Schule.* Frankfurt am Main, Germany: Suhrkamp.

Didi-Huberman, G. (2011). *Wenn die Bilder Position beziehen. Das Auge der Geschichte I.* Translated by Markus Sedlacek. München, Germany: Fink.

Grimm, R. (1975). Marxist emblems: Bertolt Brecht's *War Primer. Comparative Literature Studies, 12*(3), 263–287.

Imbrigotta, K. (2010). History and the challenge of photography in Bertolt Brecht's Kriegsfibel. *Radical History Review, 106,* 27–45.

Kebir, S., & Hörnigk, T. (2005). *Brecht und der Krieg. Wiedersprüche damals, Einsprüche heute.* Berlin, Germany: Theater der Zeit.

Kienast, W. (2001). *Kriegsfibelmodell. Autorschaft und kollektiver Schöpfungsprozess in Brechts Kriegsfibel.* Göttingen, Germany: Vandenhoeck & Ruprecht.

Knopf, J. (1986). *Lyrik, Prosa, Schriften. Brecht Handbuch.* Stuttgart, Germany: Metzler

Kracauer, S. (1993). Photography. Translated by Levin. *Critical Inquiry, 19*(3), 421–436.

Linfield, S. (2010). *The Cruel Radiance: Photography and Political Violence*. Chicago, IL: University of Chicago Press.

Long, J. J. (2008). Paratextual profusion: Photography and text in Bertolt Brecht's *War Primer*. *Poetics Today*, 29(1), 197–224.

Lotz, C. (2014). *The Capitalist Schema. Time, Money, and the Culture of Abstraction*. Lanham, MD: Lexington Books

Lotz, C. (2015). *The Art of Gerhard Richter. Hermeneutics, Images, Meaning*. London, UK: Bloomsbury Press 2015.

Lotz, C. (2017a). Representing Capital? Mimesis, realism, and contemporary photography. In D. Krier & M. P. Worrell (eds.), *The Social Ontology of Capitalism* (pp. 173–193). London, UK: Palgrave,

Lotz, C. (2017b). Fiction without fantasy: Capital fetishism as objective forgetting. *Continental Thought & Theory*, 2, 364–382.

Marx, K. (1990). *Capital: Volume 1: A Critique of Political Economy*. Translated by Ben Fowkes. London, UK: Penguin.

Marx, K. (1993). *Grundrisse. Foundations of the Critique of Political Economy*. Translated by Martin Nicolaus. London, UK: Penguin.

Mueller, R. (1989). *Bertolt Brecht and the Theory of the Media*. Lincoln: University of Nebraska Press.

Zervigón, A. M. (2010, June). Persuading with the unseen? Die Arbeiter-Illustrierte-Zeitung, photography, and German Communism's iconophobia. *Visual Resources*, 26(2), 147–164.

Chapter 3

The Poetics of Nihilism

Representing Capital's Indifference in Dickens' *Hard Times*

PATRICK MURRAY AND JEANNE SCHULER

The void at the heart of bourgeois life results in the most accomplished irony: accumulation as an infinite increase in emptiness is mistaken for a plenitude of wealth.

—Chris Arthur (2002, p. 172)

Introduction: Literature and Social Theory

Literature and film offer powerful means of disclosing aspects of commercial life. A novel makes visible social realities that are less discernible or striking in abstract analysis. Of course, as a mode of reflection, art—like philosophy—remains subject to distortion and error. Appealing to novels and other literary forms in the exposition of socioeconomic topics is not new. S. S. Prawer (1976), author of *Karl Marx and World Literature*, observes that Marx "uses incidents from specific literary works to show, as in a model, the actual or perverted logic of events in the real social world . . . Economic processes which are 'opaque' in real life may be made 'transparent' in literature" (pp. 416–417). Dante and Shakespeare are among Marx's favorite literary sources. In *Capital in the Twenty-First Century*, Thomas Piketty draws extensively on creative writers, especially the 19th-century novelists Jane Austen and Honoré de Balzac (another favorite of Marx), to call attention to 19th-century socioeconomic realities: the makeup of wealth (chiefly rent-bearing lands and interest-bearing government bonds), the negligible inflation, and the fact that work and learning could not compete with inheritance and "marrying well" as ways to become rich.[1] Of most direct relevance for present purposes is Martha Nussbaum's *Poetic Justice: The Literary Imagination and Public Life*, not only because *Hard Times* is her focus and some points she makes anticipate some of ours but also because she considers why literature—the novel in particular—plays an essential role in judging socioeconomic realities.

We focus on how Charles Dickens' novel *Hard Times* critically represents mid-19th-century industrial capitalism while uncritically adopting much of its mindset.[2] We will establish that *Hard Times* is primarily about capital's shadow forms and only secondarily about its constitutive forms and that Dickens accepts key bifurcations involved in modern conceptions of reason and society and seeks only to harmonize them or ameliorate their ill effects.

Dickens is troubled by the aggressive expansion of the utilitarian mentality into the whole social order; he wants to cordon off the political and (especially) the domestic spheres.[3] At the root of this mentality's nihilistic indifference to particularity is the reduction of the qualitative to the quantitative.[4] *Hard Times* depicts how family and schooling are mutilated through this reduction. Politics is likewise pared down to calculations: "the most complicated social questions were cast up, got into exact totals, and finally settled" (Dickens, 1990, p. 75).[5] The forces of reduction are embodied in the doctrine of two characters: Thomas Gradgrind and Mr. James Harthouse. Gradgrind leads a crusading effort to refashion society in terms of the leading ideology of the day. "Facts and figures" will triumph on the grave of traditional moral, religious, and political ideals. What appears as progress to the adherents of the Gradgrind philosophy is unmasked as nihilism by Harthouse. The Gradgrind conquest is pyrrhic, and Harthouse revels in the ruins.

The void that actually drives capitalist accumulation is treated by Dickens as an ideological abyss. His preoccupation is with capital's spreading shadows.[6] Dickens responds to social questions by upholding divisions. To maintain an intact humanity, he appeals to demarcations and separates industry from the rest of society. Imagination, love, and virtue are to be nurtured outside the factory walls not driven by Gradgrind's drumbeat: fact, fact, fact—never wonder. To set up our reading of *Hard Times*, we will briefly distinguish constitutive forms and shadow forms.

Constitutive Forms and Shadow Forms

Capitalism can be understood in terms of constitutive and shadow forms. Constitutive forms emerge from systematic analysis; they do not just pop into view. Capitalism is constituted as a self-reproducing social totality organized by the forms of the commodity, value, money, wage labor, and capital. From these forms arise the cross currents of a dynamic, crisis-prone social order directed at profit-making and the expansion of capital.[7] Money and the price system actually perform the reduction of the qualitative to the quantitative—"everything has its price"—and "money is incapable of any other movement but the quantitative one: to expand itself" (Marx, 1987, p. 495). Capital is constituted by this movement of quantitative expansion of value. At the beginning of the circuit of capital (M-C-M+ΔM), "capital exists here as yet only as a given quantum of value = M (money), in which all use-value is extinguished" (Marx, 1976b, pp. 975–977).[8] A successful (investment) circuit of capital begins with money (M)—"in which all use-value is extinguished"—and closes with more money (M+ΔM), where all particularity is likewise extinguished. The measure of success where the circulation and accumulation of capital is concerned is purely quantitative. Whether profit is gained by mining diamonds or making ice cream does not matter. In its downward spiral of disregard for particularity even as material wealth spirals upward, capital is nihilistic at its core.[9]

Powerful social forms have consequences. Marx observes that capitalism casts shadows that pervade society and shape experience. Oddly, shadow forms are often more visible than value and surplus value, the prime determinations of systematic analysis. Shadows are not restricted by the dimensions of what they track. The shadow forms crop up in social sciences, arts, and mainstream ideologies. Some shadow forms are illusory and derail efforts to understand society. Notions of utility and instrumental reason are shadows that block access to constitutive forms. They close off questions and disguise the workings of capital. Challenging these pseudo-concepts is a prerequisite to understanding capitalism. Other shadow forms illumine the workings of capital as they extend the propulsive reach of constitutive forms beyond commerce and industry into the whole of society. For example, by putting prices on almost everything, capitalism encourages a calculating mentality that can be (mis)applied to every mode of existence: What cannot be quantified cannot be trusted. Both illusory and illuminating shadow forms define capitalist society and culture; they are often easier to grasp than constitutive forms, and they lend themselves better to literary representation. *Hard Times* centers on capital's shadows, above all, indifference and the compulsion to calculate.

The early sociologist Georg Simmel called attention to the link between the money economy and the calculative, matter-of-fact mentality:

> But money economy and the domination of the intellect stand in the closest relationship to one another. They have in common a purely matter-of-fact attitude in the treatment of persons and things in which a formal justice is often combined with an unrelenting hardness. The purely intellectualistic person is indifferent to all things personal because, out of them relationships and reactions develop which are not to be completely understood by purely rational methods—just as the unique element in events never enters into the principle of money. Money is concerned only with what is common to all, i.e., with the exchange value which reduces all quality and individuality to a purely quantitative level. All emotional relationships between persons rest on their individuality, whereas intellectual relationships deal with persons as with numbers, that is, as with elements which, in themselves, are indifferent, but which are of interest only insofar as they offer something objectively perceivable. (Simmel, 1997, p. 337)

Since "all things personal . . . are not to be completely understood by purely rational methods," indifference results. Dickens portrays this indifference in the scene where Mr. Gradgrind extends Bounderby's proposal of marriage to his daughter Louisa. When Louisa has the temerity to wonder aloud, "does Mr. Bounderby ask me to love him?" her father counters that "the expression itself . . . may be a little misplaced" (p. 76). When Louisa presses her father for an alternative to the "misplaced expression," he instructs her to confine herself "rigidly to Fact."

The contrast of constitutive forms with their shadows recalls Hegel's distinction between essence and appearance: the essence of capitalism constitutes myriad appearances. Shadow forms disclose the world of capital but not the contradictory dynamism at its core. At that core lies the emptiness of value, whose supersensible substance, congealed abstract labor, shows itself in the universal equivalent, money. Marx calls the capitalist a "rational miser," dedicated to the endless accumulation of surplus value (Marx, 1976a, p. 254). In this unending process, material qualities matter only as means to money-making. In the accumulation of capital, more is never enough. This Sisyphean labor creates an emptiness that displaces concrete goals.

Not surprisingly, capital's shadow forms conceal life's specificities and spread a nihilistic mindset. Some shadow forms dismiss the reality of self and world without comprehending them. Constitutive forms track the course of accumulation cycles; they reveal how a social order renews itself. Constitutive forms are grounded in history. If shadow forms are not connected with constitutive forms, they lack historical grounding. Without recognizing their historical grounding, shadow forms appear timeless, and they lack the power to make sense of a particular social order. That saps the critical force of an analysis focused on shadow forms. Instead, the current social order appears irreversible or metaphysical; as Marx mocked the political economists: "Thus there has been history, but there is no longer any" (Marx, 1963, p. 121). Tracing shadow forms to the constitutive social forms that they are shadows of stops time from standing still.

Art and Philosophy: A Hegelian Counterpoint to Dickens

In the Enlightenment, basic distinctions often harden into logical dualities. With his sharp separations of concepts from perceptions and mind from world, Kant is the exemplar of bifurcation. Dualisms drawn from the Enlightenment shape the intellectual horizon of the 19th century and into the present. Dickens adopts this modern mindset. A rigid contrast between reason and imagination centers the plot of *Hard Times*. Gradgrind says to Bounderby, "the reason is (as you know) the only faculty to which education should be addressed" (p. 19). Dickens adopts the reason/imagination bifurcation and, likewise, splits facts from values. Another familiar divide sets knowledge apart from art and other human endeavors as what alone is objective or true.[10]

As a counterpoint to Dickens' bifurcations, consider how Hegel distinguishes art from philosophy. Hegel rejects purist splits, such as inner or outer, objective or subjective. In his philosophy, ordinary distinctions do not morph into logical disjunctions. Philosophy does not contrast with art as explication to expression or head to heart. Like science and philosophy, literature engages history, culture, and institutions. All operate within the discourse of truth, each revealing the world in its own way. Narrative reveals the matter at hand at the level of appearances. How does life unfold in commercial society? Critical social theory engages the matter at hand on the level of concepts. What forms constitute commercial society? Splitting the universal from the particular, concepts from percepts, or philosophy from art, encourages nominalism and positivism; it is always a false move. Concepts are more abstract than experience, but disclosure of the universal occurs throughout the discourse of truth.

For Hegel, art and philosophy constitute spirit in its most absolute and self-determining forms. Along with religion, each dimension of the absolute takes the totality as its object. Philosophy identifies and develops basic concepts. Art formulates sensuous ideals and paradigmatic experiences. *The Grapes of Wrath* portrays the reserve army of the dispossessed through the travails of the Joad family. The nature and vicissitudes of wage labor are analyzed by Marx. Fiction makes visible the effects of life under capitalism. At its best, philosophy investigates the social forms that produce these effects. The narrative opens up space for thinking and gives it urgency.

In Hegel, what is concrete, the actual, sets the goal of inquiry. The concrete is not immediately in our grasp, as Locke imagines simple ideas to be. To distinguish philosophy from art, it is helpful to acknowledge two meanings of concrete: conceptual determination and ideal embodiment. What is concrete in the order of thought is directed at the whole and results from analysis. Philosophy arrives at the concrete through analysis and phenomenological inquiry that makes systematic conceptual development possible. The fullest expressions of freedom and truth are most concrete. The characters and action in a novel imaginatively embody a world—Dickens' Coketown, for example. Art, properly integrated with social theory, is no intermission or seventh-inning stretch. It generates a different friction; it expands and enlivens our understanding.

Hard Times and the Gradgrind Philosophy

Hard Times is set in a factory town blackened by the soot of smokestacks and reddened by the furnaces' glare. Encircled by abandoned coal pits and dead trees, Coketown is hellish and dull:

> Coketown . . . was a triumph of fact . . . a town of unnatural red and black like the painted face of a savage . . . out of which . . . serpents of smoke trailed themselves forever . . . a black canal in it and a river that ran purple with ill-smelling dye . . . where the piston of the steam-engine worked monotonously up and down like the head of an elephant in a state of melancholy madness. It contained several large streets all very like one another, and many small streets still more like one another, inhabited by people equally like one another, who all went in and out at the same hours, with the same sound upon the same pavements, to do the same work, and to whom every day was the same as yesterday and to-morrow, and every year the counterpart of the last and the next. (p. 22)

Coketown enforces leveling and sameness from its streets to its souls.[11] Four households carry the novel's action: the Gradgrind family in their Stone Lodge; the "castle" of the self-made capitalist Josiah Bounderby; Sleary's nomadic circus performers; and the rooms of the factory worker Stephen Blackpool. The demonic force consuming Dickens' Coketown is not money or machines but the Gradgrind philosophy, an overblown amalgam of calculating self-interest and a fetish for facts. This crusading mindset dictates how household, school, church, factory, bank, and state are to run. Society in all its particulars is subsumed under Gradgrind imperatives.

In subsuming the domestic sphere—in particular the upbringing and education of children—the Gradgrind philosophy exceeds the reach of capital's constitutive forms. The households of free wage laborers cannot be formally subsumed under capital; otherwise, children would be owned by capital. What troubles Dickens is not so much capital's reach but its overreach. Only the circus resists the power of capital's constitutive and its shadow forms; no wonder it is shunned by Gradgrind and Bounderby. What revolts Gradgrind about circus members like Sissy Jupe is their embrace of imagination, fantasy, feeling, and laughter. The community of performers is not yoked to the Gradgrind regime. Generosity and friendship—anathema to the Gradgrind philosophy—are found among the scruffy performers:

> Yet there was a remarkable gentleness and childishness about these people, a special inaptitude for any kind of sharp prac-tice, and an untiring readiness to help and pity one another, deserving often of as much respect and always of as much generous construction, as the every-day virtues of any class of people in the world. (pp. 31–32)

The Gradgrind children never hear fairy tales or play make-believe. Forbidden to express feelings, they are spiritually starved. Their father orders them:

> You are never to fancy . . . We hope to have, before long, a board of fact, composed of commissioners of fact, who will force the people to be a people of fact, and of nothing but fact. You must discard the word Fancy altogether. (p. 11)[12]

Like a thought experiment, *Hard Times* follows the barren outcomes for children reared under this regimen, especially Louisa and Tom, the elder Gradgrind children. Bitzer, the "colorless" young man who excels at this training, scorns loyalty to the Gradgrinds or to anyone. He epitomizes dedication to "me, first and last."[13] Sissy Jupe, adopted by the Gradgrinds after her father, an aging clown, disappears, fails at this training. An intact human, she emerges as the family's savior.

Dickens satirizes Gradgrind's ideological use of political economy, but Dickens was less familiar with the workings of commerce and industry. In preparing for *Hard Times* he traveled north to observe the strike of textile workers in Preston, which ended in defeat after 8 months.[14] *Hard Times* follows workers trudging home at dusk but never goes inside the factory. We never learn what commodity is being produced. *Hard Times* presses no unwelcome questions about profits.[15] For Dickens, the inner workings of capitalism remain shrouded—no wonder that its constitutive forms are not in the limelight. The novel does enter the classroom, a tightly controlled production line with students called by number, not by name. Here, Sissy—Girl Number 20—confounds the facts-and-figures curriculum with the New Testament: "To the question what is the first principle of the science of Political Economy, Sissy offered the absurd answer, 'To do unto others as I would that they should do unto me'" (p. 46). Indoctrination is carried out by teachers, like Mr. M'Choakumchild, who are dedicated to eradicating the pestilence of imagination: but "dost thou think that thou wilt always kill the robber fancy lurking within—or sometimes only maim him and distort him?" (p. 12). Mr. M'Choakumchild was the product of a teacher factory: "[S]ome one hundred and forty other schoolmasters had been lately turned at the same time, in the same factory, on the same principles, like so many pianoforte legs" (p. 12). M'Choakumchild's school, like a factory, encases the "infinite grinding at the mill of knowledge as per system, schedule, blue book, report, and tabular statements" (p. 46). Here Dickens sets his sights on the calculative mentality, a shadow form whose fascination with the quantitative befits a society where prices daily reduce qualitative differences to quantitative ones. Yet Dickens looks to human nature, not political change, to offer resistance.

The Gradgrind Philosophy and Utilitarianism

Utilitarianism promotes shadow forms of the illusory kind. Dickens roughly patterns the Gradgrind system after utilitarian thinking, which comes in several varieties. Thomas Gradgrind retires from his successful hardware business to become a Member of Parliament; he shares the aspirations of Jeremy Bentham and the Mills to reform existing laws and institutions according to rules calculated to produce prosperity and happiness. Because facts, axioms, and mathematical reasoning are involved, these projects are deemed rational. Broadly following utilitarian theory, Gradgrind subscribes to a shriveled rationality whose imperial reach Dickens ridicules without first questioning its claim to count as reason. "With a rule and a pair of scales, and the multiplication table always in his pocket," Gradgrind was always "ready to weigh and measure any parcel of human nature, and tell you exactly what it comes to" (p. 8). Since Dickens allows this pinched ideology to stand as reason, his quest in the novel is to limit its scope but not to reconsider its nature. Dickens accepts the bifurcations that Hegel rejects. When reason inherently fails to fit the makeup of human beings, as it does in Dickens' reckoning, salvation can come only from outside, such as through fantasy, satire, or a circus.

Gradgrind and the utilitarian reformers promote educational as well as political reform.[16] Though references are made in *Hard Times* to the efforts of the Gradgrind party in Parliament, they are left rather vague, for Dickens' primary concern is with the outcomes of the Gradgrind educational philosophy. As John Stuart Mill came to blame his mental collapse on the defects of his utilitarian upbringing, Louisa blames her breakdown on her father's twisted, inhuman ideology.[17] Like Mill, Louisa is damaged and finds only a hole where a self should be. All her thwarted passion is spent on her brother Tom, the whelp not worthy of her devotion. Mill finds healing in poetry and love for Harriet Taylor. Louisa's wounds never heal. Those groomed to showcase utilitarian ideals bear its scars.

The Gradgrind philosophy mimics utilitarian thought, but with important omissions. Utility theory addresses a basic question posed by capitalist society: What do all commodities share that underlies their prices? Utility is put forward as the common substance attributed to all commodities: x amount of diamonds = y amount of ice cream because their utilities (or marginal utilities) coincide. Among the shadow forms, utility takes the prize for emptiness. Like value, it strips away the actual features of diamonds and ice cream, but unlike value it posits a pseudo-trait, utility, as what they have in common. Utility, a cornerstone of modern value theory, moral philosophy, and mainstream economics, is a sinkhole into which real things vanish to be replaced by phantoms.

From 1845 at the latest, Marx considered utility to be a sham concept best explained as a shadow cast by commodity circulation.[18] Marx and Engels ridicule utility while explaining its plausibility: "[T]his apparently metaphysical abstraction arises from the fact that in modern bourgeois society all relations are subordinated in practice to the one abstract monetary-commercial relation" (Marx & Engels, 1976a, p. 409).[19] In *Love's Knowledge*, Martha Nussbaum jars us with an attempt to imagine "that elusive item, utility":

It is a startling and powerful vision. Just try to think it seriously: this body of this wonderful beloved person is *exactly*

the same in quality as that person's mind and inner life. Both, in turn, the same in quality as the value of Athenian democracy; of Pythagorean geometry; of Eudoxan astronomy. What would it be like to look at a body and to see in it exactly the same shade and tone of goodness and beauty as in a mathematical proof—*exactly* the same, differing only in amount and in location, so that the choice between making love with that person and contemplating that proof presented itself as a choice between having *n* measures of water and *n* + 100. (1990, p. 116)[20]

Can we take even the first steps in this proposed thought experiment? Is there a property common to all that we desire or enjoy? We think not. The "elusive item" presupposed here does not exist. Utility is an imposter. It mimics the actual commensurability of prices, which it disguises. Commodities do share a common property: quantities of congealed abstract human labor.[21] Value is the mysterious "elusive item" that does exist.

It is not much of a leap from "everything has its price" to "everything has its utility."[22] Consider what Georg Simmel writes of money's power to level and hollow things out:

To the extent that money, with its colorlessness and its indifferent quality, can become a common denominator of all values it becomes the frightful leveler—it hollows out the core of things, their peculiarities, their specific values and their uniqueness and incomparability in a way which is beyond repair. They all float with the same specific gravity in the constantly moving stream of money. They all rest on the same level and are distinguished only by their amounts. (Simmel, 1997, p. 340)[23]

Scott Meikle writes in a similar vein that, as a consequence of capital's "subordinating use-value to exchange," "Real natures are neglected, abolished, or replaced. It is the world of Jeremy Bentham. Utilitarianism is its fitting morality, and empiricism is its fitting philosophy. The form in which we conduct our life invades and diminishes that life" (Meikle, 1991, p. 317).[24] *Hard Times* exposes the diminishment that comes with the invasion of commercial forms into real natures. Utility theory assumes that there are no definite, morally significant natures and no abiding collective good that establish the horizon for making moral judgments.[25] Liberalism insists that, for its people to be free, a society must renounce any compulsory collective good.[26] C. Welch notes the kinship between utility theory and liberalism:

> utilitarianism apparently has a special status in the evolution of modern social inquiry, not just because well-being is the modern obsession, or because the model of the "science" of economics is seductive in an age of science, but because utilitarians claim to offer a criterion of neutrality among competing conceptions of the good life in a pluralistic and antagonistic world. (Welch, 1987, p. 775)

Goals such as achieving the greatest happiness for the greatest number do not require any "thick," controversial conception of the good. There is an affinity with liberalism that adds to the attraction of utility theory.

What do all commodities share? This raises a real question for the examination of capitalist societies. By offering a phony answer to this real question, utility has staying power.[27] Capital's reach is vastly extended and amplified by forms that are shadows of its constitutive forms, the value forms.[28] Shadow forms piggyback on constitutive aspects of the world or they would not persist. Utility is a pseudo-concept while usefulness is a legitimate general concept. The proper understanding of the useful rules out the pseudo-concept of utility; it is a common mistake to equate them. Utility gains plausibility in a world where everything has its price; it conceals its falseness and emptiness behind the mask of the unobjectionable notion of usefulness, for which it purports to provide a metric.[29]

But not all shadow forms are imposters like utility. Indifference, the experience that nothing really matters, is the subjective counterpart to money, the erasure of actual differences. An economic system directed at making money is indifferent to actual commodities. Whatever makes money will do. Indifference and boredom expose the underbelly of consumer society. The "whatever" mood matches the "whatever makes money" motto. Thus, U.S. Steel gets rechristened USX to encompass "whatever" money-making enterprise. In commercial societies the emptiness of value is as real as gravity.[30] Unfortunately, the actual emptiness of value's supersensible social objectivity is trumped by the emptiness of the pseudo-concept of utility in the common understanding. Value arises from socially determinate conditions. What arises in history can disappear into history, but utility presents itself as without history: It purportedly applies across history. Utility, the imposter, makes emptiness a horizon from which there is no hope for salvation—nihilism is inescapable.

The Gradgrind philosophy delights in measurement but lacks a common substance such as utility. A hodgepodge, it includes statistics, calculation, leveling, emptiness, indifference, boredom, and—always— facts and figures. Forbidden to doubt, wonder, or understand, students rattle off facts obediently. Gradgrind's "hard facts" party in Parliament works to replace deliberation by accounting. Debate is needless, numbers alone resolve any dispute. Utility theory is propelled by an impartial mindset that calculates the greatest satisfaction for the greatest number, even if my own interests are sacrificed. But this sublime indifference to one's own interests readily flip-flops into extreme self-centeredness. Of Thomas Gradgrind's son, it is said, "As to Tom, he was becoming that not unprecedented triumph of calculation which is usually at work on the number one" (p. 51).

Sacrifice and generosity lack standing in the Gradgrind philosophy, where only the self counts. Every action is a transaction calculated to maximize one's own interests. The Gradgrind philosophy is presented as the philosophical expression of the new science of political economy:

> It was a fundamental principle of the Gradgrind philosophy that everything was to be paid for. Nobody was ever on any account to give anybody anything, or render anybody help without purchase. Gratitude was to be abolished, and the virtues springing from it were not to be. Every inch of the existence of mankind, from birth to death, was to be a bargain across a counter. And if we didn't get to Heaven that way, it was not a politico-economical place, and we had no business there. (p. 212)[31]

All reality is modeled on exchange, and the only acknowledged motivation is seeking one's own benefit.[32] The banker Bounderby combines the myth of egoism with the myth of the self-made man; he crawled out of the ditch into which his own mother allegedly dumped him. A wet ditch, sopping wet. A "self-made man" owes nothing to anyone and least of all to his parents.[33] Obligations that are not based in contracts would split the firmament of the Gradgrind philosophy.

While the Gradgrind philosophy caricatures imagination, Dickens embraces J.S. Mill's criticism of Bentham's chief character flaw. Mill observes of Bentham that

> [t]he Imagination which he had not, was . . . that which enables us . . . to conceive the absent as if it were present, the imaginary as if it were real, and to clothe it in the feelings . . . This is the power by which one human being enters into the mind and circumstances of another. This power constitutes the poet . . . the historian . . . Without it nobody knows even his own nature. (Mill, 1990, p. 317)

Imagination, in this context, is not the creative genius to design buildings or compose symphonies. This imagination involves what David Hume and Adam Smith call sympathy: our native ability to be affected by the situation of others. Sympathy is the rudder that guides our emotional understanding. Without the cultivation of emotions, practical reason cannot exist.[34] If reason actually excluded empathy, it would never establish moral rules or dispositions. We simply would not care whether refugees die at sea or children go hungry. Even so-called artificial virtues, such as promise keeping, depend on sympathy. We could not understand any action without being affected by how others feel, for example, the unpleasant sensation at dishonest treatment. Imagination allows for a self to exist, relationships to form, and reasonable judgments to be made.

In attacking imagination, the Gradgrind philosophy mounts an assault on human nature. What emerges are persons damaged in profound ways. The products of Gradgrind education are unfit for relationships or judgments. They are immobilized and isolated from the world. Faced with the marriage proposal from a man she despises, Louisa searches in vain among the "facts" to find grounds for a decision, while her father struggles to calculate her way to an answer. But facts do not make decisions for us. To make a judgment, something must matter to someone. Never allowed the luxury of a self, Louisa cannot arrive at what matters to her. In large part, her instincts and desires have no names, no handles; they move her blindly. Dehumanization in this generation of Gradgrinds begins in the cradle.[35]

Dickens employs imagination to depict imagination-starved humans. With his pale hair, skin, and eyes, Bitzer, the star student, "looked as though, if he were cut, he would bleed white" (p. 9). Ice, not blood, fills his veins, and he betrays all who get in his way. Bitzer fully assimilated the Gradgrind code: In a political-economic world there is no place for gratitude. A bargain is a bargain and nothing more. Dickens presents young Tom Gradgrind as a grotesque who, for his advancement, presses his sister Louisa into marrying the wealthy Bounderby, whom she abhors. Later, Tom betrays her confidences, enabling Harthouse to seduce Louisa. The long-suffering worker Stephen Blackpool, ostracized by the union and fired by Bounderby, is the fall guy for Tom's bank heist. Like sociopaths, Tom and Bitzer are dead to the call of conscience or human suffering. When her world is heading for collapse, Louisa flees to her father and confronts him, bitterly, with his bankrupt system. Mr. Gradgrind's moral compass is sufficiently intact. Against Bounderby's counsel, he had allowed the tumbler's child, Sissy, into his home. Faced with his daughter's accusations, he recognizes his failures and is crushed by the outcomes of his bogus ideals: He has destroyed those he most loves. Mr. Gradgrind was not reared under his system; his humanity is capable of recovery.

Louisa is not so lucky as her father. Gradgrind training has effectively hollowed out her soul. The only person who elicits her affection spontaneously is her wanton brother Tom, the comrade of her lonely youth, who uses her and ultimately rejects her. Neither walks away from the wreck that is their childhood:

> There was an air of jaded sullenness in them both, and particularly in the girl [Louisa]; yet, struggling through the dissatisfaction of her face, there was a light with nothing to rest upon, a fire with nothing to burn, a starved imagination keeping life in itself somehow, which brightened its expression. (p. 15)

When asked by her father what she (at age 15 or 16) is tired of, Louisa responds, "I don't know of what—of everything, I think" (p. 16). A disconsolate figure, Louisa is aware of her damaged psyche and its causes but is helpless to recover what she never possessed. She feels her loss strangely, as if observing a species and suddenly recognizing it as her own. Educated and wealthy, she is miffed by the pity of Sissy. But she is pitiable, and she knows it.

The Harthouse Philosophy as the
Truth of the Gradgrind Philosophy

A close look at the Gradgrind ideals discloses an abyss where nothing matters. In Book II of *Hard Times*, Dickens introduces the dark angel of indifference Mr. James Harthouse, a "fine gentleman" whose boredom with everything else left him "going in" for the "hard Fact fellows" of the Gradgrind party. "He was a thorough gentleman, made to the model of the time: weary of everything, and putting no more faith in anything than Lucifer" (pp. 91–92). Arriving in Coketown, he drifts into seducing Louisa Gradgrind, now Mrs. Josiah Bounderby. Like the Tin Man—but without his desire—Harthouse, as his name says, is a mere housing for a heart: "He was touched in the cavity where his heart should have been" (p. 172). Mr. Bounderby's scathing housekeeper, Mrs. Sparsit, imagines Louisa's seduction by Harthouse as her twisting down "the new Giants' staircase" into the abyss (p. 153, n5).[36] Louisa's education in the Gradgrind philosophy had already thrust her into a tailspin:

> Upon a nature long accustomed to self-suppression, thus torn and divided, the Harthouse philosophy came as a relief and justification. Everything being hollow and worthless, she had missed nothing and sacrificed nothing. What did it matter, she had said to her father, when he proposed her husband. What did it matter, she said still. With a scornful self-reliance, she asked herself, What did anything matter—and went on. (p. 125)

Dickens exposes the truth about the Gradgrind philosophy to be the affirmation of nihilism by the Harthouse philosophy.

In *The Sickness unto Death*, Søren Kierkegaard (1980) describes spiritual sicknesses as forms of despair. Those content with their misshapen or desiccated selves suffer least, like Bounderby and Bitzer. Those conscious of the cavern where a self belongs feel anxiety intensely. Unconscious despair is most dangerous because those unaware of their sickness do not seek help. Conscious despair is most painful because awareness without recourse brings endless torment. Conscious despair that is defiantly embraced is demonic. Louisa is aware of her missing desires but lacks recourse. She is stuck without hope of recovery, a spiritual jam that Kierkegaard calls introverted despair. Harthouse, who drops into Coketown on a lark and decides to seduce Louisa on a whim, embodies a deeper, more sinister despair. Unlike Gradgrind's utilitarian prescriptions for the nation, the Harthouse philosophy has no messianic fervor; there are no reforms to be undertaken in earnest. Louisa, the product of Gradgrind upbringing, finds a soulless mate in Harthouse, with his explicitly nihilistic outlook. What is demonic about Harthouse is the *indifference* that creates the funnel in the cavity where his heart belonged:

> And yet he had not, even now, any earnest wickedness of purpose in him. Publicly and privately, it were much better for the age in which he lived, that he and the legion of whom he was one were designedly bad, than indifferent and purposeless. It is the drifting icebergs setting with any current anywhere, that wreck the ships. (p. 135)[37]

Indifference, what Simmel calls the "blasé" or "matter-of-fact" attitude, accompanies capital's draining our world of its reality. Capital is the new, spectral giant, and the descending "new Giant's staircase" threatens our humanity. As Chris Arthur puts it in his alarming essay "The Spectre of Capital," "the void at the heart of bourgeois life results in the most accomplished irony: [A]ccumulation as an infinite increase in emptiness is mistaken for a plenitude of wealth" (Arthur, 2002, p. 172). Dickens' James Harthouse is a model of "emptiness . . . mistaken for a plenitude of wealth."

Both Harthouse and Louisa recognize the emptiness in the Gradgrind movement. That is their shared understanding: They alone realize that the emperor has no clothes. But what smothers Louisa, Harthouse cheerfully accepts as the way things are. He is ready to "go in" for any game. His arrogant indifference is limitless. Whatever promises to fill the cavity for the moment will do:

> I have seen a little, here and there, up and down; I have found it all to be very worthless, as everybody has, and as some confess they have, and some do not; and I am going in for your respected father's opinions—really because I have no choice of opinions, and may as well back them as anything else.
>
> The result of the varieties of boredom I have undergone, is a conviction (unless conviction is too industrious a word

for the lazy sentiment I entertain on the subject), that any
set of ideas will do just as much good as any other set, and
just as much harm as any other set. (pp. 98–99)

This seeming honesty—nothing really matters, including nihilism—at
first disarms Louisa. Harthouse gives voice to Louisa's disdain for her
father's great cause. But, like everything about Harthouse, this proud
indifference is a ploy meant to trap her.[38] Harthouse's despair Kierkegaard calls demonic. Harthouse arrives in Coketown, like Satan in hell,
bent—for no particular reason—on destruction. Louisa sees through inky
calculations to the nothing they add up to. Why not have an affair with
Harthouse? From the Gradgrind to the Harthouse philosophy is the slide
down the spiral staircase to the abyss at the bottom. If nothing really
matters, neither does adultery.

Dickens, *Hard Times*, and Capitalism

Dickens does not share Kierkegaard's view that true faith in God heals
spiritual sickness; he does not share Marx's view that chronic economic
and spiritual aberrations are endemic to capitalism. Dickens separates
ideology from the material conditions of production. In *Hard Times*,
overweening extremist ideologies pose the danger to humanity. Ridding
the world of the Gradgrind philosophy would bring decency to Coketown
without tearing down any factory walls: The factory school concerns
Dickens more than the factory. If the Gradgrind philosophy signifies the
spirit of capitalism, it is the subsumption of life as a whole under the
calculating eye of capital that Dickens fears, not the honestly conducted
search for profits:

My satire is against those who see figures and averages, and
nothing else—the representatives of the wickedest and most
enormous vice of this time—the men who, through long years
to come, will do more to damage the useful truths of political
economy than I could do (if I tried) in my whole life.[39]

Dickens's attitude to capitalism is ambivalent. On one hand, the union
leader Slackbridge is vilified for ordering Stephen Blackpool to be ostracized for not supporting the union. But faced with Bounderby's demand

that he spy on the union, Stephen refuses and defends the workers'
right to act in common—just as the owners do. For that bit of truth,
he loses his job. The life of a worker is endless toil without hope for a
better future, sighs Stephen:

> Look how we live, an' where we live, an' in what numbers, an'
> by what chances, and wi' what sameness; and look how the
> mills is awlus a goin, and how they never works us no nigher
> to onny dis'ant object—cepten awlus, Death. Look how you
> considers of us, and writes of us, and talks of us, and goes up
> wi' yor deputations to Secretaries o' State 'bout us, and how
> yo are awlus right, and how we are awlus wrong, and never
> had'n no reason in us sin ever we were born. . . . (p. 113)

For Stephen, there is no way out but death. It's a muddle.

Dickens satirizes an extreme, unbending capitalist mentality throughout the novel. The pompous Bounderby excoriates labor—the Hands—at
every turn. Dickens calls Bounderby's "hard facts" the "fictions of Coketown." Bounderby propounds them to the newcomer Harthouse—who
assents to each in turn—just in case he is tempted to be moved by the
plight of the workers:

> First of all, you see our smoke. That's meat and drink to
> us. It's the healthiest thing in the world in all respects, and
> particularly for the lungs. If you are one of those who want
> us to consume it, I differ from you. We are not going to wear
> the bottoms of our boilers out any faster than we wear 'em
> out now, for all the humbugging sentiment in Great Britain
> and Ireland.
>
> Now you have heard a lot of talk about the work in
> our mills, no doubt. You have? Very good. I'll state the fact
> of it to you. It's the pleasantest work there is, and it's the
> lightest work there is, and it's the best-paid work there is.
> More than that, we couldn't improve the mills themselves,
> unless we laid down Turkey carpets on the floors. Which
> we're not a-going to do.
>
> . . . as to our Hands. There's not a Hand in this town,
> Sir, man, woman, or child, but has one ultimate object in
> life. That object is, to be fed on turtle soup and venison with

> a gold spoon. Now, they're not a-going—none of 'em—ever
> to be fed on turtle soup and venison with a gold spoon. And
> now you know the place. (p. 96)

While he ridicules this capitalist humbug, Dickens repudiates class conflict. In his view, class differences are to be sensibly reconciled, not abolished. In a speech given in Birmingham in 1853, Dickens proclaims that industrial peace lies

> in the fusion of different classes, without confusion; in the
> bringing together of employers and employed; in the creat-
> ing of a better common understanding among those whose
> interests are identical, who depend upon each other, and who
> can never be in unnatural antagonism without deplorable
> results. (p. 270)

At bottom, the interests of capital and labor harmonize. If Dickens were asked how this harmony is to be achieved, however, he might have had to echo Stephen's words: It's a muddle.

Dickens' dire warning returns us to the "key-note" of *Hard Times*, namely, Gradgrind's utilitarian stifling of imagination:

> Utilitarian economists, skeletons of schoolmasters, Commis-
> sioners of Fact, genteel and used-up infidels, gabblers of many
> little dog's-eared creeds, the poor you will always have with
> you. Cultivate in them [the common people], while there is
> yet time, the utmost graces of the fancies and affections, to
> adorn their lives so much in need of ornament; or, in the day
> of your triumph, when romance is utterly driven out of their
> souls, and they and a bare existence stand face to face, Reality
> will take a wolfish turn, and make an end of you! (p. 123)

As the circus master Sleary says in his parting, slurred words to Thomas Gradgrind, "People muth be amuthed. They can't be alwayth a learning, nor yet they can't be alwayth a working, they an't made for it. You muth hav uth, Thquire" (p. 215). Thus, Alexander Welsh writes of *Hard Times*, "Although for industrial conflict Dickens and his spokesman Stephen Blackpool do not have a solution other than kindness and for-bearance, the novel is rather more assertive about entertainment—and entertainment, variety, imagination may at least alleviate factory work and the conditions it brings with it" (2000, p. 186). Dickens may not dig into capital's constitutive forms, but his narrative of the Gradgrind philosophy imaginatively takes on capital's shadow forms, which exert power in their own ways.

Conclusion: Taking on Capital's Shadow Forms

In *Hard Times*, the malaise of capitalism is chiefly encountered as the Gradgrind philosophy; it does not concern commodities, money, or profits but rather a soul-deforming subsumption of life under forms that we call capital's shadows. In *The Poverty of Philosophy*, Marx identifies egalitarianism as a shadow stretching the equality constitutive of the actual world of commodity exchange well beyond it:

> Mr. Bray does not see that this equalitarian relation, this corrective ideal that he would like to apply to the world, is itself nothing but the reflection of the actual world; and that therefore it is totally impossible to reconstitute society on the basis of what is merely an embellished shadow [*ombre* in the French original] of it. In proportion as this shadow takes on substance again, we perceive that this substance, far from being the transfiguration dreamt of, is the actual body of existing society. (Marx, 1963, pp. 78–79)

Shadow forms are cast by the underlying constitutive social forms, such as value, money, wage labor, and capital. Capital's shadow forms open a window onto Marx's account of bourgeois ideologies. *Capital* (including *Theories of Surplus-Value*) is the closest that Marx comes to a treatise on bourgeois ideology. With its focus on capital's constitutive forms, however, *Capital* leaves plenty of room for elucidation. We can think about the shadow forms as extending capital's reach. Shadows may go where the value forms may not; for example, utility theory may be applied to the family, as Gary Becker does, whereas the value forms must be excluded if there are to be free wage laborers. The subsumption of Coketown under the hard facts and calculations of the Gradgrind philosophy, which results in the nihilism of the Harthouse philosophy, illustrates capital's shadows spreading over human affairs beyond the commercial sphere.[40]

For Dickens, this transgressing of demarcations—capital's overreach—is what is so disturbing.

Shadow forms reflect capital's constitutive forms in one way or another. We distinguish reflection that illumines from reflection that conceals. Some of capital's shadow forms extend a constitutive feature beyond the commercial sphere. Equality constitutes commodity exchange; egalitarianism extends it.[41] The U.S. Supreme Court's affirmation of "marriage equality" may be seen as an egalitarian expansion of equality to the domestic sphere. Other shadow forms involve pseudo-concepts, that is, concepts whose purported referent does not exist. They pretend to describe reality, but instead they distort and block our view of the world. Like a maze of mirrors, these reflections lead nowhere. They produce confusion, if not always the nihilism depicted in *Hard Times*. Encased in these categories, thought cannot advance. Utility is a pseudo-concept identified by Marx and one of the most pervasive notions in contemporary social theory. Other shadow forms that are pseudo-concepts include instrumental reason and efficiency, the purely subjective and purely objective, facts as opposed to values, economics (understood as a generally applicable human science), and egoism (understood not as selfishness but as an anthropological claim). A telling feature of pseudo-concepts is their ahistorical character. They eliminate negation, critique, and emancipation. Unmasking these categories is the task of critical theory. Dickens' satire of the quantitative, calculative mentality that comes with utility and instrumental reason brings out the emptiness of Coketown ideology but does not ground it historically in the constitutive social form capital.

Because of the strange, abstract character of its constitutive social forms, the value forms, capitalism presents itself as the economy-in-general, where "wealth" (of no determinate social form) is created by "labor" (of no determinate social form) in a production process that is likewise deemed generic. As Martha Campbell puts it, capitalism "claims to create wealth pure and simple and [to be] organized by this purpose" (Campbell, 2004, p. 86). But there is no "wealth pure and simple"; there is no economy-in-general. Economics as ordinarily understood is a pseudo-science because it takes this illusion of the economy-in-general as its object of inquiry. What is more, "wealth" and "production" each shadow capital's telos of endless accumulation, and each appears as a fetishistic end in itself: "material wealth for its own sake" and "production for production's sake" (Marx, 1976b, p. 1037). We call "production for production's sake" *productivism*. By the same token, we call productivism's counterpart, "wealth for wealth's sake," *wealthism*. These ideologies of productivism and wealthism arise naturally as participants in a capitalist society represent their society to themselves (Marx, 1976a, p. 742). As ways to represent the capitalist mode of production, both notions reveal and conceal truth. Productivism and wealthism mimic the abstractness, quantitative focus, and indifference characteristic of the value forms, but they fail to identify the peculiar social form and purpose of the wealth being produced. The all-important concept of capital is missing.

Instrumental reason separates means from ends; it posits the task of reason as to determine the best (most efficient) means to any designated end. Founded on a false separation, instrumental reason and efficiency are pseudo-concepts, shadows of capital's preoccupation with profit-making. The Weberian fear of the complete domination of instrumental reason is capitalism getting unnerved by its own shadow. The Kafkaesque idea of the "totally administered society" smacks of science fiction. It supposes either that no collective good organizes the society or that the collective good is something formal and empty like self-preservation (Max Horkheimer), control (Niklas Luhmann), or self-maintenance (Talcott Parsons). But those phrases dodge these questions: Preservation of what form of life? Control over what? Self-maintenance of what sort of society? No society is generic—that idea is a fiction of the capitalist imagination. In truth, human labor is always concretely purposive and animated by definite, and morally weighty, social forms and purposes. As Marx succinctly puts it: "All production is appropriation on the part of an individual within and through a specific form of society" (Marx, 1973, p. 87). So the worry about "the totally administered society" is a worry that we will wriggle ourselves out of our own predicament.[42] It will never happen! Better to worry about our actual quandary.

The disconnection of shadow from constitutive forms gives rise to the neo-Weberian notion of McDonaldization.[43] Like every business, McDonald's seeks to make money. But McDonaldization ignores this goal and puts the emphasis on how production of fast food is standardized. Efficiency, not making money, is said to be the goal. McDonaldization includes shadow forms that appear in *Hard Times*. Calculability "is an emphasis on the quantitative aspects of products sold (portion size, cost) and services offered (the time it takes to get the product)" (Ritzer, 2000, p. 12). In McDonaldized systems, quantity and velocity have become surrogates for quality: A lot of something, or the quick delivery of it, means it must be good. American culture accepts that, in general, bigger is better. Sooner is also better.[44] Quantitative bigness—giganticism—and the preoccupation with calculability that Max Weber calls "the romanticism of numbers" (Weber, 1997, p. 71) belong on the list of capital's shadow forms.[45] Picture McDonald's tallies of the billions of hamburgers they have sold or Apple's Tim Cook standing on-stage before a 50-foot iPhone 7 as totems of capital's accumulation.

Constitutive forms can be reduced to shadows of themselves, which offers another way of keeping them out of sight and mind. Capital is the constitutive social form of capitalist societies, but the way that the term "capital" is now tossed around turns it into a shadow of itself. Stripped of all its determinate social content, the concept of capital is reduced to that of "whatever" resource. Capital is then ready to play its part as a shadow form. At the same time that so little thought is given to capital as the key constitutive social form of capitalist societies, talk about human capital, conceptual capital, social capital, natural capital, and even spiritual capital clogs our discourse.

Capital's shadow forms abound in our towns, as they did in Dickens' Coketown. When we focus on shadows rather than constitutive social forms, what results is predictably a muddle.

Notes

1. Piketty (2014) appeals to contemporary literature to bring home the fact that, in the 20th century, inflation became a part of life, a precarious development that he refers to as "the loss of monetary bearings" (p. 106). In contrast to Austen's determining the social position of her characters by their yearly income in pounds, "the novels of Orhan Pamuk, set in Istanbul in the 1970s, that is, in a period during which inflation had long since rendered the meaning of money ambiguous, omit mention of any specific sums" (p. 109). When they watch a custody court hearing in the film *Kramer vs. Kramer* (1980), our students don't know what to make of the information that Joanna Kramer is employed as a sportswear designer in New York City for $31,000 a year.

2. In *Dickens Redressed: The Art of* Bleak House *and* Hard Times, Alexander Welsh (2000) goes so far as to say, "Dickens's fast and loose satire of the preaching of fact should not be allowed to obscure how close his thinking is to mainline Victorian philosophy, even that of utilitarianism" (p. 199). In *Poetic Justice*, Martha Nussbaum (1995) sees Dickens' contrast between reason and imagination as succumbing to the Gradgrind philosophy.

3. Georg Simmel (1997) observes: "It has been the money economy which has thus filled the daily life of so many people with weighing, calculating, enumerating and the reduction of qualitative values to quantitative terms" (p. 338).

4. Martha Nussbaum identifies the foremost element of the broadly utilitarian Gradgrind philosophy to be commensurability, and "by *commensurability*, I mean . . . regarding all the valuable things under consideration as measurable on a single scale that itself exhibits differences only of quantity, not quality" (p. 14).

5. Note that future references to *Hard Times* will give just the page number.

6. In the Preface to their unfinished book *The German Ideology*, Marx and Engels (1976) described their purpose as "to ridicule and discredit the philosophic struggle with the shadows of reality, which appeals to the dreamy and muddled German nation" (pp. 23–24).

7. Here is a passage where Dickens does bring the constitutive form capital to light in commenting on Bitzer, that "excellent young economist": "[T]he only reasonable transaction in that commodity [referring to the tea that he, out of weakness, gave annually to his mother, after he sent her to the workhouse] would have been to buy it for as little as he could possibly give, and sell it for as much as he could possibly get; it having been clearly ascertained by philosophers that in this is comprised the whole duty of man—not a part of man's duty, but the whole" (p. 89). Here we have the spirit of capital, as Max Weber called it, as well as its basic concept.

8. Marx was struck by this indifference toward particularity already in his first studies of political economy, his comments on James Mill: "Within the presupposition of division of labor, the product, the material of private property, acquires for the individual more and more the significance of an *equivalent*, and as he no longer exchanges only his *surplus*, and the object of his production can be simply a *matter of indifference* to him, so too he no longer exchanges his product for something directly *needed* by him. The equivalent comes into existence as an equivalent in *money*, which is now the immediate result of labor to gain a living and the *medium* of exchange" (Marx, 1975b, p. 221). The indifference toward the product extends both to the capitalist and the wage-laborer.

9. Capital's disregard for particularity, then, is only one aspect of the story, since, as Marx reminds us of the double-character of the commodity, "nothing can be a value without out being an object of utility [that is, a useful thing]" (Marx, 1976a, p. 131). The particular features that make commodities useful must always be important to capitalists, workers, and consumers at the same time that their being produced for the purpose of making money bleaches out their distinctiveness.

10. John Stuart Mill, in *A System of Logic*, splits "Science" and "Art" as follows: "[T]hough the reasonings which connect the end or purpose of every art with its means, belong to the domain of Science, the definition of the end

itself belongs exclusively to Art, and forms its peculiar province" (as quoted in Welsh, 2000, p. 201). See J.S. Mill, 1974, pp. 943, 949.

11. The Monkees' hit song "Pleasant Valley Sunday," written by Carole King and Gerry Goffin, satirized a suburban Coketown, where the smoke rises from backyard grills: "Another pleasant valley Sunday; Charcoal burning everywhere; Rows of houses that are all the same; And no one seems to care."

12. In *Harrison Bergeron* (1961), Kurt Vonnegut's farcical send-up of capital's shadow form egalitarianism, Diana Moon Glampers, the Handicapper General, who enforces equality at all costs, echoes Dickens' "commissioners of fact."

13. When Bitzer's father dies, he grabs the inheritance and sends his mother to the workhouse.

14. See Dickens' report on the Preston strike, in Dickens, 1990, pp. 285–97.

15. Alexander Welsh notes, "Dickens' principal thoughts about industrial differences [are] aired in front of Bounderby. If these thoughts are less than incisive, that is because Dickens carefully avoids taking a taking a position on any of the economic issues, such as what portion of profits in textiles should accrue to the owners and what portion to the workers, or how much surplus ought to be reinvested" (Welsh, 2000, p. 161). Where profits come from in the first place is no topic for Dickens.

16. The three Books that compose *Hard Times*—Sowing, Reaping, Garnering—liken the cultivation of children in this brave new world to growing crops. You reap what you sow.

17. Alexander Welsh connects *Hard Times* with Mill's *Autobiography* and points out that the mere appeal to "the exercise of feeling" is not a sufficient answer to its suppression: "The recovery of feeling is construed as corrective in both texts; in neither the autobiography nor the novel is it certain why the exercise of feeling tends to the good" (Welsh, 2000, p. 200). In *Poetic Justice*, Martha Nussbaum addresses Welsh's concern, arguing that feelings must be properly cultivated in order to result in a capacity for right judgment.

18. That Marx rejects the very idea of utility—in abstracting from all particularity, utility amounts to a false conception of usefulness—is evident from his barbed observation: "The usefulness of a thing makes it a use value. But this usefulness does not dangle in mid-air. It is conditioned by the physical properties of the commodity, and has no existence apart from the latter" (Marx 1976a, p. 126). Utility dangles in mid-air.

19. They precede this statement with the observation: "The extent to which this theory of mutual exploitation, which Bentham expounded ad nauseam, could already at the beginning of the present century be regarded as a phase of the previous one is shown by Hegel in his *Phänomenologie*. See there the chapter "The Struggle of Enlightenment with Superstition," where the theory of utility is depicted as the final result of enlightenment" (Marx & Engels,

1976a, p. 409). Utility, the false concept of the useful, claims that all useful things are commensurable and quantifiable—every useful thing can be assigned a quantity of utility—the legitimate, generally applicable concept of usefulness makes no such assumptions.

20. Of course utility, "that elusive item" (Nussbaum, 1995, p. 14), is nothing actual, as water is. Perhaps this is a joking reference by the classicist Nussbaum to the reductionist natural philosopher Thales, who imagined that everything is water. Marx's neo-Aristotelian stance, rejecting the numerical comparability of diverse goods, is clear in the following passage from *The German Ideology*, where Marx and Engels argue that the bogus notion of utility is a disguise for commercial (capitalist) society: "Hence the actual relations that are presupposed here are speech, love, definite manifestations of definite qualities of individuals. Now these relations are supposed not to have the meaning peculiar to them but to be the expression and manifestation of some third relation attributed to them, the relation of *utility or utilisation*. This *paraphrasing [Umschreibung]* ceases to be meaningless and arbitrary only when these relations have validity for the individual not on their own account, not as spontaneous activity, but rather as disguises, though by no mean disguises of the category of utilisation, but of an actual third aim and relation which is called the relation of utility" (Marx & Engels, 1976b, p. 409). Utility is the fiction. The "actual third aim" is surplus value, a constitutive capitalist form. Later in the text, Marx and Engels write of the absurdity of the sort of comparison that goes on under the mask of utility: "[E]ven though this absurd comparison has a real basis in the absurdity of present-day relations" (1976b, p. 440). Bernard Williams makes the connection between commerce and utility: "Utilitarianism is unsurprisingly the value system for a society in which economic values are supreme; and also, at the theoretical level, because quantification in money is the only obvious form of what utilitarianism insists upon, the commensurability of values" (Williams, 1972, p. 89).

21. This assertion needs to be qualified, since, in a monetary society, useful things that are not products of labor can and do have prices. Marx addresses this issue in his theory of rent.

22. Actually, in capitalism, not everything has a price, nor can it. Unlike portions of their labor power that are for sale, free wage laborers do not have a price. And without free wage laborers there is no capitalism. Since capitalist society is organized around the collective "good" of capital accumulation, and this goal is achievable only on the basis of free labor, a capitalist society is in no position to treat the (abstract) integrity of persons as a sum of utility that could be traded off for some greater utility. This makes it hard to imagine utilitarian ethics getting the upper hand over Kantian ethics in a capitalist society. There is more respect for the human person in capitalist social forms than in utilitarian ethics.

23. Marx calls money "a born leveller and cynic" (1976a, p. 179).

24. Compare Marx's observation in 1843 that money "has, therefore robbed the whole world—both the world of men and nature—of its specific value. Money is the estranged essence of man's work and man's existence, and this alien essence dominates him, and he worships it" (1975a, p. 172).

25. On Marx's phenomenology of the human condition, utility theory engages in false abstraction. There are no such free-floating utilities or preferences (independent of all specific social forms of wealth and production) because an authoritative collective good already exists. It is one thing to challenge that good, as Marx does in the case of capital; it is quite another to pretend it does not exist.

26. Friedrich A. Hayek insists that only a society free of every compulsory collective good can be just (Hayek, 1997, pp. 399–416).

27. The question that Marx poses, and answers, in *Capital* concerns societies where wealth generally takes the commodity form. It is a question about what makes *commodities*—not all useful things—commensurable. It is a question specific to capitalist societies, as is the answer: value. Utility, by contrast, is not socially specific: It purports to answer the question, what makes all useful things commensurable? Marx's neo-Aristotelian answer to *that* question is: nothing!

28. Scott Meikle writes, "to extend by conscious design the rule of exchange value into regions of human personality and intimacy that it has not hitherto succeeded in entering by less conscious means . . . is grotesque in itself" (1991, p. 317). For the most part, only the shadows of exchange-value, utility, for example, can be extended into those intimate regions.

29. This disguise is all the more effective because the word "utility" is often used to mean usefulness.

30. Marx ominously compares value to gravity: "[I]n the midst of the accidental and ever-fluctuating exchange relations between the products, the labor-time socially necessary to produce them asserts itself as a regulative law of nature. In the same way, the law of gravity asserts itself when a person's house collapses on top of him" (Marx, 1976a, p. 168).

31. This may be Dickens' send-up of a famous passage from Adam Smith's observations on the human propensity to "truck, barter, and exchange": "Man has almost constant occasion for the help of his brethren, and it is in vain for him to expect it from their benevolence only. He will be more likely to prevail if he can interest their self-love in his favour, and shew them that it is for their own advantage to do for him what he requires of them. Whoever offers to another a bargain of any kind, proposes to do this. Give me that which I want, and you shall have this which you want, is the meaning of every such offer; and it is in this manner that we obtain from one another the far greater part of those good offices which we stand in need of. It is not from the benevolence of the butcher, baker, brewer, that we expect our dinner, but from their regard to their own interest. We address ourselves, not to their humanity but to their self-love,

and never talk to them of our own necessities but of their advantages" (Smith, 1997, p. 183). In that passage on bargaining, Smith repeatedly contrasts humans and dogs: "Nobody ever saw a dog make a fair and deliberate exchange of one bone for another with another dog" (Smith, 1997, p. 183). Because dogs don't bargain, they are of no use to one another, whereas "Among men . . . the most dissimilar geniuses are of use to one another"; they build up a common stock "where every man may purchase whatever part of the produce of other men's talents he has occasion for" (Smith, 1997, p. 185). The irony that Dickens sets up at the end of Hard Times is that Thomas Gradgrind Sr. cannot get Bitzer, whom he bred on bargaining, to save his son Tom; instead, "the learned dog" (p. 213) from Sleary's circus saves young Tom. Sleary names the alternative to the calculating, self-interested Gradgrind philosophy, "the wayth of the dogth" (p. 215).

32. Nobel laureate in economics Gary Becker takes the Gradgrind modeling of all reality on commodity exchange in earnest. He recognizes the limits to the sphere of the market but suspends them by introducing the concept of "shadow" (imputed) prices: "The economic approach is clearly not restricted to material goods and wants, nor even to the market sector. Prices, be they the money prices of the market sector or the 'shadow' imputed prices of the nonmarket sector, measure the opportunity cost of using scarce resources, and the economic approach predicts the same kind of response to shadow prices as to market prices" (Becker, 1976, p. 6). Encompassing all human affairs under the price form—whether actual or imputed ("shadow") prices—enables Becker to adopt the Gradgrind philosophy in full: "I have come to the position that the economic approach is a comprehensive one that is applicable to all human behavior, be it behavior involving money prices or imputed shadow prices, repeated or infrequent decisions, large or minor decisions, emotional or mechanical ends, rich or poor persons, patients or therapists, businessmen or politicians, teachers or students. The applications of the economic approach so conceived are as extensive as the scope of economics in the definition given earlier [Lionel Robbins's seminal definition] that emphasizes scarce means and competing ends" (Becker, 1976, p. 8). Ironically, Becker notes that Robbins drew back from the implication of his sweeping definition: "Even Robbins, after an excellent discussion of what an economic problem is in the first chapter of his classic work on the nature and scope of economics (1962), basically restricts his analysis in later chapters to the market sector" (Gary Becker, 1976, p. 4, n. 5). Martha Nussbaum quotes Becker's teacher George Stigler as saying, "all of man's deliberative, forward-looking behavior follows the principles of economics" (Nussbaum, 1995, p. 47). On shadow forms and neoclassical economics, see Murray and Badeen (2016).

33. It turns out that Bounderby has been spouting lies about his origins, presenting an ironic contrast with the prized virtues of commerce: honesty and fairness. The explosive Mr. Bounderby is the sort that would provoke Georges Bataille to remark: "[T]he bourgeois are incapable of concealing a sordid face, a

face so rapacious and lacking in nobility, so frighteningly small, that all human life, upon seeing it, seems degraded" (Bataille, 1997, p. 373).

34. See Chapter 3, "Rational Emotions," in Nussbaum (1995), which concludes: "Sympathetic emotion that is tethered to the evidence, institutionally constrained in appropriate ways, and free from reference to one's own situation appears to be not only acceptable but actually essential to public judgment. But it is this sort of emotion, the emotion of the judicious spectator, that literary works construct in their reader, who learn what it is to have emotion, not for a 'faceless undifferentiated mass,' but for the 'uniquely individual human being.' This means, I believe, that literary works are what [Adam] Smith thought they were: artificial constructions of some crucial elements in a norm of public rationality, and valuable guides to correct response" (p. 78). Note the crucial difference here between Dickens and Nussbaum: Where Dickens insists that "reason" must be *complemented* by "fancy," Nussbaum shows why "sympathetic emotion" is "essential to public judgment."

35. Dickens' narrator points out that this painful interview between father and daughter concerning Bounderby's proposal was a missed opportunity for Mr. Gradgrind, one that he will redeem only at the end of the novel, when Louisa has skipped out on her adulterous rendezvous with Harthouse and is at the end of her wits. In this earlier scene, Louisa turns to her father, who "leaned back in his chair, and bent his deep-set eyes upon her in his turn, perhaps he might have seen one wavering moment in her, when she was impelled to throw herself upon his breast, and give him the pent-up confidences of her heart. But to see it, he must have overleapt at a bound the artificial barriers he had for many years been erecting, between himself and all those subtle essences of humanity which will elude the utmost cunning of algebra until the last trumpet ever to be sounded shall blow even algebra to wreck. The barriers were too many and too high for such a leap. With his unbending, utilitarian, matter-of-fact face, he hardened her again; and the moment shot away into the plumbless depths of the past, to mingle with all the lost opportunities that are drowned there" (pp. 77–78).

36. In his essay "The Spectre of Capital," Chris Arthur cites Cynthia Willett's essay "The Shadow of Hegel's *Science of Logic*" (1990), in which she pictures the dialectical development of Hegel's logic as an upward spiral of Being and a downward spiral of Nothing. Arthur appropriates this image to capture the two-fold development of the upward spiral of capital accumulation and the downward spiral (the "New Giant's Staircase") into nihilism, as value hollows out everything it touches (Arthur, 2002, pp. 164–165).

37. At the bottom of the ninth circle of Dante's inferno, ringed with giants, is ice created by the flapping of Satan's wings. We take it that Marx had this in mind in describing commodities, in so far as they are values, as "merely congealed quantities of homogeneous human labour" and "crystals of this social

substance" (Marx 1976a, p. 128). Marx explicitly associates the sphere of commerce, simple commodity circulation, with Dante's plain of Acheron and the realm of capitalist production as the inferno (Marx 1976a, pp. 279–280). On Marx and Dante, see Roberts (2017).

38. With his handsome face, charm, and "assumed honesty in dishonesty, most effective and most patronized of all the deadly sins" (p. 125), Harthouse calls to mind Geryon, Dante's monster of fraud.

39. Charles Dickens in a letter to Charles Knight, January 30, 1855.

40. Martha Nussbaum calls attention to this "spill over": "As the novel suggests, seeing people in the way recommended by economics does tend to spill over into the conduct of life and the choice of policies: Gradgrind's vision of the world is in that sense not an innocent 'as if' operation, but a way of restructuring the human world that has, if thoroughly and habitually carried out, profound significance for the shape of human societies" (1995, p. 47).

41. A bumper sticker now popular in the United States is simply an equals sign: "=."

42. That fact that this worry looms so large in Jürgen Habermas's work, as evidenced by his antagonism toward the social engineering approach of Niklas Luhmann and, conversely, by his passion for communicative action as a counterweight to instrumental action, attests to his failure to recognize instrumental action as a shadow form of value-producing ("practically abstract") labor, which turns out to be surplus-value producing labor. Frankfurt School discourse around the notion of instrumental reason turns on a miscomprehension of Marx's labor theory of value, which, as a theory not of "labor" but of the specific social form of labor in capitalist societies, represents a profound critique of the traditional (Ricardian) labor theory of value. The "traditional Marxism" (Postone, 1993) of most members of the Frankfurt School has more in common with the neo-Kantian concepts of Weber than the neo-Aristotelian ones of Marx.

43. See George Ritzer, *The McDonaldization of Society* (Ritzer, 2000). Ritzer's book has in common with *Hard Times* a preoccupation with capital's shadow forms, though constitutive forms turn up toward the end of the book.

44. In volume 2 of *Capital*, Marx (1978) shows how shortening turnover time raises the rate of profit.

45. On giganticism, see also Simone Weil (1997).

References

Arthur, C. (2002). *The New Dialectic and Marx's "Capital."* Leiden, UK: Brill.
Bataille, G. (1997). *The Accursed Share* (excerpts). In P. Murray (ed.), *Reflections on Commercial Life: Classic Texts from Plato to the Present* (pp. 375–381). New York, NY: Routledge.

Becker, G. (1976). *The Economic Approach to Human Behavior*. Chicago, IL: University of Chicago Press.

Campbell, M. (2004). Value objectivity and habit. In R. Bellofiore & N. Taylor (eds.), *The Constitution of Capital: Essays on Volume I of Marx's "Capital."* Basingstoke, UK: Palgrave Macmillan.

Dickens, C. [1854] (1990). *Hard Times* (2nd ed.). Edited by G. Ford & S. Monod. New York, NY: W. W. Norton & Company.

Hayek, F. A. [1973] (1997). The discipline of abstract rules and the emotions of the tribal society (excerpts from *Law, legislation and liberty*). In P. Murray (ed.), *Reflections on Commercial Life: Classic Texts from Plato to the Present* (pp. 399–416). New York, NY: Routledge.

Kierkegaard, S. [1849] (1980). *The Sickness unto Death*. Edited and translated by H. V. Hong & E. H. Hong. Princeton, NJ: Princeton University Press.

Marx, K. (1963) [1847]. *The Poverty of Philosophy*. New York, NY: International Publishers.

Marx, K. [1857–58] (1973). *Grundrisse*. Translated by M. Nicolaus. Harmondsworth, UK: Penguin Books.

Marx, K. [1843] (1975a). On the Jewish question. Translated by C. Dutt. In *Karl Marx, Frederick Engels: Collected Works, Vol. 3: Marx and Engels: 1843–44* (pp. 146–174). New York, NY: International Publishers.

Marx, K. [1844] (1975b). Comments on James Mill's *élémens d'économie politique*. Translated by C. Dutt. In *Karl Marx, Frederick Engels: Collected Works, Vol. 3: Marx and Engels: 1843–44* (pp. 211–228). New York, NY: International Publishers.

Marx, K. [1894] (1976a). *Capital: Volume 1*. Translated by B. Fowkes. Harmondsworth, UK: Penguin Books.

Marx, K. [1863–64] (1976b). Results of the immediate production process Translated by R. Livingstone. In *Capital: Volume 1*. Harmondsworth, UK: Penguin Books.

Marx, K. [1885] (1978). *Capital: Volume 2*. Translated by D. Fernbach. Harmondsworth, UK: Penguin Books.

Marx, K. [1858] (1987). "Original text" (*Urtext*) in Economic manuscripts of 1957–58. In *Karl Marx, Frederick Engels: Collected Works, Vol. 29: Marx: 1857–1861*. London, UK: Lawrence & Wishart.

Marx, K., & Engels, F. [1845–46] (1976). The German ideology (C. Dutt, W. Lough, et al., Trans.). In *Karl Marx, Frederick Engels: Collected Works, Vol. 5: Marx and Engels: 1845–47*, New York, NY: International Publishers.

Meikle, S. (1991). History of philosophy: The metaphysics of substance in Marx. In T. Carver (ed.), *Cambridge Companion to Marx* (pp. 296–319). Cambridge, UK: Cambridge University Press.

Mill, J. S. [1843] (1974). A system of logic ratiocinative and inductive. In J. M. Robson et al. (eds.), *The Collected Works of John Stuart Mill*, Vols. 7 and 8. Toronto, Canada: University of Toronto Press.

Mill, J. S. [1838] (1990). The mind and character of Jeremy Bentham. In G. Ford & S. Monod (eds.), *Hard Times* (2nd ed.). New York, NY: W. W. Norton & Company.

Murray, P., & Badeen, D. (2016, November). A Marxian critique of neoclassical economics' reliance on shadows of capital's constitutive social forms. In A. Hamza and F. Ruda (eds.), "Critique of Political Economy," a special issue of *Crisis and Critique*, 3(3), 8–28.

Nussbaum, M. (1995). *Poetic Justice*. Boston, MA: Beacon Press.

Nussbaum, M. (1990). *Love's Knowledge: Essays on Philosophy and Literature*. Oxford, UK: Oxford University Press.

Piketty, T. (2014). *Capital in the Twenty-First Century*. London & Cambridge, MA: Harvard University Press.

Postone, M. (1993). *Time, Labour, and Social Domination: A Reinterpretation of Marx's Critical Theory*. Cambridge, UK: Cambridge University Press.

Prawer, S. S. (1976). *Karl Marx and World Literature*. Oxford, UK: Oxford University Press.

Ritzer, G. (2000). *The McDonaldization of Society*. Thousand Oaks, CA: Pine Forge Press.

Roberts, W. C. (2017). *Marx's Inferno: The Political Theory of "Capital."* Princeton, NJ: Princeton University Press.

Simmel, G. [1903] (1997). *The Metropolis and Mental Life* (excerpts). In P. Murray (ed.), *Reflections on Commercial Life: Classic Texts from Plato to the Present* (pp. 335–347). New York, NY: Routledge.

Smith, A. [1776] (1997). *The Wealth of Nations* (excerpts). In P. Murray (ed.), *Reflections on Commercial Life: Classic Texts from Plato to the Present* (pp. 176–203). New York, NY: Routledge.

Vonnegut, K. (1961). *Harrison Bergeron*. In *The Magazine of Fantasy and Science Fiction*, J. W. Ferman, publisher.

Weber, M. [1905] (1997). The spirit of capitalism. In P. Murray (ed.), *Reflections on Commercial Life: Classic Texts from Plato to the Present* (pp. 350–364). New York, NY: Routledge.

Weil, S. [1958] (1997). Sketch of contemporary life (from *Oppression and Liberty*). In P. Murray (ed.), *Reflections on Commercial Life: Classic Texts from Plato to the Present* (pp. 385–395). New York, NY: Routledge.

Welch, C. (1987). Utilitarianism. In J. Eatwell, M. Milgate, & P. Newman (eds.), *The New Palgrave: A Dictionary of Economics*, in 4 volumes. London, UK: Macmillan.

Welsh, A. (2000). *Dickens Redressed: The Art of Bleak House and Hard Times*. New Haven, CT: Yale University Press.

Willett, C. (1990). The shadow of Hegel's *Science of Logic*. In G. di Giovanni (ed.), *Essays on Hegel's Logic*. Albany, NY: State University of New York Press.

Williams, B. (1972). *Morality*. Cambridge, UK: Cambridge University Press.

Chapter 4

The Repressed Returns

Mann's *Doctor Faustus* and the Fugue of Capital

DAN KRIER

Mann's Life and *Doctor Faustus*

Thomas Mann's *Doctor Faustus* is *poiesis* about *poiesis*, a creative work of the highest caliber that highlights the centrality of ethically infused callings in modern capitalism. In the burgherly calling, "work is the purpose and meaning of life . . . [it is] the melody and everything else is mere accompaniment" (Lukacs, 2010, p. 76). To work within a burgherly calling is to concern oneself entirely with the "holy everyday" (p. 85), seeking nothing more than "consciousness of work well done" (pp. 79–80). Total devotion to work of highest quality becomes the central focus of life, the realm of freedom and meaning. As in other of Mann's works, the vicissitudes of callings determines the life-trajectory of characters. Like the legendary Faust, Mann's protagonist wagers his soul to realize his desires, but unlike in other variants of the legend, he renounces wealth, power, and sensual pleasure in pursuit of absolute creative potency in his calling. The protagonist of this Faust legend lives an almost entirely sinless, even blameless life to ascetically commit himself to the most intensive creative work. Leverkuhn's fate is a strange sort of tragedy because he "gets what he bargained for," a life without "cow warmth" but thoroughly infused with creative achievement.

The shape of Thomas Mann's (1975–1955) early life was marked by the declining fortunes of his burgherly family, the death of his father, and the liquidation of the family's Lubeck-based commodities trading firm in 1892. Mann retraced the arc of that decline in his first novel, *Buddenbrooks* (1901), a masterpiece that brought Mann fame, a modest fortune, and eventually, a Nobel prize. The novel portrays the Buddenbrooks family across four generations, with characters, settings, and events transplanted into the narrative from Mann family lore, scarcely masked by the thinnest of fictional veils. The Buddenbrooks, like the Manns, traded grain in the Hanseatic city of Lubeck. Like waves lapping the Baltic shore, each generation of Buddenbrooks swelled, crested, and died into their children, who then swelled and crested in structurally altered historical moments that prevented them from reproducing their parent's burgherly ways. Beginning in 1835, the burgherly ways of the first Buddenbrooks resounded with the French overtones, secular philosophy, and cosmopolitan culture of the German Enlightenment.[1] The second generation was marked by intense religious piety of the Weberian kind that ascetically restricted life within the confines of ethically weighted callings. This was the golden age of the German burgher, and this generation's business acumen, ethical conduct, and public service elevated the family to high position within Lubeck society. The next generation lost its inner conviction of religious piety, a conviction necessary to unify burgher life within ethical callings. None of the children in this generation "found their calling," but suffered fractured, fragmented, and increasingly desperate lives, while struggling to "keep up appearances" and sustain profits against rising competition from new breeds of boorish, ungentlemanly capitalists (the Hagenstroms). The fourth generation of the family washed out in disgrace, the patriarch dead, the family firm lost, and the social conditions necessary to the burgherly way of life vanished amid barbarism, militarism, and anomic disintegration. The book ends when the last of the Buddenbrooks, an artistic, sensitive, musical boy named Hanno, is snuffed out.

This retrospective, historical quality was common to all of Mann's best works. In Mann the historical dimension was never merely a psychological, Proustian persistence of memory, but a sociological *insistence of structure*, in which the *sequencing and direction of historical change is structurally determined by the return of the repressed*. In *Buddenbrooks*, each generation unified a historically determined burgherly way by negating incompatible symbols, disruptive fantasies, and disturbing drives. These un-burgherly elements were negated but preserved, and uncannily reappeared when structural conditions changed. Historical development was not a random shamble but a dialectical unfolding of structure determined by the return of the repressed. In *Buddenbrooks*, each generation was utterly unable to reproduce their parents' ways regardless of conscious striving precisely because historical conditions made these ways impossible. Capitalism's dark dynamism destroyed the conditions that shaped parental traits of character and culture, flooding children's lives with the uncanny return of drives, desires and symbolic forms repressed by previous generations. Mann's fiction, from *Buddenbrooks* through *Doctor Faustus*, depicted accelerating rates of historical change under capitalism that destabilized structural forms and shortened the half-life of each succeeding burgherly way of life.

Buddenbrooks further introduced music as a primary structuring device in Mann's writing. He returned again and again to music as the source of symbolic analogues and imagery to convey the immanent structure of the social world (more on this below). *Buddenbrooks* also introduced Mann's critique of capitalism as inescapably ambivalent: Progress unleashes retrogressive coarsening, and advances in high culture unleash barbarism and reaction.

At the center of *Buddenbrooks*, *Doctor Faustus*, and most of Mann's other works was the fictional depiction of the calling as the unifying structure of burgherly forms of life.[2] *Buddenbrooks* anticipated Weber's great essay on the centrality of the calling, *The Protestant Ethic and the Spirit of Capitalism* (1905), by several years. Mann's writings frequently depicted characters whose lives became deranged when they stepped outside of the protective magic circle of their calling, when they exposed themselves to the sacred impure by yielding to repressed drives, desires, and longings that had been renounced upon entrance into vocational life. Other characters were determined by the loss of their calling through failed inner conviction, or by inability hear a call or find a "place" of recognition in the structural order; in short, by not finding a regulatory calling to structure their lives. Finally, Buddenbrooks introduced characters who suffered physical and psychological maladies (including the ache of unfulfilled desire) that intersected in complex ways with callings, often unleashing a strange "productiveness of illness." Indeed, characters debilitated by illness were often forced to withdraw from social activities, avocations, and family duties, dwelling in twilight states where nothing disrupted total devotion to production in a calling.[3]

Variations on Mann's Recurring Themes

The vicissitudes of callings were explored throughout Mann's works. In his (1912) novella, *Death in Venice*, the protagonist Gustav Aschenbach (loosely based on the composer Gustav Mahler) is depicted as a man in late middle age who successfully found his calling as a writer and, like a good burgher, unified his life in the pursuit of his craft. At the beginning of the book, Aschenbach has achieved high honors and professional recognition but has begun to lose that religiously tinged inner conviction that fueled his previous production. Aschenbach is drawn out of the orbit of his calling by a chance encounter with a young man who disturbs his capacity for work. On health-restoring holiday to Venice, Aschenbach is overwhelmed by the return of the repressed when a youth of notable beauty becomes the object-cause of aching, extra-vocational desire. Stepping outside the calling's magic circle, Aschenbach no longer prudently self-regulates his activities and ignores repeated warnings to flee Venice, which is not only hot and fetid, but in the grip of a full-blown cholera epidemic. Aschenbach soon succumbs, a suicide of extra-vocational desires that were fanned into a flame when he stepped outside his calling to restore his health. Themes that propel action in Mann's *Death in Venice*—the centrality of the calling for self-regulation, the sacrifice of health and well-being in pursuit of productivity in a calling, the ascetic sublimation of desire as means to mobilize energy for high achievement in a calling—reappear as core themes in Mann's *Doctor Faustus*.

The protagonist of Mann's grueling (1924) *The Magic Mountain*, Hans Castorp, was a fresh, healthy college graduate who had just completed his professional training and accepted a position with an employer who prepared an office him to inhabit. Before assuming his duties, before being securely "installed" in his calling, Castorp briefly stepped outside its protective circle to visit a military cousin residing in an Alpine tuberculosis sanitorium. Castorp's plans for a 3-week visit morphed into an open-ended stay when he became "caught" in the temporal and spatial warp of the asylum. He found himself installed, not in his engineer's profession, but in the calling of a tuberculosis patient. Castorp assumed his vocation as tuberculosis patient when a doctor located a "soft spot" on his lungs

and recognized him as a patient of high promise. The calling of tuberculosis patient involved the same kind of ascetic renunciations as other
burgherly callings, constricting the orbit of life to a disciplined regime of
production. But while engineers produced plans and drawings, Castorp
and the other patients devoted themselves to the production of symptoms
(fevers, mucous, rashes, chills). The moral career of tuberculosis patients
requires the free participation of the subject in the progression of their
illness: Good patients are not cured, nor do they leave the sanitorium
alive, but rigorously work the therapeutic regimen to produce symptoms
of increasing refinement and complexity. Inmates of the sanitorium devote
themselves wholeheartedly to their patient calling, seeking fulfillment
in recognition from doctors and fellow patients as virtuoso producers of
symptoms unto death. In Mann's narrative, illnesses do not progress from
organic causes, but from hypnotic suggestion: Patients produce mucus,
lung spots, and other tuberculosis symptoms in an agonistic striving for
recognition. Mann writes about illness with the same vivid detail as
music: His descriptions of coughs, hacks, phlegm, and excretions are so
vivid, and his depiction of patient's desire for recognition in the elaborate regime of symptoms and treatment so powerful, that one develops
sympathetic tuberculosis while reading the book.

Mann's recurrent motifs—the insistence of structure, immanent
ordering, return of the repressed, the unifying structure of callings for
burgherly life—resound throughout *The Magic Mountain*. Success in the
calling requires the renunciation, or at least sacrifice, of extra-vocational
desire. Castorp's desire is awakened in the sanitorium and fixated upon
an impossible object-cause, a young woman who (almost) always remains
out of grasp, and hence keeps him firmly installed in place. It is only
after her death, and the structural rupture of the great war, that Castorp
escapes the Magic Mountain, assumes the calling of soldier, and rushes
to sacrificial death in the trenches. Engineer, soldier, tuberculosis patient:
The search for recognition in the burgherly way of life drives characters
into callings with such masochistic intensity that they renounce desires,
monastically deanimate their bodies, and ritualistically produce symptoms
in a therapeutic regime. Success in callings requires the sacrifice of robust
health. Sickness, especially chronic and progressively severe disease, is
productive and socially honorific. The patients in the Alpine asylum,
removed from the hurly-burly of profane, lowland life and submitted to
the authority, routine, and moral order of the sanitorium develop symptoms and die as if on cue. Castorp and the other inmates were called

to the ultra-vocation of tuberculosis patient, a return of the repressed in the form of a pure, but inverted, Weberian calling. Their deaths were not symptomatic of psychological persistence of private memory, but sociological insistence of immanent structure.

These motifs recur in Mann's "Mario and the Magician" (1930), a short story that depicts a German professor who leaves the protective circle of his calling and travels with his family to an Italian beach resort, arriving at the historical moment when fascists consolidated power. Vacations to these beaches had been a routine part of the family's life, but changed structural conditions fundamentally altered the meaning of "normal" avocational activities. When the family's 8-year-old daughter removed her sandy swimsuit to rinse it in the sea, the family was mobbed by local beachgoers. They were soon arrested and charged by authorities with public indecency. Following this disturbing event, the family attended a magic show featuring an Italian magician named Cipolla, whose act was devoid of typical sleight-of-hand magic tricks and conjurings, and was instead an exhibition of hypnotic domination over the assembled audience. Cipolla cut an ambivalent figure on stage. His buttocks were strangely deformed (another illustration of the inverse relationship between moral power and robust physical health), and he wielded a phallic riding crop. He engaged the audience in sado-masochistic banter with consummate skill, calling forth a symphony of emotions while generating currents of moral energy that he collected, concentrated, and deployed as weapons against singled-out members of the audience who were commanded and humiliated. Mann describes Cipolla's ability to invert his chosen victim's resistance into compliance, to use victim's own moral weight against them. The story ends when Mario, a waiter and friend of the family who was publicly humiliated by Cipolla on stage, returns to avenge himself upon his tormentor. Mann's story powerfully depicts Freudian mass psychology in ideal-type form. Individuals removed from their callings and assembled into mass formations unleash demonic energies, projective displacements between ego and ideal, and transferential distortions. The insistence of structure, the return of repressed sociological drives and desires, shines through when the surface tissue of civility disappears in a flash, revealing barbarism and cultural recrudescence. The innocent act of a child rinsing a swimsuit unleashes pent-up energies and punitive power, the entertaining pleasures of a magic show unleashes sado-masochistic aggression, submission, and destructiveness. In Mann, these monstrous "flashes" are not locally generated or psychologically determined but reveal the insistence of immanent structure and the return of the social repressed.

Mann's writings leading up to *Doctor Faustus* include many variations on these themes. In manifold layerings, Mann's narration generates ideal-typifications in imaginary form that become congruent with Hegelian absolute idealism, Marx's dialectical materialism, Durkheim's social realism, and the best strands of contemporary critical social theory. Central to Mann is the unavoidable dialectical nature of history, determined by an insistence of immanent structure, whose symbolization is always incomplete and whose consistency is maintained through negation of discordant elements that nevertheless persist and return. In *Doctor Faustus*, Mann recognizes that the insistence of structure that determines historical change is comprehended within the realm of music through the compositional form of the *fugue*. The protagonist of *Doctor Faustus* masters the immanent order of music by comprehending and transcending the fugue form, a type of music that, like history itself, is structurally determined by the introduction of themes/motifs that repeat, transform, modulate in sequential returns of the repressed. Comprehending the phrasings and movements of the musical fugue necessitates not only conscious understanding of intoned, harmonic passages, but also unconscious grasp of impossible variations, silences, and discordant tones. The movements of the fugue are not random play with notes, but systematic variation on themes whose movements are determined by the insistence of structure, unheard and unconscious. In Mann's *Doctor Faustus*, the protagonist pursues musical composition as the ultimate calling, a vocation whose highest achievement required mastery of the most complex system of symbolic coding and a comprehension of the immanent structural order that it failed to encompass. Mann wrote *Doctor Faustus* in close collaboration with leading critical social theorists (especially Theodor Adorno), and came to recognize that the insistence of structure in modern capitalism echoed the compositional form of the musical fugue. To comprehend dialectical historical development, one not only must understand the current moment but the sequence of prior moments that are remembered and carried forward in a social unconscious.

Like modern symphonies based on folk tunes, Mann's late novels, *Lotte in Weimar* (1939), *Joseph and His Brothers* (published in four volumes between 1933 and 1943), *Doctor Faustus* (1947), and *The Holy Sinner* (1951), reconstruct and retell iconic historical legends in modern

mode. The story of Faust's deal with the devil is rooted in folktales of
great antiquity but achieved iconic form in reformation era chapbooks
(see Spies, 1587) that became immensely popular in the time of Luther.
Faust's legendary adventures were set in and circulated throughout German
Heartland regions that bore the full, brutal brunt of the Reformation, the
Thirty Years War, Pietist and Anabaptist purges. The legends described
the adventures of an alchemist/ doctor/negromancer who signs a pact
with the devil to acquire supernatural power and obtain extraordinary
ends. The devil's avatar (Mephistopheles) grants Faustus his period of
self-expansion but invariably returns to make good on the bargain,
claiming Faust's soul as his own. Allen (1985) correctly identifies Faust
as an inversion of Christ, an anti-hagiography, a negative morality tale,
and reversal of the *imitatio christi*. The Faust chapbooks were the source
of Christopher Marlowe's (1592) play, the highly successful *The Tragical
History of Doctor Faustus*. Goethe famously reimagined and redeemed this
tragic figure in his masterpiece, *Faust, Part 1* (1790) and *Faust, Part 2*
(1832). Goethe's *Faust* has become a master narrative of modernity and
an ongoing source of critical theories of capitalist development (e.g., see
Berman, 1982, pp. 37–85; Carter, 2014; Marx, 1977, pp. 161, 180, 302;
Worrell, 2015). Echoes of the Faust legend were still resounding in German literature, for example in Herman Hesse's (1927) *Steppenwolf*, when
Mann began writing *Doctor Faustus* in 1943, and his reconstruction of
the legend has been enormously influential, generating a secondary literature of commentary and analysis of immense proportions (Fetzer, 1996).
Mann's *Doctor Faustus* has a close affinity with critical social theorists
due to the influence of Theodor Adorno on Mann's vision of the book.
Mann read Adorno's study of Wagner (Adorno, 2005) and his *Philosophy
of New Music* (Adorno, 2006), discussing them at length while living
as near neighbors in the 1940s (Mann, 1948). Mann memorialized his
debt to Adorno within the diegesis of *Doctor Faustus* when, at a critical
juncture, the devil assumes Adorno's appearance and speech patterns.

Fugue Structure in *Doctor Faustus*

> I call the piece a fugue, and it gives the impression, yet the
> theme is not faithfully repeated, but rather develops with the
> development of the whole, so that a style is loosened and in
> a way reduced *ad absurdum* . . . to the archaic fugal forms of
> certain *canzoni* and *ricercari* of the pre-Bach time, in which

the fugue theme is not always clearly defined and adhered to. (Mann, 1948, p. 360)

The fugue structure of *Doctor Faustus* opens with the thematic distinction of "pure and impure genius" that parallels Durkheim's (1965) contrast of the pure and impure sacred. Adrian Leverkuhn's diabolical augmentation of his natural "god-afflicted" talents thematically organizes the book. Though Leverkuhn possessed remarkable aptitude for musical achievement, it was corrupted when he bargained with the devil to become possessed of a second, impure, and overmastering genius (Mann, 1948, p. 5). Leverkuhn had a "learning head and a lighting brain" (Mann, 1948, p. 32) whose particular *ingenium* lay in instantaneous comprehension of systems of symbolic coding, that once understood, enabled him to leap ahead of lessons with "swift, strangely sovereign and anticipatory" understanding as if the entire structural order had been intuitively assimilated (Mann, 1948, p. 33). Leverkuhn recognized early that music was one structured order among many, subject to rapid mastery once law-like rules were apprehended. Mann clearly possessed remarkable musical talent as well, since he frequently "wrote" music into words, translated virtuoso musical performance and technically complex composition into sentences and paragraphs of glistening clarity. Mann, like his protagonist, was possessed by a similar genius to transpose symbolic coding from one structural order to another, capturing musical effects and technical movements in words.

The contrapuntal structure of *Doctor Faustus* begins with Leverkuhn's first exposure to the "sphere of music" in the peasant polyphony of traditional rounds sung by the stable girl at his farm. Her singing opened a window into music as a symbolic order by singing music "more artistically organized than that of mere unison songs . . . [with] interweaving voices and imitative entries . . . [in which the] second singer fitted itself very pleasantly point for point to the continuation sung by the first." (Mann, 1948, p. 28). Up to four singers all singing in various harmonics and sequence could be incorporated in one of these rounds, "always separate from each other in time, but the melodic presence of each kept together pleasantly with that of the others and what we produced made a graceful web, a body of sound such as unison singing could not, a texture in . . . polyphony" (p. 28). This is an excellent description of initiation into a structured social phenomena, one not improvised, but embedded in a culture of long historical duration, that had arrived at a "plane of musical culture already relatively very high, in a realm of imitative polyphony, which the fifteenth century had to discover in order to give us pleasure" (28–29). The round, like traditional peasant culture, returned its singers back in rotary motion to their point of departure, in song that could be repeated without end, music that did not conclude but had to, at some point, merely cease.

While the round repeats, the fugue literally takes flight, a form of polyphony that introduces a theme that returns transformed, an uncanny double of itself. Such doubling occurs everywhere in Mann's *Doctor Faustus*: Settings, characters, and plot sequences recur in new variants as the novel unfolds. The setting, household, and family structure of the pleasant farm near Buchel where the novel's protagonist spends his childhood uncannily reappears in slightly altered form on a farm near Pfeffering, where he lives in adulthood. The many doublings were reproduced in astonishing detail: a community bench on a hill; a pond for bathing; a great tree in the farmyard; a pipe-smoking father; the appearance and manner of a mother; a family dog; even a hired cowgirl with shaking bosoms, dung-caked feet, and a harmonic singing voice. As in other Mann novels, the parallels were not absolute, variations on a theme rather than precise repetitions, but the past clearly bled into his present. Leverkuhn's life was structured as a fugue, the return of the repressed, in which "certain correspondences, transposed, as it were, into another but not far removed key" (Mann, 1948, p. 204). Throughout the book, new characters are introduced who displace existing ones, never precise duplicates, but fugue-like variation. The parallel structures were not consciously chosen, but unconsciously reappear, as in Leverkuhn's holiday rental in Italy, in a farmhouse that was strangely familiar in form, character, people, animals only slightly transformed from the other "peasant baroque" settings in which he dwelt (p. 202).

Time in the novel was also doubled: The novel was written as a first-person narration by Leverkuhn's friend, the philologist and retired teacher, Dr. Serenus Zeitblom, and most chapters begin with clear reference to the precise time, place, and historical context unfolding while Zeitblom composes (between 1943 and 1945). This contrasts with the temporality of the diegesis that was being narrated, which covered Leverkuhn's lifespan (1880s through his death in 1940). Mann generated harmonic resonances by juxtaposing events in these two temporal series: sometimes consonant, sometimes dissonant. The novel, in short, was composed in counterpoint, a polyphonic, fugue-like structure full of complex harmonics. In Chapter 21, battles fought nearby were consonant with the struggle underway in the narrative, air raids were underway and the narrator writes with "trembling hands" while bombs rocked his home. The density grew in moments, as the "quite extraordinary interweaving of time-units, destined moreover, to include even a third, the day the courteous reader will take for the reading of what has been written" so that the novel contained a threefold ordering of time: his own, that of the chronicler, and historic time (Mann, 1948, p. 252). Ultimately, the novel brought the time series together in consonant tragedy at the end, when both Germany and Leverkuhn met their tragic fate in the climactic battle for Berlin coincided with Leverkuhn's final frenzied composition, after which both passed from "deep night into the deepest night of all" (p. 3).

Polyphony was further introduced in the novel by the stark personality contrasts of its two main characters, the gifted but sickly protagonist, Adrian Leverkuhn, and the book's narrator, Serenus Zeitblom, a healthy humanist. Leverkuhn was the brilliant younger son of smallholding farmers in deepest Germany, "the place of witches and strangelings" (Mann, 1948, p. 82). Leverkuhn was gifted and capable of quick mastery of symbolic orders, the book is structured by turning-points in his journey through mathematics and theology before finding his "calling" in musical composition, and his dealings with the demonic, including the famous pact with a Mephistopheles-like phantasm. Sequences of Leverkuhn's life loosely parallel Nietzsche's (failed sexual dalliance, syphilitic infection, productive illness ending in a crescendo of manic achievement, ultimate collapse), while other sequences parallel that of the composer Schoenberg, whose atonal 12-tone system of composition forms the real-world referent for Leverkuhn's creative breakthrough.

Zeitblom by contrast was a sunny and reasonable man without taste for the "daemonic," a man who refused all intercourse with the "powers of darkness" (Mann, 1948, p. 4). Out of tune with National Socialism, Zeitblom resigned his teaching position after Nazis came to power and became increasingly estranged from his ardent Nazi sons. Throughout the book, he feared "a German victory more than a defeat" (p. 30). Zeitblom shaped his life to remain connected to Leverkuhn, forestalling his own life plans, changing universities, taking extraneous courses, and altering vacation plans to keep within Leverkuhn's orbit. Zeitblom felt that he had a calling for humanistic studies, and completed a doctorate in philology, but his interest in language was professional, rational, and technical, while his avocational interest in music was heartfelt, irrational,

intense and emotional. While Zeitblom never fully committed in a burgherly fashion to a single calling, Leverkuhn's commitment to his was
all-too-total and he sought to augment his inborn talent by resorting to
perverse demonic bargaining. Leverkuhn was already gifted with a "pure
and genuine, God-given, or shall I say God-inflicted genius" augmented by
a second "acquired kind" of genius, resulting from a "horrible bargain" a
"sinful and morbid corruption of natural gifts" (p. 4). This double genius
enabled extraordinary production and achievement in Leverkuhn's calling
as a composer. His calling led Leverkuhn to spurn careerist measures of
worldly success (immediate fame, popular accolades, enrichment) and to
completely abandon affection, warmth, and companionship. Working in
a dedicated frenzy, Leverkuhn wrote music that his contemporaries found
nearly impossible to either perform or enjoy. Like the whispered prayers
of an isolated hermit, his music constituted symbolic love songs tuned
to the ears of his Lacanian Big Other, the negative Valhalla of absolute
music. Leverkuhn's life was similar to ascetic Calvinists in Weber's writings,
who endeavored mightily in a cold abyss, striving for recognition by a
long-absconded God. Like these Puritans, everything in Leverkuhn's life
was sacrificed to the absolute pursuit of his burgherly calling.

The Calling in Doctor Faustus

In Mann's *Doctor Faustus*, like Weber's (1958) writings on the capitalist spirit, the burgherly calling, the "holy everyday" (Lukacs, 2010, p.
85), defined the boundaries of meaningful, ethical activity. The calling
particularized individuals determining the confines of action and the
individual's relation to the Social Big Other. While callings appeared in
all variants of ascetic protestantism as the site of ethically justified activity, in Calvinism-Puritanism, the purest form of ascetic protestantism in
Weber's work, believers were driven into their callings with exceptional
force. Pietists, Quakers, and members of other sects that emphasized
the heartfelt spirit of brotherly love lived in an ontological world that
vibrated with the sacred pure. For these believers, the demonic, sacred
impure was vanquished and drained from the immanent world by the
savior's redemptive power. In Calvinism-Puritanism, however, the sacred
pure Creator abandoned the immanent world that vibrated with the
demonic sacred impure. For these believers, the devil stalked the world,
seeking the destruction of souls. In Calvinism-Puritanism, the burgherly
calling functioned as a magic circle drawn around believers, protecting

them from the wiles of the devil while providing a particularized altar upon which to sacrifice human time and energy.

In Mann's *Doctor Faustus*, after making his deal with the devil, Leverkuhn withdrew to an old monastery, occupying the Abbot's room, where he productively composed music while living an ascetic, even monastic, existence. The suggestion of a pentacle was visible on the floor of Leverkuhn's room (Mann, 1948, p. 486). He worked, quite literally, within the magic circle of his calling and suffered debilitating migraines when he left. The burgherly calling circumscribed life and became the site of capitalist sacrifice, the ethically justified location for redeeming spent human energy in creative production.

Leverkuhn sought productive solitude. For him, inspiration came not "from the world' but from the demonic genius that possessed him with greater force when he was removed from ties and activities. Achievement required isolation from society's stimulating moral energies. Leverkuhn lived "the life of a saint" . . . not because of the "ethos of purity but from the pathos of impurity" (Mann, 1948, p. 220). He maintained a monastic *anti-relationship* to the world, a complete withdrawal from the universal into the particular. Possessed of the ultimate burgherly calling, Leverkuhn lived productively but austerely, and remained sexually ascetic in a "community of chastity."

Finding one's calling required struggle and strife. Talents were tested, tastes sampled to find a particular position in the world. In Mann's work, many characters failed to find their calling. Even Leverkuhn, who surely was an archetype of the man solidly installed in a vocation, pursued training in two other professions (mathematics and theology) before hearing the call, before embracing the composer's vocation. Unlike other literary Fausts, Leverkuhn's tarrying with the negative, his deal with the devil, was strangely consistent with the burgherly way of life. His break with typical burgher morality lay in his willingness to achieve success through demonic inspiration, magic, even miracle, rather than purely through ascetic work and avoidance of sin. Leverkuhn's accursed inspiration turned him into the ultimate burgherly hero: He desired success in a calling with such fervor that he was not only willing to ascetically sacrifice his life in its pursuit, he was willing to be damned. In the phrasing of Weber, no saint ever wore a tighter cloak, renounced this-worldly pleasures, or experienced the steel-hard casing of vocational striving more than Leverkuhn. Like a fugue, Mann's *Doctor Faustus* did not repeat already extant Faust legends but dialectically modulated them. While previous

Faust demonically bargained to gain riches, glory, wide-ranging experience, universal knowledge, unrestricted sensual enjoyment, Leverkuhn wanted what every good burgherly subject desired: success in his calling.

The Calling: Playing with an Immanent Structural Order

Throughout *Doctor Faustus*, Leverkuhn remained fascinated with immanent structural orders, and was especially interested with things that hovered indeterminately on the edge of categorical boundaries. He inherited aptitude for comprehending symbolic structures from his father. Though a farmer by vocation, the elder Leverkuhn was an avocational alchemist who maintained an enthusiastic "libertine traffic with forbidden things" and whose deepest desire was to "speculate the elements" (Mann, 1948, p. 13). Such daring ventures were contrary to Protestant condemnation of creation as "morally depraved," and god-forsaken. Impiously enthralled with obscure natural phenomena, his practices were "not altogether remote from magic," as he sought out "freaks and fascinations" that disturbed commonsense categories, revealing nature's "equivocal moods, weird, half-hidden associations" (p. 13). Behind the analytic concern with border cases and limit phenomena was a desire for understanding and mastery of the structural order that defined them. The search for categorical antinomies that were ontologically real but outside the currently defined symbolic order signaled "a rash overstepping of ordained limits" and a willingness to "traffic with the forbidden" (p. 13).

Hence, burgherly callings do not merely divide workers into narrow specializations to perform alienated labor. Instead, the possession of a burgherly calling requires the sublation and transcendence of the vocation's entire structural order. Burgherly callings require more than the possession of talent, aptitude, and taste for the particular work tasks to be performed. One also must manifest an aptitude and desire to comprehend the structural coding upon which the profession is based. Those with a calling know the history and structure of their vocation, understand it genetically, even philologically, as a structural system of codes. It is this comprehension of immanent structure that enables creativity. High achievement comes not from inspiration or naïve discoveries, but from comprehension of structural rules, the capacity to play within them, and a willingness to go beyond them. The mark of the calling is the God-afflicted capacity to comprehend and play with the historical structure of a field.

Music as an Immanent Structure

Max Weber's (1958) book, the *Rational and Social Foundations of Music,*
originally an appendix to *Economy and Society* (1978), describes the
immanent structure of music in the mathematical relationships built
into the real of sound. Musical harmonics of the octave (ratio of 1:2),
the fifth (ratio of 2:3), and the fourth (ratio of 3:4) are structurally
determined by the physics of sound. The structural real of sound generates impossibilities, such as the inability to divide an octave into two
consonant equal intervals and the impossibility of bringing the circle
of fifths to consonant conclusion without remainder, even if the fifths
are extended in perpetuity. The geometry of sound determines that the
twelfth perfect fifth exceeds the seventh octave by an interval, known
since ancient times, of the Pythagorean comma, an "unalterable state
of affairs" that "forms the core of facts for all musical rationalization"
(1958, p. 3). Different civilizations have developed systems of musical
notation and conventions to represent and domesticate music produced
under these structurally determined conditions. In the West, intervals
of fourths and fifths predominate, as well as consonant harmonic triads.
The intervals of harmonic triads are consonant, all other intervals are
dissonant, but "dissonance is the major dynamic element of chordal music,
and dissonant chords like the seventh "demand resolution into a new
chord representing the harmonic base as consonant focus" (p. 6). This
closed system of chords would create wooden, over-rationalized music
but for the charisma of free melody: "[W]ithout the tensions motivated
by the irrationality of melody, no modern music would exist" (p. 11).
Further, the real of sound makes fully rational music impossible, as the
"failure of rationalization can in no way be eliminated" by any symbolic
system due to the immanent irrational structure of music, reflected in
the "unresolvable opposition of thirds/fifths" and the inability to create
perfectly tempered musical instruments (p. 11).

In Mann's *Doctor Faustus,* Leverkuhn lived for a time above a
musical warehouse that traded in archaic, superseded instruments whose
unique tone and temper was "embodied" in them with lost artisanship and
whose sound could not be reproduced with the rationalized instruments
current to the late 19th century. Orchestral instruments were the real,
material bodies that gave tongue to sound and made music. Manufacturing these instruments required mastery of acoustics, an artistic if not
scientific comprehension of the symbolic rules necessary to produce a

particular instrumental voice. Music was not a transcendent symbolic system, residing in the noumenal ether, but an immanent structural order resistant to full symbolization.[4]

The bearer of Leverkuhn's call to musical composition was his teacher Kretschmar, who articulated this central theme of the book: Callings with great complexity in their symbolic structure possess high levels of emotive or "elemental" power. Composers, especially composers of highly complicated polyphonic compositions, "speculate with the elements" of music. Music was the most elemental, or primitive, of all arts because it "never got rid of a religious attitude towards her own beginnings; a pious proneness to call them up in solemn invocation—in short, to celebrate her elements" (Mann, 1948: 62). Good composers speculated with the elements, the immanent structure, of music.

The Calling and Productive Sickness: Dying into Work

Leverkuhn's creative production increased with sickness rather than health: "[C]reative, genius-giving disease . . . is a thousand times dearer to life than plodding healthiness" (Mann, 1948, p. 242). Mann's fascination with productive sickness, with the need to "die into" work was fundamentally linked to the burgherly calling. High achievement in a calling required mastery of the structural history of its structural order, which involved a massive sacrifice of time and energy. To find a burgherly calling was to find a particular place and way to die.

Leverkuhn was fully at play in the symbolic order of music, fascinated with ambiguities, indeterminate relationships between chords, telescoping into complex harmonics. He found himself at play in the structural order, focused upon inner-laws of progression, to understand how chords are "meant" to follow others, how chords are decomposed into component notes/voices that move. Leverkuhn learned to "despise chords" to pursue pure polyphony . . . "the polyphonic character of the chords is the more pronounced, the more dissonant it is. The degree of dissonance is the measure of its polyphonic value. The more discordant a chord is, the more notes it contains contrasting and conflicting with each other, the more polyphonic it is, the more markedly every single note bears the stamp of the part already in the simultaneous sound combination" (Mann, 1948, p. 74). This is music as magic square, the stuff of modern jazz, of modern society, of capitalism itself, rendered into the field of music.

Leverkuhn kept an image of a magic square on the wall of his study. The magic square represented an immanent structure, a symbolic order that "completes itself." Leverkuhn's magic square was a 4-by-4 table containing 16 numbers precisely arrayed so that every column, row, and diagonal summed to the same total. Once the first numbers are laid down, the structural order completes itself. The remaining numbers must occupy one and only one exact position. The structural order of the magic square is overdetermined: Each number is fixed in position on every side. The immanent order of music functioned as a magic-square: Consonance, dissonance, chord progressions were immanent in the structure of sound.

Leverkuhn "loved to put mysteries, magic formulas, and charms into his work" (Mann, 1948, p. 155). Like his father, he was fascinated with limit phenomena, with music that hovered just at the very limit of playability. Leverkuhn produced virtuoso music of incredible technical complexity that was nevertheless unlovely to the senses (p. 160). Speculating with the elements of music, he pushed a compositional logic right to the point of its impossibility, to the point where antinomies were at peak tension (p. 218). Leverkuhn, like all virtuosos who master the symbolic order of their chosen calling, created technically elegant works that were scarcely understood. His music became technique, "nothing but the solving of technical puzzles" (p. 239).

The Polyphony of Callings and the Technical Frontier

Throughout the book, Leverkuhn continued his life as an inverted saint, a man without vice, who worked almost constantly. As his mastery of music grew and his achievements mounted, he found himself striving for technical perfection that was musically impossible. He struggled to "keep within the limits of the possible" (Mann, 1948, p. 259). As Leverkuhn pushed contrapuntal-fugue technique as far as possible, it was no longer music for the ear, "more to be read than to be heard" (p. 262), producing "glorious pieces . . . almost unsung" and in all likelihood, unsingable (p. 264).

Capital's monstrous expansion of symbolic orders accelerated parabolically since the early 20th century. The scale and scope of symbolic systems have exploded in a whole universe of specialized fields—science, arts, humanities, math, physics—without a compensatory expansion of the universal imaginary to comprehend such highly particularized experience. No connection between this universe of particulars, no verstehen, just symbolic orders expanding exponentially into a "monstrously extra-human" (Mann, 1948, p. 269). Under the anomic force of capital, symbolic orders have become "ungraspable . . . overwhelmed by size" causing a "deafening bombardment of our intelligence" (p. 271). For the humanist Zeitblom, "there is in all this monstrousness nothing that could appeal to the likes of me as goodness, beauty, greatness" (p. 271).

As each particularized sphere advanced, each symbolic code pushed technical frontiers beyond their capability to connect with the universal. Atomized individuals sought "romantic movements" to generate an illusory "union of the advanced with the popular, the closing of the gulf between art and accessibility, high and low" (Mann, 1848, p. 320). Of course, such movements were impossible, since each symbolic sphere was destined to experience "new and deeper cleavage and alienation between the good and the easy, the worthwhile and the entertaining, the advanced and the generally enjoyable" (p. 320). And since each sphere was accelerating away from others (despite new links, bridges, and crossovers), a virtuoso in one sphere remained a person who sacrificed understanding of all other spheres, and was therefore reduced to the same stupefied enjoyment of the base and "sentimental" as the uneducated masses. Genuine appreciation across particularized symbolic systems was no longer possible. Each cultural sphere, each expanding system of symbolic coding existed in "pompous isolation . . . being alone with an elite of culture," particularized to the point of singularity (p. 322). Without meaningful contact between particularities, no appreciative audience for elite, technically advanced cultural productions could exist. The consequence: "[A]rt will be entirely alone, alone to die, unless she were to find her way to the folk" (p. 322).

The Return of the Repressed: The Totalization and Return to Folk Aesthetics

Such immediate emotive connections to the atomized "folk" can occur only through retrogression and extreme simplification: Art that "goes in unto the folk, which makes her own the needs of the crowd, of the little man, of small minds, arrives at wretchedness, and to make it her duty is the worst small-mindedness, and the murder of mind and spirit" (Mann, 1948, p. 322). Members of the folk were not particularized into burgherly callings: They were singulars who identified immediately with the emotive universal. To Mann, the folk were "anachronistic and alarming . . . you need only tell a crowd they are "the folk" to stir them up to all sorts of reactionary evil" (pp. 37–38). Explosive expansion of particularized systems impoverished and massified individuals. The "flashes" or "breakthroughs" of direct emotive unification of singularities into universals were moments of immense danger. Praxis was often conceived as the building of mass political movements emotively mobilized toward (often) irrational ends. Under capital, the explosive fragmentation of particularized spheres of creative production (*poiesis*) was fated to push technical frontiers farther apart, while romantic political movements (praxis) sought to emotively override these divides and bring together something approximating a folk. Such aestheticization of culture and politics tends to end badly. *Doctor Faustus* depicted history's dialectic as a fugue-like "insistence of structure" in which motifs, even when repressed, return in variant form. This should give pause to critical theorists who desire after-capital: We must be careful lest the thing we destroy returns in even darker form.

Notes

1. This chapter views the calling as the central sociological construct of the burgherly way of life, for the calling forms a protective magic circle that provides a portal for redemptive, sacrificial use of time while simultaneously shielding the laborer from demonic influences in a god-forsaken world. This view largely agrees with Lukacs's synthetic image of the "bourgeois way of life," the "cutting down the conduct of one's life to a strictly and narrowly bourgeois measure . . . asceticism . . . renunciation . . . a kind of forced labor, a hateful servitude . . . the whip that drives the life-denying man to work without cease . . ." (Lukacs, 2010, p. 74). I prefer to use Mann's term "burgherly" rather than bourgeois in this essay to maintain a greater emphasis on the particularity of 19th- and 20th-century German middle-class life that formed the immediate biographical and cultural background of both Mann and Weber. Thomas Mann's essay on "Burgherly Nature" is also relevant here (1982, pp. 71–106).

2. Weber (1958a) is the classic statement of the centrality of the calling to protestantism, as in his discussion of Luther's translation of Sirach 9:20, 21: "Persevere in your duty, take pleasure in doing it, and grow old in your calling." Cranmer's translation of the Bible, echoed in King James, contains Corinthians 7:20: "Let every man abide in the same calling to which he was called." The importance of the calling to Puritan theological speculation is apparent in Perkins (1603), and in Hieron, who writes: "He that hath no honest business about which ordinarily to be employed, no settled course to which he may betake himself, cannot please God" (Hieron, 1620, p. 246). On literary representations of the

calling, see Barrett (1989), Danon (1985), Mint (1978), and Ridley (1994). The fate of particularized callings in after-capital is discussed in Worrell and Krier (2015) and Krier and Worrell (2017).

3. Mann experienced in his own life, including during the writing of *Doctor Faustus*, "the curious divergence between biological and intellectual vitality . . . a sinking of vitality as the cause and precondition for a creative effort that absorbs into itself the stuff of an entire life" (Mann, 1961, pp. 5–6). This would seem to place Mann on the Romantic side of Goethe's famous formula: "Classicism is healthy, romanticism is sick."

4. Weber's book is foundational to any grasp of social determinations of musical notation disciplined by the immanent structure of sound. See also Heller-Roazen (2011), Helmholtz (1895), Mann (1987), and Adorno ([1946] 2006). Adorno's extensive writings on music reveal strong overlap between musical theory and critical social theory.

References

Adorno, T. W. (2005). *In Search of Wagner*. London, UK: Verso.

Adorno, T. W. ([1946] 2006). *Philosophy of New Music*. Translated by Robert Hullot-Kentor. Minneapolis: University of Minnesota Press.

Agamben, G. (2016). *The Use of Bodies*. Stanford, CA: Stanford University Press.

Allen, M. D. (1985). *The Faust Legend: Popular Formula and Modern Novel*. New York, NY: Peter Lang.

Aristotle. (1908). *Aristotle's Politics*. Translated by Benjamin Jowett. Oxford, UK: Clarendon Press

Barrett, D. (1989). *Vocation and Desire: George Eliot's Heroines*. London, UK: Routledge.

Berman, R. (1982). *All That is Solid Melts into Air: The Experience of Modernity*. New York, NY: Penguin.

Carter, W. H. (2014). Faust's Begehren: Revisiting the history of political economy in *Faust II*. *Goethe Yearbook, 21*(1), 103–128.

Danon, R. (1985). *Work in the English Novel: The Myth of Vocation*. London, UK: Croom Helm.

Durkheim, E. ([1915] 1965). *Elementary Forms of the Religious Life*. Translated by J. W. Swain. New York, NY; Free Press.

Fetzer, J. E. (1996). *Changing Perceptions of Thomas Mann's Doctor Faustus: Criticism 1947–1992*. Columbia, SC: Camden House.

Heller-Roazen, D. (2011). *The Fifth Hammer: Pythagoras and the Disharmony of the World*. New York, NY: Zone Books.

Helmholtz, H. (1895). *On the Sensations of Tone as a Physiological Basis for the Theory of Music*. London and New York, NY: Longmans, Green & Co.

Hieron, S. (1620). *The Sermons of Samuel Hieron*. London, UK: John Legate.

Krier, D., & Worrell, M. P. (2017). The organic composition of Big Mama. *Continental Thought & Theory*, 1(4), 636–652."

Lacan, J. (2015). *Transference: The Seminar of Jacques Lacan Book VIII*. Translated by Bruce Fink. Cambridge, UK: Polity.

Lukacs, G. (1978). *Essays on Thomas Mann*. Translated by S. Mitchell. New York, NY: Howard Fertig.

Lukacs, G. (2010). The bourgeois way of life and art for art's sake: Theodor Storm. Translated by A. Bostock. In J. T. Sanders & K. Terezakis (eds.), *Soul & Form* (pp. 73–97). New York, NY: Columbia University Press.

Mann, A. (1987). *The Study of the Fugue*. New York, NY: Dover.

Mann, T. (1948). *Doctor Faustus*. Translated by H. T. Lowe-Porter. New York, NY: Alfred A. Knopf.

Mann, T. (1951). *The Holy Sinner*. Translated by H. T. Lowe-Porter. New York, NY: Alfred A. Knopf.

Mann, T. (1961). *The Story of a Novel: The Genesis of Doctor Faustus*. Translated by Richard & Clara Winston. New York, NY: Alfred A. Knopf.

Mann, T. (1982). *Reflections of a Nonpolitical Man*. Translated by W. D. Morris. New York, NY: Ungar.

Mann, T. (1989). *Death in Venice and Seven Other Stories*. Translated by H. T. Lowe-Porter. New York, NY: Vintage.

Mann, T. ([1901] 1994). *Buddenbrooks: The Decline of a Family*. Translated by John E. Woods. New York, NY: Everyman.

Mann, T. (1995). *The Magic Mountain: A Novel*. Translated by John E. Woods. New York, NY: Vintage.

Marx, K. (1977). *Capital, Volume 1*. Translated by B. Fowkes. New York, NY: Vintage.

Mint, A. (1978). *George Eliot and the Novel of Vocation*. Cambridge, MA: Harvard University Press.

Perkins, W. (1603). *A Treatise of the Vocations, or Callings of Men*. DigitalPuritan. net. Retrieved from www.digitalpuritan.net/Digital%20Puritan%20Resources/Perkins,%20William/Treatise%20of%20the%20Vocations%20(OTW%20Version).pdf

Plato. (1902). The Symposium. In *The Dialogues of Plato, Vol. 1* (pp. 449–514). Translated by Benjamin Jowett. New York: Scribner's.

Ridley, H. (1994). *The Problematic Bourgeois: Twentieth-Century Criticism on Thomas Mann's* Buddenbrooks *and* The Magic Mountain. New York, NY: Camden House.

Spies, J. (1587). *Historia and Tale of Doctor Johann Faustus, Wolfenbuttel Manuscript*. Retrieved from www.lettersfromthedustbowl.com/msE.html

Weber, M. (1952). *Ancient Judaism*. Translated by H. H. Gerth & D. Martindale. New York, NY: Free Press.

Weber, M. (1958a). *The Protestant Ethic and the Spirit of Capitalism*. Translated by Talcott Parsons. New York, NY: Charles Scribner.

Weber, M. (1958b). *The Rational and Social Foundations of Music*. Translated by Don Martindale. New York, NY: Stratford Press/Southern Illinois University Press.

Weber, M. (1978). *Economy and Society*. Edited by G. Roth and C. Wittich. Berkeley: University of California Press.

Worrell, M. P. (2015). Imperial homunculi: The speculative singularities of American hegemony. *Current Perspectives in Social Theory*, *33*, 217–241.

Worrell, M. P., & Krier, D. (2015). Atopia awaits! A critical sociological analysis of Marx's political imaginary. In *Critical Sociology* (pp. 1–27). doi: 10.1177/0896920515620476

Zizek, S. (1999). *The Ticklish Subject: The Absent Centre of Political Ontology*. London and New York, NY: Verso.

PART II
DAWN

Chapter 5

"Shakespearian Politics" and World History

Tony Smith

It is pointless to speculate on Shakespeare's own political views. But we do have the plays, and one dimension of these multidimensional works is the way they include extended thought experiments on the nature of political rule. The first part of this chapter explores three main political themes that I believe can be found in these works. The second, more speculative, section presents what I take to be a conclusion that can be taken to follow from these themes regarding the essential nature of the political sphere. Since we cannot claim anything about Shakespeare's own political views, I shall refer to these theses and conclusion as a form of "Shakespearean politics." This political worldview is neither a conservative endorsement of traditional political authority, nor an endorsement of a radical political alternative. It centers instead on the fundamental ethical irrationality of the political realm, and the idea that the normative satisfaction that cannot be found in politics must be sought instead in the private domestic sphere, where the great dramas of reconciliation of husband and wife, parents and children, birth and death are played out. From this standpoint, the greatest political dramas in world literature endorse an apolitical mode of being in the world. The final section of the chapter, however, presents and defends an alternative version of "Shakespearian politics."

147

Three Themes in a "Shakespearian Politics"

The plays are set in a number of different historical contexts, including the warrior aristocracies of ancient Greece and Troy, the republic of ancient Rome, the Roman empire, the early English and Scottish kingdoms of medieval feudalism, the mercantile republic of Renaissance Venice, and the nascent absolute monarchies of Shakespeare's own Britain and elsewhere. If common themes are found in the plays, it is reasonable to assume we should take the scope of "Shakespearean politics" to apply to political life throughout world history. I shall not consider here whether considering non-Western cases, or incorporating the greater knowledge of the historical periods depicted in the plays that we possess today, would call into question the scope of "Shakespearean politics." It will simply be assumed here that the plays do indeed capture features of political life common to different political forms from the beginning of world history through the Renaissance.[1]

Theme 1: Political Authority Is Not Determined by A "Natural" Hierarchical Order, But by Power Struggles between Competing Elites

The dominant ideology of Shakespeare's day (and long after), has been aptly captured with the phrase "the great chain of Being" (Lovejoy, 1936). According to this view, a natural hierarchical order in the cosmos extends from prime matter on the lowest rung to an "Unmoved Mover" (Aristotle) or personal God (Christianity) at its pinnacle. Everything that exists has a proper place in this hierarchy, with those on lower levels "naturally" subordinate to those above. Plants are naturally subordinate to animals; animals are naturally subordinate to humans; all creation is naturally subordinate to God.

The social world is a part of this metaphysical order, its hierarchy a part of the natural hierarchy of beings. Women and children are naturally subordinate to husbands and fathers. Slaves, serfs, and peasants are naturally subordinate to masters and lords. And those subject to political rule are naturally subordinate to rulers. If the Great Chain is taken to culminate in a personal deity, these hierarchical relationships are thought to be divinely sanctioned. If the rightful order is disrupted by willful actions, chaos results, and continues until order is reestablished.

Perhaps the single most powerful expression of the Great Chain of Being motif is found in Ulysses's great speech at the beginning of *Troilus and Cressida*:

> The heavens themselves, the planets and this centre
> Observe degree, priority and place,
> Insisture, course, proportion, season, form,
> Office and custom, in all line of order . . .

His powerful expression of the chaos following the willful disruption of the natural hierarchical order is worth quoting at length:

> O, when degree is shaked,
> Which is the ladder to all high designs,
> Then enterprise is sick! How could communities,
> Degrees in schools and brotherhoods in cities,
> Peaceful commerce from dividable shores,
> The primogenitive and due of birth,
> Prerogative of age, crowns, sceptres, laurels,
> But by degree, stand in authentic place?
> Take but degree away, untune that string,
> And, hark, what discord follows! each thing meets
> In mere oppugnancy. . . .
> Then every thing includes itself in power,
> Power into will, will into appetite;
> And appetite, an universal wolf,
> So doubly seconded with will and power,
> Must make perforce an universal prey,
> And last eat up himself. (*Troilus and Cressida* 1.3, lines
>   85–124)

If this bleakest of bleak ends is to be avoided, all must accept their proper place and its obligations.

Almost every subsequent event in *Troilus and Cressida* mocks Ulysses's speech. If the natural difference of degrees in society had the absolute metaphysical status Ulysses claims, shouldn't it be widely recognized? Political authority among the Greeks seems to have a much different foundation. Authority appears to be based instead on a rough social rule of thumb: whoever has the greatest number of troops, ships, and other material resources, should be considered preeminent. Agamemnon has brought more resources than the others, and so prominent figures like Nestor and Ulysses acknowledge him in public settings as king among the warlords. Little evidence can be found that anyone truly believes Agamemnon is at the head of a natural "line of order" defining "degree, priority and place."

When the play begins, Achilles has refused to recognize the natural authority of King Agamemnon, Agamemnon's authority to determine how spoils will be divided up, or any duty to follow the King's order to cease sulking in his tent and recommence killing Trojans. As the greatest warrior among warrior chieftains, Achilles can see no reason to accept a subordinate status with its obligation of obedience. Even worse, Achilles offers protection to Thersites, an especially vitriolic political satirist who viciously mocks Agamemnon's speech and demeanor, eroding whatever respect for the king's authority his audience might retain. Tellingly, Ulysses does not attempt to bring Achilles to believe in a natural order of society with Agamemnon at its summit. He plans instead to manipulate Achilles's return to the battlefield by rigging a lottery so that Ajax will receive the glory from meeting a challenge from Hector clearly intended for Achilles. Agamemnon plays no directing role in these machinations. If the plan had worked, and Achilles's pride led him to reassert his status over Ajax as the preeminent Greek killing machine, that would hardly imply he now accepted a subordinate position in a metaphysically grounded social hierarchy. As it happens, the plan fails utterly. Achilles is indifferent to the lottery, whose only result is that now Ajax too believes no one possesses a "natural" superiority over him.

A striking illustration of the utter failure of the supposed metaphysical order to have substantial force in concrete political life comes immediately after Ulysses's speech. Aeneas arrives at the Greek camp to deliver Hector's challenge. He asks where he can find Agamemnon, apparently unaware that the person he is asking is the person he seeks. If Agamemnon possessed natural authority, shouldn't that be apparent? It is not; he lacks any distinguishing feature setting him apart from the other Greek warriors. Perhaps Aeneas merely pretends to not recognize the king; perhaps he truly fails to distinguish the supposed highest authority from all the others. Either way, the effect is to call into question the claim that a natural hierarchical order compels recognition.

Troilus and Cressida, Shakespeare's most cynical play, is hardly the only one to call into doubt the assumption that an objective hierarchical order can be discerned in the social world. Every claim to authority appealing to a "natural" order of things by other characters in other plays is systematically undercut, even if the undercutting is not always highlighted on the plays' surface levels.

Julius Caesar is set in the historical moment when the Roman Republic was about to be overthrown by the acclamation of Caesar as king. Nothing in the play suggests a metaphysical justification for Caesar being granted this absolute form of political authority. If this vain and increasingly infirm man is made king, it will be due to the prestige and wealth won in military campaigns, not his place in an immutable "natural" order. The members of the republican elite who conspire against him refuse to accept that military success is a sufficient reason to abandon republican practices and institutions. In their view, the "natural order of things" is for equals to share authority with equals (Hadfield, 2012). By the standards of the Roman Republic they are Caesar's equals, and so his appropriation of absolute power would be profoundly "unnatural." The audience's knowledge that both the Roman republic and the conspirators were doomed utterly undercuts the republican view about the natural order. The social world at the end of the play is determined instead by the power of Antony and Octavius's troops, and the strategic and tactical mistakes of their opponents.

Antony and Cleopatra continues the story after Caesar's assassins have been defeated. The question whether Octavius or Antony has superior authority must now be settled. Neither Octavius nor Antony acknowledges the "natural" preeminence of the other. Nothing in the play suggests that some metaphysical principle would justify one or the other's claim to ultimate political authority; no answer can be read off the nature of things. Octavius emerges victorious because he proves able to mobilize superior forces and use them with a strategic discipline and shrewdness the impulsive Antony cannot match. There is no other political reality.[2]

What of monarchies, where political authority is fixed by rules of *natural* succession? Wouldn't they have a more plausible claim to be a *natural* order than the loose alliance of Greek warlords who hoped to plunder Troy, the Roman republic of aristocrats Brutus and his comrades hoped to preserve, or the empire Octavius created by destroying the substance of republican forms? If Ulysses's general claim regarding the place of society in the cosmic hierarchy is reformulated as the claim that political authority is determined by the natural line of succession extending over time, conflicts over who possesses authority should not be as inevitable and irresolvable as the conflicts in the Greek camp, or in the last days of Julius Caesar, or in the struggle between Octavius and Antony. With a hereditary monarchy in place, it should be easy enough to establish who occupies the ultimate place of authority in hierarchical order "by nature": the rightful heir.

Plays set in the Christian period added a sacred quality to kingship supervening on the "natural" metaphysical superiority of monarchs. In *Richard II* the Bishop of Carlisle proclaims that overthrowing a rightfully anointed king, "the figure of God's majesty, / His captain, steward, deputy elect," is "so foul a wrong" that "Disorder, horror, fear, and mutiny/ Shall here inhabit, and this land be called / The field of Golgotha and dead men's skulls." (*Richard II* 4.1, 105 ff.). Civil wars do in fact break out soon after Richard II is disposed by Henry IV. While they had been all but extinguished prior to his son's rule, internecine fighting recommenced immediately after Henry V's death, culminating in Henry VI's loss of the throne usurped from Richard by his grandfather. Many have seen the sequence of plays depicting these events as a theodicy, confirming the Bishop's prophecy (Tillyard, [1943] 1959). Macbeth's seizure of power can be condemned as both unnatural and unholy from this perspective, along with Richard III's.[3]

Hereditary kingdoms have often avoided conflict in the transition from one ruler to another, with the natural heir succeeding the parent without incident. But the plays show that political rule will regularly be contested in them too.

Sometimes when this happens, the normatively correct (from the standpoint of the plays) result occurs. Malcolm defeats Macbeth; Richard III falls to Henry Tudor. In other cases, matters aren't so clear. Who has the stronger claim, King John or Arthur? Bolingbroke or Richard II? Henry IV or the former allies who later question his right to rule? Richard of York or Henry VI? Fortinbras or whoever has the strongest hereditary claim to rule Denmark after Hamlet's death? In all these cases political authority ultimately rests on power considerations, that is, the ability to mobilize military and financial resources and to develop effective strategies and tactics for employing those resources.

Another issue regarding monarchies can be discerned below the surface of *Troilus and Cressida*. The principle of natural monarchy has been established in Troy, resulting in a far more stable social order than the Greek camp. In stark contrast to Agamemnon's precarious authority, the legitimacy of Priam's rule is unquestioned by any Trojan. Yet there is nothing "natural" about Priam's coming to power. The original audience of this play was not the public at large that frequented outdoor theaters, but the highly educated lawyers and state officials who attended enclosed playhouses. Shakespeare's audience knew the story of the origin of Priam's rule, which had nothing to do with any natural order of succession. Hercules had sacked the city for a slight, killed the king who had slighted him along with those following next in the line of succession, and placed the infant Priam on the throne by hand. Priam's authority, in other words, is rooted in political violence, not any abiding metaphysical order in the cosmos. How could rule determined by a chain of succession following Priam be considered legitimate by "nature" when the chain was established by a forcible destruction of the previously supposed "natural" ruler and heirs?

This is, of course, precisely the problem that plagued the Lancastrian linage. Richard II was unquestionably taken to be the rightfully anointed ruler, legitimated by the natural order of succession. Perhaps at some point a monarch's illicit actions undermine any claim to legitimacy; perhaps Richard exceeded that point. But even if this were the case, it only follows that Bolingbroke was justified in forcing Richard's abdication. It does not establish the former's right to rule as Henry IV, since he had no claim to be next in the order of succession (three Mortimers and a Percy came before him). Henry planned to crusade in Jerusalem as penance for what he himself understood to be the sin of seizing the throne (and perhaps also the sin of encouraging—or at least not doing enough to discourage—Richard's execution). The supposedly guilt-expunging crusade never took place. If it had, perhaps believers could think it benefitted Henry's immortal soul. But no theological doctrine affirms that a crusade transforms the offspring of a usurper into a divinely sanctioned ruler. Henry V's position as his son is therefore quite problematic, as he well understands. He is the legitimate son of an illegitimate monarch, according to the rules of succession. In Ulysses's terms, does his position at the top of the social hierarchy illustrate how social relations "Observe degree, priority and place, / Insisture, course,

proportion, season, form, Office and custom, in all line of order"? Or is
not rather a case haunted by Ulysses's prophecy, "Take but degree away,
untune that string, / And, hark, what discord follows"? On the surface
level of *Henry V*, the former judgment is difficult to resist. If we attend
to it with Shakespeare's earlier Henry VI plays in mind—as most of his
audience would have—the latter judgment cannot be dismissed; the
Henry VI trilogy depicts a period racked by discord.

This issue would not be a serious problem if cases of lines of succession being violently interrupted were rare. The plays suggest otherwise.
To return to *Troilus and Cressida* for a moment, we know not only that
Priam's line began in political violence, but also that it will end that
way as well, with the victorious Greeks installing a new ruling lineage.

There is also the problem that natural lines of succession may come
to a biological end. What does the "natural" order of things determine
then? The power considerations that are always just below the surface
now threaten to erupt. This provides a clue why the dying Hamlet
endorses Fortinbras as the future ruler of Denmark. Fortinbras does not
have any "natural" claim over the country as a whole, and it is highly
disputable whether he even has a legitimate claim over the part ceded
to Denmark when his father lost his battle with Hamlet's father. When
we recall that Norway and Denmark were in a Cold War threatening to
become hot at the start of the play, another hypothesis seems far more
plausible. After Fortinbras had been forced to stop his attacks on Denmark by his uncle, he received permission to travel through Denmark to
Poland, where he engaged in what Hamlet took to be pointless battles.
As the final tragic events in the Danish royal family were taking place,
Fortinbras was in the process of passing through Denmark on his return
from these battles. In other words, at a time when Danish troops had
been demobilized by Claudius, Fortinbras was in Denmark with what was
in effect an experienced occupying army, able to seize power by force.[4]
Hamlet's endorsement of him avoided the suffering that probably would
have occurred otherwise. Certainly, no natural right of succession is in
play here, and certainly no natural justification for Fortinbras's descendants to claim rule of Denmark as a birthright granted to them by the
metaphysical order of things.

Another point relevant to the first theses of "Shakespearian
politics" concerns the difference between official political power and
actual rule. The two are most often conjoined in the plays, but not
always. In Priam's case, while his place at the summit of Trojan society

is unquestioned, in actuality his power is more formal than substantial. There are two moments in the play when the Trojans must make a crucial political decision. The first occurs when the Greeks offer peace in return for Helen, the second when it must be decided if Hector will return to the field despite clear omens he shouldn't. Priam exerts no real authority in either case. The first issue is dominated by the debate between Troilus and Hector, concluding when Hector accepts Troilus's view that honor rules out accepting the offer, however strong reasons for acceptance might be. Priam is silent throughout. The second case is not a matter of concern to Hector alone. It goes to the very heart of Trojan strategy and prospects. And yet the king does not have the final say; Hector explicitly disobeys Priam's directive to remain home. When and how did ultimate authority seep away from Priam? No answer can be found in the metaphysical nature of things. Hector has the power to disobey, and he uses it.

Other problems are raised when foreign alliances are accepted by a rightful heir. In *King John*, having reached maturity Arthur, not John, has the stronger claim to legitimacy. Does Arthur's alliance with a foreign power undermine his claim to legitimacy? The rhetoric of *King John* suggests the answer is yes. The narrative arc of *Titus Andronicus*, however, suggests the opposite. In that play, the rightfulness of the rightful heir's claim is reinforced, not undermined, by an alliance with foreign tribes against Rome. Once again, the rules of natural succession apparently cannot do what they are supposed to do, and provide a secure metaphysical foundation for political authority. Once again political violence determines the result.

The examples discussed in this subsection establish that a first political theme in "Shakespearian politics" is that no "natural" hierarchical order in the cosmos determines who comes to have political authority. While metaphysical justifications appealing to such an order may play an important role in the belief that this or that ruler is legitimate, the rule itself directly or indirectly rests on the results of power struggles between competing elites in either the distant or recent past.

It seems appropriate to conclude this subsection by referring to the beginning of *Coriolanus*, where something very close to a *reductio ad absurdum* of the thought that the social hierarchy is part of the metaphysical hierarchy of being can be found.

When the play begins, the Roman populace has been suffering from a horrible famine. Patricians are widely thought to be hoarding food and gorging food prices, and a plebeian riot has broken out in response. A member of the ruling caste, Menenius, is sent out to quiet the rebellion. He attempts to do so with an analogy. For plebeians to rebel against the Senate of Rome, he argues, is as senseless as other parts of the body rebelling against the belly for its consuming all the food. The belly, he continues, would respond to the rebelling organs,

> "True is it, my incorporate friends," quoth he,
> "That I receive the general food at first,
> Which you do live upon; and fit it is,
> Because I am the store-house and the shop
> Of the whole body: but, if you do remember,
> I send it through the rivers of your blood,
> Even to the court, the heart, to the seat o' the brain;
> And, through the cranks and offices of man,
> The strongest nerves and small inferior veins
> From me receive that natural competency
> Whereby they live . . ."
> "Though all at once cannot
> See what I do deliver out to each,
> Yet I can make my audit up, that all
> From me do back receive the flour of all,
> And leave me but the bran." (*Coriolanus* 1.1, 128–144)

Perhaps a more ludicrous defense of a hierarchical social order could be given, but I do not know what it would be. When ruling elites are fully sated, while ordinary members of the society starve, the few are fed, the many are famished, and that is that. Nothing remotely like the organic process of transferring energy throughout an organism takes place. If this argument by analogy is the strongest case that can be made for the claim that the social hierarchy is natural, the case is weak indeed.

We turn next from acquiring political authority to its exercise.

Theme 2: Once Acquired, Political Authority Tends to Be Maintained through Normatively Questionable Means

Some cases of exercising political power depicted in the plays are transparently unacceptable from a normative point of view. Richard III's deceptions and murders clearly fall under this category, as do the expropriations of others' "rightful" property for personal gain by the second Richard (and most likely an order to murder Gloucester). Less extreme cases explore the theme in a more interesting fashion.

Troilus and Cressida may be the most powerful deconstruction of the aura of political authority in world literature. The heroic mode is mocked in every line. In contrast, *Henry V* has been widely interpreted as a dramatic presentation of a Christian hero. Yet it too effectively disenchants the heroic mode of rule. The very techniques of power that undermine the normative pretentions of the leaders of the Greek camp play a crucial role in Henry's rule as well. In the course of the Trojan war, Ulysses informs Achilles that his collusion with the Trojans is known to the Greek authorities (he is negotiating to receive the Trojan princess Polyxena in return for permanently withdrawing from fighting). Prefiguring the Edward Snowden revelations of our own NSA, Ulysses informs Achilles this is standard political practice, giving those with political power something approaching divine omniscience:

> The providence that's in a watchful state
> Knows almost every grain of Plutus' gold,
> Finds bottom in the uncomprehensive deeps,
> Keeps place with thought and almost, like the gods,
> Does thoughts unveil in their dumb cradles.
> There is a mystery—with whom relation
> Durst never meddle—in the soul of state;
> Which hath an operation more divine
> Than breath or pen can give expressure to:
> All the commerce that you have had with Troy
> As perfectly is ours as yours, my lord. (*Troilus and Cressida*
> 3.3, 189–199)

Henry V demystifies but also corroborates this assessment. When Henry passes incognito in the campfire of his own troops, he is spying on his subjects, even if serves the purpose of assessing the state of mind of the army before an important battle. In a similar vein, Octavius's system of spies throughout the length and breadth of the Roman empire is not the least of the underlying reasons he is able to seize undisputed power in *Antony and Cleopatra*, while the level of surveillance in Claudius's court in *Hamlet* approaches Foucault's panopticon.

If surveillance is by definition a hidden aspect of political life, *the spectacle* dominates the lived experience of everyday politics. As Ulysses patiently explains to Achilles, what a person's actual capabilities and accomplishments are matter far less than how that person appears to others. What Ulysses does not mention is that he has himself engaged in the systematic manipulation of appearances when he fixes the lottery selecting the respondent to Hector's challenge. By ensuring that Ajax is chosen, Ulysses aims to create a public spectacle making Ajax the privileged object of social praise, displacing Achilles from his accustomed place in the public imaginary. Achilles certainly got the general point. At the conclusion of the play, he knows that his future status as a warrior will be tremendously enhanced if the image of him killing Hector circulates throughout society. Whether or not he has actually killed Hector will not matter. Achilles acts accordingly. He watches passively while his minions butcher Hector, and then claims the deed for himself, ensuring that the image of him as the victor circulates through the ages.

Whatever his other virtues might be, Henry V is a true master of the politics of the spectacle, far more successful than Ulysses. He has in fact made his entire life into a spectacle for public consumption. Years have been spent preparing for a carefully designed public display of emerging from a misspent youth into the bright light of mature monarchical authority, as the sun emerges from clouds into its full glory (Holderness, 2000, p. 163). There is more than a little deception here. Hal was never as dissolute as he led spectators to believe, nor is Henry V as virtuous as he wants to be perceived. A truthful person would not devote such efforts to a fraudulent manipulation of his image. A politically shrewd person for whom truthfulness is secondary would undertake these efforts.

A quite different example of the politics of the spectacle is offered in Henry's speech before the town of Hafleur. Henry piles graphic image upon horrific graphic image, forcing citizens to picture their town pillaged and burning, the males massacred, and mothers, wives, and daughters brutally raped. Few horror movies are packed with more disturbing images. There is deception here, but it is not that the depicted events cannot occur. The lie is that if they do, the city bares full responsibility, and Henry none. If the town does not open its gates, it will be Henry who utters the command resulting in pillaging and raping. It is bad faith of the highest degree for him to erase his own causal agency, even as he exercises agency with his threat.

Examples of the necessity of mastering the politics of the spectacle are sufficiently numerous in other plays to warrant considering it a major dimension of the "Shakespearian" view of the political sphere. Mark Antony seems to understand this as well as anyone. He first puts the body of the slain Caesar on display, proclaiming each slash a mouth encouraging "the stones of Rome to rise and mutiny" (*Julius Caesar* 3.2, 225). He then withholds Caesar's will from the sight, transforming it into a fetish object representing Caesar's great love for common citizens. Finally he displays it with apparent reluctance. The social effect is orders of magnitude more powerful than any theoretical argument Antony might make against Caesar's assassins (Wills, 2011). By the time of the events in *Antony and Cleopatra*, however, the politics of the spectacle works against Antony. He has lost control of the image circulating of him in Rome, where his liaison with Cleopatra is portrayed as a decadent indulgence, incompatible with the masculinist ethos of the Roman psyche. Once this has happened, his subsequent defeat is all but assured.

The case of Coriolanus exemplifies the importance of the spectacle in a different setting. He merely must show his wounds to the plebeians to be acclaimed as ruler. What matters is only that he appears to acknowledge the plebeians as his fellow citizens in public display. His refusal to create the necessary spectacle disqualifies him for political rule. No attentive reader of Shakespeare could think the "politics of the spectacle" commenced with the mass media of the 20th century.

Surreptitious surveillance and the manipulation of the spectacle are hardly the only normatively problematic means for exercising political authority. The single most reliable means for maintaining power depicted in the plays is to wage war against an external foe. At the nadir point of King John's legitimacy, when many nobles have turned against him, thinking him responsible for the death of the rightful heir, his authority begins to be reestablished as soon as he mobilizes forces against the invading army from France.

After his break from Falstaff and crew, Henry V is far more esteemed than John ever was. Nonetheless, the legitimacy of his reign is comparably precarious, given his father's deposition of Richard II and seizure of his throne. Unlike John, a war against France is not forced upon the fifth Henry. Following his father's deathbed advice, he strategically ensures it will happen by pressuring (more accurately, by blackmailing) the Archbishop of Canterbury into asserting that war is justified. (The implicit threat is that church lands might otherwise be confiscated.) For good measure, the Archbishop also agrees to cover an unprecedented portion of the costs of the military excursion.

On the surface level of *Henry V*, it is easy enough to be swept along by the great speech before the battle of Agincourt, when Henry proclaims that differences of status have been erased, and the British forces are now a "band of brothers." But the doubts about the enterprise shared with the disguised King the previous night are not completely erased. As Henry conversed with ordinary soldiers around a campfire, he was reminded in the sharpest of tones that the military conflicts of political elites in the great game of geopolitics invariably inflict horrible suffering on ordinary soldiers,

> . . . some swearing, some crying for a
> surgeon, some upon their wives left poor behind
> them, some upon the debts they owe, some upon their
> children rawly left. I am afeard there are few die
> well that die in a battle; for how can they
> charitably dispose of any thing, when blood is their
> argument? (*Henry V* 4.1, 137–140)[5]

We should also recall Henry's speech at Halfleur, which so graphically expressed the misery imposed on towns caught between the rival claims of elites. From a normative point of view, a very high price must be paid to maintain Henry's political authority.

Of course, rulers are not the only ones operating the levers of political power. Once the state has reached a certain level of complexity, a ruler's decrees must be carried out by a political apparatus, whether made up of administrative staff or nobles holding offices at court. In the history plays, we are shown almost continuous in-fighting among the leading counselors of the land. It soon becomes obvious that success in this arena does not necessarily go to those who fulfill the obligations of their offices most scrupulously. The "rules of the game" of factional intrigue select for those most capable of building factions. Building factions successfully often involves deception in some form or other. It always involves possessing and employing bargaining power. The naïve faith expressed by Gloucester in *Henry VI, Part 2* that no harm can come to him from enemies at the court because he has always acted nobly is mercilessly mocked by his wife. Subsequent events confirm how correct she was.

We also learn from the plays that it is often impossible to discern when someone exercising political power has engaged in ethically suspect activities. And even when this can be discerned, it will often prove impossible to know the degree of the wrongdoing. Disputes on these matters are bound to arise. Part of the measure of success of normatively problematic methods of exercising power, after all, is the ability to hide that these methods have been employed. Success in displacing suspicions onto others, or in creating suspicions when they do not exist, is a form of success in strategic political action.

Richard II illustrates these points. Wrongs have undoubtedly been committed during Richard's reign, not least the killing of Gloucester. To what extent does the blame fall on Richard's cronies? To what extent is the King personally responsible? Richard has undoubtedly abused his office, engaging in illegitimate appropriations of property, arbitrary decrees, and so on.[6] How bad must such behavior be before the line is crossed separating a legitimate (if imperfect) monarch from a tyrant? There is obviously vast indeterminacy here. There will inevitably be recurrent and irresolvable conflicts over where exactly the line should be drawn, and recurrent and irresolvable conflicts regarding whether it has been crossed in particular cases. Within the context of the play, it is not at all clear whether Richard's behavior has caused him to lose the right to rule granted him by his place in the order of succession. Given this indeterminacy, what else besides force can decide?

Legitimate authority can also be lost by incompetence in the most fundamental task of rule, maintaining order. At the end of the day, this is as central to the Yorkist justification for seizing the throne from Henry VI as the interruption of the natural order of succession by Henry's grandfather. It is also the justification for Henry VI's wife Margaret and her anti-Yorkist allies taking away Henry's VI's de facto political authority, despite their nominal acceptance of his rule. Others, however, deny that Henry's obvious ineffectualness implies that his rightful claim to the throne inherited from his father has dissolved. Power, not rightness, determines which of these competing and irreconcilable perspectives prevails.

What of cases in which abuses reach a point where a strong and widespread consensus has been reached that the normative legitimacy of the ruling power has been thoroughly eroded? Nothing will be done about this in the absence of forces in the society with sufficient power and motivation to seek redress. In the social world of the history plays, the estates and retinues of the nobility give them a separate source of power from the king. While the king is more powerful than any of them, he is not more powerful than all together, or even certain subsets of them. This gives the nobility the capacity to address a king's abuse of political authority. In Shakespeare's plays, this objective possibility provides the material for high drama. The motivation to employ this capacity is, of course, quite another matter.

The plays constantly remind us of the high risks involved in rebellions, most obviously the risk of being executed for treason. When Hotspur's closest relatives fail to show up for his crucial battle with the forces of Henry IV, it is because of the serious free rider problems involved in coalition building. If we generalize from this case, we must conclude that systematic abuses of power tend *not* to be addressed effectively, even when there are agents that are individually motivated and collectively have the capability to do so.

Finally, elites with the capability to challenge rulers will not be motivated to do so when they too inflict and benefit from the same sort of injustices rulers inflict and benefit from. A third theme in "Shakespearean politics" is that this has been the normal state of affairs in world history.

Theme 3: Oppression is the "Normal" Condition of Political Life

From the standpoint of Shakespeare's plays there seems to be no effective check on the abuses of authority suffered by ordinary persons. They tend to continue indefinitely, to the benefit of monarchs and nobility.

Normalized oppression without hope of redress may not be the stuff of high drama. It is also not the sort of theme we would expect playwright in London in the late 15th and early 16th century to explore, given the ideological pressures and threat of punishment writers faced. It is a theme of "Shakespearian politics" nonetheless.

Is there a more powerful critique of social injustice in world literature than the moment in the storm when Lear realizes that he has paid too little attention to the plight of those at the bottom of the social hierarchy?

> Poor naked wretches, whereso'er you are,
> That bide the pelting of this pitiless storm,
> How shall your houseless heads and unfed sides,
> Your looped and windowed raggedness, defend you
> From seasons such as these? O, I have ta'en
> Too little care of this. Take physic, pomp,

Expose thyself to feel what wretches feel,
That thou mayst shake the superflux to them,
And show the heavens more just. (*King Lear* 3.2, 28–36 Folio)

Perhaps when these lines were written the playwright himself regretted how often his plays had overlooked the all-too-normal condition of most human beings in order to focus on extraordinarily tragic or comic interactions. Still, passing references to everyday deprivations can be found in earlier texts, notably Hamlet's soliloquy referring to,

The oppressor's wrong, the proud man's contumely,
. . . , the law's delay,
The insolence of office and the spurns
That patient merit of the unworthy takes . . .
. . .
To grunt and sweat under a weary life . . . (*Hamlet* 3.1, 72–79)

The economic desperation leading an impoverished apothecary to sell poison to Romeo is another reminder of a condition the privileged usually prefer to ignore, neglected as completely by the political authorities in Renaissance Verona as in the ancient times of Lear. Corin, the shepherd in *As You Like It*, is in somewhat better circumstances. But still,

. . . I am shepherd to another man,
And do not shear the fleeces that I graze.
My master is of churlish disposition,
And little recks to find the way to heaven
By doing deeds of hospitality. (*As You Like It* 2.4, 77–81)

And however chilling Cade's plan to "kill all the lawyers" might be, it cannot be denied that law was an instrument used effectively against ordinary people to trap them in debt and take from them ("enclose") the "commons" that their economic independence depended on:

. . . Is not this a lamentable
thing, that of the skin of an innocent lamb should
be made parchment? that parchment, being scribbled
o'er, should undo a man? Some say the bee stings:

> but I say, 'tis the bee's wax; for I did but seal
> once to a thing, and I was never mine own man
> since. (*Henry VI, Part 2* 4.2, 79–84)

The food riots in *Coriolanus* were also rooted in the material oppression of class politics. The deprivation caused by a famine was only an extreme expression of the everyday vulnerability of ordinary citizens.

A last example from *Timon of Athens* goes to the heart of this theme. The fact that the speaker, Timon, is pathologically bitter does not prevent his words from ringing true:

> Raise me this beggar, and demit that lord,
> The senator shall bear contempt hereditary,
> The beggar native honour. Who dares, who dares
> In purity of manhood stand upright,
> And say "This man's a flatterer"? If one be,
> So are they all, for every grece of fortune
> Is smoothed by that below: the learnèd pate
> Ducks to the golden fool . . . (*Timon of Athens* 4.3, 11–18)

In this section I have explored three themes regarding the nature of the political sphere running through Shakespeare's plays. First, political rule is not determined by a metaphysical hierarchy inscribed in the very nature of things. No appeal to a "natural" order is able to resolve political disputes about who should rule at the very time such resolutions are most needed. Power is acquired through power struggles.

Second, once political power has been acquired, the means employed to exercise it will regularly be deeply problematic from a normative point of view. This point holds with special force when the state apparatus is captured and used for predatory purposes and the eradication of opponents. But even in more "normal" cases of rule, maintaining power appears to require systematic invasions of privacy, a willingness to be less than completely truthful, a self-interested manipulation of images circulating in the social imaginary, and an acceptance or even aggressive pursuit of conflicts involving significant human suffering whenever these conflicts promise to enhance the ruler's political authority.

Third, there is every reason to think that those exercising political authority will typically be either indifferent to the everyday oppression of those in the lower stratums of the social hierarchy, actively complicit in it, or—the usual case—both.

What general conclusions regarding the political sphere should be drawn from these three themes?

The General Content and Practical Orientation of "Shakespearian Politics"

A general consideration that might be drawn from the themes just discussed can be approached indirectly by considering two other aspects of the plays that might seem at first to point in a different direction.

There are, first, plays where the audience is presented with a political sphere operating in a normatively attractive manner. The forest of Ardenne in *As You Like It* can serve as an example. The authority of Duke Senior is recognized as legitimate by all member of the political community in Ardenne on the basis of both hereditary right and the Duke's evident possession of all the virtues of a good political leader: compassion, openness to others, sincere concern for the well-being of all within his territory, unwillingness to impose his will by violence, and so on. This political setting is no Garden of Eden. There is no guarantee everyone gets whatever they want all the time. Someone may love someone else who does not love them (Silvius). A melancholy disposition may prevent enjoyment of life (Jaques). Those who once lived in more opulent surroundings may regret their loss (Touchstone). Labor is still required to provide necessary preconditions for human life. Ardenne is not a perfect utopia. Nonetheless, human dramas and human comedies are played out within a political context of order, stability, compassion, and fairness.

As the play continually reminds us, however, this happy place does not resemble any real political world. The inhabitants of the forest are not citizens of a functioning polity. They are either exiles whose citizenship has been revoked, or members of a rural labor force without time or energy to engage in active political citizenship. The continued existence of the little community has less to do with its own virtues than with the contingent fact that Duke Frederick, who usurped the throne and now controls the coercive apparatus of the state, has left them in peace for the moment. In the final act of the play this changes, and

Frederick's troops invade the forest. They undoubtedly have the power to obliterate the forest settlement. But *As You Like It* is a comedy. Frederick meets a charismatic religious figure, who miraculously converts him to a life of spiritual meditation, away from the power politics of the world. He abdicates, returning rule to the deposed Duke and his happy band of followers.

There is no denying the pleasure of this narrative arc. Who would not like to believe that in the end good will triumph? Just a moment's reflection, however, transforms the pleasures of comic resolution to something more foreboding. How many rulers ever have renounced power voluntarily? How many ever will? Wasn't the usurping Duke's conversion completely inconsistent with his character? Doesn't social psychology teach us how rare acts so completely out of character are? Doesn't this make the resolution of conflict depicted in the play utterly irrelevant to actual political life? To place hopes for a normative acceptable political order in the spiritual conversion of rulers seems entirely misplaced. In only happens in the realm of fantasy.[7]

The Tempest presents another narrative of reconciliation. Again, an unjust usurpation of power defines the context of the play's beginning, and is reversed at its conclusion, when Prospero returns to Milan to reclaim the Dukedom to which he has a "rightful" claim. Here the means accomplishing the reversal is not a spiritual conversion of the usurper, but the magic of the usurped. No doubt the acceptance of alchemy in the Renaissance predisposed people to consider magic a possible way of gaining power over the world and other people. Nonetheless, *The Tempest* is not a counterexample to the claim that the political realm is generally *not* defined by a politics of reconciliation.

For one thing, Prospero destroys the text providing instructions how to evoke and harness magical powers, so any chance to right political wrongs through their use again is gone forever. More importantly, using them to right wrongs is itself wrong. The powers are so extreme—they include the ability to raise the dead—that by the standards of Shakespeare's day it was blasphemous to want to possess them and impious to use them. Finally, their use inflicts suffering and manipulates the free will of others. Most importantly, the thought that a magic formula can reestablish the proper hierarchical order in the world is as much a fantasy as the idea that a tyrant dedicated to the physical destruction of his enemies would suddenly be converted to a life of holy contemplation. The utter implausibility of the events required to prevent *As*

You Like It and *The Tempest* from becoming tragedies suggests indirectly, but unmistakably, that there is an inherently "tragic" dimension at the heart of the political sphere.

Might belief in a divine providence governing human affairs allow us to avoid this conclusion? If we cannot rely on human agency to bring about normatively acceptable political results, might divine intervention alleviate our concerns? An appeal to providence is central to many of the late "romance" plays such as *The Winter's Tale*. The concatenation of highly unlikely events required to reestablish social harmony within the polity after Leontes's tyranny has such little probability of occurring that a sense of wonder arises in many readers and viewers. Does this wonder point toward some transcendent force mysteriously operating beyond our comprehension? Or does it not instead pose the question: Why does God intervene to direct some narratives to a pleasing end and not others? The negative consequences of Leontes's tyranny may be overcome. But Antigonus is horrifically killed after having played a crucial role in making the moment of reconciliation possible. It is natural to forget about him (and the others who drown on the ship he had taken) as we are swept along by the movement of the play from discord to harmony. Nonetheless, a providence this arbitrary does not remove ethical arbitrariness from the world. Our willing suspension of disbelief does not transform the unbelievable into the believable.

Nor does the happy ending of *The Winter's Tale* weaken the force of the brutal counterargument against the thesis that good must eventually, if mysteriously, prevail: the sight of the dead Cordelia in Lear's arms.

In my estimation, then, neither utopian nor providential appearances in Shakespeare's plays modifies the force of the three themes considered in the previous section. The general content of a "Shakespearian politics" is that the political realm is essentially characterized by a fundamental *ethical irrationality*. Despite the efforts of conservative critics over the course of many generations, Shakespeare's plays are not best read as a normative affirmation of the established social order. Success in struggles to obtain political power are not necessarily correlated with ethical desert in the plays, to put it mildly. Neither is success in maintaining political power once it has been obtained. There is an obvious and immense gulf between the strategic rationality that (along with luck) underlies political success and what is rational from a normative viewpoint. Shakespeare's plays do not teach us that political power cannot ever be won or exercised without conflicting with substantive normative values. But they do suggest that this conflict tends to arise regularly, and that when it does this is not merely due to the contingent personal defects in rogue individuals. It is a systematic pattern of politics, an essential property of political systems.

What do the plays propose as an appropriate practical response to this ethical irrationality of the political realm? One possibility is to take the "realist" option, defined in this context as a ruthless pursuit of self-interest in political life, excluding all normative considerations unless they serve self-interest (promises should be kept, for example, so long as doing so is in one's self-interest).

It remains reasonably clear that amorality is not the last word on politics in the plays. Issues of profound normative concern regarding politics are continually raised with great seriousness in the Shakespearian corpus. Does the past seizure of power that established the chain of succession resulting in the ruler depicted on the stage undermine the legitimacy of that ruler? Has he or she engaged in tyrannical acts to the degree required to cause a loss of legitimacy? Has the present ruler proven to be incompetent past an acceptable point? Audiences are invited to answer these questions in the course of making substantive normative assessments of the actions presented on the stage. They are not encouraged to dismiss such questions as pointless in light of self-interested politics. The fact that determinate answers to such questions cannot always be given establishes that the political sphere is regularly condemned to conflicts normative reasoning cannot resolve. Nonetheless, as long as these sorts of questions must be posed, we cannot say that the political sphere lacks a normative dimension beyond the scope of "realist" politics.

There is a strong "realist" component in "Shakespearian politics." Unlike other forms of "realism," however, success in the pursuit of self-interest is not affirmed as the only, or even as the ultimate, measure applicable to individuals, coalitions, or nations. In specific, the plays strongly endorse the applicability of normative principles to rulers. They ought to be virtuous: wise, compassionate, loyal, honest, generous, and just. They ought to avoid the vices of excessive anger, vengeance, partiality, and greed. The force of these normative demands is even greater on those exercising political authority than ordinary citizens, given the scale of the damage their vices can inflict, and the scale of benefits that flow when they are virtuous. These demands are unfortunately what Hegel would term "abstract oughts." The plays point to no mechanism ensuring that those emerging victorious from political struggles tend to be the most virtuous among the competing parties. If rule is determined simply by a power struggle (Octavius versus Antony), victory will almost surely go to the shrewd, capable of mobilizing the greater power. If rule is determined by hereditary succession, the regal line will have begun with political violence, and the order of succession will coincide with an order of virtue only by accident. When the truly virtuous are placed in positions of power, the result will often be political incompetence (Henry VI). And when those occupying positions of power are only apparently virtuous, systematic hypocrisy tends to be especially reprehensible (e.g., the puritan Angelo's attempts to use the coercive powers of the state to force sex from Isabella in *Measure for Measure*).

"Shakespearian politics," then, advocates neither utopianism nor realism. It instead ambiguously accepts normative demands while recognizing just how limited their relevance is. Its practical implications differ for different groups.

For rulers, the best and only realistic hope is that they are strong enough to impose domestic peace, protect the community's international interests, and not be too abusive. It is notable that the incredibly powerful criticism of social injustice in *Lear* is not accompanied by a call for a radical rupture from the given social structures. It is simply a plea for powerful rulers to show more concern for those in the greatest need.

When disputes among elites arise, supporters of a side should be aware that there are no guarantees of success, however strong their arguments and whatever their claim to virtue. If success does come, they should be cognizant that the struggle to rule has likely eroded whatever virtues they may have claimed before, and that ruling is likely to erode them yet more. Those facing defeat will find themselves in the position of Antony's lieutenant Enobarbus, torn by incompatible duties of loyalty, on the one hand, and concern for self, on the other. When defeat does come, they must be prepared to suffer the consequences, even if they are less guilty of wrongdoing than those inflicting the punishment.

The unhinged irrationality of the Cade rebellion (reminiscent of the horrors of Pol Pot), the fickleness of the crowd hearing the speeches at Caesar's burial, the relationship between the Tribunes and plebeians in *Coriolanus*, all suggest that any attempt to replace the given social order with a different one would sooner or later (and sooner rather than later) become at least as problematic from a normative point of view as the order it replaced. Cases suggesting the contrary, like Duke Senior's happy little polity in *As You Like It*, occupy a space of romantic fantasy.

The space of political reality is a space of tragedy interspersed with a few precarious pockets of luck. Those participating in it will eventually find themselves ethically compromised, if not fully corrupted, by the inner logic of power. Or else they will find themselves pushed to the margins of political life, or destroyed altogether, by those who are.

The political realm as conceptualized by "Shakespearian politics," then, is a space where normative principles are in play, but where they coincide with power considerations only in fantasy. The political dimension may be an inescapable aspect of social life. But it is not a realm where we can be "at home." It is not a sphere where we can expect to find what Hegel termed "rational satisfaction," that is, social practices that can be affirmed from a normative point of view. For most of us, the best way of being in this imperfect world is to keep as much distance from power struggles as possible, and attempt to create as best we can a space of decency protected from political intrigue. Politics can be left to elites, who will be at best ethically compromised, at worst completely corrupt. In face of the ineluctably tragic dimension of public political life, the best chance for true human happiness is found in the dramas of reconciliation in the domestic sphere, where love between adults, and between parents and children, can be rediscovered and renewed across the years. In the final instance, "Shakespearian politics" is apolitical.

Only a fool would identify the speech of a minor character in a Shakespeare play with the author's views. And yet it is difficult to refrain from thinking that when Iden expresses his worldview at length in the second part of *Henry VI*, an echo of Shakespeare's own voice can be heard (Bate, 2009, p. 315). No comparably minor character has a comparably extensive soliloquy in any other play. Walking in his garden, Iden reflects,

> Lord, who would live turmoiled in the court,
> And may enjoy such quiet walks as these?
> This small inheritance my father left me
> Contenteth me, and worth a monarchy.
> I seek not to wax great by others' waning,
> Or gather wealth, I care not, with what envy:
> Sufficeth that I have maintains my state
> And sends the poor well pleased from my gate. (*Henry VI,*
>   *Part 2* 4.9, 16–23)

To abandon political action is to accept the political status quo and thereby participate in its ethical irrationality. The apolitical option is just another way to be political, and not an abandonment of political agency. Immediately after affirming his supposedly depoliticized life, Iden kills Cade, whose desperate hunger forced him into the precious private garden. By bringing the Cade rebellion to its final conclusion, Iden props up the very world of the nobility he has attempted to withdraw from. His is not an ideal solution to the tragic dimension of politics. But that is precisely the point. I take "Shakespearian politics" to center on the denial that there is *any* ideal solution. The great political dramas leave us with a melancholy just this side of despair, alleviated only by a turn to the domestic romance of reconciliation.

"Shakespearian Politics" Today

"Shakespearian politics," as the term has been understood here, emerges from the Bard's dramatic exploration of the warrior aristocracies of ancient Greece and Troy, the republic of ancient Rome, the Roman empire, the early English and Scottish kingdoms of medieval feudalism, the mercantile republic of Renaissance Venice, and the nascent absolute monarchies of Shakespeare's own Britain. At the turn of the 17th century, of course, the knowledge of these historical periods was not what it is today. If Shakespeare illuminated essential features of political life in those periods that does not necessarily matter much.

Suppose we grant that the main political themes of the plays are in fact applicable to the political forms of Shakespeare's day and before. Are they applicable still? In the present section I shall call on the testimony of the plays to make a case that they are.

Shakespeare lived in the midst of one of the most important transitions in world history, from feudalism to capitalism, and from the Renaissance state with its vestiges of feudalism to the modern capitalist state (Archer, 2012). Many people who witnessed the execution of Charles 1 and the accompanying shift of political power to a Parliament controlled by wealthy merchants, investors, and landlords, would have been living when Shakespeare walked the earth. The Glorious Revolution consolidating this shift, and the founding of the Bank of England, the first instance of a crucial institution of modern capitalism, occurred within a century of Shakespeare's death (1688 and 1694, respectively). What, if anything, do the plays have to teach us about either the capitalist state or the modern capitalist economy?

In states today leaders cannot claim legitimacy by birth, or any other natural quality they might be thought to possess. Abstracting for the moment from any democratic element states might possess, political legitimacy will generally tend to be a matter of (1) the ruler's capability to establish and maintain a domestic "rule of law" that protects property owners from arbitrary confiscations, enforces compliance with contracts, disciplines the labor force so that wages are low enough to allow an "acceptable" level of profits, and so on; and (2) the ruler's capability to further the geopolitical interests of the polity, including access to foreign raw materials, foreign markets, foreign investment opportunities, as well as strategic military alliances and conflicts (Smith, 2017, Chapter 8). In some respects, these challenges differ greatly from those facing Renaissance dukedoms, feudal monarchs, the emperors of ancient Rome, the warlords of Homeric myth, and the other types of political rule presented in Shakespeare's plays. This, however, does not make the central themes of "Shakespearian politics" less relevant.

- It remains the case that there is no "natural" way to discern the "rightful" holder of political authority. There will be power struggles to determine who is selected. These struggles will not be based on the tension between the centralized political authority of monarchs and emperors and the quasi-independent regional powers of a land-based aristocracy, the structural source of dramatic conflicts in so many Shakespeare plays. But the tension between the centralized capitalist state and the various political factions representing the interests of various sectoral and regional factions of capital are no less intense. The resulting political conflicts will not take the same form as the multigenerational War of the Roses that afflicted late feudal England. But success in these struggles will also tend to not reflect preeminence is either personal virtue or normatively defensible policies.

- Nor does the history of the nondemocratic capitalist states provide any reason to expect that once political authority has been attained it will tend to be exercised in a more normatively acceptable manner than in the precapitalist period. Deception, mastery of the politics of the spectacle, and a willingness to engage in foreign conflicts to mobilize domestic support, all remain central means of political rule.

• Finally, Lear's complaints about economic injustice have far less to do with some imaginary feudalism lost in the historical mist of ancient Britain than they do with the rapid rise of a modern market society, already well under way in Shakespeare's era. Any restructuring of the state apparatus reflecting this rise and designed to spur the further growth of capitalist markets could only make Lear's laments more applicable.

Does the institutionalization of (formal) democracy in leading regions of the capitalist world affect the continued relevance of "Shakespearian politics"? When universal adult suffrage is adopted, political authority can be legitimated by popular consent. Other matters of normative import will be affected as well.[8] Nonetheless, another recurrent theme in Shakespeare's plays suggests that this matters less from a normative point of view than we might think. The plays in effect anticipate the Schumpeterian thesis that political democracy can never be more than a competition among competing elites resolved by a plebiscite acclamation, a thesis fully compatible with "Shakespearean politics" as sketched above.

Over the centuries, conservatives have complained that "the masses" are too easily swayed this way and that, a complaint Shakespeare has often been taken to endorse. In *Julius Caesar*, the crowd that had just been convinced by Brutus's defense of the assassination is made to erupt in a killing frenzy against the conspirators by Antony's rhetoric. Laertes's ability to turn the crowd storming Claudius's palace in *Hamlet* on and off makes the same point. Given the way the plays show how public opinion can abruptly and incoherently shift in response to manipulative emotional appeals, they provide reason to fear that the outcomes of democratic plebiscites in the capitalist state may prove even *less* substantively rational than more overt forms of elite rule.

On the rare occasion in the plays where "the masses" engage as agents on the political stage there is always a faction of the political elite behind their mobilization, shaping the form and direction of their activities in ways unknown to them. Cade's rebellion in *Henry VI, Part 1* successfully mobilized the widespread anger at the enclosure of the commons and other predatory acts by the nobility. But it was the nobleman Richard of York who set the rebellion in motion with his secret support of Cade, and Richard no more shares the concerns of oppressed and exploited peasants than any other nobleman. York's goal is simply to use social chaos to undermine Henry's rule. A straightforward extrapolation from the play would be to conclude that politics in democratic capitalism will tend to revolve around attempts by factions of the political elite to mobilize grievances against other factions on a mass scale, while leaving the root causes of those grievances unaddressed. Nor need we extrapolate much from the desperate chaos of Cade's revolt to predict that mass political activity against elites in more democratic societies will also prove incapable of effective strategic rationality, also be driven by incoherent fantasies, and also dissipate quickly, leaving the social order in place (with, perhaps, a new ruling faction).

Further, we have little reason to think political rulers in societies with universal suffrage will have any more difficulty "manufacturing consent" through nationalist appeals than the rulers appearing on Shakespeare's stage did. Both King John and Henry V consolidate their rule by playing the nationalist card in wartime. Precious little historical evidence suggests the mechanisms of formal democracy have weakened the effectiveness of this move.

Coriolanus suggests yet another reason for thinking that the adoption of formal democracy does not make "Shakespearian politics" outmoded. The ordinary citizens of Rome have obviously justified concerns regarding the proposed promotion of Coriolanus to the pinnacle of political power. He has scorned plebeians his entire life. Nonetheless, he will be granted the power he seeks as long as he goes through the formal motions of acknowledging the plebeians as fellow citizens. Coriolanus cannot bring himself to do what is required, proving (as if additional proof were required) that his rule would be utterly opposed to the interests of ordinary citizens. In the play, his distain prevents him from coming to power. But under the surface the deeper point remains: winning acclamation may take only a little pretense. Here too we have an anticipation of the Schumpeterian thesis that formal democracy is merely a way to organize and resolve the struggle for power among elite groups, rather than an effective mechanism for ensuring that the substantive interests of the vast majority determine the direction of political life.

I do not think Shakespeare's plays show that that the masses are inherently less rational and consistent than the ruling class, however often elites in the plays make this complaint.[9] The plays are replete with cases where the powerful act in ridiculously irrational ways. And for all their pious talk of loyalty there are too many cases where alliances among them abruptly shift to think that they are any less prone to inconsistency. The apparent intellectual superiority of members of ruling elites is easily explained by their access to a much higher general level of education, as well as opportunities to be far more informed about what is going on in the political realm, who is doing what, and why they might be doing it. Their real advantage is simply that they can mobilize far more resources to affect political life, and so have a wildly disproportionate influence on the polity. This remains the case even if the populace engages in mass collective action, as in the Cade rebellion, and even if there are formal procedures in place enabling ordinary citizens a political voice, as in *Coriolanus*. From this perspective, we have little reason to think that the rise of formally democratic political forms in the modern capitalist state undermines the force of "Shakespearian politics."

A similar conclusion can be drawn from the fact that modern capitalism is the most monetarized society in human history. Shakespeare's plays do not lack for denunciations of the social power money grants to its holders, most strikingly in *Timon of Athens*:

> Gold? yellow, glittering, precious gold?
> . . . Thus much of this will make
> Black white, foul fair, wrong right,
> Base noble, old young, coward valiant.
> Ha, you gods! why this, what, this, you gods? Why, this
> Will lug your priests and servants from your sides,
> Pluck stout men's pillows from below their heads.
> This yellow slave
> Will knit and break religions, bless th' accursed,
> Make the hoar leprosy adored, place thieves,
> And give them title, knee and approbation
> With senators on the bench. . . . (*Timon of Athens* 4.3, 26–38)[10]

This power, great as it was in Shakespeare's day, has been tremendously exacerbated in contemporary society, where the accumulation of money capital has become the dominant imperative of social life.

The Comedy of Errors depicts an especially significant example of social relations mediated by money. Each of the twin merchant brothers (both named Antipholus) employs one of a pair of twins, both named Dromio. Each Dromio is beaten throughout the play. On the surface, this is just comic slapstick. But the serious point should not be ignored: Those with sufficient funds are able to purchase and control the activity of others for most of the latter's waking life. This immense social power remains in place even if legislation eliminates the infliction of physical punishment. This asymmetrical power relation remains in place after formal democratic mechanisms have been adopted in the state.

I would like to conclude this section by examining the relationship between merchants and states presented in the plays. The way this relationship is treated strongly reinforces the thesis that "Shakespearian politics" remains relevant in today's republic of capital. In a subplot in *The Comedy of Errors*, an unnamed "second merchant" has lent money to Angelo, who in turn expects to be repaid for a chain he has sold for payment on delivery to Antipholus of Ephesus. It is mistakenly given to Antipholus of Syracuse. When Antipholus of Ephesus refuses to pay for the undelivered (to him) chain, Angelo cannot repay the second merchant. The latter then calls on state officials to arrest Angelo, who in turn insists that the Antipholus of Ephesus be arrested. Underlying the comic confusion there is a serious point: The web of personal relationships in a market society is mediated by circuits of money flows, and behind these monetary flows lies the coercive power of the state, ready to intervene whenever they are interrupted, and ready to punish those responsible for the interruption.

The threat of the state's coercive power haunts *The Merchant of Venice*. When Antonio proves unable to repay Shylock, all characters expect that the penalty for nonpayment will be enforced. They all agree that a state wishing its merchants to prosper must maintain formal-legal rationality, whatever the resulting substantive irrationality from a normative point of view. As Antonio himself believes,

> The duke cannot deny the course of law,
> For the commodity that strangers have
> With us in Venice, if it be denied,
> Will much impeach the justice of the state,
> Since that the trade and profit of the city
> Consisteth of all nations. (*Merchant of Venice* 3.3, 26–31)

It is quite noteworthy that while members of the domestic merchant elite are threatened with state coercion in both *The Comedy of
Errors* and *The Merchant of Venice*, in neither play are any actually
punished. *The Comedy of Errors* begins with the Duke of Ephesus
informing Egeon, a merchant from Syracuse, that he must be executed,
in accordance with a law proclaimed in retaliation for the execution
of merchants from Ephesus by the Syracusan state. He is given a long
speech to stress the point that exceptions cannot be granted without
undermining the social order.

> Hapless Egeon, whom the fates have marked
> To bear the extremity of dire mishap,
> Now, trust me, were it not against our laws—
> Which princes, would they, may not disannul—
> Against my crown, my oath, my dignity,
> My soul should sue as advocate for thee. (*Comedy of Errors*
>   1.1, 140–145)

At the conclusion of the play, it turns out that matters are not quite so
fixed. Egeon's sentence is overturned, the supposedly impossible somehow
now possible. In *The Merchant of Venice*, the judge in Antonio's case,
the disguised Portia, interprets the contract in an arbitrary fashion that
neither of the parties (nor any other observer) took it to mean (Lemon,
2012). In this case, as in *The Comedy of Errors*, viewers and readers
very much want the law's evident dictates to be averted somehow. We
instinctively endorse their cancellation as the triumph of the spirit of
the law over its letter. Hamlet's and Lear's reflections on injustice make
explicit what goes unsaid here: this "spirit" will generally turn out to
be the power to interpret laws in a way benefitting "insiders" of the
business elite (Antonio), or those able to establish networks with such
insiders (Egeon now allied with his son, Antipholus of Ephesus). Hamlet
and Lear in effect anticipate how the capitalist state will regularly allow
members of the economic elite to escape the coercive power of law, while
ordinary men and women face its full force.

In many respects, then, there are good reasons to think that the
rise of modern capitalism and the formally democratic capitalist state
has not brought us beyond the "Shakespearian politics" presented above.
In my view, however, this should not be the final word regarding the
political dimension of Shakespeare's plays.

A "Shakespearian Politics" beyond Shakespeare?

So far, "Shakespearian politics" has referred to a political worldview combining critique and acceptance. On the one hand, human flourishing and the avoidance of avoidable suffering matter from a normative point of view, and so a critical assessment of social practices that undermine human flourishing and inflict avoidable suffering is an appropriate response to them. The plays include many instances evoking such a critical response. On the other hand, human nature being what it is, some people will always want to get or retain power over others, and a significant subset of them will be willing to undermine human flourishing and inflict avoidable suffering when doing so appears to further that agenda. As a result, the political realm is not a place where we can be "at home," so to speak. It cannot provide the normative satisfaction we crave as rational beings, the sort of rational satisfaction Hegel believed could be found was present in the institutional framework of modern society, and Marx thought was possible in the future. The best we can reasonably hope for is an institutional order that is not excessively predatory, accepting that if we live in such an order that is mostly a matter of luck, unlikely to last. Given this bleak assessment, we should turn away from politics and toward the private domestic sphere, and attempt to find normative satisfaction where it is possible, in the drama of reconciliation between spouses and between parents and children.

Can there be a different sort of "Shakespearian politics," based on the plays yet resisting the conclusions they appear to push us toward? It could not be based on yet another critique of the all too obviously ethical irrationalities of political life in our own day. That would only echo Lear. Nor could it merely propose yet another political utopia. That would simply imagine another Ardenne. How, then, might it be developed? In this final section, I shall argue for a "Shakespearian politics" beyond Shakespeare, so to speak, based on three claims. First, despite the undoubtedly deep pessimism of Shakespeare's great political dramas, alleviated to only a small degree by excursions into romantic political fables, it is possible nonetheless to affirm that normative advances have in fact occurred, measured by standards internal to the plays. Second, it can be shown that cultural products like Shakespeare's plays can play some role, however small, in bringing about normative advances when the right background conditions are in place. Third, and most important, there are reasons to think that cultural products like Shakespeare's plays might again play some role, however small, in bringing further normative advances about, again measured by standards internal to the plays. If these points are accepted, they would provide reasons to refrain from dismissing anyone believing normative advances are possible in history as a naïve dreamer. And they would provide reasons to refuse to join Iden in retreating to a private garden, away from social struggles.

1. There have been a number of limited but still significant normative social advances since Shakespeare's day, measured by standards embedded in his plays. Many characters in the plays assume that they are inherently superior to other human beings, not in this or that capability but in all essential respects, simply due to the accident of being born into this family rather than that, or having this gender identity rather than that. His plays depict a world where supposed superiors do not have to recognize any common human dignity shared with their supposed inferiors. This belief was an essential feature of both common sense and law in Shakespeare's own period, and the plays correctly reflect how pervasive this idea has been in human history.

We have already noted that the plays undermine the claim that a sociopolitical hierarchy can be justified as part of an immutable metaphysical hierarchy. We can add now that there are many instances in the plays where the ludicrousness of the claim to innate superiority is on full display. In *Henry VI, Part 2*, for example, Suffolk, an especially fervent holder of this view, expresses utter disbelief that it might be possible a lowly commoner could kill him. Nonetheless, he is killed. In *Lear*, it is the fool who best understands the folly of dividing the kingdom; Lear's great superiority of birth does not provide superiority of insight. The belief that women are by nature inferior to men, a commonplace of Western thought for millennia, is also taken as unquestioned and unquestionable by almost all male characters. Yet throughout the comedies and late romances the women in the plays have a mature understanding of reality that the men only win with great difficulty.

In the period separating us from Shakespeare, the belief that some have an inherent superiority over others simply because of the group they were born into has lost its force in many parts of the world. From the point of view of the plays, I believe this must be seen as a normative advance. Unfortunately, the principle of our inherent equality in dignity has in practice been institutionalized in a profoundly partial and precarious manner. But some normative advance has been made in some places in some respects, and that is enough to make the point at hand.

Shakespeare's political dramas are haunted by rulers who do whatever they wish, whenever they wish. It is far too easy to find far too many examples of such rulers today. Nonetheless, in some regions of the global the behavior of those holding sovereigns power has been constrained by constitutional rules, such that at least the worst abuses depicted in Shakespeare's plays have become far less prevalent. Far too many loopholes enabling far too many abuses of political power persist in constitutional republics. Nonetheless, from the standpoint of the plays, there has been normative advance, even if this progress has not brought the return of the Garden of Eden, and even if there is no gain that cannot be reversed.

Laws and customs granting fathers close to absolute power over their offspring are shown in many plays to lead to abuses that playgoers and readers find unacceptable from a normative point of view (e.g., Leontes's treatment of Perdita in *The Winter's Tale*). The erosion of patriarchal power manifested in the widespread consensus today that children should be protected from such abuses must also be seen as a normative advance from the perspective of the plays, even if the erosion has been far from complete across the globe.

The fate of the aged is raised in many Shakespeare plays. When servants are abandoned by their masters after a lifetime of service as Kent is in *Lear*, the audience is clearly meant to emphasize with them, not their masters. Few if any readers or playgoers do not feel that the fate of these servants is not merely poignant, but wrong. Since Shakespeare's day, the principle that the elderly should not be abandoned to radical economic insecurity has been implemented in at least some public policies in at least some regions. Here too the advance in normative rationality has been partial and precarious. But here too it has been real nonetheless.

These cases show that ethical irrationality is not an all-or-nothing matter. There are degrees. If normative advances have happened to at least some degree, a political worldview that takes the ethical irrationality of the political world as immutably fixed rests on a faulty premise. And if normative advances have occurred before, there appears no good reason in principle to assume they cannot occur again. In this sense, Shakespeare's plays point beyond "Shakespearian politics" as that term has been used so far.

2. It is obviously impossible to give a comprehensive account here of how normative advances occur. In every case a multitude of contingent factors are bound to be in play simultaneously, with culture just one of

many factors in the mix. But the role of culture must have its due, as Shakespeare's plays illustrate. Hegel insisted in *The Phenomenology of Spirit* that when an unexamined social practice is transformed into an *examined* social practice by being objectified in a cultural product, a collective learning process may occur, transforming a social practice assumed to be natural and legitimate to one that has lost the appearance of being either natural or legitimate.

Numerous social practices whose naturalness and legitimacy were taken for granted were objectified on Shakespeare's stage. Hamlet affirms this as a project of theater when he urges the players to not diverge from "from the purpose of playing, whose end, both at the first and now, was and is, to hold, as 'twere, the mirror up to nature, to show virtue her own feature, scorn her own image, and the very age and body of the time his form and pressure." (*Hamlet* 3.2, 20–24). A list of specific examples from the plays would include the scenes mentioned above, where we see objectified a nobility convinced of its inherent superiority over all other human beings, or rulers, husbands and fathers with close to absolute powers, and radical economic insecurity imposed on the elderly after a lifetime of care labor for others. Insofar as Shakespeare's own plays objectified these social practices, they contributed in some small way to the learning process that led to the denaturalization and delegitimation of what had been taken as natural and legitimate social practices.

3. If normative advances have occurred before, there is no good reason to assume they cannot occur again. If cultural products have played some role in bringing about those changes, there is no good reason to assume they cannot contribute again, if the right general background conditions are in place. A "Shakespearian politics" beyond the horizon of the plays it is based on would point to other normatively questionable social practices objectified in these plays, and note that by objectifying them, a space is opened for their denaturalization and delegitimation. Shakespeare's plays include numerous depictions of the power of the spectacle. The power of the spectacle holds most strongly among those who do not have a concept of the spectacle. For those who do, its force dissipates (although its fascination may linger.) The objectification of its workings potentially makes the continuation of the power of the spectacle more difficult. *Julius Caesar*, *Henry VI, Part 2*, and other plays depict how the less privileged can be co-opted by ruling elites. An objective depiction of cooptation in a powerful cultural product makes it more difficult for the audience to take the claims of some alleged defender of

the underprivileged at face value. If the understanding that a Cade can be manipulated by a Richard of York were to become part of collectively shared knowledge, would it not be more difficult to some degree or other for the future Cades and future Richards to control events in the same way? *King John* and *Henry V* depict how easy it has been in the past for rulers to manufacture consent to their rule through appeals to nationalism in times of military tensions. By depicting this process, it may become just a bit more difficult for this appeal to work in the future. Mechanisms of manufacturing consent also work best when they are hidden, losing their force the more they are brought into the open.

Of course, no plays by themselves can change history, not even Shakespeare's. That is not the issue. The issue is also not whether progressive change is inevitable. It surely isn't, and the odds are surely against significant normative advance in our bleak historical moment. The issue is instead whether normative advances are possible in principle, aided in some measure by the collective learning process set off when social practices taken as natural and legitimate are denaturalized and delegitimated in cultural works. Insofar as Shakespeare's plays provide reasons to insist that the answer to this question is "yes," a second form of "Shakespearian politics" begins to emerge, distinct from the version endorsing an apolitical mode of being in the world. The latter captures profound truths about the all too evident ethical irrationality pervading political life from ancient warrior aristocracies through Renaissance dukedoms and monarchies, to the merchant republics and the formally democratic capitalist states of modernity. There are, however, other truths too.

In some all-too-limited and precarious, but nonetheless real, ways, political life has advanced in normative rationality as measured by Shakespeare's plays. We can therefore be "at home" in the polity world to some extent, even if we cannot find the full "rational satisfaction" in modern society Hegel thought we could affirm. It is a realm where the denaturalization and delegitimation of the beliefs, practices, and institutions that are most responsible for that ethical irrationality is possible in principle, as Marx thought. From this standpoint, there can be a "Shakespearian politics" contributing to a collective learning process that dismantles the power of the spectacle, the transparent manipulation of popular energies by regressive ruling factions, and the rhetorical power of reactionary nationalist appeals.

If we accept a "Shakespearian politics" denying that any transformation of the political realm could possibly make a normative difference, wouldn't that be acting like those in Shakespeare's day who could not imagine that social and political rights could ever extend beyond a small ruling caste, or that young adults could be freed from the control of patriarchal fathers, or that constitutional limits could be place on rulers?

The "Shakespearean politics" the plays appear to point toward restricts the scope of political imagination. But there is another, pointing beyond the horizon of the plays, that refuses that restriction.

Notes

1. This section, and the chapter as a whole, has been greatly influenced by Lake (2017).

2. The background plot of *Hamlet* is similar in relevant respects. Nothing in the metaphysical nature of things justifies the authority of the Danish king over the territories won from Norway by Hamlet's father in his challenge match with Fortinbras senior. They were taken by a contingent act of violence. As far as Fortinbras junior is concerned, they can be retaken by force as well.

3. Hamlet's infamous delay is not entirely due to an idiosyncratic individual psychology making him unsuited to decisive action. If he killed Claudius and the testimony of the ghost proved false, he would not only have committed murder. He would be guilty of the even more grievous sin of assassinating God's representative on earth. This would place Hamlet in the same moral category as Macbeth and Richard III.

4. Was that Fortinbras's plan all along? The play stresses how old and close to death his uncle was, the only person capable of stopping Fortinbras's planned attack on Norway. Are we to think that perhaps Fortinbras went to Poland so that when his uncle died he could return to Denmark with an experienced army in place and ready to go? If so, the battles in Poland were not as pointless as Hamlet assumes. See Shapiro (2012, pp. 308–12).

5. The "band of brothers" bluster is undermined after the battle as well, when the toll of the battle is taken. Only the names of the nobility who fell are read; the common sort die anonymously, their names not worth mentioning.

6. Richard II went a step too far when he confiscated Bolingbroke's estate. The future Henry IV was too dangerous and powerful. Too many nobles had too much sympathy for him, and too much fear of suffering the same fate at Richard's hand.

7. In *As You Like It*, the event that switches the path of the plot from tragic to comic was a chance meeting with a priest. If there is one thing we learn from the history plays, it is that spiritual confessors to rulers do not regularly turn political rulers into monks. As a rule, they have their own political agenda, and use whatever influence they have over ruling elites to further it.

8. The constant threat and sporadic reality of physical abuse of workers discussed below with reference to the *The Comedy of Errors*, for example, will tend to be eliminated in principle.

9. See, for example, the interchange between Flavius and Murellus at the beginning of *Julius Caesar*.

10. Marx's economic manuscripts of 1844 can be seen as an extended commentary on this passage.

References

Archer, I. (2012). "Economy." In A. Kinney (ed.), *The Oxford Handbook of Shakespeare* (pp. 165–181). New York, NY: Oxford University Press.

Bate, J. (2009). *Soul of the Age: A Biography of the Mind of William Shakespeare*. New York, NY: Random House.

Hadfield, A. (2012). "Republicanism." In A. Kinney (ed.), *The Oxford Handbook of Shakespeare* (pp. 587–603). New York, NY: Oxford University Press.

Holderness, G. (2000). *Shakespeare: The Histories*. New York, NY: St. Martin's Press.

Kinney, A. (Ed.). (2012). *The Oxford Handbook of Shakespeare*. New York, NY: Oxford University Press.

Lake, P. (2017). *How Shakespeare Put Politics on the Stage: Power and Succession in the History Plays*. New Haven, CT: Yale University Press.

Lemon, R. (2012). "Law," In A. Kinney (ed.), *The Oxford Handbook of Shakespeare* (pp. 554–571). New York, NY: Oxford University Press.

Lovejoy, A. O. ([1936] 1990). *The Great Chain of Being: A Study of the History of an Idea*. Cambridge MA: Harvard University Press.

Shapiro, J. (2012). *A Year in the Life of William Shakespeare: 1599*. New York, NY: Harper Collins.

Smith, T. (2017). *Beyond Liberal Egalitarianism*. Leiden, UK: Brill.

Tillyard, E. ([1943] 1959). *The Elizabethan World Picture: A Study of Order in the Age of Shakespeare, Donne, and Milton*. New York, NY: Vintage.

Wills, G. (2011). *Rome and Rhetoric: Shakespeare's Julius Caesar*. New Haven, CT: Yale University Press.

Chapter 6

The Radical Implications of Hölderlin's Aesthetic Rationalism

Michael J. Thompson

Lern im Leben die Kunst, im Kunstwerk lerne das Leben,
Siehst du das eine recht, siehst du das andere auch.

—Friedrich Hölderlin

I

At about the same time as the *Institut für Sozialforschung* was beginning its work, Thomas Mann writes an essay in 1928: "I maintain that all would be well in Germany, and Germany would find its true self, the day that Karl Marx reads Friedrich Hölderlin . . . a one-sided acquaintance would remain sterile." Mann, like many of his contemporaries, was aware of the need for a humanization of modern culture, but also of the need for a concept of social justice that could incorporate humanistic ideals. Exploring Mann's basic proposition will not be an easy one. For one thing, Hölderlin's reception in nonliterary circles is not well established and, although Adorno did much to counter the existentialist reading of his work popularized by Heidegger, the image persists of a Romantic without practical concerns, without relevance for politically minded theorists and philosophers. But what I want to suggest here is that Mann's insight compels us to return to Hölderlin's aesthetic-philosophical project

186   Michael J. Thompson

and his engagement with the hubristic dilemmas of modern reason that went unheeded. In the end, what Hölderlin asks us to consider is the extent to which modernity confronts us with a choice: between a life of one-dimensionality, of domination and unrealized potential and what he sees as a "new world" or "new age"—a way of living, thinking, feeling able to encompass the full potentialities contained within nature.

I want to argue that Hölderlin's aesthetic theory seeks to encompass a more holistic and more ambitious conception of rationality than the predominant *Aufklärung* ideas about reason during his own time. More specifically, my thesis is that Hölderlin's conception of aesthetic reason encompasses and deepens not only our cognitive but also our practical capacities for reason. His ideas were, from the start, engaged with the problem of instrumentality that he saw inherent in the 18th-century ideas about reason. What Hölderlin is able to provide for us is, in this sense, a deeply anti-reificatory conception of rationality and human reflection that provides the framework for a theory of the "good" and truth that can help expand the concept of critical agency and contribute to a critical theory of human reflection and judgment. Through his engagement with thinkers such as Plato, Spinoza, Kant, and Fichte, Hölderlin is able to introduce a more compelling, more comprehensive idea about the nature of human freedom and our pursuit of the good life.

Hölderlin poses a new conception of thought and the idea that the whole must be experienced before it can be known. He seems to be concerned to defend a human experience against the mechanistic, the subjectivistic, and the dualistic. His conception of an aesthetic is one that senses the reified stale reality that pervaded his time. Of the rise of instrumental reason, of the division of labor, of the rise of the market mentality, and the increasingly shallow culture of bourgeois life. He sees the seeds of what will become an alienation of human life and the deformation of human reason and culture because of the wayward direction to which modern culture has succumbed. This is a conception of reason and individuality that is expanded, one that is connected to the whole, a vital, organic conception of the totality that connects the subject and object, and which prevents the separation of man from himself and from nature. But his poetry probes the dilemma of a kind of consciousness that cannot grasp this; it is a tragic art that shows the limits of everyday experience, of constrained life and thought. It is the tragedy of modernity: to be caught between the potential experience of the expanded self and the constrained world of subjectivism. Beauty and truth are thus connected, and the lack of aesthetic experience thereby limits exposure to truth. The regeneration of modern culture will come about only once man and nature are once again reconciled.

Indeed, it can be said that Hölderlin's problematic was similar to that explored by Horkheimer and Adorno in *Dialectic of Enlightenment*. It is man's separation from nature—and hence his separation from himself—and his domination of nature—and hence his systematic domination of himself—that Enlightenment reason has spawned. For Hölderlin, the Enlightenment is therefore a necessary but deficient development in human culture. It requires that we expand the circle of reason—expand it to the extent that is encompasses beauty as well as truth. That our ability to know truth is only possible once we can experience the absolute, the "unconditioned," and overcome the radical separation between the subject and the object. Once this is done, a new man will emerge: a new form of subjectivity, of agency, of culture, society and a true kind of freedom. In the end, Hölderlin's critique of modernity is not a regressive, Romantic movement to the past, as Lukács and others have seen it.[1] It is, rather, a critique of an age that has lost touch with humanism but at the same time allows us to glimpse a new world, a new conception of what human culture can become. Through the efforts of Kant's and Fichte's critical philosophy, the political efforts of the French Revolution, and the gradual secularization of ethical Protestantism, the paradigm of the Greeks can now be seen to be a renewable, achievable goal. Now man has the potential to grasp the "absolute," the deeper reality of his relation to nature, the totality of rational existence. What Hölderlin offers us is an aesthetic-philosophical vision of a form of being that exists *in potentia* within us. It is an emancipatory form of reason that seeks to overcome what he thought was the narrow Enlightenment conception of the rational subject. For Hölderlin, the new man will create the new culture—a culture that will live without the dichotomies and contradictions of subject and object, hope and despair, freedom and necessity and individual and community.

II

To understand Hölderlin's project, we have to grasp why he thinks that aesthetics grants us access to a higher sense of our unity with nature, and how this is conceived as a pathway to an emancipated form of being.

Reason for Hölderlin has different gradations relating to how humans relate to the whole, to the unity of subject and object. He therefore presages a distinction between the instrumental use of reason, that which is circumscribed by utility, by function, by operationalization on the one hand and the kind of emancipatory rationality that can allow for a creative form of agency that can embody the full, developed powers inherent within human being. For Hölderlin, the world is a totality, it is organic, it is dynamic, and it is constituted by different levels of organization. Our capacity to perceive and to experience this and these higher levels of organization entails a different relation of the part and the whole, but not only in a conceptual, but also an actual sense. For one of Hölderlin's great problems with Kant's philosophy—something rooted in the *Kritik der Urteilskraft*—was the distinction between regulative and constitutive powers of reason and the aesthetic. For Hölderlin, the experience of art and nature (of the sublime more broadly) was not something merely captured by the regulative powers of the understanding, a mere phenomenon given shape by subjective consciousness alone. Rather, aesthetic ideas, those conveyed particularly by poetry itself, are *constitutive of the world itself*: It possesses a creative power, a power to transform oneself into a subject ready to unite with nature, with one's essence. To perceive beauty, to articulate aesthetic ideas, was to convey the organic, rational structure of nature and to aid the infinite striving of the ego not against nature, not to dominate or subjugate it, but to expand itself to be able to unite oneself with it. To be able to experience the sublimity of nature is to experience "pure being" (*reines Seyn*), the true structure and substance of nature. Once we experience this, we have the capacity to return to it, to create a culture that can embody true being.

Beauty is thus more than an aesthetic category; it also encompasses truth. The reason for this is that once we are able to see what nature really is—that it is characterized by growth, development, differentiation and organization—what we come to see in experiencing nature is the very substance of all being itself. We as human beings are therefore the ultimate expression of nature, of its most highly organized, self-conscious manifestation: We possess the creative powers that manifest the most developed form of nature. Beauty therefore has a wider scope of meaning than a mere aesthetic category—indeed, not unlike classical Greek culture, which used the term καλός (beauty) to describe not only objects relating to art and nature, but also those aspects of human life that expressed the "Good" (τὸ ἀγαθόν), that is, those things that contributed to the well-being, the goodness of the whole community, and to the flourishing of the individual. Like Plato, the Good (τὸ ἀγαθόν) and the Beautiful (τὸ καλόν) are pursued not for the sake of some other good, but for themselves—because in so doing, we express a self-determination that manifests the fullness of nature and our Being. What beauty is and why it plays such an important role for Hölderlin can be seen once we understand his opposition to Fichte. For modern rationalism, knowledge is posed as the problem of the subject's relation to the object. This entails that thought is about the object, that the thinking subject is external to and sealed off from the object, the *Ding an sich*. What Hölderlin proposes, in his philosophical fragment "Judgment and Being" (*Urtheil und Seyn*), is that this separation is an original unity. As Dieter Henrich remarks on this point, "Yet we would not even seek after it if that infinite unification, that being in the only sense of the word, were not present to us. It is present—as beauty" (Henrich, 1997, p. 84).

Beauty is now more than merely a feeling and more than mere cognition. It is deeper experience of that basic unity of the self with the totality of nature and the ability to see that the ego and nature, the subject and object, are both unified parts of a larger totality. "Holy nature!" he writes in *Hyperion*, "you are the same within me and outside of me. It need not be so difficult to unite what is outside of me with the divine within me" (GW, p. 392).[2] This unity of nature is not mechanistic, however, as it was for Spinoza. The key here is that nature be understood as organic and dynamic, that the subject comes to relate to the objective world of nature once it realizes that it is an integral part of it, that subject and object constitute to facets of the same substance, that any true knowledge must encompass nature since nature is itself the essence of subjectivity itself—subjectivity that is fully realized, fully developed. Human freedom therefore can be construed as the realization of this capacity in man, the development of these powers of creation as free beings aware of their essential, substantial being.

This necessity is one that yields freedom for the self once there is the realization that this beauty represents the lost memory, inscribed in our intuitions, that a broader relation with the world is not only possible, but also the true essence of our being. To properly grasp nature is to properly grasp ourselves. To come to this kind of knowledge is therefore to overcome the subject-object divide, between the thinking agent and nature. We must make this turn toward nature, Hölderlin suggests, because not to do so would restrict us to our own subjectivity; it would rob us

of the normative, aesthetic, and intellectual ground for truth. And this
is not simply a philosophical choice; it is also a cultural condition. To
be dirempted from nature is tantamount to the isolation of the self from
the source of real value and therefore marks a slippage into nihilism.[3]
This is the fate of Alabanda in *Hyperion*, who cannot bear to see the
fate to which humans are locked into:

> When I look at a child, he cried, and think how shameful and
> corrupting is the yoke that it will bear, and that it will starve
> as we do, that it will seek men as we do, search as we do for
> the beautiful and the true, that it will pine away fruitlessly,
> because it will be alone as we are, that it—O take your sons
> from the cradle, compatriots, and cast them into the river, so
> as to rescue them at least from your disgrace! (GW, p. 334)

The nihilist is one that denies not only the essential relation that the
self, that each ego, has with nature—a relation that exists ontologically
but of which he is unaware. It is also to be caught within the circle of
the ego, to either not see, or have frustrated the capacity to see that
aesthetics grants us not simply experience, but an experience that possesses *constitutive power* rather than merely *regulative power*. What this
means is that aesthetic experience is the experience not of an idea, but
of "Being" itself, the source of all that is beautiful and all that is good
and worthy of our strivings. The subject is only saved by his comprehension of the object, a full comprehension that is able to see past mere
atoms, mechanisms and static facts and into process and dynamism. Art
is the reflection of this truth back into nature; it alone can complete
the relation of subject and object, the ideal and the real, and it at once
perfects nature—insofar as human reflection is nature reflecting on and
completing itself as organized matter—and completes the reflective subject
as a constituent part of that whole. Art is related to reason, and hence
to truth-content, insofar as we see that the power of art is the power
to constitute the world, to put us in touch with that same capacity that
nature possesses: to constitute the world through the process of making
chaos into form, of making coherence from what is incoherent. This
becomes the very nucleus of Hölderlin's powerful idea that aesthetics
and philosophy, beauty and truth, operate on the same plane.

   This will require a different conception of the subject and object,
of self and world, and of reason and feeling than modern culture has

brought forth to us. The basic formula for this form of reason—a rationality that attains the status of beauty—is described in *Hyperion* with
the Greek phrase, borrowed from Heraklitis, ἐν διαφέρον ἐαῦτῳ: or "that
which is differentiated in itself" (*das Eine in sich selber unterschiedne*). The
individual's return to nature is not done out of resignation, nor is it an
absorption of the subject, the ego, into the manifold of nature. Rather, it
represents the achieved status accomplished through the realization that
there is a deeper truth than what our own subjective cognitive powers can
reveal to us. To be "differentiated in oneself," therefore means that the
ego has undergone a transformation via aesthetic experience wherein his
agency is now rooted not in his own atomistic and subjectivist confines,
but through his conscious, rational relation to nature, in a real, rational
totality. One's freedom is therefore the result of this capacity to have
this relationship with nature, with the source of what is truly rational.
For now, the free person is one who is transformed, constituted by the
knowledge that the subject and object belong to the same structure and
are in fact interdependent aspects of higher totality.

The individual is now brought back to nature through his own
strivings, his own choice, his own direction once he sees his own fragmented, deformed state by being estranged from nature, from the essence
of his being. A new individual has now emerged, one who can integrate
the self and its essential nature. Since Kant and especially Fichte had
made it the hallmark of their respective philosophical systems to chart
the ego as the center of reason, Hölderlin's opposition to this was to see
the necessary linkage between the ego and nature; to perceive that this
unite of man and nature was not some static unity, but one of self-dif-
ferentiation. The richer form of reason that can be achieved is one that
dialectically sublates (to employ Hegel's later language) the atomic ego
with the rational, organic and dynamic structure of nature—a structure of
nature which is also constitutive of himself. The problem with modernity
was its confusion about the source of reason: It was not contained in
us, as Kant and Fichte had claimed. This mistake led to the problem of
stripping reason of its relation to the whole. "From mere understanding
(*Verstande*) comes no philosophy," he writes in *Hyperion*, "for philosophy
is more than the limited knowledge of what exists. . . . From mere reason
(*Vernunft*) comes no philosophy, for philosophy is more than the blind
demand for an interminable progress in the unification and differentiation of a particular material." Rather, he continues, "when the divine
ἐν διαφέρον ἐαῦτῳ, striving reason's (*Vernunft*) ideal of beauty, shines

forth, so it demands not blindly, and knows why, wherefore it demands" (GW, pp. 386–387).

This means that the concept of the subject, of agency has to be reconstructed. The new kind of agency and subjectivity that emerges from Hölderlin's ideas is one that takes the "eccentric path" between the poles of reflection and organized experience on the one hand and a fundamental unity with nature, on the other. But the new, integrated self is only capable of this Hölderlin's ideas matured as a reaction to his studies of Kant and Fichte on the one hand and Spinoza and Leibniz on the other. What he saw was that the subjective Idealism of Kant and Fichte was problematic because it restricted reason to the rational subject, excluding the entirety of nature. Reason was restricted to the noumenal, broken off from the "phenomena" of nature and the world as a whole. With Spinoza, who recognized the absolute character of nature, but saw it as defined by mechanism and causation, there was a denial of the power of the will and what Fichte called the "eternal striving" of the self. For Fichte, the "eternal striving" was done by the ego against nature, nature being the field within which the ego was to posit its freedom. But Hölderlin's radical proposition is that we synthesize these two poles of philosophy—that we see the subject not as the antithesis to nature, nor as simply absorbed into the totality of rational nature. Rather, the idea is that the rational subject now represents that part of nature, of organic, rational matter that is most highly organized, capable of reflecting on itself. In this sense, the Fichtean "eternal striving" is not to be construed as acting against nature, but seeking to be part again of that whole from which it has been alienated, dirempted. Nature itself is not a static totality; it is an organic, developmental, self-differentiating whole. This growth of things from that which is inchoate to that which is organized and developed—resonant with Aristotle's metaphysical concepts of δυνάμις (*potentiality*) and ἐνέργεια (*actuality* or *activity*) and with Hegel's later distinction between *Dasein* and *Wirklichkeit*—entails a distinction between that which is fully developed and realized and that which is defective or stunted. This forms the basis of Hölderlin's critique of modernity, in that since he sees the relation between subject and object as continuous rather than discrete, so too the relation between what is real and ideal have an organic relation.[4] The ideal is not a regulative principle, but is constitutive of reality, and it is this that provides him with a critical conception of modernity. Our culture can be critiqued not from the standpoint of an *a priori* or transcendental principle, but rather from what is constitutive of that reality itself. The ideal is present *in nuce* within reality. It is our relation with the absolute, with the true essence of nature that determines the relative perfection or imperfection of man.

But even more, this leads us to a point of view—philosophical but also accessible, according to Hölderlin—only through aesthetic experience that the absolute, the whole is to be understood as the totality of the vital, systemic organization of nature. And this is something that cannot be grasped through conceptual thought alone. It must be *experienced*. Love—a theme made trite by its overuse in Romanticism—is no mere sentiment, but is the force, the emotional drive, that draws us out of our subjectivity and gives us the feeling of the need to reunite with others, with the whole itself. As Frederick Beiser puts it: "The feeling of the sublime, the longing to reunite ourselves with all things, and the experience of love, in which I see myself in others as others see themselves in me, show us that we know an other that transcends our own circle of consciousness" (Beiser, 2002, p. 373). Love now becomes, for Hölderlin, the supreme creative force, the experience of which requires the other, and which is satisfied only by one's unification with an other. When animated by love, man begins to reach a status of perfection, reaching beyond his narrow subjectivity: "Yes! Man is a sun, all-seeing, all-illuminating when he loves, and when he loves not, he is a dark dwelling in which a smoking little lamp burns" (GW, p. 378). It is also the ground for friendship, the kind of sociation that reflects the actual substance of human nature, the truth of our being, one reason why Hölderlin holds that: "It is a better time, for which you seek, a more beautiful world. Only that world you embraced in your friends, you were with them in this world" (GW, p. 371). But even here, friendship retains a political valence. In *Hyperion*, Hölderlin references, as a classical idea of friendship, the memory of Harmodius and Aristogeiton, the two lover-friends who overthrew the Peisitratid Hipparchus in Athens paving the way to the Democracy: " '[T]here Harmodius and Aristogeiton lived!' someone finally cried, 'back then there was friendship in the world' " (GW, p. 367). The narrowness of modern social relations is contrasted with the engaged, common life envisioned by classical Athens. What Hölderlin increasingly seems to be calling into question is the brittle, shallow, vacuous nature of modern social relations—a shallowness that can only be overcome by reconciling ourselves with the whole, with what is true and sublime.

Hölderlin's critique of modernity is therefore not a Romantic escapism, but a critique from within. Modern rationality is itself to blame, but not rationality itself. Hölderlin sees a deficiency in the nature of Enlightenment reason in that it takes the form of instrumental, analytic, and atomistic rationality. It is a paradigm of reason that advocates the separation of man from nature, that entails his domination over nature, and is consequently, as Adorno and Horkheimer pointed out in *Dialectic of Enlightenment*, the terminus of a kind of rationality that Hölderlin sought to stop in its tracks, to, in effect, block before it grew out of control. For Adorno and Horkheimer saw the way that this narrow, reified form of Enlightenment reason refracts back to us the world as a field for our domination: "Myth turns into enlightenment, and nature into mere objectivity. Men pay for the increase of their power with alienation from that over which they exercise their power. Enlightenment behaves toward things as a dictator toward men. He knows them in so far as he can manipulate them" (Adorno & Horkheimer, 1972, p. 9). But for Hölderlin, this is the outcome of what he saw already predominant in his own time—a modernity that has divorced reason from beauty, intellect from feeling. "Understanding (*Verstand*) without beauty of spirit," he writes in *Hyperion*, "is like a subservient journeyman who constructs the fence out of coarse wood as sketched out for him, and nails the carpentered posts together for the garden that the master shall cultivate" (*GW*, p. 386). For Hölderlin, the overcoming of the subject-object problem, the move toward an aesthetic experience granting us access to that which is absolute, which is "unconditioned," provides us with a wholly different way of conceiving the powers and the purposes of reason. Contrary to the domination of nature because of our separation from it, Hölderlin's claim is that we must explode the confines of the anthropocentric, sub-jectivist model of reason and expand what it means to think and feel.

But one important theme that emerges from *Hyperion* is what can happen to the actually lived experience of the modern subject who struggles with the complexity of this insight. This is why he refers to the ἐν διαφέρον ἑαυτῷ as "striving reason's idea of beauty," since it is only when reason has been mediated by the experience of the sublime that an expanded ego can be free, can be truly self-determined because it has incorporated within itself the structure of the universal: "When the sun of the beautiful shined upon the understanding (*Verstande*) at its business as a May day shines into the artist's workshop, then it does not rush out and abandon its makeshift work, yet it thinks fondly of the festive day when it will wander in the rejuvenating spring light"

(GW, p. 387). It is as if Hölderlin is portraying for us a vision of man on the cusp of some great ontological shift, on a precipice between the present, dirempted condition and the possibility of the new realization of a totality, the ἐν καὶ πᾶν, the "one and all," that he sought as the great regenerative tonic for modern culture. By moving beyond the confines of the self-sufficient ego, of self-consciousness itself as the basis for human knowledge and experience, Hölderlin posits "being" (Seyn) as the "single universal substance of which thought and extension, the subjective and objective, are only manifestations or appearances."[5] The content of true thoughts, of beauty, therefore are constitutive of reality, of nature of being itself. Once a culture no longer cultivates this basic truth, man is lost, a mere fragment, and no longer possesses of his true powers: "[O]ne who is a man," he writes in Hyperion, "can he not do more than hundreds who are only fragments of men?" (GW, p. 392).

III

But it is precisely of this that Hölderlin's critique of modernity consists. Modern man, the modern subject, is, for Hölderlin, a tragic figure. "Nothing can grow," he writes in Hyperion, "and nothing so profoundly waste away, as man" (GW, p. 348). The great problem of modernity is that the kind of rationality that it embodies chases out what he sees as the higher capacity of the subject to experience and to grasp the absolute and reconcile subject and object. This is a core theme of Hölderlin's work and points to a core, living theme in modernity: namely, the loss of meaning, the loss of the individual's connection with the world as a whole. Modernity has killed off the premodern religio-communal frame-work of life that once guided us.[6] Now, after the French Revolution, after Spinoza, Kant, Fichte, and the Enlightenment, we stand at a juncture, a juncture where the old culture has been destroyed and the new has yet to take shape— not unlike Matthew Arnold's narrator in "From the Grande Chartreuse," who "wanders between two worlds, one dead; The other powerless to be born." Hölderlin's modern man is one who suffers from the limits of the Cartesian-Kantian worldview where the individual ego is the sole font of reason.

    The alternative is for us to see that aesthetic experience provides us with the proper transcendental deduction necessary for man's capacity to grasp truth. Hölderlin's argument here is that aesthetic judgment and experience is necessary so as to prevent the slippage into nihilism and skepticism; it is also necessary to anchor the expanded form of reasoning and judgment that Hölderlin saw as capable of grasping true being, of nature and its rational, dynamic structure. And this is of importance because without aesthetic judgment as a ground for human reason, we will drift into a blind instrumentality, split what is human from what is will become merely "technical," and block our achievement of a higher form of being. Intellect, reason, requires beauty since without it, it will be unable to grasp truth. "From mere understanding (*Verstande*) comes no philosophy, for philosophy is more than the limited knowledge of what exists" (*GW*, p. 386), he writes in *Hyperion*. And this is meant to convey the idea that a self-sufficient epistemology is a defective approach to the world no less than the rigors of moral perfectionism and the categorical imperative; it is so because it does not—it cannot—adequately grasp the true essence of nature and of life since it attempts to do so from a one-sided and hence deficient vantage point.

Not unlike Rousseau, whose Emile learns of the proper ways of being before the deformative powers of socialization, Hölderlin's view of youth is one that is full of potentiality. But the spirit of the age is what gives even the young the basic pattern for a life of truth and beauty—a free, emancipated life that grasps the absolute. As Hyperion laments: "I had grown up like a vine without a pole, and the wild tendrils spread aimlessly over the ground. You know how so much noble strength perishes among us because it is not used" (*GW*, p. 320). It is the fate of modern culture to produce individuals unable to realize that higher truth and the tragic nature of modern culture is that it is unable to provide the foundation, the ground for the developed self. In his lyric poem "Hyperion's Song of Fate" we are told this explicitly:

> Doch uns ist gegeben,
>   Auf keiner Statte zu ruhn,
>   Es schwinden, es fallen
>   Die leidenden Menschen
>   Blindlings von einer
>   Stunde zur andern,
>   Wie Wasser von Klippe
>   Zu Klippe geworfen,
>   Jahr lang ins Ungewisse hinab.

But to us it is given
　　To find no place of peace,
　　　And suffering mortals
　　　　Dwindle and fall
　　　　　Headlong from one
　　　　　　Hour to the next,
　　　　　　　Like water from cliff
　　　　　　　To cliff thrown
　　　　　　　　Downward for years into the unknown.

Hölderlin makes his relation to Rousseau explicit in his poem "Rousseau,"
which paints a picture of the citizen of Geneva as a kind of prophet:

How narrowly confined is our day-time here.
You were and saw and wondered, and yet, darkness falls.

Rousseau's message goes unheeded by modern man, for what he can be
and what he contains within him he is unable to grasp:

Des Lebens Überfluß, das Unendliche,
　　Das um ihn　　　　　und dämmert, er faßt es nie.
　　　Doch lebts in ihm und gegenwärtig,
　　　　Wärmend und wirkend, die Frucht entquillt ihm.

Du hast gelebt!　　Auch dir, auch dir
　　Erfreuet die ferne Sonne dein Haupt,
　　　Und Stralen aus der schönern Zeit. Es
　　　　Haben die Boten dein Herz gefunden.

Life's abundance, its infinity
　　That teems and glimmers around him, he'll never grasp.
　　　And yet it lives in him, and is present,
　　　　Warming and effective, the fruit springs forth from him.

You have lived! And you, your head
　　Rejoices by the light of a distant sun,
　　　The radiance of a more beautiful age.
　　　The messengers have discovered your heart.

The age of reason predisposes us to a fragmented view of life. It spawns a culture and institutions that deform humanity, severing us from the link between aesthetic experience as the ground for a proper form of cognition that can place the unity of being as the telos of human life. But this is no mere ideal, it is real in the sense that aesthetic experience grants us access to the powers of unified nature, of its organic, teleological structure.

With the power of love, that force that is within us seeking unity with the whole, that which seeks the reconciliation of opposites within the self, that force which can grant us experience of the true nature of the whole—that force, represented by Diotima in *Hyperion*, is alienated from him. Indeed, after losing Diotima, Hyperion laments that "My soul is like a fish cast out of its element onto the sandy shore, and it writhes and flings itself about until it dries up in the heat of the day" (*GW*, pp. 363–364). The regeneration of man, the restoration of what was prefigured in classical Athens, is dependent upon returning to human experience as a whole experience, not simply to cognition. Aesthetics and philosophy must be brought together and the point of this is to be able to grasp the whole, the experience of the sublime is not mere feeling, it possesses philosophical power as well. The whole man, the full, developed self is one who has perfected this capacity and who belongs to a culture that embodies these capacities. These people would be capable of free being and free activity; without an integration of aesthetic experience of beauty, our science, our politics, our philosophy—all will degenerate leaving man fragmented. From *Hyperion* again: "Where divine nature and its artists are so insulted, oh there life's best pleasure is gone, and every other star is better than the earth. There the men become ever more barren, more desolate, though they were all born beautiful; servility grows, with it impudence, intoxication grows with worries, and with plenty grow hunger and fear of famine; the blessing of every year becomes a curse, and all gods flee" (*GW*, p. 454).

This is why Hölderlin sees Athens—classical Greece, in general— as the idealized paradigm for culture and the whole man. In *Hyperion*, the contrast between classical Greece and the Germans represents this opposition between the two poles of humanity. Greek culture was the product of a people who were able to merge feeling with thought, to grasp true being. Their art and their politics were expressions of a people that thought and felt widely. The Germans, the "people of the North," as he refers to them in *Hyperion*, are different. They have shorn thought from feeling, fragmented man, and stultified him:

> In the North, a man must already be reasonable (*verständig*) even before a mature feeling is in him, he imputes guilt to himself for everything even before ingenuousness has reached its beautiful end; he must become rational, become self-con- scious spirit before he is a man, must become a shrewd man before he is a child; he does not allow the unity of the whole man, beauty, to thrive and ripen in him before he cultivates and develops himself. Mere understanding (*Verstand*), mere reason (*Vernunft*), are always the kings of the North. (GW, p. 386)

The critique of modernity is thus a critique not of reason itself, not a reactionary retreat into sentiment and feeling, but of a kind of reason that lacks the necessary moorings in aesthetic experience that can grant us access into the fullness of true being. The division of labor between man's capacities—between his labor, art, thinking, feeling, all instantiate a kind of decadence. The rejuvenation of modern culture can come about only after this fragmentation has been restored to a coherent unity; only once reason is once again resonant with a harmony with nature rather than a persistent one-sidedness.

IV

What must be emphasized is the way that Hölderlin views the connec- tion—indeed, the essential connection—between the act of the poet and the conception of truth he is working with. Indeed, we must be clear that the radicalness of Hölderlin's ideas rests here in this idea of the nature of truth and its relationship to the aesthetic act because it grants us insight into the very structural essence of all truth-claims: namely, that we must see the totality of things as the product of a dynamic, creative process. His indebtedness to Plato here and his reworking of Platonic ideas in the light of Spinoza, Kant, and Fichte, in particular, means that he is seeking to grasp a conception of truth that unites what he saw as the fragmented quality of modern reason and modern society and man.

Unlike the Greeks who, he would have said, viewed the totality of human experience and did not divide knowledge from beauty and the Good, modern man has divided these concerns. The result is the fall into despair and nihilism that he explores in vicissitudes of *Hyperion*. But if we go back to Hölderlin's Platonic roots, then we begin to see a very different set of ideas emerge—ideas that can, I think, give to critical theory and critical philosophy more generally a more radically humanistic set of ethical and intellectual goals and purposes.

To be more specific, Hölderlin's relevance for critical theory can be grasped only once we are willing to see that he is pursuing a form of rationality that achieves two interdependent aims. First, an expanded capacity of the subject to grasp a truer, more comprehensive account of reality as a whole, as a *totality*. Second, and related to this, an account of rationality that mitigates against forms of reason that can lead to the fragmented and instrumentalized form that he saw implicit in the narrower conception of reason championed by the *Aufklärer*. The dichotomy between the Enlightenment ideas of the 18th century and the "Romantic" ideas of the late 18th and early 19th centuries needs to be called into question. Indeed, the *Frühromantik* defense of the aesthetic, which Hölderlin championed, was in fact seeking to complete the ideas started by the *Aufklärer*. As Frederick Beiser has forcefully put the matter: "The goal of art was to achieve one of the *Aufklärung's* most cherished ideals—namely, the closing the gap between theory and practice so that the principles of reason could be realized in public life. The value of art was that it could inspire the people to act according to the principles of reason" (Beiser, 2003, p. 57).

This latter point is of prime importance, for without understanding what kind of rationality Hölderlin was seeking to articulate, specifically, we will fail to understand his idealization of classical Greece and its emphasis on the Greek ideas about the synthesis of theory and practice, of the realization of the individual through the solidaristic community, of the aesthetic quality of this process of self-formation, and the full, flourishing form of life it envisioned for members of the political community. In this respect, Hölderlin's connection with Platonic ideas is thus of prime importance because he sees in Plato's ideas a conception of reason that unites the polarities of modern thought and culture. The most signifi-cant polarity is that between—not only theory and practice, as Beiser points out—but also between the realm of theoretical knowledge, moral judgment, and aesthetic quality. Put differently, Hölderlin grasps on to

Plato's complex thesis that the True, the Good, and the Beautiful are all to be synthesized into a single conception—that the chasm between these three realms of thought, made explicit by Kant, was to be overcome. The implications of Hölderlin's project are what make him so centrally significant today, for in his emphasis on the aesthetic function of reason, we see the importance of an anti-instrumental, humanistic expression of reason. Hölderlin's project was not to escape into emotivism and feeling but to fill out it out with the actual purposes of developing human life and creating the conditions for a kind of human reflection that would allow a more humane, more emancipated form of self and society to emerge.[7] "*Ohne Dichtung nie ein philosophisch Volk gewesen*," Hölderlin says in his *Hyperion*, and it is this fundamental problem he wishes to address and to solve for modern man via Plato.

We can take the idea of aesthetic creation as an entry point. For Hölderlin's claim is, as I have shown above, that aesthetics and truth are bound together, indeed, two facets of the same faculty. In the *Symposium*, Plato's understanding of the concept of poetry (ποίησις) is greatly expanded beyond the act of literary production. Both Agathon and Diotima in the dialogue stress the original concept of the term *poiesis* (ποίησις) as "creation." Plato's Diotima goes on to say: "[Y]ou know that poetry is many things; for any thing that passes from nonbeing into being, the whole cause is poetry (ποίησις), with the result that all arts (πάσαις ταῖς τέχναις) are kinds of poetry, and their craftsmen (δημιουργοί) are poets" (205C).[8] Plato's thesis here is an important one for Hölderlin: He is saying that creativity is the essence not only of literary poetry, but that poetry itself is an expanded notion that captures the creation of any thing by any craftsmen.[9] Poetry is the source of the *ens creatum*, that realm of all that is created. To grasp nature as creative, to see that man, too, has the power to create, means that the aesthetic plays a central role in the cognition of truth and in the constitution of the beautiful as perfection.[10]

But at an even more important level, the capacity to create, the power of ποίησις, is directly related to that of truth. In the *Timaeus*, Plato makes this link between creation and truth explicit by invoking the idea of creation as an organization into coherence from chaos.[11] This idea of creation is an important one for another reason. For Plato, the relation between the Good (τὸ ἀγαθόν) and Truth (τὸ ἀλήθειον) is synthetic, by which is meant they are both terms that *explain* the same object because both categories *constitute* the same object. At the heart of the Platonic thesis about truth and beauty, however, is the idea that the form of the good is the very precondition for genuine knowledge. The thesis here is that the "form of the good" (ἡ τοῦ ἀγαθοῦ ἰδέα) is one that comes to govern truth. In his *Republic*, Plato further explores the thesis that rational knowledge (i.e., knowledge capable of cognizing Truth) is rooted in the Good and that these, in turn, are related to the Beautiful or that, as Socrates puts it:

> As fair as both truth and knowledge are, you will be right in esteeming this other nature as more beautiful than either; and, as in the previous instance, light and sight may be truly said to be like the sun, and yet not to be the sun, so in this other sphere, knowledge and truth may be deemed to be like the good, but not the good; the good has a place of honor yet higher. (509a)

This relation between the Good and Truth conveys a conception of reason that seeks to capture a much richer and more complete grasp of the totality of any thing. The Platonic Idea (ἰδέα) is therefore not only a nonmaterial thing, it is more importantly an infinite pattern and source for creation of all things. It is not simply that, but perhaps more importantly, it is the very principle, the first cause of what any thing actually is. This is both beautiful and good and true at the same time since Plato does not separate cognition into epistemic, evaluative, and aesthetic spheres, à la Kant, but instead sees that the idea of the good is the pattern and form that allows knowledge of the truth which is never properly manifest in the world of phenomena. The idea of the Good allows us access to a higher form of truth because the Good and the Beautiful in this context mean the fully functioning, perfected form of any thing. To know a true X entails knowing the perfect, fully functioning and developed X. For Plato, the Idea or Form (ἰδέα or εἶδος) is not transcendent and separate from any object, as is too often assumed; it is, rather, the creative principle that *constitutes* the object. The thesis here is that the concept of the Good relates to the notion of truth in the sense that the fullness and completeness of what anything is a condition of its goodness and its truth.

Reason is therefore not an instrumental capacity of the mind, something to be used for the mastery over things and the analytic power to break it down in order to be able to utilize it, in some Baconion or

Cartesian sense of reason. Nature is not mechanism, but process; it is not a machine, but, as the *Timaeus* tells us, a living creature. Even more, Truth is not simply the collection of empirical facts and hypotheses. Rather, Plato's thesis is that the Good and Truth are united concepts insofar as the processual structure of nature is also the very process of aesthetic production. To know truth is to know beauty. This becomes the Good only once we see that the Good of any thing is its truth, its true, complete manifestation, its relative approximation of the ἰδέα, of the formal principles that are inherent in what any thing truly is. Plato employs a neologism, ἀγαθοειδῆ, which means literally the "good-form," and which Plato seems to have invented to capture this complex philosophical concept. This is no doubt why Plato says in the *Republic* that "we can say that the things that are known are known not only because of the good, but also their being (τὸ εἶναι) and essence (τὴν οὐσίαν) come from it as well" (509b). What can this mean? For one thing, it means seeing that the essence of any thing, its truth-content, is dependent on it being what it is, in fulfilling its essential (ideal) structure. Similarly, for something to be good, it must also realize this structure. Trees that do not manifest their ideal form of tree-ness are "bad" trees, they are defective trees. Similarly, trees are beautiful when they manifest this ideal form. The Good, the Beautiful and the True are interdependent dimensions of any object. They constitute the highest status that any object can attain. In this sense, we cannot separate, as Enlightenment rationality sought to do, the relation between these three dimensions of reality.

Separating fact from value, cognition from judgment, can lead us only to the sterile path that Hölderlin is diagnosing and to which he is reacting in *Hyperion*. Reason must attain a higher, more complete and comprehensive grasp of the world. For Hölderlin, this is the core aim of his aesthetic-philosophical project: to show that the overcoming of the subject-object divide can only truly be done through a grasp of aesthetic process. For only the aesthetic—viewed as a process of creation, of the move from chaos to order—actually captures the true structure of the objective world. To understand the process of creation is also to understand truth; we are no longer held under the spell of atomism, empiricism, nominalism, or utilitarianism—aesthetic reflection brings us into the core of being and, in so doing, unites beauty with truth. For these cannot capture the whole, cannot capture process, cannot capture what truly is. The ideal and the real are now reconciled and brought into a new revitalizing force. The subject and the object, once reconciled, constitute a new totality that expands the horizons of the agent and allows him to grasp the true, actual nature of himself and reality. This reconciliation of subject and object is therefore not the *absorption* of the subject into nature, but a *realization* of one's part within a system of creation and becoming.

Plato's argument therefore holds, in its own way, a key to those who would seek an alternative form of rationality that (1) does not abandon the principles of reason and (2) allows for reason to be under the guidance of the principle of the good. Plato's argument is a difficult one, but I think Hölderlin's reception of this thesis is one that seeks to expand the compartmentalized conception of human reason that Kant had delineated and instead insist upon a *synthetic understanding of the capacity for reason*, one that would overcome the split between *noumena* and *phenomena*, *Sein* and *Sollen*, and ultimately lay the foundation for a more critical conception of human reflection and judgment. Now we are to see reason and creation as aspects of the same faculty, as a faculty that can peer into the essential nature of truth as dynamic, total, processual and objective.[12] The reason is that, Hölderlin suggests, the poetic faculty is the form-imposing faculty. It creates reality not *ex nihilo*, but through the organization of form from chaos. It is able to create truth, knowable objects, and nature itself is the most primordial exemplar of this same capacity. As the *Timaeus* made clear, the key to creation was the higher organization of what was already existent. For Hölderlin, the aesthetic was now further allied to the capacity to know truth.

We need to make this move because by doing so we see that the evaluative concepts of the Good, the epistemic concepts that delineate Truth, and the aesthetic concepts that describe the Beautiful are all now describing the same reality. What Hölderlin saw as problematic was the way that modern Enlightenment rationality divided reason into theoretical, practical, and aesthetic forms of cognition. Plato's path was to see that these three spheres of human thinking converged in the domain of real truth. This is because the Good is a prerequisite of any kind of true thing or form. It is "good" in this sense that the stomach secretes digestive enzymes; it is "good" that it does this, it is not only a "fact" that it does it. And we know real truth when we know this kind of good because we know what things are in their most ideal, formal sense. We are able to apprehend the ideal pattern that generates the changing forms of empirical reality. The good and the true are thus united. Proper knowledge, the highest form of intellect—*dianoia* for Plato—is the capacity to grasp the infinite ideal that lies behind the plethora of empirical, temporal manifestations of being. True knowledge of a tree is also knowledge of the best tree, that is, a tree whose functions and properties are near perfection and, in this sense, closer to the ideal pattern of tree-ness. In this sense, it can also be seen to be beautiful. To know and to judge are the same capacity. As Plato puts it in the *Republic*: "This thing that gives the truth to things that are known and grants the knower the capacity to know is, we can say, the form of the good" (508e).

How well this fits with Hölderlin's project of refuting the narrow and instrumental impulse of Enlightenment rationality. Indeed, he is concerned not with the refutation of reason itself and with a Romantic return to feeling and to the mystical. He is concerned that the narrowing of reason will lead to the degradation of man, not his expansion and fulfillment. The unity of aesthetics with rationality therefore means a thicker form of reasoning that is granted critical ballast. The analytic, instrumental force of modern reason is now contrasted with reason as a vehicle not of control and dominance over nature, but rather as the vehicle for the expansion of human flourishing and well-being. Here we can glimpse a kind of rationality that resists the reificatory tendencies of technical reason. For Hölderlin, the Enlightenment must therefore be *critiqued from within*; its principles must be deepened and enriched if they are not to fall into the various problems that he probes in *Hyperion*. Where later critical theorists would react to the alliance between instrumental reason and administered capitalism, Hölderlin sees that the solution to this is to impose an alternative form of rationality, one able to capture the capacity to think and to judge. A culture that severs the relation between fact and value, between what is and what ought to be, can no longer perceive what the true, good forms of life can be. Aesthetics is therefore, for Hölderlin, a means out of the iron cage, a path out of the incomplete and stunted world of human nihilism sustained by the problematic chasm between subject and object as well as idealism and realism that causes the degeneration of the modern world.

V

The core insight here is not to see that Hölderlin's project is an escapist return to nature or some illusory form of vitalism. His project was to make aesthetics into the framework for human understanding, one that would be able to overcome the narrow, more instrumental form of reason that dominated Enlightenment thought. Since he saw the two philosophical poles of his time as Kant and Fichte on the one hand and Spinoza, Schiller, and Leibniz on the other, what was crucial was the way that the development of the ego, of the modern self, is shaped and developed through his erotic striving for unity with nature. This attempt at unity leads to persistent failures, but is only saved from nihilism by the ultimate possibility that man can be regenerated through aesthetic experience. Hölderlin's position is radical and rational insofar as it is both an embrace of reason and impulse toward cultural progress. This is an expanded form of reason that will explode the narrow, egoist market world of the bourgeois, a form of reason that no longer has human unity and perfection in view. The age of reason is being critiqued from within: It is a realization that the Enlightenment project requires a conception of nature for it to be oriented toward the good.

This is what is meant, after all, by ἐν διαφέρον ἐαῦτῷ, or the differentiation of the self within itself: For the basic idea here is that we as aesthetic-rational subjects are not passive aspects of the totality, the whole of nature, but we can create our relation to nature. Our status as free beings, the nature of free activity itself, is now to be understood as the striving for a unity within life, that unity for which nature is the paradigm. We never merge with nature, we come to see ourselves as aspects of it, as unique parts of it. As such, the free life is achieved through being, not activity—a being where man's integration confers upon him the highest potentialities of nature. What Hölderlin does not want is for us to surrender our subjectivity, to retreat into tradition, memory, moral perfection or into the mystical. Unlike his contemporary Novalis, who in 1799 writes his *Die Christenheit oder Europa* in response to a similar diagnosis of modern culture, Hölderlin wants to maintain the powers of the subject, but to see that their full development and actuality can only come about through their grounding in nature, not simply as a set of regulative principles, but rather as constitutive of what their lives should actually be. The end of our culture, our institutions, our activities, all should be seen as constituted by rather than regulated by our relation to the higher, integrated self that can only come about through a conscious relation to the totality of nature. Novalis sees that modern reason has also had deformative effects: "The members were unceasingly occupied with purging poetry from nature, from the soil, from human souls and from the sciences, exterminating all traces of the sacred, polluting the memory of exalting events and men by means of their sarcasm, and robbing the world of all its motley ornamentation."[13] We become one with nature, but only once we have come to see that this is the proper, correct, and rational harmonization of the self and its broader nature. Once we come to see ourselves as organic, dynamic, developmental beings with proper ends and purposes; once we come to see ourselves as potentially able to achieve unity, to overcome the diremption brought about by our estrangement with nature, only then will we attain some degree of perfection.

Indeed, we are not passively resigned to our natural state, in some Spinozist sense, but are rather transformed by our struggle *with* nature. In vain we seek our freedom as autonomous selves, as individuals in tension with nature. We cannot be free through the domination of nature, or by seeing nature, as Fichte did, as the field for our activities and projects. The ego must evolve, must developmentally bring to realization that which it possesses *in potentia*, what has been given to it by nature. The ontological thereby displaces the practical or the epistemic as the highest mode of judging human life. It is for this reason that the paradigm of innocence, of the child, must become the free being, the one who has evolved his rational and aesthetic faculties—faculties that create a new conception of the self. In this sense, Hölderlin's ideas retain their salience within the critical theory tradition, in particular. The pathologies of alienation, reification, and so on all can be understood as generated by the one-sidedness of a deficient form of reason that pervades our self-understanding as well as the institutions of our society. The purposes and ends of our culture no longer provide a home for the kind of unified self that Hölderlin insists exists within us. Only the noninstrumental conception of reason that seeks our development and the higher forms of being of which we are capable are worthy of what we can call a critical social rationality with emancipatory and transformative intent.

For this reason, Hölderlin's conception of nature and of human freedom possesses compelling weight for critical theorists. For unlike the concept of utopia put forward by Ernst Bloch, it is not some kind of "anticipatory illumination" playing a regulative function in relation to our ideas. Rather, for Hölderlin, *it is constitutive of our status and activity as free beings.* We are free only when we create the kind of selves, the kind of culture, that is guided by beauty, by the striving to fulfill the unity of ourselves with nature and to see that the experience of beauty is *constitutive of what nature actually is* in its highest, most developed form and, therefore, what a realized, free humanity can actually become. But this relation between the ego and nature should be understood in deeper terms: It is not a *merging* with nature—it is the realization that the "eccentric path" of the individual is to see the deeper essential truth of what it means to be human, to see the organic, dynamic, purpose of human existence, and that modern culture must give way to a "springtime of humanity" where each individual will operate under the constitutive guidance of nature. "Love bore thousands of years of living men, friendship will give birth to it again (*GW*, p. 367)."

In this sense, we can perhaps return to Mann's proposal about the necessary relation between Hölderlin and Marx: that a nonanthropocentric humanism is not only an ethic, but a foundation—a foundation for our culture, our ethics, our philosophy, the ends and purposes of our institutions, and so on. Indeed, if Marcuse, in his book *The Aesthetic Dimension*, makes use of Schiller's conception of *Spiel*, or "play," as a central category of an aesthetics with emancipatory potential, then perhaps we can see Hölderlin's conception of an aesthetic-philosophical form of reason as a way to rejuvenate the critical force of critical theory. For although Marcuse saw Schiller and his concept of the "play drive" (*Spieltrieb*) as an emancipatory force, Hölderlin's alternative is able to posit for us more than a drive within the self, it is also able to provide for us a much more expanded criterion for our reasons, laws, culture, art, institutions, and such.[14] For Hölderlin, eros plays a role not of subjective creation only, but *an expanded role in actually constituting the good*: It is only when we strive for the absolute, when we can experience the beauty of nature and our inherent connection (*Verbindung*) with it that we can constitute new sensibilities, new powers, and new creations—in short a new way of being. And this is because, as I have sought to demonstrate above, anytime we have aesthetic experience, we are also having a cognitive experience about the true, essential nature of reason and the rationality of the structure of the world: that it is created, dynamic, processual. The beauty is the good because the true nature of the world should be seen as its optimum creation. That which is ugly, which is bad, is therefore an expression of defective creation, lacking the expression of its full potentiality, and therefore its full, true form. Hölderlin is thus no wayward Romantic; he is offering a more compelling idea about the nature of art and its relevance for our epistemic and moral reasoning.

A humanized critical theory would therefore be able to keep in view the irreducibly human ends and purposes of our social world and culture, and these human ends can perhaps be turned into normative-critical categories. It would possess a wider, more encompassing view of reason oriented toward nondestructive purposes and aims—a form of reason circumscribed not in the epistemic subject or congealed in technological objects, but embedded in a developmental and teleological conception of the species and our relation with nature as a whole, making it capable of serving as the ground for a truly radical transformative paradigm. But as I have labored to show in this chapter, this is not to be conflated with some mystical flight from reality or some return to nature; it is rather to be understood as the expression of a kind of reason that grasps the whole, the *totum*, and which, thereby, accords itself to a deeper, more expansive form of rationality. And, even more, it is to understand that the mechanistic expression of reason, of *Verstand*, and of the analytic attitudes are to be governed by a higher set of rational categories. It is this expanded form of reason that allows us to gain insight into the experience of a new, more compelling kind of freedom. Indeed, perhaps then the words of *Hyperion* will resonate with individuals who one day will inhabit a freer, more evolved age:

> We are like fire that sleeps in the dry branch or in flint; and in every moment we struggle and seek the end of our narrow confinements. But they come, they make up for eons of battle, the moments of liberation, when the divine bursts open the prison, when the flame frees itself from the wood and surges victoriously over the ashes, ha! when we feel as if, the sorrows and servitude forgotten, the unfettered spirit returned in triumph into the halls of the sun. (GW, p. 357)

Notes

1. Although the conservative nature of much of Romanticism must be accepted, it cannot be applied to Hölderlin's work and his aesthetic-philosophical project. Lukács's critique can be found in his essay "Hölderlins Hyperion," in his *Goethe und Seine Zeit.* (1947), 110ff.

2. GW = Friederich Hölderlin, *Gesammelte Werke.* Hans Jürgen Bals (ed.). Munich: Carl Hanser Verlag, 1990. Translations from the German are my own.

3. Cf. the discussion in Beiser (2002, p. 397ff.).

4. The resonance here with certain themes in Marx should not be overlooked, in particular the normative categories that ground his critical ideas about capitalist society. See Thompson (2015).

5. Beiser (2002, p. 387).

6. Franz Gabriel Nauen claims: "Following Rousseau and Kant, Hölderlin believed that if man would only consult the beauties of nature, he—retarded by centuries of despotism and superstitious religion—could find his place in the league of free spirits" (Nauen, 1971, p. 52). Although I agree with Nauen on this broad point, it must be pointed out that the need to consult the beauty of nature has a richer purpose than a merely aesthetic-contemplative one. It is Hölderlin's bold aesthetic-philosophical project to merge the categories of truth, beauty, and the good into a united concept. Only in this way would modern man be able to achieve freedom and to move beyond the forces of modernity that were fragmenting him.

7. Nathan Ross insightfully comments on Hölderlin's project as one that urges modern man "to think of an ideal state of freedom, in which the subject does not command itself but enters into a fruitful interplay with the world, and to think of the experience of beauty as the transformative experience that would allow us to cognize and realize such a state" (Ross, 2017, p. 82).

8. All references to Plato's works employ the relevant Stephanus numbers. Translations from the Greek are my own.

9. See the important discussion of the Platonic ἰδέα and its function as a creative process by Chambers (1936).

10. As Hölderlin remarks in his essay "Grund zum Empedokles": "Nature and Art are only opposed harmoniously in pure life. Art is the blossom, the perfected completion (*Vollendung*) of nature; Nature first becomes divine through the conjunction with the diverse, but harmonious art; when everything is what it can be and one conjoins itself with the other, compensates for the defects of the other, which that one necessarily must have, in order to be that which it can as a particular, then there exists completed perfection (*die Vollendung*), and the divine rests in the middle of both" (GW, p. 560). The aesthetic reflection of man therefore helps to complete the brute facts of raw nature. In the process, man is brought to perfection as well since he is brought into the realm of perfection and into the realm of the universal thereby overcoming his particularity as his aesthetic reflection overcomes the particularity of the object of nature.

11. See *Timaeus* D 33 and *passim*. In particular, Plato points to the idea that the creation of the cosmos by God was intended to be like a living creature as well as being a whole, composite of all other wholes. "These were his intentions: first, in order for it to be whole, it would be like a grown creature perfected from its perfected parts (ὅ τι μάλιστα ζῷον τέλεον ἐκ τελέων τῶν μερῶν εἴη)" (D 33). The idea of the cosmos as a living creature, of nature as a living organism with the ends and processes of life, is what Hölderlin refers to as the subjective factor of man and his ability to complete and to cognize this truth in nature. This truth is also, at the same time, constitutive of the Beautiful and the Good.

12. As Beiser aptly puts it: "It is indeed more accurate to regard understanding and reason as distinct functions of a single faculty rather than distinct faculties: they are ultimately the same faculty because they have the same source and object, namely, the striving toward the infinite. It's just that they approach their object in different ways" (Beiser, 2003, p. 61).

13. Novalis (1955, p. 134).

14. See the discussion of Marcuse's use of Schiller by Paul Guyer, who argues that "in spite of his Kantian language he meant to praise Kant himself only as a precursor of Schiller. That may be, but then the important point is Schiller too understands the free play of our powers in aesthetic experience in more narrowly cognitive and metaphysical and less globally psychological terms than Marcuse does." Guyer (2008). Also cf. the discussion by Charles Larmore (2000, p. 141ff).

References

Adorno T. W., & M. Horkheimer (1972). *Dialectic of Enlightenment*. New York, NY: Continuum.

Beiser, F. (2002). *German Idealism: The Struggle against Subjectivism, 1781–1801*. Cambridge, MA: Harvard University Press.

Beiser, F. (2003). *The Romantic Imperative: The Concept of Early German Romanticism*. Cambridge, MA: Harvard University Press.

Chambers, L. P. (1936). "Plato's Objective Standard of Value." *Journal of Philosophy, 33*(22), 596–605.

Guyer, P. (2008). "Marcuse and Classical Aesthetics." *Revue Internationale de Philosophie, 246*, 349–365.

Henrich, D. (1997). *The Course of Remembrance and Other Essays on Hölderlin*. Stanford, CA: Stanford University Press.

Larmore, C. (2000). "Hölderlin and Novalis." In Karl Ameriks (ed.), *The Cambridge Companion to German Idealism*. Cambridge, UK: Cambridge University Press.

Lukács, G. (1947). *Goethe und Seine Zeit*. Bern, Switzerland: A. Franck AG, Verlag.

Nauen, F. G. (1971). *Revolution, Idealism and Human Freedom: Schellng, Hölderlin and Hegel and the Crisis of Early German Idealism*. The Hague, Netherlands: Martinus Nijhoff.

Novalis (1955). *Die Christenheit oder Europa*. In *The Political Thought of the German Romantics*. Oxford, UK: Basil Blackwell.

Ross, N. (2017). *The Philosophy and Politics of Aesthetic Experience: German Romanticism and Critical Theory*. New York, NY: Palgrave.

Thompson, M. J. (2015). "Philosophical Foundations for a Marxian Ethics." In M. Thompson (ed.), *Constructing Marxist Ethics: Critique, Normativity, Praxis* (pp. 235–265). Leiden, UK: Brill.

Chapter 7

From Mirror to Catalyst

Whitman and the Literature of Re-Creation

JAMES BLOCK

The great novelists of the 19th century, perhaps none more powerfully and pitilessly than Flaubert and Melville, held up a mirror, a vast canvas, to the failure of individuals to make use of their liberation from traditional society with its ascribed castes and rigid markers of status. When placed alongside the exemplary novels portraying the ever-heightening class distinctions in the emerging world of industrial wealth and poverty, modern literature appeared to have in the main succumbed to providing a record of what was not possible. In this age, it seemed to be saying, the extravagant claims about the potentialities of modernity were just that: misguided and misleading claims.

Things at the beginning of the 21st century are somewhat different. To be sure, class differentiations now are not only more extreme but seemingly more intransigent than ever, a perspective persuasively advanced by Thomas Piketty in *Capital in the Twenty-First Century* (2014) with evidence of a return to patrimonial capitalism (or neo-feudalism). At the same time, unlike the 19th century, there are few who claim this shift to be more than a vast grasping for power and control by plutocratic elites. In other words, the terms of the discourse have shifted dramatically, and with the powers of insight provided by the new moral paradigm we can now recognize in Flaubert and Melville (the *Pequod* goes down), in Balzac and Austen, Mann and Eliot, a devastating critique of hierarchy and domination. What was once taken to be a mirror is now more accurately regarded as a veiled bill of indictment.

A major catalyst in this discursive transformation has been literature itself. The novel, once regarded as constrained by its rhetoric of verisimilitude, was long thought to be less flexible a site for advancing social vision. This view has been challenged more recently in novels by Margaret Atwood, Marge Piercy, Ursula LeGuin, and others, going back even to Melville's *Billy Budd* and Bellamy's *Looking Backward*, which have stretched the possibilities of the medium. Yet, it is perhaps in poetry, from Rimbaud to Rilke to William Carlos Williams, that the project of imaginative re-creation has been more fully advanced. And a central figure in that project, perhaps its great epical voice, is Walt Whitman. In our time, when hegemony and cynicism feed upon each other in a death spiral, his voice speaks with unequalled power, fierce intensity, and dogged insistence that *what is* is not *what can and shall be*, and that the literary voice must serve as a guide and catalyst to the pathways of transformation.

Whitman's timeliness takes on special meaning in an age in which the forces of transformation have lost their way. Unable in the spirit of Marx to absorb the great achievements of the modernist age and to dialectically subsume them within a greater vision of human possibility than liberal and neoliberal capitalism, these impulses have been stymied. In order not to appear entirely bereft, theorists of the left—when they can resist the easy temptations of apocalypse—have settled for a resolute naysaying. What neoliberalism asserts the theorists of negation reject, offering only a film negative mirror of the arrogant displays of raw late modern power and hegemony, that is, of the world they resist. Ignoring the clamor for alternatives, they resist acknowledging that "no" is not an alternative to "yes."

Progressive forces have given up the language of liberation—the very concepts of individual and individualism, autonomy and freedom, development and self-development and self-realization, consent and genuine democratic citizenship, recognition and self-recognition, with which it can be announced. In so doing, they have whittled away the very ground on which a future age of emancipation could rise. Whitman perhaps more than anyone foresaw this crisis as the modern age struggled to chart a course of postliberal transformation. He prophesied in *Democratic Vistas* that the coming age was at hand, forestalled by the incapacity of individuals raised in earlier and more repressive orders to grasp the great potentialities lying all about to be seized.

This new age, Whitman believed, would occur in the United States, because the United States had—through its prior history—laid the groundwork most fully for a just and realized late modern society. Having already achieved what at the time existed nowhere else, the two essential precursors to transformation, political democracy and material abundance, Americans were poised to undertake the third and decisive step, the spiritual and psychopolitical transformation of values to a genuine inclusive democracy of self-actualized individuals. This new world would build upon, and appropriate, the deeper spiritual aspirations of the modernizing quest for the good life and the good society. Within the language of liberalism already developed lay incipient possibilities for transformation. By utilizing the practical achievements of this earlier liberal age and expanding the vision it could suggest but not realize, the deeper potential of modernity would become accessible.

This project is given powerful conceptual form in *Democratic Vistas*, but would achieve its fullest evolution and expression in the epic poetry of *Song of Myself*. Whitman knew the power of literature, advocating in *Democratic Vistas* for poets of the new to lead the way as only literature could (once religion had declined), creating the characters, self-hoods, and identities that would help Americans and others shape themselves for full democratic life. Poetry could also as no other form of expression call each through its incantatory power to the popular journey toward a world where all were to be included in the achievement of new selves and new bonds. Poetry (as literature), in other words, was a form of activism.

The incantatory voice in *Song of Myself* works by a continually heightening call (and response, which is the reader/hearer's responsibility). In order to suggest this prophetic, sermonic power, I will group some of the myriad and irrepressible calls on specific themes. As the poem reaches out to its participant audiences, the responsibility of each to take this transformative journey to a new form of selfhood—and the responsibility of the poet to point out the path—is clearly announced:

"I launch all men and women forward with me into the
   Unknown" (Stanza 44).

"I tramp a perpetual journey, come listen all . . .
Not I, not anyone else can travel that road for you,
You must travel it for yourself.
It is not far, it is within reach,
Perhaps you have been on it since you were born and did
    not know,
Perhaps it is everywhere on water and on land.
. . . let us hasten forth" (St. 46).

"You are also asking me questions and I hear you,
I answer that I cannot answer, you must find out for yourself."
    (St. 46)

"If you want me again look for me under your boot-soles. . . .
Failing to fetch me one place search another,
I stop somewhere waiting for you." (St. 52)

In part, this nurturing of individual responsibility and self-mastery
is one of the capacities literature possessed, and is the reason the poet
gave up theory, "creeds and schools in abeyance," (St. 1):

"Stop this day and night with me and you shall possess the
    origin of all poems. . . .
You shall no longer take things at second or third hand,
nor look through the eyes of the dead, nor feed on the
    spectres in books." (St. 2)

"Backward I see in my own days where I sweated through fog
    with linguists and contenders,
I have no mockings or arguments, I witness and wait." (St.4)

"I know this orbit of mine cannot be swept by a carpenter's
    compass. . . .
I do not trouble my spirit to vindicate itself or be
    understood,
I see that the elementary laws never apologize." (St.20)

"Hurrah for positive science! Long live exact
    demonstration. . . .

Your facts are useful, and yet they are not my dwelling."
   (St. 23)

"I do not give lectures . . .
When I give I give myself." (St. 40)

The first goal of a literature of re-creation is to take us beyond existing boundaries and boxes (an image used in *Democratic Vistas*), beyond the known and expected, the conventional and taken for granted:

"I wear my hat as I please indoors or out." (St. 20)

"Unscrew the locks from the doors!
Unscrew the doors themselves from their jambs!'" (St. 24)

"Inland and sea-coast we go, and pass all boundary lines,"
   (St. 38)

"Behavior lawless as snow-flakes . . .
I force surfaces and depths also." (St. 39–40)

"And I swear I will never again mention love or death inside
   a house,
And I swear I will never translate myself at all. . . .
No shutter'd room or school can commune with me,
But roughs and little children better than they." (St. 47)

"I too am not a bit tamed, I too am untranslatable,
I sound my barbaric yawp over the roofs of the world." (St.
   52)

This function of literature, as anthropologist Michael Jackson develops in his recent philosophical inquiry *Hanrattan*, is to open us up to spaces and dynamics beyond the city walls, what in Africa is the "bush," the untamed everywhere. In part, this involves what I call in the spirit of Whitman the process of *unnaming*, of dissolving the established definitional systems in place and opening language and meaning. In part, as well, beyond the liminal state after unnaming is what for Whitman becomes the role of literature and poetry that theory cannot access, and yet is necessary to even begin the process of transformative theorizing. Whitman calls this "the unseen" (St. 3) all in the previous language "forbidden," (St. 24) "Less the reminders of properties told my words, And more the reminders they of life untold" (St. 23), gained through this process of "freedom and extrication." (St. 23)

The deepest function of the poetic imagination is to "turn from gazing after and down the road" (St. 3) at the facts, and to the *unseen*. Here Whitman distinguishes newly between the process of causation and the process of apprehension. Without perceptual access to the unseen, we cannot determine directly the first causes of meaning and spirit, but as we dwell among the results, we must infer the unseen, which can be "proved [only] by the seen." (St. 3) We must discern the "origin of all poems" (St. 2) from our own first-hand experience, rather than posit a first cause in the unseen, a divinity or primum causum, to fill the blind spot and thereby persuade ourselves that we are in touch with the causal process. We must take back this god projection as a product of our own drive to become our own first causes of meaning.

We must then, "already a creator" (St. 41) by "Accepting the rough deific sketches to fill out better in myself," find "as much or more" insight "in a framer framing a house" (St. 41) and in our everyday world. In this way, we can constitute ourselves as first causes:

> "Divine I am inside and out, and I make holy whatever I touch or am touch'd from." (St. 24)

> "And I know that the hand of God is the promise of my own,
> And I know that the spirit of God is the brother of my own." (St. 5)

> "I am the mate and companion of people, all just as immortal . . . as myself." (St. 7)

> As first cause, I "now and always send sun-rise out of me." (St. 25)

> "Walking the old hills of Judea with the beautiful gentle God by my side. . . .
> I take part, I see and hear the whole." (St. 33)

"And nothing, not God, is greater to one than one's self
   is . . .
And I say to mankind, Be not curious about God . . .
I hear and behold God in every object . . .
Nor do I understand who there can be more wonderful
   than myself. . . .
In the faces of men and women I see God, and in my own
   face in the glass,
I find letters from God dropt in the street, and every one is
   sign'd by God's name." (St. 48)

At the same time, creation is by no means a physical act of constituting the cosmos. Rather, bringing values into the world is the work of the poet, as one with access to Eros, to the primary process by which meaning emerges, erupts, out of our libidinal center. This is Walt as his most Whitmanian, evident in the rhythms, the vast waves and tides embodying the epic, a libidinal epic, as he tells us from the outset:

"I harbor for good or bad, I permit to speak at every hazard,
Nature without check with original energy. (St. 1)

"I will go to the bank by the wood and become undis-
   guised and naked." (St. 2)

"Urge and urge and urge,
Always the procreant urge of the world,
Out of the dimness opposite equals advance, always sub-
   stance and increase, always sex,
Always a knit of identity, always distinction, always a breed
   of life." (St. 3)

"All goes onward and outward, nothing collapses." (St. 6)

The goal of the poet, then, is to craft a "new tongue." (St. 21) Through "new forms" that "descend . . . from the tips of his fingers," that are "wafted with the odor of his body or breath" and "fly out of the glance of his eyes," (St. 39) the poet can make our unseen first cause as creator seen, the liberating and empowering unseen that must be recovered in order to effect the process, the journey of transformation.

This journey, which is the path that the poem helps us to identify, is not a process of institutional transformation. For Whitman, the
institutions that will facilitate the process of transformation have already
done the preliminary work. A full and genuine democracy will come only
after each journey to a more encompassing self. What he sings to us, the
result of the song he has written for himself ("I celebrate myself, and sing
myself") (St. 1), is the "chant of dilation or pride," the effort to "show
that size," our full size, is the result of "only development" at which will
"arrive there everyone" (St. 21). Too long "We have had ducking and
deprecating about enough" (St. 21), "Long enough have you dream'd
contemptible dreams," making oneself smaller and retarding one's growth
in order to fit alongside those who stifle their own growth. We must
be a "bold swimmer," and "habit yourself to the dazzle of the light and
of every moment of your life" (St. 46). We must make "higher claims"
and "special revelations" as "Magnifying and applying come I" (St. 41).

As we walk toward the hills of Judea, toward our own special
revelation, we become individuals, fully developed, with autonomy and
freedom, as liberalism ambiguously offered and retracted, living a new
form and speaking a new language in a world where there will be "never
any more perfection than there is now, Nor any more heaven or hell
than there is now" (St. 3). The poem helps us to rename these capacities
toward which we shape firsthand our stories of self-development as we
become authors of our own meaning systems, enunciated most clearly in
his bold declaration, "Walt Whitman, a kosmos" (St. 24), in a universe
of authorial suns and meaning system.

This new world will involve a moral transvaluation. Evil is no
longer to be feared but to be understood:

> "I am not the poet of goodness only, I do not decline to be
>   the poet of wickedness also.
> What blurt is this about virtue and about vice?
> Evil propels me and the reform of evil propels me. . . .
> My gait is no fault-finder's or rejectors gait;
> I moisten the roots of all that has grown." (St. 22)

Evil is the product of inadequate or stifled growth, it is the *result of
privation*, and thus not to be condemned or judged but suffered with and
surmounted. We are, he says, "Wicked rather than virtuous out of con-
formity or fear." (St. 47). Thus, the poet of democratic selfhood is "No

sentimentalist, no stander above men and women or apart from them," singing also the "Voices of the diseas'd and despairing and of thieves and dwarfs" so that they can be "by me clarified and transfigur'd." (St. 24)

As Whitman enables us to rename our moral code and our own journey to selfhood beyond the boundaries of the older moral, psychosocial order, so too do we achieve the capacity and moral resolution to rename our common world and our lives together. Following out the logic of the poem, the political achievement of democracy and of its two principal components, equality of worth, which in *Democratic Vistas* he will call justice (in Plato's expansive and comprehensive sense of a political cosmological first principle of desert and entitlement), and consent, are only possible with and among self-realizing and self-loving authors.

Neither is possible, as Rousseau understood, in the liberal age: Given its construction of selfhood as an earned achievement, differential rewards are accorded necessarily in a competitive, nearly zero sum system. That some—it turns out many—must and will in sociologist Howard Becker's analysis lose in order to emphasize the link between striving and well-being, is the cost of mobilizing conventional instrumental productiveness. So, when some people lapse, fall behind, have trouble, that is taken as a judgment (originally divine, now societal) of their worth, there can be no call for help or facilitation or nurturance but rather their use as an object lesson of the costs of failure for all, but particularly the young, to ingest.

For Whitman, contrarily, our universal, incommensurable (who self-loves more?—the very question is a failure of self-love, a form of Rousseau's hollow vanity) self-worth makes just distribution and care imperatives. This does not mean that the issues of justice are somehow resolved as in a weak reading of Rousseau's General Will. Rather, well-meaning, self-loving Authors can still reason together about the ends of the society and what the common priorities should be given the inevitable limits on resources. Consent in turn, the capacity to promise—"I know that the hand of God is the *promise* of my own" (St. 5; emphasis added)—and to covenant in the sense of Hannah Arendt is only possible between and among self-derived equals: "The boy I love, the same becomes a man not through derived power, but in his own right" (St. 47).

And recognition, that bane of our time, is anchored in our own self-recognition as authors that enables us to recognize others and—evident in all of Whitman's work—the potential of others as authors in the making. That is, recognition has a necessarily self-referential foundation and in turn a critical—or rather, I would say, aspirational—center in moving us beyond perceptions of surfaces, of appearances and poses, to the deep human core of self and social reconstruction.

Realizing that assertions of privilege and unequal forms of power invalidate the possibility of justice, democratic society is an inclusive project, "This is a meal equally set. . . . I will not have a single person slighted or left away" (St. 19); "Not one kneels to another" (St. 32). Here we are free because we are equal and thus not dependent for our leverage on the psychological and functional deficits imposed on others.

A society constituted in mutual self-recognition and self-empowerment, nurturing the many diverse journeys of self-actualization, is the Song we weave individually and together, the transcendence of the liberal age even as the tools and resources of that age are redeployed toward heightened ends. From this point, filling out the project requires theory, though less of it, than the work of individual and mutual growth to fill out our "rough deific sketches" as they are fueled by our Eros, our natural energy, released to the task of self-actualization. Just as Plato provided us with a world structured by the superego, and Hobbes and liberalism dissolved the superego and provided a world structured by the ego, so have Rousseau and his great poets, Emerson and Whitman, called us to a world that rises from our primal human energy. Joining in this radical project is the path forward.

References

Piketty, T. (2014). *Capital in the Twenty-First Century*. Cambridge, MA, and London, UK: Harvard University Press.

Whitman, W. (1964). *Leaves of Grass and Selected Prose*. New York, NY: Holt, Rinehart and Winston.

Chapter 8

The City of Brothers

Mark P. Worrell and Dan Krier

Society is a thing of thought, a syllogism that is either wrong or right. The key to any syllogism is mediating particularity, and mediation is, as Bataille saw, the product of human aggregation and the necessary precondition for every form of interaction. However, for Bataille, the "inevitable middle term" was also, inevitably "terrifying" (1988, p. 107). The notion of an alien social nucleus, where inversion transforms mana into taboo (a negative mana roughly synonymous with pure heteronomy and swift, automatic, and harsh punishments), is more or less compatible with, say, Zizek's vision of the radical ambiguity of the Lacanian Big Other. However, this is not faithful to the even more ambiguous nature of the Hegelian Universal with respect to its appearance within the disjunctive syllogism. Where, for example, Zizek sees Christ as an ambiguous monstrosity, Hegel's finite (open) universal container filled with individuality, particularity, and universality (universality itself *redoubled*) made possible the negation and resublimation of universality onto the same ontological plane as the individual and particular, the reduction of a "god" to an empirical object of love requiring ongoing completion through the act of sustained mediation with empirically real others. Here, the enjoyment of the third is in line not with Bataille and Zizek but with Nietzsche, where "the third is the cork that prevents the conversation of the two from sinking into the depths" (1982, p. 168). However, we need

223

more than a cork to prevent sinking into nonbeing. What is needed is an Other that prevents wasted energies, human degradation, and also prohibits charismatic self-exaltation and tyrannical ascendency of, say, a tangerine oligarch over a mass of dupes.

What does a society regulated by such a Big Other, or, here, (an)other, sans neurosis or psychosis, a world with a mediating term but without reification (The Thing) or alienation (The Monster) look like? A strong case can be made that the most popular American effort to produce such an imaginary is found in Walt Whitman's *Leaves of Grass*. Whitman was, in his own way, not only *the* poet of democracy and the poet of the working person but also the *Hegelian* poet. Hegel makes a few appearances in *Leaves* and within his correspondence, but Whitman was also friends with the Saint Louis Hegelians, a reader of their *Journal of Speculative Philosophy*, and dabbled in German philosophy and literature from time to time. Lastly, his impact crossed the Atlantic to influence German thinkers and European revolutionaries; in Germany, Whitman was also a hit with Marxists (Erkkila, 1980; Grünzweig, 1995). Thomas Mann was so enthused by *Leaves of Grass* that he not only elevated Whitman to the same rank as Goethe but conceived of them as necessary counterparts:

> . . . for me this book has been nothing less than a gift from heaven, for now I really see that what Whitman calls "*democracy*" is nothing other than what we, in an old-fashioned usage, call "humanity"; just as I also see that it cannot be done with Goethe alone, that a shot of Whitman will be necessary to achieve the feeling of the new humanity, even though these two fatherly figures have much in common, above all the sensual element, the "Calamus," a sympathy with the organic. (2007, p. 109)

What the good gray poet lacked as far as the grasping of fine-grained details he made up for in terms of his comprehension of the overall arc of the program and, importantly, its aesthetic implementation. His friend Traubel recounted a conversation he had with Whitman in 1890 in which the poet said of Hegel: 'I have held Hegel the top of the heap so far because of his acceptivity: it seems to me he fit better than any other to America, to its democracy, its aspiration, its future. And that was a big key for a big door' (1992, p. 63). In "The Base of all Metaphysics,"

Whitman concluded that "Having studied the new and antique, the Greek and Germanic systems, Kant having studied and stated, Fichte and Schelling and Hegel. . . ." that under it all resides "The dear love of man for his comrade, the attraction of friend to friend . . ." (1992, pp. 91–92). However, Whitman's affinity for German philosophy was alloyed with other currents of thought, including, to name just two, Comte's positive sociology (Erkkila, 1980, p. 41) and Emersonian transcendentalism. In a nutshell, few thinkers were as eclectic (in the positive sense of, say, Plato or Victor Cousin) as Whitman. Whitman's basic problem came down to capitalism. As Erkkila says,

> At the same time that Karl Marx was making his revolutionary critique of Western capitalism, Whitman began mounting his own attack on American capitalism from the viewpoint of the laboring class. Like Marx, he recognized that the economics of capitalism "enters every transaction of society" and "taints its soundness," but by focusing on the problem of monopoly and corporate wealth, he avoided the potential contradiction between the free-enterprise society he lived in and the harmonious and egalitarian democratic society of his dreams. (1989, p. 37)

Here, though, the critical critic will suspect a creeping mysticism; is not Whitman guilty of promoting a religion in the guise of poetry? There is no need to hide from the facts and, really, are we not all after a religion (or cult) of reason anyway?[1] Whitman thought of himself as religious and definitely held up *Leaves* as new scripture for Americans. But even though Whitman himself believed he was creating a new religion, in fact, literally nobody recognized what he was doing as religiously valid—far from it; his work was commonly seen as not only base or sacrilegious but even pornographic. *Leaves* is, if you believe Whitman's own statements, a "sacred" text (and perhaps it is best to see the *book itself* as Whitman's god descended) but his version of "religion" was so eclectic and radical that, as a religion, it was anathema to even religiously eclectic America.

As a youth, Whitman was marinated in virtually every theological current circulating in Brooklyn, but those that appealed most to him were freethinkers, Deists, and, importantly, Hicksite Quakers—such an extreme form of Quakerism that the blood of Jesus was held to be no better "than that of a bull or a goat, a heresy even more extreme than

Emerson's later rejection of the Unitarian communion" (Reynolds, 1995, p. 37).[2] Here was Whitman, then, creating what he hoped was a new kind of biophilic scripture (cf. Fromm, 1964) that was, as it turns out, repulsive to virtually all religious people then and, especially, now. The irony, of course, is that Whitman's religious aim resulted in a purely down-to-earth manifesto of human solidarity that is philosophically and sociologically coherent, while scientific and humanist Marxism, to put it bluntly, often falls into its own form of theology—little wonder, then, why Durkheim waved off Marxist socialism as "a cry of grief, sometimes of anger, uttered by men who feel most keenly our collective *malaise*" (Durkheim, 1958, p. 41). Far from pulling the wool over the eyes of dupes, *Leaves* contains a rational philosophy, political economy, anthropology, sociology, and a psychology as it calls together the masses in a unique form of solidarity and brotherly love; it is a product of its time but, like all great works, it also transcends the 19th century, and, most important, it contains something essential found in Hegel that was lacking in Marx that helps us comprehend the gap between Marx's immaculate sociological critique of the commodity and his merely "pragmatic" delineation of postcapitalist society.

Like nobody since Hegel was the speculative philosophy of the imagined other of humanity better articulated than by Whitman. In "Are You the New Person Drawn Toward Me?" we see the crucial immanence and finitude of the mediating nucleus:

> Are you the new person drawn toward me?
> To begin with take warning, I am surely far different from what you suppose;
> Do you suppose you will find in me your idea?
> Do you think it so easy to have me become your lover?
> Do you think the friendship of me would be unalloy'd satisfaction?
> Do you think I am trust and faithful?
> Do you see no further than this facade, this smooth and tolerant manner of me?
> Do you suppose yourself advancing on real ground toward a real heroic man?
> Have you no thought O dreamer that it may be all maya, illusion? (1992, p. 93).

Love is not conditional, and perfection is not required: You are perfect, because I love you.[3] "None but has found you imperfect, I only find no imperfection in you, None but would subordinate you, I only am he who will never consent to subordinate you, I only am he who places over you no master, owner, better, God, beyond what waits intrinsically in yourself" (1992, p. 177). As far as selves go, you have a good one, and everyone is capable of locating their self in *Leaves*, it invites all, but poetic selfhood is a collective and regulative project, and more than nominally independent monads and dyadic frivolity are required for the project of human actualization. Together, we are perfect and free.

In the poem "To You," Whitman's great other says, "Whoever you are, now I place my hand upon you, that you be my poem." We have, here, a poetic subject-object identity. The retrospective unity of Whitman and Hegel lies in the Platonic conception of *poiesis*. Marxism in various forms has championed praxis as the unity of thought and action, but praxis is far less sublime than *poiesis*, creativity in general. The "passage of non-being into being" says Plato, "is poetry or making, and the processes of all art are creative; and the masters of arts are all poets" (1945, p. 335). And music is one of the many forms of poiesis. The underlying thread that connects everything in *Leaves* is the collective song—singing, chanting, the chorus. (Hegel's *Phenomenology* introduces music and song as important markers of *turning points* in the development of Spirit). We have a model of currents of collective ebullience creating strong bonds of solidarity minus self-degradation and minus charismatic exaltation. We have no need for a categorical imperative or external laws levied from above; ascetic self-torture is anathema, and *piacular* violence is evil. The bond is the common song and the unique occupation.

Whitman's construct was many things. Above all, perhaps, the great self of *Leaves* was the common companion or (br)other or (an) other of its readers. Whitman's *Leaves* was the brother *and* sister of every member of humanity. The universal sibling of love was the foundation for the expansion of the sociological second family. Inspired by the German romantics and by Hegelianism, broadly conceived, as well as other native movements and international currents of thought, Whitman constructed what is, arguably, the most comprehensive, poetic condensation of the speculative logic as it pertains to the problem of social mediation. Where Marxian praxis has led to nothing but failure on top of failure, critical *poiesis* offers new possibilities.[4]

Marx's historical materialist (social realist) theory of the commodity does not rest on the same ontic ground as his theory of communism—the latter, more or less, relies on a set of "pragmatic" assumptions that are appropriate for two moments within an overall sociogonic arc: toward the beginning and toward the end. In *Capital*, Marx caught exchange value in its full trinitarian splendor, yet, his representation of communism is that of comrades either milling about the cafe or zealots engaged in collective suicide; Marx had no image of mature communism. Marx's "pragmatic" or constructionist representation frees him from responsibility for something like Stalinism (the portrait of the Communard is one that goes little further than the "law of the heart" in Hegel's *Phenomenology*), yet, we find that his vision of communism is also, due to what it lacks, not *logically inconsistent* with terrifying devolution. To prevent a social space from degenerating into a war of all and the ascendency of the strong over the weak, where might makes right, some authoritative and universal substance is required to mediate the passions of individuals. Without this universal, "they lose everything" (Hegel, 1977, p. 227). Marx was a critical disciple of Hegel's dialectical method, but what apparently escaped his notice was that a key part of Hegel's logic, the syllogistic procession that leads from subjectivity to objectivity, contains more than he thought it did; it seems he was hung up on universal mediation as only resulting in the kind of society capitalism creates where money, the universal social substance, mediates all intercourse and reduces humans to brutes. Marx presents us with an everything-or-nothing choice: either no universal mediation leading to some kind of vague "pragmatic" freedom, or, alternately, universal mediation leading, inevitably, to servitude under some inhuman, absolute other. Marx could not imagine, apparently, that his own "pragmatic" immediacy could also leave an opening for terrifying personifications. We argue that Hegel offers another, weirder form of universal mediation neglected by Marx and that a lack of universal mediation would render any possible transparent, postcapitalist utopia a psychotic atopia. Critical praxis, today, hardly more than a stale crouton, is not, nor was it ever, the panacea that most theorists believe. Critical *poiesis* offers an intriguing alternative because it opens up a way to grapple with immanent universal social mediation and also exposes a major flaw in Marxology: a lack of an "anthropology" of energy that can account for more than labor and combat.

Notes

The chapter's title is from Whitman: "I dreamed in a dream of a city where all the men were like brothers" (quoted in Parker, 1996, n.p.).

1. As Caillois says, religion is merely the "administration of the sacred" (1959, p. 20) and do we not hold reason to be sacred?

2. Whitman's Quaker antecedents are important and suggestive. While many analysts have singled out Calvinism-Puritanism as the source of bourgeois economic theology, Weber dwelt with equal intensity upon Quakers and Pietists. The Religious Society of Friends and German Pietists, the "other" Protestant ethics, shared an orientation to brotherly love (rooted in part in the heart-religion of German mystics like Boehme), practical piety, and ethical workaday conduct with a profound commitment to egalitarian social relations. Both deemphasized God the Father (supramundane, remote, inscrutable) in favor of an egalitarian, accessible spiritual immanence imagined as the "inner light" by the Quakers and "brother Jesus" by Pietists (especially Zinzendorf). These religions of brotherly (and sisterly) love were not granular but social: Access to the spirit was mediated (focused, enhanced, amplified) by egalitarian community (the Quaker meeting and Pietist conventicle). In both Quakerism and Pietism, spiritual mediation was not accomplished through ritual sacrifice to imaginary totems, but through the transparent presence "in the real" of a moral community. The journey from such a religious society of friends to a postcapital society of comrades is a short step. Though some have found a relationship between Pietism and political authoritarianism, especially in Prussia (Gawthrop, 1993), we note that folkway systems rooted in Quakerism-Pietism (U.S. North and Midwest; Northern European Social Democracies) tend to correlate with egalitarian political and economic systems (see Krier & Amidon, 2015, p. 358).

3. You are not loved due to positive qualities, rather, positive qualities are the product of love.

4. Novalis, in such thoughts, is very close to Whitman, who once said that at the core of democracy, finally, there resides a religious element, and who shows himself to be in love with the words "en masse" in both his prose and his poetry. That is, like Novalis, who turns it into nothing more and nothing less than a mystical formula. He dreams of human immortality, "en masse," and of a higher, composed human being, the genius. Plurality, he says, is genius. Every person who is composed of several persons is a person to the second power or a genius. . . . He offers observations on living and thinking "en masse," and finds that if symphilosophy or thinking in common were possible, then a common will would also be possible, the realization of great, new ideas. "Community, pluralism is our inmost essence, and perhaps everybody has a certain share in what I am thinking and doing, just as I have in the thoughts of other human

beings." "Just as philosophy, by means of systematic thinking and the state, strengthen the powers of the individual with the powers of humanity and the world as a totality, so poetry, with respect to life. The individual lives in the whole and the whole in the individual. From poetry stems the highest sympathy and shared activity, the most intimate community of the nite and in nite. 'Salut au monde!'" (Mann, 2007, p. 124).

References

Bataille, G. ([1938] 1988). Attraction and repulsion I: Tropisms, laughter and tears. In D. Hollier (ed.), *The College of Sociology* (pp. 103–112). Minneapolis, MN: University of Minnesota Press,

Caillois, R. (1959). *Man and the Sacred*. Urbana: University of Illinois Press.

Durkheim, E. (1958). *Socialism*. New York, NY: Collier.

Erkkila, B. (1980). *Walt Whitman among the French*. Princeton, NJ: Princeton University Press.

Erkkila, B. (1989). *Whitman: The Political Poet*. New York, NY: Oxford University Press.

Fromm, E. (1964). *The Heart of Man*. New York, NY: Harper and Row.

Gawthrop, R. L. (1993). *Pietism and the Making of Eighteenth-Century Prussia*. Cambridge, UK: Cambridge University Press.

Grünzweig, W. (1995). *Constructing the German Walt Whitman*. Iowa City: University of Iowa Press.

Hegel, G. W. F. ([1807] 1977). *Phenomenology of Spirit*. Translated by A. V. Miller. Oxford, UK: Oxford University Press.

Krier, D., & Amidon, K. S. (2015). Critical theory and the limits of academic economics: Resolving the political in Piketty's *Capital in the Twenty-First Century*. *Critical Sociology*, *41*(2), 349–358.

Mann, T. (2007). On the German Republic. *Modernism/modernity*, *14*(1), 109–132.

Nietzsche, F. (1982). *The Portable Nietzsche*. New York, NY: Penguin.

Parker, H. (1996). The Real "Live Oak, with Moss": Straight talk about Whitman's "Gay Manifesto." *Walt Whitman Archive*. www.whitmanarchive.org/criticism/current/anc.00157.html

Plato (1945). Symposium. In *The Works of Plato*, Vol. 4 (pp. 293–358). New York, NY: Tudor.

Reynolds, D. (1996). *Walt Whitman's America*. New York, NY: Vintage.

Traubel, H. (1992). *With Walt Whitman in Camden, Vol. 7*. Carbondale: Southern Illinois University Press.

Whitman, W. ([1892] 1992). *Leaves of Grass*. New York, NY: Book of the Month Club.

Chapter 9

Critical Theory, Sociology, and Science-Fiction Films

Love, Radical Transformation, and the Socio-Logic of Capital

HARRY F. DAHMS

Introduction

Since the beginning of the modern age, as accelerating social, political, economic, and cultural changes have been imposing on human beings an ever-greater need to adapt to new conditions different from those they were born into, human existence has been fraught with awareness of and concern about the future. The inauguration and proliferation of the capitalist mode of production, combined especially with industrialization as it required and fostered ongoing organizational changes and technological innovations, at the same time promised and threatened the prospect of an array of *possible* futures, typically associated with the binary distinction of *utopia* and *dystopia*, especially since the early 20th century (e.g., Kumar 1987). Realistically speaking, though, and contrary to the hopes and fears of many, *likely* futures will be located somewhere between the extremes of utopia and dystopia, along more or less disorienting, haphazard, even chaotic and nonlinear lines, within a range of

possibilities determined by various and varying, and more or less conflicting, structural and organizational path dependencies. The latter are
likely to be influenced by the inconsistent range of norms and values
according to which individuals are supposed to orient and organize their
lives, and individuals are just as likely to be caught up in persistent
and mostly futile efforts to interpret the direction, speed and impetus
of social change in terms of those norms and values.[1] Presumably, the
emotional, psychological, and intellectual limitations of human beings,
along with the limitations contradictory (as identified by Karl Marx; see,
e.g., Grossman, 2017; Wilde, 1989) and irreconcilable (as stressed by Max
Weber; see, e.g., Schluchter, 1996a, published in English as Schluchter,
1996b) features of modern social, political, and economic life have been
imposing on individuals, are conducive neither to the emergence of a
full-fledged dystopia, nor to the realization of utopian conditions (as
the term itself suggests: "no-place"—an imagined, nonexistent place or
society). Hybrids that comprise elements of both utopia and dystopia,
and which will take the form of more or less socially, politically, and
culturally destructive perversions of the promise of the modern age, are
much more likely to characterize the human condition for the foreseeable
future, if not for the remainder of its existence. Contrary to the kind of
optimistic perspectives that were allowed to flourish during much of the
post–World War II era, both in the East and West, to whatever extent and
in whatever form, and despite tensions relating to myriad circumstances
and trends—such as the Cold War, looming nuclear threat and economic
recession, space race and exploration, major advances in medicine and
economic productivity, and so on—in the medium term (and possibly
even the long term), there will be ample occasions for concern, as the
challenges individual countries and global civilization are facing in the
21st century have the potential of becoming overwhelming.

Historically, religion, philosophy, literature, entertainment, and
culture frequently have propagated *love* as a means to alleviate, soften,
or cope with burdens, dreads, and threats endemic to human existence
and social life in many different ways and for an array of reasons, typically either in terms of "love of humankind" or "love of other (human
beings and living creatures)" (especially with regard to the importance
of family), or at least of one other human being.[2] Science-fiction stories—and even more so, films—often rely on the desirability of *love* (or
romance) to tell stories about fateful or existential choices individuals
in *modern* everyday life confront, must make, and in fact have been

making on an ongoing basis, in social contexts whose basic configuration usually is beyond their grasp. Many of these choices have far-reaching and tangible, though unpredictable, consequences for those making (or refusing to make) them, others, and the world they inhabit, and especially *for their shared future*.[3] As I will emphasize in this chapter, in many instances, scriptwriters and filmmakers employ love as a framing device to relay "messages" they regard as important to audiences, and which explain at least in part why especially directors go through the arduous process of making a film. Without explicitly acknowledging the function of *love*, it often would be difficult, if not impossible, to explain and appreciate the narrative structure of many films, especially in the science-fiction genre. In their determination to relay important insights to audiences, as in many other regards, there are parallels between the intent and the imaginaries of social theorists and science-fiction film makers. Regarding the status and role of love in science-fiction films, though, and for the most part, viewers are oblivious to the links between personal dilemmas, ideas, desires, and practices, and how the latter, and they themselves, reflect, support, are embedded in and representative of, and through their actions feed back into concrete socially and historically specific circumstances, even when viewers are disturbed by their own moment in time, their place in space—and their complicity with concrete sociohistorical circumstances. Viewers often are unfamiliar with, but also intrigued by, the challenge of pondering and critically assessing problems and myriad experiences of cognitive dissonance associated on an ongoing basis with modes of reconstructing historically specific social structures and processes, as they are being concealed by the veil of the deceptively bland and purportedly innocent and innocuous conduct of life in everyday modern society.[4] This is true even and especially since many have started living their lives in increasingly noisy desperation (e.g., Crary, 2013; Ehrenberg, 2009, 2010).

As commentaries on the dynamism, complexities, and contradictions of the modern age, the parallels between classical social theory, classical critical theory, and sociology, on the one hand, and science fiction, on the other, are most apparent in that they have been addressing similar issues. Industrial revolution, capitalism, the accelerating destruction of nature and natural environments, totalitarianism, atomization, the subversion of human decision-making power and responsibility, the predictability of social, political, and economic patterns and problems that are in conflict with shared norms and values extending from the past into the future, the simuiltaneous encouragement and subversion of efforts directed at bringing about a better world—all of these phenomena appear in classical social and critical theory and sociology. Yet only science fiction tells stories that extrapolate from these trends and features since they appeared 2 centuries ago and have been shaping human sociality ever since, into the more or less distant future, in ways that speculate about what it will mean to be human if some trends continue as opposed to others—practically, theoretically, and existentially. Still, given the similarities and differences between social theory and science fiction, we must ask: In terms of concrete narratives, does science fiction tell a specific and consistent story as far as the problematic nature of modern societies is concerned, in a manner that is consonant with social theory generally, and critical theory, in particular? Due to their mass appeal, the focus here will be on science-fiction films, especially in the United States, with an emphasis on *social relations*, and issue that frequently is alluded to, but which to date has not received the focused consideration and scrutiny it deserves.

Theorizing Modern Society:
Critical Theory, Sociology, and Science Fiction

The crux of studying modern society—especially with an eye toward the development of a related theory—is easily identified, but due to the nature of this type of society, impossible to resolve once and for all: Which aspects, phenomena, and dimensions warrant our consistent and careful attention and consideration, and which may be neglected without peril? Even preliminary answers to this question will be much less clear-cut than its formulation suggests. Regardless of when and where exactly we locate its inception, modern society undoubtedly is a social formation whose dynamic, complex, and contradictory character presents unique analytical and theoretical challenges.[5] Yet, these characteristics are inversely related to the prospect of arriving at a satisfying answer to the question of what demands close attention and what does not, since they make it impossible even to formulate a working definition of modern society that would be acceptable to most social theorists and social scientists. Worse still, modern society has proven to become more dynamic, complex, and contradictory as time goes by, thus continuously heightening the need to address and, if possible, to prepare an answer to the above question, while thwarting related efforts.

Sociology is the discipline that emerged in the 19th century in response to accelerating social change and scholars' and researchers' determination to identify, delineate, and illuminate the defining features of modern society. Though early sociologists such as Auguste Comte (1798–1857) in France and Herbert Spencer (1820–1903) in England refrained from (or consciously avoided) acknowledging this unwelcome fact, modern society may well be the most baffling of subject matters. Indeed, modern society constitutes the reference frame in which sociologists are situated, are conceiving of and conducting what should rank as important social research about modern society as a whole or in its minutest details, and as a reference frame whose workings and patterns are manifested not only in social, political, and cultural forms, but also in the spectrum of possible identities embodied by most of its members.[6] As a discipline that drew on social philosophy and initially relied on social theory to circumscribe its purpose and rationale, sociology produced an array of theories and methodologies to engender an entirely new type of knowledge about modern society, the role of the economic system within it, new forms of organization, technology, and the place of the individual.[7] Regrettably, though, since the 1970s, the majority of sociologists rejected the notion that integration of the rapidly proliferating forms of knowledge they produced was imperative for the discipline's mission, purpose, and success.[8]

Alongside the fragmentation of worldviews that has accompanied the history of the modern world, sociologists devised increasingly fragmented perspectives on the social world everyone inhabits. As a result, even sociologists perpetually were and continue to be in danger of losing sight of the discipline's specific charge within the academic division of labor—to illuminate the workings of modern society especially where those workings, and the constitutional logic they are based upon, fly in the face of everyday assumptions. Thus, sociologists risk contributing to the subversion of whatever willingness and ability may remain among members of society to confront the proverbial "big picture" (see Dandaneau, 2001). Especially under the sway of neoliberalism, economic and career incentives have been proliferating in professional and social life that discourage efforts to ensure that social research will remain cognizant of, rather than falling prey to, the trend in modern society to fracture, and to thwart at an accelerating pace, the ability of educated and informed members of society, social scientists and social theorists to accept that this most dynamic, complex, and contradictory social formation, paradoxically, still may be so *in ways that are specific, discernible, and scrutable.*

As a critique of traditional Marxism of sorts, even though elements remained, critical theory emerged to confront the question of whether it is possible to develop a framework designed to illuminate dilemmas and challenges related to the dynamism, complexity, and contradictions of modern society, by relying on and combining different traditions of thought in the social sciences and the humanities, especially philosophy (see Postone, 1993; Dahms, 2005a). In doing so, critical theory both relied on certain aspects and criticized other aspects of sociology, and was especially critical of the agenda that began to define the latter as it became increasingly professional, and integrated into the academic division of labor.[9] As a transposition of Marx's critique of political economy to the reconfiguration of capitalism and especially the link between economy, culture, and society that occurred during the early decades of the 20th century, the first generation of critical theorists maintained a systematic interest in the role of the economy in social life.[10] By contrast, at the same time, sociology—which had begun with an explicit interest in the role of the economy in modern society—was moving further and further away from studying economic issues (and would not return to it, under the aegis of economic sociology, until the 1980s). In response, critical theory not only maintained a stated interest in economic matters, but also, especially in the writings of Adorno and Löwenthal, continued to delineate what sociology would look like, if it were to draw lessons from critical theory. The issue of how to communicate key insights about the nature of modern society to larger audiences was very much on the mind especially of those critical theorists who conceived of their tradition as translating the importance of insights that increased with the inscrutability of modern society into a more effective approach to education.[11]

The shape and outlines of modern society continue to keep changing all around us, and morphing in more or less mysterious ways into a world we were socialized and educated to assume ought to be familiar to us, but which is turning out to be increasingly mystifying. In recent years, this sense of mystification, particularly with regard to the vicissitudes of globalization, for a growing number of individuals appears to have been sufficient cause to disregard the bar against aggressive, noncompromising and violent reactions, coping mechanisms, and actions.[12] This bar, which never was especially high, had characterized the post–World War II era to an unusual extent, especially in countries of the northern hemisphere, in imperfect form, and the recent related disregard expressed and displayed certainly is far from a new phenomenon.[13] There are mounting indications that the combination of persistent adherence to largely traditional modes of socialization, on the one hand, with the more or less organized repression and undercutting of those educational paradigms that were designed to enable students explicitly and forcefully to face up to proliferating experiences of cognitive dissonance characteristic of life in modern societies, on the other, has been conditioning growing segments of the population in many countries to abandon the precepts of the Enlightenment, modernity, democracy, and justice (along with *social justice*), if not to actively reject them altogether, along with efforts to "make sense of it all," since such efforts to a growing number of individuals seem to be too burdensome to accept and confront constructively. Evidently, this trend—along with many others—does not bode well for the future.

Among literary and film genres, the social sciences, and the many distinct traditions in social theory developed since the 19th century, the affinities between science fiction, critical theory, and sociology are most apparent. This applies especially with regard to the classics of social theory, above all Marx, Durkheim, and Weber; to the well-known writings of the first generation of Frankfurt School theorists; and to theoretical (as opposed to empirical) sociology. Yet, in classical theory, the critical theory of the Frankfurt School, and sociology, science fiction rarely is mentioned or alluded to. There is no evidence that the classical theorists ever directly acknowledged or discussed science fiction as what was then an emerging, yet contested literary genre. Most sociologists appear to have been regarding science fiction as a frivolous and illegitimate subject matter undeserving of serious consideration (for the most noteworthy exception, see Kumar, 1987), despite the obvious affinity between perspectives on societies being "socially constructed" (Berger & Luckmann, 1966; also Couldry & Hepp, 2017) and speculative constructions of alternative societies (esp. Gunn & Candelaria, 2005). Critical theorists, to the extent that they addressed science fiction, considered it—as in Adorno's case—"sub-artistic."[14] In one of the more amusing passages toward the end of *Negative Dialectics* (1973), referring to Schönberg's last tonal masterpiece before turning to atonality—the Second String Quartet op. 10 completed in 1908—Adorno chided Schönberg for having opened the door to making the intent behind the string quartet, especially the fourth movement, and by implication the thrust of George's poem it is based upon, commensurable with what by the 1960s had become part of the human experience, relating science fiction to religion and vice versa,

> Decades after Arnold Schönberg set Stefan George's "Rapture" to music, he wrote a commentary praising the poem as a prophetic anticipation of the feelings of astronauts. In this naïve reduction of one of his most important works to the level of science fiction he was involuntarily acting out the metaphysical need. The subject matter of that neo-romanticist poem, the face of a man setting foot on another planet, is beyond doubt a parable for something internal, for an ecstasy and exaltation recalling Maximinus. The ecstasy is not one in space, not even in the space of cosmic experience. But precisely this shows the objective ground of the excessively earthly interpretation.
>
> Taking literally what theology promises would be as barbarian as that interpretation. . . . poetic exaltation has been pilfered from the theological realm. Religion *à la lettre* would be like science fiction; space travel would take us to the really promised heaven. Theologians have been unable to refrain from childishly pondering the consequences of rocket trips for their Christology, and the other way round, the infantile interest in space travel brings to light the infantilism that is latent in messages of salvation.[15]

The common disregard for science fiction in social theory and social science, as well as elsewhere, is not surprising, as much of it was either written or produced for purposes of entertainment or profit-making, though even in "cheap" instances a modicum of imagination and creativity was required. Moreover, during the 1960s, just when Adorno was completing *Negative Dialectics*, a virtual explosion of serious science fiction books and films began to be published and released that warranted close reading and repeated viewing, and careful interpretation and examination. A growing number of authors and directors began to reflect on the human condition under rapidly changing circumstances, on social structure, political order, and bureaucratic economic organizations, the power and prevalence of ideology, and the increasing inescapability of ever more sophisticated and all-embracing systems of control, in both the East and West.[16] Many novels, short stories, and films resonated with social theory, and even more so with critical theory. Prominent writers included Isaac Asimov, Arthur C. Clarke, Philip K. Dick, Robert Heinlein, Frank Herbert, Ursula K. LeGuin, Frederick Pohl, and especially the Polish philosopher, essayist, and science-fiction writer Stanisław Lem (1921–2006). Many science-fiction enthusiasts and experts have been regarding Lem as one of the most sophisticated and important science-fiction authors to date, and the above themes, along with an array of related and unrelated ones, appear in his novels and essays, including the issue of humans not being able or willing to control themselves, and their inclination to create systems of control that produce myriad unintended consequences which in turn subvert reason and rationality—particularly in his most important work, *Solaris* (1970). The novel, which provided the basis for three feature-length films, including one of Russian director Andrei Tarkovsky's major works, was not translated into German until 1972—3 years after Adorno's passing.[17] If Adorno would have been familiar with Lem's novels or had had the opportunity to experience Tarkovsky's film, his verdict about science fiction might have been less harsh.[18]

Two years after the publication of Adorno's *Negative Dialectics*, Kubrick's *2001: A Space Odyssey* (1968) made it onto the big screen, profoundly transforming public perceptions and the self-understanding of the narrative and visual (as well as visionary) possibilities contained in film (as well as television, to a lesser extent). The rejection or science fiction as a serious subject matter even in its early stages, as in the writings of Mary Shelley, Jules Verne, Edward Bellamy (esp. *Looking Backward*), Charlotte Perkins Gilman (esp. *Herland*), and H.G. Wells, is ironic in many ways, not just because of its proximity to narratives about utopia (as *promise*) and dystopia (as *warning*), but because the time horizon of classical theory, critical theory, and sociology does not just comprise the past and the present, but also—and very much so, in many different ways—the future. Although, as far as it possible to make related determinations, the classical theorists never seriously thought (nor thought seriously) about science fiction, there is an emerging literature on how science fiction, including films, parallels or illustrates themes identified and addressed by the classics (e.g., Leigh & Durand, 2013, Mazierska & Kristensen, 2014). The early critical theorists occasionally referred to science fiction, and acknowledged early films, especially Lang's *Metropolis* (1927), but strictly speaking, the literature on critical theory and science fiction has remained scant at best.[19] Sociology of science fiction and sociology of film have remained rudimentary, especially in the United

States, and sociology of science-fiction film virtually is nonexistent.[20] On top of all this, critical theory also is much less prominent especially in American sociology than in philosophy, literary studies, and a few other fields, which adds one further wrinkle to the tense relationship between sociology as the social science of modern society, and sociology as rigorously critical practice related to and reflection on modern society.

Specifically, critical theory and science fiction, and certain traditions of theoretical sociology, constitute efforts to address and convey to audiences the importance of acknowledging the role of deception in modern social life, the tendency in modern societies to produce ever more all-embracing systems of control, and the problematic link between technology and human beings (e.g., Lemert, 2011). In different, yet related and even complementary ways, critical theory and science fiction encourage the development and the application of critical perspectives on modern society and modernity—especially so in the science-fiction subgenre of "alternate futures" (Booker, 2006; Fuhse, 2003). With regard to more recent versions of critical theory, such as those of Jürgen Habermas, Nancy Fraser, Axel Honneth, Hartmut Rosa, and Rahel Jaeggi, as well as in the broader sense of poststructuralist, feminist, and postcolonial approaches, among others, the similarities are also apparent, but less conspicuously so, or in different or more specific ways. By contrast, *as a discipline, sociology relies on the concept of critique only loosely, and largely without systematic intent.* At the same time, the issue of utopia has been a recurrent theme in critical theory, but less so in science fiction, or mostly as a set-up, to then turn to concern with dystopia (with a few notable exceptions, including *Star Trek*); in sociology, to the extent that the distinction plays a role at all, it does so almost exclusively with regard to, but not in explicit terms of, dystopia. Moreover, social theorists, philosophers, and social scientists who were closely associated with critical theory, even though they never belonged to the core, strictly speaking, and less so sociologists, did examine and discuss or touch upon science fiction, either in literature or film, or both, such as the philosopher of utopia *par excellence*, Ernst Bloch (1995), as well as Siegfried Kracauer (2004, 1960), Fredric Jameson (2005), Slavoj Žižek (2006), Alain Badiou (2013), Martin Seel (2018), and especially Darko Suvin (1979, 1988, 2010).

Critical theory and science fiction are oriented toward the future, inspired by the potential of modern society to prepare social, political, cultural, and economic conditions qualitatively different from and superior to the past and present, and concerned that this potential is being undercut on a continuous basis, both actively by identifiable individual and institutional actors, as a consequence of negligence and disregard for an array of "others," and especially by forces that sustain the constitutional logic of modern societies and shape societal conditions, usually without being accessible from within everyday life circumstances. Typically, with a constructive rather than a reactive (or especially a reactionary[21]) stance, both critical theory and science fiction take as their starting point the dialectic between the social, political, economic, and technological achievements of modern societies, and past, present, and future catastrophes that were and tend to continue to be predictable. Both critical theory and science fiction extrapolate from achievements and catastrophes in ways that translate into or amount to warnings about the likely consequences resulting from naïve faith in progress, especially in technology, and the inclination of humans to reject responsibility for their own and each other's actions, not just individually, but especially collectively. The challenge of conceiving of what the latter—*collective responsibility*—would look like, along with strategies to promote or engender related ideations and practices, is daunting indeed, particularly when reduction of related conceptions to the scope and framing of any of the amply available, largely regressive ideologies is to be avoided. The incipient literature in sociology on social relations, which harkens back to an aspect of Marx's critique of political economy, as it drew on the antagonism between the bourgeoisie and the proletariat, provides a suitable venue for delineating the idea of collective responsibility.

Sociology and Science Fiction as Responses to Modernity

Regardless of when and where *exactly* we pinpoint the beginning of science fiction as a literary genre, and of the notion of sociology as a social science, both emerged within and from similar sociohistorical circumstances in the mid–19th century, in France and England, in response to comparable yet distinct experiences of accelerating social and economic change, the proliferation of new types of cultural, political, and organizational challenges and means of transportation and communication, and the problem of "progress," including especially technological progress.

In England, as the society where the Reformation triggered a rapid erosion of shared worldviews and, in combination with an expanding colonial empire, precipitated the onset around 1800 of industrialization, the formation of markets, and the spread of the capitalist mode of production, a peculiar and contradictory mindset took hold which, at the same time, was embedded in and in many ways expressive of a stratified system of social relations, with segments of the population that benefited from these processes in peculiar ways being blind to the human, social, cultural, and political costs that came with them, especially for others. The drama of rapid social change was recognized, but predictably and immediately rationalized by those who benefitted, with the consequence that in incipient social theories, greater effort was directed at justifying the specific pattern of "progress" taking hold, rather than critiquing it. In art, especially literature and painting, the momentous changes were felt more strongly, but tended to be rendered aesthetically, as in the famous paintings of J.M.W. Turner depicting the incursion of industry into nature, or in the nostalgic transfigurations of idyllic nature and rural life in John Constable's work (see also Hemingway, 2017). To the members of the emerging industrial working class, whose experiences initially were not regarded as legitimate or justified by the wider society, the costs were much more concrete and manifest. Conspicuously, though, sociology—especially as represented by Herbert Spencer—did not emerge in this context as a critical response, but rather as an expression and rationalization of the acceleration of societal change. The concepts of alienation, anomie, and especially the Protestant ethic, though they transformed England first and from there radiated to the rest of British Isles and then to the world, was not theorized on location, but in France and Germany. Still, there is widespread agreement that the first modern science-fiction novel was written and published in England, Mary Shelley's *Frankenstein* (2007), to be followed a century later by the novels of H.G. Wells.

By contrast, in France, in the aftermath of the Revolution of 1789, the clash between the emerging world market and established religious, cultural, and political traditions and practices (and ways of "reading the world") was much more intense, and awareness of the costs much greater, across the social hierarchy, along with willingness to confront the contradictions of the modern world, due presumably in part to the fact that the Protestant ethic since the notorious Massacre of St. Bartholomew's Day (August 24/25, 1572) was alien to the dominant culture. Sociology as a social science thus emerged in response to the above processes, in no small measure mourning the erosion of the stable order of the feudal world, especially in Auguste Comte's conception of the discipline. It was under these circumstances, in France, that science fiction as a genre emerged in the writings of Jules Verne.

In Germany, at the same time, in the wake of Idealism, especially of Hegel's writings, social theory began to form as a distinct response to the incursion of economic and industrial change into a predominantly agricultural society divided into Catholic and Protestant regions and populations. Whereas Herbert Spencer rose as a proto-Darwinian proponent and ideologue of free-market capitalism, Auguste Comte conceived of sociology as a discipline dedicated to protecting the existing social and political order from the destructive economic forces propelling proliferating modernization processes. In Germany, Karl Marx, who first lived and worked in Germany, then in France and Belgium, and finally in England, dedicated his entire oeuvre to the need to scrutinize the underlying economic logic of the newly emerging, contradictory bourgeois social and political order—a logic that both Comte and Spencer merely touched upon, without examining it carefully. Precisely during the time period when the economic logic of capital forcefully started to rear its head in England, and subsequently spread across Europe and the globe, Marx's critique of political economy as an "aesthetic theory of capital" preceded by decades the formation in Germany of sociology as a social science.[22] While some consider Johannes Kepler's *Somnium* (1634)—an attempt to imagine the Earth from the vantage point of the moon—the first European novel with a science-fiction theme of note, published in Latin, the first modern science-fiction novels published in German did not appear until the early 20th century.

As a genre located, in recent decades, in the field of tensions between politics, culture, society, on one side, and the capitalist economics-neoliberalism nexus, on the other, science-fiction films have come to play a most paradoxical role in perpetuating, amplifying and concealing the logic of capital, while also drawing attention to, and criticizing, its centrality to modern life. At least since the 1970s, through their importance to the film industry, science-fiction films have been fulfilling a key role in supporting the logic of capital (Beller, 2006). On the other hand, by relaying a type of subversive and largely overlooked or misunderstood message relating to the link between love and radical transformation, science-fiction films also have been pointing out and illustrating the social, political, cultural, and ecological destructiveness of the logic of capital.

By recognizing explicitly and explicating the peculiar message about "love" that is built into and at work in the narrative structure of most acclaimed science-fiction films, the opportunity opens up to access an aspect of modern societies that has been unduly neglected in social, political, and philosophical thought and social science (including in critical theory), and in much of Marxist and Marxian discourse (but *not* in Marx): *the entwinement of the system of modern social relations and the logic of capital.* This neglect has been detrimental to both *theory*—to think what is supposed to be "unthinkable" (Lemert, 2007) to members of modern societies—and to *praxis*: to conceive of practical and political strategies that will remain "unimaginable" as long the link between the logic of capital and the system of modern social relations implicitly is taken for granted even in most efforts at critical reflection, including as it pertains to *praxis.* Appreciating explicitly the message about love and radical transformation in science-fiction films reveals a powerful aesthetic vision of the modern age and opens up perspectives on the future that have been—and that are supposed to be (from the vantage point of modern society as a system that is evolutionary on *its* terms, rather than on our human terms)—too audacious for social scientists and social theorists to entertain with any measure of seriousness.[23]

In recent years, an expansive literature has emerged on science-fiction film from a philosophical perspective (e.g., Constable, 2009; Grau, 2005; Litch, 2002; Sanders, 2008; Schneider, 2009; see also Diocaretz & Herbrechter, 2006, for a set of "theoretical" perspectives). Yet, by comparison, the literature from a sociological perspective has remained scant, especially in the United States, where the genre of science fiction is especially popular and prolific both in cinema and television. In this context, part of the purpose of this paper is to sketch a critical-theoretical perspective on science-fiction film that goes beyond related writings in both philosophy and sociology. Put simply, the *philosophy* of science-fiction film suffers from a neglect of how most science-fiction films and television series are historically and geographically situated, and how they constitute socially oriented commentaries on the vicissitudes and contradictions of modern society at different points in time. The *sociology* of science-fiction film (or of science fiction, or even of film generally), on the other hand, is so underdeveloped that it is not possible to situate it clearly with regard to modern society. Moreover, sociology's concern as a social science is so concerned with neutrality, balance, and the chimera of objectivity—"researchers and research captured in a labyrinth of busy irrelevance," as Helmut Dahmer (2001, pp. 8) put it—many of its proponents do not recognize how immersed they as well as the discipline are in sociohistorical specificity. In fact, social researchers may be so embedded that they are not able to study how exactly a large segment of the population is being entertained with ideations relating to the future, in the interest of profit-making, as long as film continues to constitute an important sector of the industry, before video games and virtual reality take it over more or less completely, while most people are not in the position to shape their collective future.

Rather than outlining what a sociology of science-fiction film might look like, however, it will be more productive to delineate a critical-theoretical perspective on science-fiction films that (1) highlights their sociohistorical embeddedness and (2) appreciates that there are many films that have been released since the 1980s which, more or less explicitly, convey a message of radical transformation. Typically, such messages center on the theme of "love" as the focal point for a critique of alienated social relations in the modern age, and for envisioning—in *inflationary* fashion—qualitatively superior kinds of social relations that point beyond both alienation and capitalism. Toward this goal, a critical theory of science-fiction film must rely on philosophy *and* sociology, and integrate both so as to enhance either, beyond what they are capable of addressing and examining under present circumstances. Concordantly, it will not be sufficient to conceive of a critical philosophy or a critical sociology without specifying *critique*, and how critical approaches are different from noncritical approaches.

Critical Theory and the Logic of Capital

As a distinctive tradition of social and philosophical thought, the critical theory of the Frankfurt School emerged to tackle a confounding challenge related to determining the role of the logic of capital in and to modern society. This logic is not only counterintuitive, but flies in the face of an array of prevailing assumptions in and about modern societies, including in academia, without which societies of this type would not be able to function or maintain order, especially regarding the link between individual and society. This logic also continuously transforms the tools individuals employ to relate to, make sense of, and intervene into the world to which they belong and of which they are parts. The challenge of determining the importance of the logic of capital in and to modern society involves three distinct steps which must be kept in mind when assessing the contribution of critical theory to the history of social thought, even though the members of the Frankfurt School did not explicitly employ this kind of language.[24]

In the first step—despite occasional efforts to update Marx's critique of political economy to later conditions, and after a hiatus of nearly half a century of futile efforts of doing so successfully—the early critical theorists observed in the 1930s that the *economic* logic of capital no longer was a viable target of critique, since this logic had become submerged in social forms.[25] Theorizing and critiquing the logic of capital above all as an economic logic—which, to be sure, according to Marx, it never was (see Postone, 1993)—could be effective only as long as there was a clearly discernible difference between economic and social dimensions of individual and public life. Yet, by the 1930s, "society" and social forms and modes of co-existence had ceased to be conceivable independently of the logic of capital, so much so that even if it still would have been possible to reveal, effectively and compellingly, the "nature and logic of capitalism" (Heilbroner, 1986) as separate from processes of individual identity formation and the constitutional logic of modern society, it no longer would have been possible to overcome "capitalism" without deconstructing and reconstructing on new foundations individual identity as well as social structure. Even if it would have been possible to make accessible and intelligible to well-educated and informed members of modern societies—including workers as the original target audience of Marx's *Capital*—that the logic of capital was no longer confined to the economic sphere, it would have been difficult, and more likely impossible, for most to grasp how the link between society and capital had become too pervasive for the kinds of efforts social groups and movements set out to pursue, and the goals they endeavored to achieve, to be successful and, in effect, transformative; instead, the logic was likely to persist, and to deepen further.

In the second step, critical theory set out to scrutinize how—over time, during the second half of the 19th century—the economic logic of capital had begun to become ingrained in politics, culture, and society, thus transforming and subverting the latter into epiphenomena, functions, and means of its further proliferation at an accelerating pace, in the process turning into an increasingly mystifying and obscure social logic whose impetus is almost impossible to discern and circumscribe, since science in general, the humanities and the social sciences, as well as individual identities, are permeated by this logic also, though not entirely shaped by it, or determined in the strict sense. In the related literature, this concern with the social rather than the underlying economic logic of capital frequently has been framed and described—if not dismissed—as a "cultural turn" in critical theory. Yet, this turn was neither a matter of choice or preference, but an imminent necessity in light of the ongoing, structural transformations of modern societies, and indicative of their counterintuitive constitutional logic, as it conflicts with everyday perspectives and notions about the links between politics, culture, society—and the increasingly bureaucratic capitalist economy. Thus, the importance of developing a rigorous critique of the *culture industry* was not merely an expression and surface manifestation of the logic of capital, but its medium und amplifier. The culture industry also is a social and political coping mechanism inasmuch as it provides a pressure valve for conflict and frustration, and a space for creativity that feeds back into the logic of capital, not least because it is incapable of slowing or altering the direction of its impetus.[26]

In the third step, exemplified especially in Horkheimer's famous programmatic essay, "Traditional and Critical Theory" (1972), the distinguishing feature of critical theory emerged as the commitment to discern and delineate how the gravity concrete sociohistorical circumstances in modern (capitalist) societies exert on efforts to illuminate the constitutional logic of those societies increases with every generation, thus concealing the warped dialectic of modernity, by seemingly "naturalizing" it.[27] By implication, social research turns out to be located in a field of dynamic, complex, and contradictory tensions that thwart efforts to assess whether and to what extent the specific forms of particular social, political, or cultural practices, organizations, or institutions are expressive of human sociality, or of human sociality mediated by the increasing prevalence of the economic logic of capital. Before opportunities emerge to engage in focused and careful empirical social research relating to social, political, or cultural forms, it is necessary to ensure that such research and the knowledge it produces will not replicate and aggravate further dimensions of the constitutional logic of modern societies that are detrimental to those modes of social integration and that they do not aggravate further alienation and anomie. Typically, those dimensions of the constitutional logic are related, but neither identical with nor limited, to the economic logic of capital, and located at the intersection of dynamic systems of economic power and persistent structures that have been fostering alienation and anomie (see Dahms, 2006). With configurations of power and inequality that are at the core of modern societies being inversely related to individuals endeavoring to grasp the forces and patterns that facilitate social stability, the unavoidably first order of business is to conceive of what would amount to social research oriented toward "emancipation."

The program of early critical theory stressed the need to assess how, in modern societies, economic logic (in its capitalist vein) and social logic are prone to becoming interlinked in increasingly specific and less and less fathomable ways, and its proponents pursued this program from a variety of angles, but in two ways, above all. On the one hand, efforts were directed at conceptualizing and explicating the difficulties that predictably would accompany the development of critical theory with "practical intent," as Habermas would later put it. Recognizing and examining the gravity sociohistorical circumstances in the modern age exert on social research directed at identifying the defining features of social reality required possession of a viable theory of modern society, even though—paradoxically—delineating (though not necessarily *formulating*, as doing so successfully would require reliance on traditional theory at least to some extent) such a theory was the stated goal of critical theory. On the other hand, as the representatives of the early Frankfurt School confronted the ongoing challenge of conceiving of a theory of modern society, while appreciating the likelihood that such a theory would reflect sociohistorical circumstances without critically reflecting *on* them, they discerned that modern societies encourage or compel their members to subscribe to assumptions about the nature of this type of society in ways that facilitate the problematic conversion of economic and social logics into the logic of capital. They pursued many different strategies to illuminate and verbalize the proliferation of impediments to individuals' efforts to maintain sanity (and to avoid aggravating further, for themselves and others, alienation and anomie, though their actions and modes of existence) and to prospects of modern society becoming more "sane" over time (to allude to the title of one of the books of the erstwhile member of the Institute for Social Research, Erich Fromm (1955). *De facto*, even though they did not use this exact language, the early critical theorists also were concerned that the conversion of economic and social logics into the logic of capital would be detrimental to solidarity in the formal and in the substantive sense—for "organic solidarity" as identified by Emile Durkheim, and for sociocultural and political solidarity as a proactive and transformative transposition of norms and values into novel practices, forms of organization and institutions—as both are based on norms and values according to which members of society either are supposed to lead their lives and relate to each other (or would prefer to do so). In the final analysis, though, and for a variety of reasons, they succeeded only to a certain point.

Indeed, what many social theorists began to recognize more or less explicitly as a new kind of economic logic that took hold during the 19th century, by the early the 20th century had morphed (and needed to be grasped) as the social logic of modern "society" (centered on corporate capitalist forms of organization) in its many forms turning into the conduit for capital establishing itself as the unavoidable force to be reckoned with in all human, social, cultural, and political affairs, as it started spreading at an accelerating pace around—and thus transforming the surface of—the planet. Yet, precisely during the same time-period when this transformation started gaining momentum, sociologists began to establish the discipline as a social science and professional field concerned with the study of human social relationships and institutions: *sociology* as the study of society as opposed to the study of the *socio-logic of capital*. For the most part, they did so either by implicitly abstracting from, or by explicitly disregarding, how especially in modern societies, all social forms were turning into parts and parcels of the social logic of capital, at varying levels of intensity, and thus could neither be explained nor understood on their own terms, but instead as products of the tension between the underlying forces (capital accumulation, division of labor, rationalization, etc.) that shape modern society, and how these forces are observable (only) at the level of surface manifestations, the level sociologists—as opposed to social theorists, and especially critical theorists—are concerned with. Put differently, contrary to the early social theorists, sociology for the most part, and especially as a professional discipline, focuses on the surface level of modern society, implicitly working with the supposition that it is the task of sociologists to regard and study social customs and practices and forms of social aggregation on their own (i.e., sociological) terms, and to "explain" one social phenomenon (i.e., surface manifestation) as the unintended result or the intended—as in the case of social movements—product of interaction between other social phenomena (i.e., surface manifestations). Yet, what is being ignored actively or neglected passively is that what appears as "social" phenomenon must be scrutinized within modern society as located within the field of tensions and at the intersection of different, more or less closely related underlying forces, on the one hand, and efforts of human actors at the level of surface manifestations (e.g., in the context of social movements, in politics, in large organizations, etc.) to influence the form, importance, and gravity of other surface manifestations. More interestingly, though, and unknowingly, but still *in effect*, human actors set out to "control" at least some of the underlying forces (or the impact they have on social phenomena, or social life in general), and thus—by definition—to alter the combined dynamics that co-determine the thrust, impetus, and relative power of those forces, respectively, even though, as a matter of principle, such efforts are less and less likely to be successful as time goes by, even if such efforts would be explicit, intentional, and cognizant of the dynamics, complexity, and contradictions that define the modern world.[28]

Thus, from the outset, sociology as a social science—as a profession as opposed to a vocation—was in danger of neglecting, misreading, or even concealing and thus extending further invisible forces whose reach and concrete manifestations were in plain sight and increasingly impossible to deny. On the one hand, sociology emerged as a *reluctant* form of "anti-economics" or "counter-economics" of sorts that emphasized the social dimension of human coexistence over the economic dimension, both from a descriptive and a normative vantage point. From an empirically grounded, descriptive vantage point, sociologists contended that a society centered entirely on an economic system only could arise as the consequence of a long-term societal reconfiguration of "everything existing" that is revolutionary in nature, and which even economists like Polanyi and Schumpeter stressed would not be desirable. Ironically, such a reconfiguration would parallel, in inverted form, the long-term transformation required for the establishment for a well-functioning communist society. As it turns out, though, it appears that the *economic rationalization of society* will take far less time than early sociologists would have considered possible, considering the success to date of the neoliberal project that began during the 1970s, no doubt in part due to the fact that modern society is centered on the capitalist economy, and that in modern society, economic power exceeds all other forms of power, including social and political power. From a normative vantage point, early sociologists posited that the economic dimension should be framed and contained by and embedded within the social dimension, rather than vice versa, for an array of reasons—and that the most important contribution sociology could possibly make is to facilitate the *societal rationalization of the economy* (see Dahms, 1992, 1995). Thus, while *the social* was being subverted (and to some extent, supplanted) by *the economic*, early proponents of the discipline set out to study modern society as an expression and consequence of human sociality, rather than focusing on how in modern society, human sociality is mediated through (and increasingly warped by) economic imperatives and forms of organization in the specific register of capital, and increasingly expressive of the latter.

To the early critical theorists, by contrast, sociology should have been concerned above all with the process of the economic logic of capital morphing into a *social logic*, as the discipline established a foothold at universities right before or after the turn from the 19th to the 20th century, within the academic division of labor especially in the United States, France, the United Kingdom, Germany, and Italy. De facto, even if they did not do so directly, sociologists from the outset focused on the intricacies and recorded the process of the social being transformed by the logic of capital, while devising tools, strategies, categories and methods designed to interpret and analyze this process *sociologically*. Thus, sociology embraced as its charge the delineation and study of "the social," precisely during the time period when its dissolution began to gain momentum. By the early 21st century, the language of the social as independent of the economic still prevailed, but the gulf between the terminology being employed to capture "reality"—the empirical process of "society" reconstituting itself—concealed the progressive assimilation of the social to the economic, with the economic becoming even more elusive than it had been during the 20th century. The early critical theorists saw the promise as well as the failure of sociology as fraught with the potential of fulfilling key ideological functions by framing the process of the economic logic of capital turning into the social logic of capital in exclusively sociological terms, and set out to conceive of and to integrate *critical* sociology into the interdisciplinary agenda of critical theory.

Yet, the commitment of later critical theorists—such as Habermas, Offe, and Honneth—to confront these challenges has been weakening with each subsequent generation, with its representatives increasingly running the risk of "embodying" implicitly how the logic of capital shapes and orients processes of ego-formation, socialization, organization, and social integration generally—and currently, many critical theorists indeed did so, typically by downplaying or abstracting from the specificity of sociohistorical circumstances in their own society (see Dahms, 2017b). The neglect of psychology and psychoanalysis in recent versions of critical theory is symptomatic of the assimilation of processes of identity-formation to capital, as this assimilation has continued to intensify (e.g., Allen, 2015; Dahmer, 1994). The willingness to confront the "unthinkable" in modernity has been declining precipitously in critical theory at least since the 1970s, more so it seems with each successive generation, especially among the tradition's "official" representatives, and in proportion with the growing eagerness with which its most prominent proponents endeavored to reconcile critical theory with traditional approaches, and the corresponding conceit that there is nothing truly mysterious or mystifying at work in modern societies which would necessitate radical and innovative theoretization.[29] Yet, the latter notion is inversely related not only to Marx's efforts at formulating the critique of political economy as the precondition for a theory of modernity that is not itself a manifestation of modern society as devoid of critical reflection upon the latter, but to the program of the early Frankfurt School, and the "new Marx reading" that was inspired, above all, by Adorno's version of critical theory, and his take on Marx.[30] The suggestion that anyone, on the basis of everyday assumptions about social life that are consonant with prevailing and more or less shared norms and values—which used to be espoused regularly in modern societies until a few years ago, in ways that were rarely contested—ought to be able to recognize and grasp the baffling nature of this type of society, is incompatible with the thrust of both classical social theory and classical critical theory. Recent political and cultural developments, such as the erosion and retreat of democratic culture and institutions, have been possible only as a consequence of the widespread but paradoxical notion that the workings of modern societies should be transparent to all, where in fact they require a major effort not only at facing undesirable facts, but also at deconstructing one's own self to the extent that it is the product of unseen forces which maintain social order and facilitate ongoing social changes, including those that are neither compatible with established identities, nor with purportedly shared norms and values (e.g., Kaplan, 1997; also Kurlantzick, 2013; Diamond & Plattner, 2015; Diamond, Plattner & Walker, 2016; The Data Team, 2018).

Over the course of the last 2 centuries, especially in those societies that began to industrialize during the 19th century, social practices and relationships have been permeated and transformed, from generation to generation, to an ever greater and more intense degree by the logic of capital, via the "reloading" of alienation that is foundational to the ongoing reconfiguration of the relationship between human beings and the world. Rather than alienation emerging as a problem only once, at the beginning of the modern age, the pattern that appeared then has been recurring with every subsequent generation, each becoming more alienated from nature and from *social* relations as they are supposed to prevail in modern societies, and accustomed to relations as they are endemic—following Marx—to bourgeois society as it is based on the capitalist mode of production. This presents the problem I alluded to earlier, as the second step the early critical theorists were concerned with: How do we know that how we relate to each other is expressive of our social nature, as opposed to successive mediations that have transformed what we experience as human sociality in ways that have very little to do with what the latter would be, if the response to the crises of legitimacy and democracy and "ungovernability" of the early 1970s would have been *further* democratization, rather than retreat from the latter and neoliberalism (see Dahms, 2009). If the historical opening that occurred with the Enlightenment and the trajectory of continuously growing prosperity would not have narrowed the horizon of present and future possibilities to the requirements and the underlying logic of modernity as defined by the capitalist mode of production and the pattern of industrialization that came with it—and corresponding "world-relations" (Rosa, 2016)—as thematized from Marx to Horkheimer and Adorno's *Dialectic of Enlightenment* (2002)—how would humans coexist, and what would "society" denote?

Critical Theory, the Problem of Futurity, and Science Fiction as the Genre of the 21st Century

From the outset, critical theory was oriented toward the prospect of a better future. Without the supposition that modern societies have the capacity to undergo qualitative transformations, the program of critical theory would not be intelligible, and lack its vanishing point. Those transformations would need to be consonant with the *emancipatory* norms and values according to which we are *both* supposed and would want to live—as opposed to the *regressive* norms and values that correspond with structural patterns and systemic imperatives which govern our lives—as the latter norms and values are in more or less manifest conflict with the former, and reliant on a set of warped human, social, political, and cultural conditions fraught with proliferating experiences of cognitive dissonance. Whereas the prospect of a better future appears to have been one response to the intensifying desire among growing numbers of individuals to reduce the frequency of such experiences and to overcome the material conditions that sustain and foster them—by appreciating the modern age as what may well be the singular era and window of opportunity in history to reconcile "facts and norms," to whatever extent possible, at successive points in time—it is undeniable that in the 21st century, experiences of cognitive dissonance are proliferating rapidly, as the ability of institutions in charge of socializing and educating younger members of society to confront those experiences constructively, appears to be eroding just as rapidly.

The appeal of critical theory, at least in part, has been a reflection of its commitment to the "utopian impulse," the stance that the socially consequential source of existential meaning in the modern era is located, and located *only*, in lived participation in ongoing collaborative, ideally collective efforts directed at preparing and pursuing, if not bringing about, more livable conditions for everyone in one's own society and on Earth generally, which includes *all* living creatures.[31] Absent real human beings in sufficiently large numbers making tangible, circumspect and determined efforts to activate and keep alive modern societies' capacity for qualitative social change, this capacity—to whatever extent it may exist, and in what ways and regards—will remain dormant, if not lying fallow, and be conducive to civilizational regression. Humanity, especially in the double sense of *human and humane*, if conceived of in the narrow and confining sense of existing circumstances, replicates and duplicates the central role of power and inequality in and to the historical process; in the 21st century, as the coming of a posthuman era looms large (see Braidotti, 2013; Crombez & Dahms, 2015), acknowledging and taking on the challenge of transcending the organizationally and technologically mediated political and especially economic constructions of social and cultural forms is as important as ever, and more disturbingly daunting. Yet, even though allusions to a better future, and less so, to "utopia," are not uncommon in the writings of critical theorists, there have been few instances of this theme being developed further or fully (e.g., Benhabib, 1986; Whitebook, 1995).

To be sure, the cursory and generally latent nature of explicit references to the idea of a "better future" should not be surprising, since the stated and distinctive contribution of critical theory Max Horkheimer delineated in his programmatic essay (1972) did not address existential concerns, nor refer to concrete forms of practice (especially political practice), but instead belongs to the realm of the philosophy of social science concerned with analytical challenges resulting from the specificity of modern society. Modernity promises the reconciliation of facts and norms, of material circumstances with the norms and values according to which we are to organize our individual and social lives. Yet, at the same time, the constitutional logic of modern society inevitably undercuts and perverts the prospect and the reality of such reconciliation. Initially, this was the guiding paradox that oriented the work of the early critical theorists, in a variety of ways, in the effort to face this paradox directly and uncompromisingly, without "overriding" or sidelining related analytical, theoretical, and empirical challenges by proposing and then pursuing "constructive" approaches based on one "paradigm" or another. Such paradigms, as they were developed in the later 20th century in terms of communicative action (Habermas, 1983, 1987), recognition (Honneth, 1995), or acceleration (Rosa, 2015), and in the interest of "resolving" the paradox, however, are incompatible with Horkheimer's concept of critical theory, not least because each of these paradigms combines elements of critical theory and traditional in ways that pervert the former. Effectively, and as long as treated indirectly—as has been the case in more recent versions of critical theory especially in Europe which refrain from "tuning" critically into the link between the peculiar dynamics, complexity, and contradictions that constitutes a feedback loop with the logic of capital—this paradox is conducive to modern society maintaining itself in a manner likely to increase the prospects of its undoing—a prospect which, within the tradition of critical theory, only members of the first generation were willing to contemplate in earnest.[32]

To rely on Baudrillard's (1994) terminology, the early critical theorists understood that modern society must turn into a version of itself that is not limited to and satisfied with being a simulation, but a version that is open to the possibility of actualizing the reconciliation of facts and forms as an ongoing project, from the past, via the present, to a qualitatively superior future. Yet, if various trends that have been taking hold in the 21st century to date—such as the retreat of democracy, the resurgence of authoritarianism and fascist ideas, and the decline of solidarity both as a concept and as a practice—will continue, three scenarios suggest that we are headed toward the end of social, political, and cultural "progress" (see Allen, 2016, and the discussion of Allen's book in Dahms, 2020).

First, if modern society as represented by a sufficiently large segment of the population in societies of this type is to abandon firm commitment to socially progressive principles, postmodernity is likely to take hold more or less along the lines predicted during the 1980s, as a hybrid of premodernity and modernity that hovers between the past and the present, while perverting the social, political, and cultural achievements of modernity, and supplanting them with technological, organizational and economic progress. The result in some fashion certainly is likely to be novel in various regards, but there is no relationship between novelty and improvement, and the very idea of progress is incompatible with this kind of hybrid of past and present as a perpetual state of regression that may well lead to societal catastrophe. Second, postmodernity in this sense will not constitute the overcoming of the deficits and faults of modernity, but their aggravation, as a type of progress that produces such an intense condition of structural schizophrenia that the vast majority of individuals will reject all notions pertaining to the prospect of "grasping" the circumstances of human existence in this de facto postmodern age. Third, in retrospect, the present situation will turn out to have been indicative of and foreshadowed the erosion of modernity as a direct consequence of the unwillingness of individuals, social groups, social movements, organizations, and institutions to make the requisite effort to anticipate in their actions, practices, and operations the actualization of modernity's progressive principles, and instead be contended with projections of such actualization and progress, while facilitating the hollowing-out of both from the inside.[33] Yet, the distinction between utopia and dystopia may still apply, as it is likely—as alluded to earlier—that combinations of both will characterize the perimeter of the species' existence.

In one, more or less utopian, future, humans will experience continuous improvements, be subject to the forces of nature (including their inner nature, especially as far as it is regressive and disabling) to an ever-decreasing extent, and find themselves in circumstances in which to a greater extent than in the past their fate will be tied to (and an expression of) their talents, aspirations, decisions, and ability to cooperate with others. In the other, more or less dystopian, future, humans will pay the price for having unleashed purportedly anonymous forces (e.g., the capitalist market economy, bureaucracy, etc.) whose workings they neither understand, nor are interested in or capable of controlling, and for accepting and even eagerly submitting to the choices of the powerful, or the workings of both seen and unseen forces deemed to be necessary for maintaining social order and for sustaining "society," or the whims of nature, and *de facto* more or less "natural" catastrophes. Both futures are foreshadowing the disappearance of established notions of "humanity" and "humankind": either in the sense of progressive transformations of humankind and corresponding concepts of what it used to mean to be human, or in terms of the persistent erosion of the modern commitment to "humans as the measure of all things," either in the anthropocentric sense or in terms of the humanity-humanism nexus, to the point of humans possibly literally vanishing from the face of the Earth, or being replaced by a "more advanced" species, such as cyborgs, replicants, or humans who exist in such a miserable "natural" environment that they cannot live without mobile air-filtration systems they carry with them, or the like.

In the first, utopian, future, Earth civilization increasingly will resemble a world of free, self-determining, conscious and responsible individuals who are flourishing most as social beings fully cognizant of and committed to membership in their social group, community, and society, with political, economic, and social structures as functions of liberated and self-determining human existence capable of constructively confronting and embracing a multiplicity of challenges. In the second, dystopian, future—especially if neoliberalism is any indication of things to come—the disappearance of humanity and/or humans/humankind will be precipitated by a process of individuals obliviously assimilating to economic forces and processes, politico-administrative forms of organization of their (or their ancestors') own making, and the system of social relations that correspond with the former. Corporate capitalism, technology, and mass-organizations increasingly will shape and determine the concrete "nature" of human existence and social coexistence, and human sociality—purported to continue to be consistent with democratic ideas and ideals and notions of rational collective decision making—will become incompatible with *modern* human and social standards and principles, which will remain as the echo of a receding past.

In both cases—either in the interest of pursuing and amplifying opportunities toward the goal of inaugurating the "human millennium," or in the interest of averting doom and disaster and the end of humanity—humans still would have to take responsibility, for their own choices and actions, as well as for the choices and actions of others. The decades immediately following the catastrophe of World War II were characterized by unwillingness to take responsibility for the well-being of others being reigned in, within the confines of national borders, by the imperative to survive, if not "win," the Cold War, and the related need to avert another world war, nuclear holocaust, or debilitating internal social conflict. Arguably, these decades represent a notable and historically unique exception in the history of the modern age. Beyond this exception, the evidence appears to suggest that the number of those who would rather not take responsibility for themselves, and especially not for others, must be assumed to be much higher than it was thought to have been during the postwar era, and too high to foster steps toward the actualization of a "human millennium" and for the species to conduct itself and especially its business, in a manner that will be conducive to the well-being both of the planet and its inhabitants. In any case, as there is no legitimate basis for certainty of knowledge about "the future," in light of the history of the modern age, there are indications aplenty that the impending future will continue to be fraught with ambivalence, ambiguity, hesitation, as well as a mixture of hope and fear, of optimism and pessimism.

Combined with memories of the catastrophes of World War II beginning to fade at least as early as during the 1980s—catastrophes that had made possible the pursuit and implementation of public policies and social legislation which, realistically speaking, would have been inconceivable without those catastrophes[34]—indications of the "exhaustion of utopian energies" (Habermas, 1989) decried in the mid-1980s already at that time began to point in the direction of the surge of right-wing policies whose consequences are observable today, in the United States and elsewhere. Absent modes of socialization and educational curricula being conducive to laying the requisite groundwork (and possibly even then), humans are neither necessarily, nor "naturally" willing to face the future constructively; most humans would rather resist doing so, as the structure of identities is entangled with the specific social, political, and economic structures of society (Dahms, 2017c, 2018, forthcoming), contrary to what progressives prefer to presuppose, and to what the liberal mindset posits as being the case. Ironically, in this regard, both liberals and neoliberals miss the mark: just as many individuals do not appear to be particularly fond of limiting their choices and opportunities by concern for and consideration of "other" (in the sense of others outside of their family, social class, race, religion, religious organization, and of animals, nature, the planet, etc.), many individuals also are not willing or able to dedicate their lives to the single-minded pursuit of prosperity. In part, both of these stances are reflective of the prevalence of the logic of capital, in terms of which individuals are only supposed to care for themselves, but in ways that undercut the pursuit of profit as it would be conducive to agency beyond the logic of capital. Liberals assume that those needing help will welcome it when it is being provided, while neoliberals claim that all should be able and eager to help themselves before seeking help from others—but solely within the existing framework. Yet, growing evidence suggests that both inferences are incorrect. Many of those who would benefit from help refuse to see themselves as belonging to those who need help, and resent it when it is being offered (Hochschild, 2016). Given the existing economic, political, and social structures, it is "objectively impossible" for all to be successful and to take care of themselves, even if they would make the requisite efforts. In any case, most humans are much more likely to look to the future in a highly ambivalent and weary, even fearful, fashion. What, then, does "future" stand for, in our endeavors as critical (and) social theorists and sociologists, as well as in our personal lives?[35]

In *Claims of Knowledge—On the Labor of Making Found Worlds* (1989), and in allusion to Hans-Georg Gadamer's work, Lawrence Hazelrigg observed that "futurity—not 'the future,' which is a progeny of that rule of 'the past,' but the potentiality of futureness" is what is primary for "the whole of our history."[36] "This 'primacy of futurity,' which maintains all pastness in a secondariness, means not that we do not know how 'to draw our poetries' from futureness . . . but that we do just that"—meaning that even though we do not have a clear sense that and how we draw "our poetries" from the future, we nevertheless do draw them from the future, even if we are oblivious to this fact, or insufficiently cognizant of it.[37]

> Even when the poetries we draw are alienated, when they are drawn in/as conditions of alienation and our drawing is occulted as a discoverable effect of the rule of "the past," they are still poetries of/from futurity; for it is we, in historical conditions of here-and-now, who make tomorrow's world, even if we make it still again as alienated product. Futurity, the potentiality of futureness, our "superiority over what is actually present," is, in Gadamer's phrase, "the distinguishing feature of man."[38] So we must insist.
>
> We must insist against the attitude of retrospection, the attempted erasure of historicity, and for projection. We must

insist for potentiality and against those practices that enact "the word 'realism' as if reality were already entirely constituted (whether for good and all, or not) when the writer comes to the scene," as if the latter's role is limited to 'explaining' and to 'expressing' the reality of his period."[39] (Hazelrigg, 1989, p. 225)

In other words, we moderns cannot *not* see ourselves through the future, through what we—individually as well as collectively—hope, expect, want, would wish, desire, and fear to be(come). The more important issue may be whether this fact is being acknowledged, denied, or ignored. Especially in the United States, arguably throughout its history the most consistently dynamic society on Earth (while struggling persistently, and *with futility*, with growing complexity and proliferating contradictions), the connection to *future* is part and parcel of the fabric of social, political, economic, and cultural life, much more so than in all other societies, where the inclination to relate to "the" future as a continuation and extension of the present and the more or less distant past *in time* is likely to be much greater and much more pronounced, and buffered by a concern with order. Especially in the United States, it is a given that "nothing will be left unturned," that nothing will remain as it was, that nothing will last, as human beings (really, *white men*, as products and also primary beneficiaries of established structures) cannot but apply themselves to the world in ways that perpetually transform the surface and climate of the planet we all inhabit, for better and for worse.

> The interest in futurity, in which our "superiority over what is actually present" is projected, is in the interest of a world-to-be-made. It is the interest of facticity-to-be-made—that is, of a *factum* (a deed, an act; past participle of *facere*: to do, to make) and a *fictio* (something made; from *fingere*: to form, invent, feign)—and therefore is a projection of value. And it is from this projection of making, this value-projection of world-to-be-made, that actuality ("the realm of fact *and* fiction") must submit to judgment of truth or falsity, good or evil, beauty or ugliness. But always as a making of life/world/history. (Hazelrigg, 1989, p. 226)[40]

When Hazelrigg put his observations on paper, the decade was drawing to a close that saw the onset of neoliberalism, the end of European socialism, even the "end of history" (though evidently not the end of history).[41] Rather than the opening of an era of global opportunities to pursue greater social equality, social justice, and public policies directed at reconciling the human species with nature, the environment, and Earth to an ever increasing extent, what ensued was a process of retraction and contraction, a shying away from possibilities to bring about more rational societies (see Cook, 2012), a more humane and fair world, except at the individual level, framed in an intensifying matrix of social class that many had assumed was in the process of being overcome, especially in Europe, as the dark side of the dialectic of enlightenment started to come to the fore in an ever less deniable fashion.[42] The "value-projection of world-to-be-made" turned out to be mostly economic value—in its capitalist mold and ever more vulgar fashion, no less, as has been documented in the literature (see Verhaeghe, 2014)—and the utopia implied and expressed in this value turned out to be a world in which the market mechanism no longer was taken to apply to the economic sphere of activity only, but to all areas of human and social practice.

How does the notion of poetries of the future apply to the genre—especially in literature, but also in film—that is most directly concerned with the world(s) we are making, science fiction? How does science fiction, how do especially science-fiction films, reflect and reflect upon conditions in the 20th and 21st century, as a context in which economization, marketization, and capitalization, along with alienation, commodification, and reification no longer are abstract theoretical concepts designed to capture what used to be the hidden workings and the consequences of processes which, as it were, keep rumbling under the surface of both modern everyday and public life, but which are now in plain view? Indeed, these concepts refer to empirically observable processes whose prevalence has become utterly undeniable, and whose power over what we refer to as "social," "cultural," and "political" makes it difficult to conceive of the latter as anything but realms in which the workings of the nexus between economy, organization, and technology can be observed directly.[43]

To begin to tackle the social-theoretical significance of science-fiction films today, I will focus on treatments of the phenomenon of *love* as the most personal of social relationships. With "love" as a type of practice of world-making in the fields of tension between personal life and global capitalism, and between individual aspirations and desires and collective imperatives and objectives, I will examine how "love" plays a role in science-fiction cinema as a genre directly concerned with the fact that inevitably and undeniably, future will be different from present in imaginable and unimaginable ways. How do science-fiction films constitute a surprising and largely ignored venue for thematizing how alongside the history of modern society, the status, meaning, and importance of love has been undergoing continuous transformations? How is acknowledging and recognizing those transformations is a necessary precondition for working toward a kind of love that is not merely a reflection and extension of the workings of modern society as capitalism, instrumental technology, and warped democracy, but as a type of social relationships that points beyond the status quo and the established system of social relations?

The foremost theorist of science fiction, Darko Suvin, insisted that as a genre, it has been geared toward visualizing and criticizing the degree to which the world that resulted from the spread of the capitalist mode of production and industrialization is fraught with and by alienation, and shaped to varying degrees by what I have been referring to as the logic of capital. While other genres alternatively accept, rationalize, glorify, hypostatize, or illustrate the prevalence of alienation, science fiction stands alone in the explicit way in which it points it out and criticizes it, within the coordinate system of *estrangement* and *cognition*, with conscious counter-alienation (aka, *estrangement*) as the necessary and inevitable precondition for knowledge of any kind, of any degree of importance (aka, cognition). As Suvin put it:

> I will argue for an understanding of SF [science fiction] as the *literature of cognitive estrangement*. This definition seems to possess the unique advantage of rendering justice to a literary tradition which is coherent through the ages and within itself, yet distinct from nonfictional utopianism, form naturalistic literature, and from other non-naturalistic fiction. It thus makes it possible to lay the basis for a coherent poetics of SF. . . . [A] spectrum or spread of literary subject matter . . . extends from the ideal extreme of exact recreation of the author's empirical environment to exclusive interest in a strange newness, a *novum*.

In referring to and employing the concept of *novum*, Suvin explicitly cites Ernst Bloch (1995) as a source (see ch. 4: "SF and the Novum," pp. 63–84), and reaffirms his debt to Bertolt Brecht: " 'alienation' [*Entfre-*

mdung] evokes incorrect, indeed opposite connotations [to Verfremdung]: estrangement was for Brecht an approach militating directly against social and cognitive alienation."[44] Without a novum, science-fiction stories or films would be impossible:

> [I]t is not only the basic human and humanizing curiosity that gives birth to SF. Beyond an undirected inquisitiveness, which makes for a semantic game without clear referent, this genre has always been wedded to a hope of finding in the unknown the ideal environment, tribe, state, intelligence or other aspect of the Supreme Good (or to a fear and revulsion from its contrary). At all events, the possibility of other strange, covariant coordinate systems and semantic fields is assumed.[45]

In a manner that harkens back to the theme of Horkheimer and Adorno's *Dialectic of Enlightenment* (2002) as it pertains to the tense link between enlightenment and myth, though without referencing it, despite the conspicuous affinity between their positions, Suvin continues:

> The use of estrangement both as an underlying attitude and dominant formal device is found also in *myth*, a "timeless" and religious approach looking in its own way beneath (or above) the empiric surface. However, SF sees the norms of any age, including emphatically its own, as unique, changeable, and therefore subject to *cognitive* view. The myth is diametrically opposed to the cognitive approach since it conceives human relations as fixed and supernaturally determined. . . The myth absolutizes and even personifies apparently constant motifs from sluggish societies. Conversely, SF, which focuses on the variable and future-bearing elements from the empirical environment, is found predominantly in the great whirlpool periods of history, such as sixteenth-seventeenth and nineteenth-twentieth centuries. Where the myth claims to explain once and for all the essence of phenomena, SF first posits them as problems and then explores where they lead; it sees the mythical static identity as an illusion, usually as fraud, at best only as a temporary realization of potentially limitless contingencies. It does not ask about The Man or The World, but which man?: in which kind of world?: and why such a

man in such a kind of world? As a literary genre, SF is fully as opposed to supernatural or metaphysical estrangement as it is to naturalism or empiricism.

> . . . SF is, then, a literary genre whose necessary and sufficient conditions are the presence and interaction of estrangement and cognition, and whose main formal device is an imaginative framework alternative to the author's empirical environment.

(Suvin, 1979, pp. 7–8)

Science fiction thus is the genre par excellence for reflecting on the flaws and dark side of modern society as well as of modernity, and in this it is similar to classical social theory, classical critical theory, and sociology as envisioned by the classics (but distinct from, to be precise, sociological practice and even most *sociological* theories (see Dahms, 2007). Science fiction tends to address the possibility of and need for radical transformation, if there is to be correspondence between the norms and values according to which moderns like to claim to want—and are supposed—to live, and the material circumstances that ground and frame their lives. In this, there is a similarity in focus between social theory regarding trends whose medium or long-term consequences humans must be warned about, and science fiction. Moreover, just as most social theorists, including critical theorists, have been reticent to advocate for revolution—given that failure is the more likely outcome, and even if it were to be "successful," exceedingly problematic in many of its consequences (e.g., under dynamic conditions of high complexity sustained through discernible contradictions internalized by individuals)—science-fiction writers and film-makers, too, tend to refrain from positing that the result of revolution either necessarily or even potentially would be better than the conditions that prepared it, even and especially if the latter made revolution an appealing prospect or an inevitability. In fact, for the most part, in science fiction, the messages relating to impending, or the need for, radical transformation more or less explicitly suggest that there has to be simultaneity between the processes of social transformation and reconstitution of the self for catastrophe to be averted. Usually, systems of social relations in place at a novel's or film's outsets, prevent such simultaneity of social transformation and reconstitution of the self. Frequently, in fact, social transformation is presented as adaptive evolution rather than political revolution, even if the stage is set for the former by the latter, or when revolution is on the horizon, because the selves that will be in charge of the new circumstances and of their own selves, and independently of their will and intentions, would be products of the regime of control and system of social relations the revolution was supposed to destroy, abolish, remedy, or supersede.

Love and Radical Transformation in Science-Fiction Films

Even and especially the most intimate personal relationships inevitably are infected by the logic of capital, in part because we suppose or take for granted that they are expressions of our selves at our most distinctive. This supposition especially applies to *love*: Like everything else that is being taken for granted, love, too, is likely to replicate and promote the invisible logic that is shaping the social context in which it is occurs and is experienced, as it tends to be overlooked in social research and by sociology, since the latter are imbued with this very same logic. Moreover, not only has there been a process of the social being assimilated to the logic of capital, the latter is not static, but has been evolving also, and more on its terms than on ours (Heim, 2013, Haskel & Westlake, 2018).

To be sure, *love* is not a singular phenomenon—not even as a word, and especially not as a concept—in terms of how certain notions and practices are integral to, and others in conflict with, existing circumstances in society. As many writers have illustrated, *love* denotes an entire spectrum of ways of relating to "other" (e.g., Keen 1997). Scholars in the humanities, the social sciences and theology have been interested in *love* as a historical and cultural phenomenon, not just in language departments, but also in philosophy, social theory, sociology, and critical theory, from Fromm's (1963) and Herbert Marcuse's (1974) related classics—both had been affiliated with the Institute for Social Research in Frankfurt and in New York, to be sure—to the systems theorist Niklas Luhmann (1986 and 2008), the critical psychoanalyst Jessica Benjamin (1988), the political theorists Drescher, Esser, and Fach (1986), the Israeli sociologist Eva Illouz (1997), the German social theorist Günter Dux (1994) and proponent of historio-genetic theory (Dux, 2011), and the French sociologist Luc Boltanski (2012), just to name a few.[46] In addition, scholars also have examined the role of love and romance in film, from various angles, including philosophy (Wartenberg, 1999; Wolf & Grau, 2014).

Especially in science-fiction films, *love* is an element that viewers and critics often ignore, neglect, or downplay as a staple of Hollywood entertainment, or notice only implicitly, despite its consistent recurrence and narrative importance in a variety of ways and contexts. In recent years, the importance of love in and to science-fiction has become all but undeniable. Yet, as a character in one prominent science-fiction franchise suggested, love just "is a word. What matters is the connection the word implies."[47] In science-fiction films, *love* tends to function as a means to illuminate and criticize one type of socially coded "connections" as they facilitate, reinforce, and deepen regressive dimensions of—and ways of relating to other and others in—modern societies, and corresponding types of social relationships, in order to delineate and promote another type of "connection"—another type of social relationship that points at a different system of social relations—which must be promoted, "if humanity is to survive." Despite some notable exceptions, most importantly Kubrick's *2001: A Space Odyssey* (1968) and Ridley Scott's *Alien* (1979)—many widely recognized and/or financially successful science-fiction films involve the theme of love, typically in a manner that is central to the plot, but by no means confined to the relationship between a man of a woman.[48] In most instances, the love theme revolves around the question of whether qualitative social or political change is possible, necessary, or desirable. Frequently, once a protagonist reaches the conclusion that change is possible, or even required, such as for the survival of humanity, for life on Earth to continue, "to save the world," and so on—even though especially the lead character (or characters) rarely start out from this proposition—the ensuing "action" turns on how to bring about what amounts to a radical transformation of the existing arrangement, usually between humans and others (aliens, machines, etc.), as code for the system of social relations between those who benefit from the social and economic structure, and those who make it work but who do not benefit, or only in the sense of their "bare life."

In science-fiction films situated in the twilight area between utopia and dystopia, love appears to be an indispensable plot device. In the remainder of this section of the chapter, I will illustrate this point with reference to two examples, one of which stresses the theme of individualism and individual transformation beyond what the established system of social relations allows for (with the latter remaining intact), the other the theme of collective identity as defined by an established and implicitly presumed system of social relations, and *its* transformation.

The first example is Robert Wise's *Star Trek: The Motion Picture* (1979), which resonates in certain regards, though certainly not in overall effect, with Kubrick's *2001: A Space Odyssey* (1968), although love plays no role in the latter; the other example is Alex Proyas's *Dark City* (1998), which openly cites from and refers back to Fritz Lang's *Metropolis* (1927), though their conclusions are radically different.[49]

Star Trek: The Motion Picture (1979)

Forty years ago, *Star Trek: The Motion Picture*, the first movie produced in the context of one of the most—possibly *the* most—economically success-ful television and entertainment franchises ever, was released.[50] The film wove together several familiar science-fiction themes and tropes whose resonance with issues addressed by social theorists since the beginning of the modern age, especially since the early 19th century, is as undeniable as it is remarkable (see Rosa, 2016). Among these themes and tropes are technology going awry, the requirement for individuals to adapt to ever newer and increasingly unexpected challenges (and technologies), the growing gulf between creativity (and self-assertion) and submission (and self-denial) as responses to an increasingly dynamic world (and the persistent problem of hierarchy in human affairs), the nature and meaning of human existence, human civilization as a field of tensions between progress and regression, the conflict between intelligence and emotion, the changing nature of social relations, and the prospects for radical transformation in modern affairs. In the history of social and philosophical thought, discussions of these and related themes (which often coincide with a variety of science-fiction tropes) have been going on for centuries, with regard to individual freedom and agency, division of labor, development, evolution, rationalization, the inertia of social order (social structures and systems of power), the desirability and difficulty of qualitative social, political, and economic change, the changing modes of economic accumulation and organization, and an array of related concepts and distinctions.

In *Star Trek: The Motion Picture*, these themes are in plain view. While the film contains many elements that prevent it from being one of the great examples of science-fiction film—such as an indulgent and overly long panning of the ship with the telling name, the U.S.S. Enterprise, at a pace that is reminiscent of Kubrick's *2001*, but much more akin to technology fetishism than conducive to serious reflection, to name just one example—this motion picture still has many serious elements, including the overall plot as it is emblematic of many films to follow that involve love and radical transformation.[51]

The story revolves around a cloud two astronomical units in diameter (one astronomical unit [AU] = the distance between Earth and the sun) with unimaginable (destructive) power that has entered our solar system from interstellar space, moving toward Earth. The cloud proceeds with intent, has the ability to respond to approaching ships and to protect itself (it destroys three spaceships and a large space station as it is getting closer to Earth), and to learn and adapt to changing circumstances. The imminent threat it poses to Earth (as "Sector 001" and the heart of the United Federation of Planets) presents a formidable challenge to the federation's flagship and its crew (a familiar cast of characters returning from the "original series" of *Star Trek*, which ran from 1966 to 1969, again with James T. Kirk at the helm, this time not as Captain but as Admiral (William Shatner). As it turns out, an artificial intelligence exists in material form at the center of the cloud, and it is approaching Earth looking for its "creator," which it assumes to be an entity similar to itself. Bothered by the fact that in order for it to complete its mysterious mission, it must content and communicate with the "carbon units" on board the U.S.S. Enterprise—the humans, whose organic nature and intelligence is incompatible with the cloud's pure logic as it is devoid of emotions—the entity takes over one of the carbon units/crew members, Lieutenant Ilia (Persis Khambatta), and replaces her with an android to facilitate more effective communication with the humans. Before her replacement with an android, Ilia functioned as the ship's navigator, was a female Deltan with the qualities of an empath who also, as required by her species, is committed to a vow of celibacy. Yet, as it turns out, Ilia has a prior history with Willard Decker (Stephen Collins), the executive captain who was designated to be the captain of the newest version of the Enterprise, before Kirk wrested command of the ship from him prior to boarding. Evidently fond of each other, Decker's feelings for Ilia were and continue to be unrequited, due to her vow. Speaking through the Ilia replica, which retains at least some of the original's memories and "carbon-based" qualities, the artificial intelligence at the core of the vast cloud that refers to itself as "V-Ger," pronounces that "the creator" must respond to its desire to complete its mission, which both are linked to Earth and humankind in some fashion. V-Ger deploys several missiles in orbit around Earth that have the capability to destroy all life, should V-Ger not receive the desired response from "the creator." Kirk and his crew recognize the danger but refuse to cooperate. The Vulcan, Spock (Leonard Nimoy), who is linked to V-Ger telepathically due to their intellectual affinity and penchant for logic, enters the cloud on his own and discovers that it is a gigantic storage facility employing a highly sophisticated visualization technology. Following Spock's suggestion that Kirk treat V-Ger like a child, he declares himself the creator, insisting that the response V-Ger is seeking will be provided only directly to V-Ger, not to the Ilia android representing V-GER. Still clueless as to how to respond to V-GER's demand, Kirk, Decker, Spock, the Ilia android, and a couple of other crew members are permitted to proceed toward the cloud's core on foot, after an oxygen atmosphere begins to envelop the Enterprise. As it turns out, the heart of V-Ger is a NASA probe ("Voyager 6"—only V and GER are visible due to damage incurred at some point), which had been sent into space during the latter part of the 20th century, but which was assumed to have been lost. The members of the Enterprise crew who were permitted to approach V-Ger in person, including Decker, conclude that during its voyage Voyager 6 encountered a planet populated by machines that repaired the probe, amplified its capabilities in line with its mission (to collect all available information), and enabled it to return to Earth. Kirk and the crew realize that V-Ger is waiting for NASA's 20th-century radio response, which was supposed to instruct Voyager 6 to send all the data collected during its voyage to Earth, and they retrieve the sequence from the ship computer's archive. Yet V-Ger engages in self-sabotage: It is not willing to provide the data it collected; rather, it expects to be *unified* with the creator. Decker steps forward and begins to be transformed, with the Ilia android joining him, as the other crew members hurry back to their ship. V-Ger and the entire cloud transform into energy and vanish. Kirk, Spock, and the other crew members on the bridge realize that they witnessed the birth of a radically new, unprecedented life-form.

Evidently, the love between Decker and Ilia is the conduit for the radical transformation that occurs at the end of the film, even though Ilia is no longer alive, strictly speaking, with human (Decker and what remains of Ilia) and machine (V-Ger and what remains of Ilia, also) forming a life-form with access to a higher dimension of existence, well beyond the three-dimensional space, the linearity of time, and the imagination and limitations of humans. To be sure, extrapolating further from this event would be difficult indeed, and speculating on the nature of the new life-form's novelty, and whether it would have any bearing on the real circumstances of real people facing concrete challenges and dilemmas, and the work they/we would have to do to implement resulting opportunities, and the social relations we are all embedded in, embody, and execute. This would not be the kind of challenge Hollywood is willing to take on—quite the opposite—but facing this challenge constructively and creatively partly was the motivation behind *Star Trek*: to show how a society not bogged down by constant internal strife and social, political, and economic problems would function and be able to move beyond itself, both at the social and the subjective level. Of course, in the *Star Trek* universe, this is the *status quo ante*: compared to how we live today, the humans who form and inhabit the federation and make it work exist in a state of actualized utopia, in many regards. As the captain of the second series, *Star Trek: The Next Generation* (1987–1994), Jean-Luc Picard (Patrick Stewart) explained to a character from the mid–21st century (in *Star Trek: First Contact* (1996; dir. Jonathan Frakes),

> CAPTAIN JEAN-LUC PICARD: The economics of the future are somewhat different. You see, money doesn't exist in the twenty-fourth century.
>
> LILY SLOANE: No money? You mean, you don't get paid?
>
> CAPTAIN JEAN-LUC PICARD: The acquisition of wealth is no longer the driving force of our lives. We work to better ourselves and the rest of humanity.

Necessarily, this kind of economics would require a de-centering of the subject/individual—human beings would have to see themselves actively through others, rather than passively, as has been the case since the earliest social forms and structures took shape—and embrace the responsibility for oneself and for others, in order to lead a meaningful and fulfilling life. It is this kind of meaning and fulfillment, however, that is inversely related to the logic of capital, except for those who thrive by "selling their soul" to the latter, or whose life-goals jive with and parallel this logic so perfectly and to such an extent that there is no need for them to sell their soul, probably at the expense of many others.

Dark City (1999)

In an essay on science fiction and *film noir*, Carl Freedman (2009), the author of the only book to date on critical theory and science fiction (Freedman, 2000), distinguishes between deflationary (disenchanting, disheartening) narratives in *film noir* and inflationary (inspiring, encouraging) narratives in science-fiction films that parallel analyses in social theory, especially in what he refers to as Marxism, and which in the context of this essay should be understood as applying to the theory of Marx. The films that Freedman relies on to set the stage for his comparison are Billy Wilder's *Double Indemnity* (1944) and Stanley Kubrick's *The Killing* (1956) as examples of *film noir*, and Robert Wise's *The Day The Earth Stood Still* (1951) and Kubrick's *2001: A Space Odyssey* (1968) for science fiction, to prepare a more specific observation of what he refers to as "ultra noir" as represented by Alex Proyas's *Dark City* (1998). Without going into the details of his analysis here, Freedman contends that

> The opposition between the deflationary perspective of *noir* and the inflationary perspective of SF recalls a dialectical tension at the heart of Marxism, which is deflationary and inflationary at once. The deflationary dimension is represented by the attempt to destroy all illusions necessary or useful to the preservation of class society in general and of capitalism in particular. . . . In the spheres of both culture and political economy, the deflation of capitalist illusions is an indispensable part of the Marxist project.
>
> But Marxism ultimately aims at the positive project of human liberation and self-realization, rather than only at the negative task of destroying capitalism and other forms of class (and other) oppression. . . . The overthrow of capitalism . . . can . . . be the prelude to the radically democratic self-organization of the human race, allowing all individuals the maximum possible fulfillment of their creative potentialities: as mankind leaps . . . from the realm of necessity to the realm of freedom (Freedman, 2009, pp. 72–73).

When comparing the importance of deflation to that of inflation, science fiction provides an opportunity to elaborate what Marx (and Engels) merely touched upon, even though in terms of visual and narrative representation and settings, depictions of dystopia are far more common than of utopia. Most of Marx's and Engels's writings were dedicated to demystification and deflation, and "the moments of inflationary positivity . . . , while fascinating and important, amount to a series of brief, sometimes ambiguous passages scattered through tens of thousands of pages of mainly deflationary scientific analysis" (p. 74). Strictly speaking, deflation and inflation "form a genuine dialectic" in Marx and Engels, which in turn corresponds with an aesthetic dialectic "between SF cinema and *film noir*" (p. 75). This is where Freedman turns to *Dark City*, a film whose feel is similar to Ridley Scott's *Blade Runner* (1982), to the Wachowskis' *The Matrix* (1999), and a number of other films, which all combine elements of science fiction and *film noir*, thus adding up to what he refers to as "ultra noir," and which has come to be discussed more frequently as "tech-noir" (Meehan, 2008; Auger, 2011).

Dark City is the story of John Murdoch (played by Rufus Sewell), who wakes up one night without knowing who or where he is, after he resisted—also unknowingly—an attempt to imprint him with different memories and a new identity (as a murderer, no less). The details of the plot are not important for present purposes; suffice it to say that he discovers that the city he inhabits is controlled by "the Strangers," a class of aliens that have kidnapped an entire city of humans who they have been manipulating—for how long, only the Strangers know—as part of an experiment designed to enable the latter to learn what enables the humans to retain the motivation to keep living, even in the "dark" conditions of their world. The Strangers have the ability to "tune," to change the city—by exerting collective mental control over highly sophisticated machines—and the identities of its human inhabitants—with the help of a human psychologist who had to erase his own memory of his and the other humans' past. For reasons not explicated (though hinted at), and contrary to the other humans who are oblivious to the fact that they are entrapped in the city, Murdoch acquires the Strangers' ability to "tune" also—in no small part motivated by his love for the woman (Emma, later Anna; Jennifer Connelly) the Strangers manipulated him into thinking is his wife who he is in love with, but who purportedly betrayed him, presumably causing him to turn into a murderer—and refuses to accept the identity he was imprinted to enact, and act out.

> [T]he entrapment is taken to a science-fictional extreme and rendered terrifyingly literal. . . . The metropolis at night

typically is the 'world' of classic *film noir*, but here it is the world in a precisely literal sense . . .

[S]cience-fictional means achieve a similarly ultra-noir effect in the film's presentation of human character. If the typical noir protagonist is a man driven by transpersonal forces like greed and lust, and equipped with only a limited grasp of his own motivations and an even more limited ability to determine his own fate [and thus performs his assigned role within the regressive system of capitalist social relations; HFD], Murdoch is that protagonist raised to a higher power. . . .

As an ultra-noir production, then, *Dark City* is deflationary and deterministic in ways that allegorize aspects of both Freudian and Marxist materialism. . . .

Yet, *Dark City* as an SF film not only raises *film noir* to a higher power but also . . . dialectically produces a powerful inflationary, and utopian, theme that is the antithesis of noir. . . .

Dark City is thus, finally, and despite its noir and ultranoir deflationary aspect, a work in the great inflationary tradition of Blake's *The Marriage of Heaven and Hell* (1790–93), Shelley's *Prometheus Unbound* (1820), and Beethoven's *Fidelio* (1805–14) . . . (pp. 78–81)

Dark City being a movie, it is important for the underlying message of inflation also to be represented with the help of cinematography. The first major part of the film is constructed

through an accumulation of discrete shots, with little tracking or panning: and the effect is one of stasis, entrapment, and determinism. But as the humans assert themselves and move against the Strangers' tyranny, the cameras begin to move as well, and a contrasting effect of progressive flow is achieved.

We leave Murdoch to begin a love relationship with the Jennifer Connelly character, who is no longer burdened with the false memories of having been Murdoch's cheating wife. It is the sort of visionary, material transcendence that has always been what SF does best—and that, of course, has, at least since the final lines of *The Communist Manifesto*, been the ultimate point of Marxism itself. (pp. 81–82)

Without Murdoch's emerging and authentic feelings toward Emma (as well as Anna, after the implantation of different memories and a new identity), which initially were the product of manipulation, but which he comes to realize he is affirming and embracing as his own, it would be much more difficult for him to go against the system of control the Strangers created and maintain, and without those feelings and the leap of faith they make possible, Murdoch would be less motivated to pursue the path he finds himself on. The link between visual representation and dialogue, especially the revelatory sequence involving Murdoch, psychologist Dr. Schreber (played by Kiefer Sutherland), and Inspector Bumstead (William Hurt), illustrates how control over perception (the inhabitants of the city are not noticing that the sun never rises), and the normalization of perpetual darkness (harkening back to the condition of proletarian laborers during the early face of industrialization, working in mines or factories, and not seeing the sun much either), projects images of control that go beyond mere "domination" or "power." Instead, control of perception molds the very soul of most human beings, in part because they are oblivious to this, as they have internalized the system of social relations that, on the one hand, rests on such internalization, and on the other hand, makes such controlled internalization possible to begin with. The system of control and social relations is truly all-embracing and inescapable, until one protagonist, the psychologist Schreber, refuses to submit to the rules of the game, setting the stage for another protagonist to appear, the purported murderer Murdoch whose fake identity produces such an extreme experience of cognitive dissonance in him that his initial, implicit willingness to submit begins to crack, which not only enables him to think by and for himself, but also to realize—partly due to his refusal to conform—that he can think *like the aliens*, that is, that he can *tune*—meaning: change the shared reality at will.

The Matrix (1999)

There are obvious parallels in the Wachowskis' *The Matrix* (1999), a film much more familiar to audiences (contrary to *Dark City*, it has become an integral part of pop-culture), and that is centered on a conventional heterosexual relationship between Thomas Anderson / Neo (Keanu Reeves) and Trinity (Carrie-Anne Moss), who both come to experience and to be committed to love. *The Matrix* suggests a similar expression of and response to the same rapidly changing sociohistorical circumstances under conditions of globalization as *Dark City*, especially with regard to the link between individuals and society, and how the latter relies on its ability to make sure that the former "think" modern society in such ways as are necessary for the latter to continue to exist without undergoing structural and qualitative transformation, despite rapidly accelerating change at the societal level that is becoming increasingly incompatible with the ideas of life and existence bestowed, in the modern age, upon individuals via primary and secondary socialization and education, and immersion in mass media. And it very much is modern society, "the world as it was at the end of the 20th century," as one of the protagonists, Morpheus (Laurence Fishburne) puts it, Chicago, specifically, where the simulated reality is situated and the narrative takes place.

In *The Matrix*, as in *Dark City*, the hero/savior Neo only appears on the scene after another protagonist, well ahead of his birth, the Oracle (Gloria Foster), set in motion and has kept alive a process geared toward finding and helping the One, who as "legend" will have it, will change the matrix. The Oracle played a key role in facilitating and sustaining an entire network of resistance fighters and their families—the City of Zion with its military social structure, whose visual presentation the audience must wait for until the beginning of the second film (*The Matrix Reloaded*; 2003)—who rely on her insights and predictions to fight for "peace." As it turns out in the end, to the disappointment of many viewers, the Oracle, Neo, and the resistance all work together to bring about a *truce* between the humans and the machines, enabling the former to establish an internal and external system of social relations that will not be a function of the war between the humans and the machines (*The Matrix Revolutions*; 2003). This conclusion, though, while a letdown in the eyes of many viewers, is entirely consistent with the underlying narrative structure of *The Matrix Trilogy* (including especially the two-part "The Second Renaissance" that forms the theoretical core of *The Animatrix*), as the trilogy and the conclusion are informed by social theory, especially Marx and Weber, but also critical theory, including Baudrillard, and philosophy, including Plato, Descartes, Hegel, Schopenhauer, William James, and Hilary Putnam (see Grau, 2005; Dahms, 2005b, 2013).

Importantly, helping the One involves helping Neo find himself: to discover what and who he is if no longer a cog in the machines' machinery, a highly sophisticated system of control and social relations set up between machines and humans (and among the latter, as modeled on the late 20th century), and maintained to turn humans into providers of energy without their knowledge. The Oracle, "a program from the machine world," was designed to study humans to enable the machines to establish a more effective system of control over those who "refuse the programming," whose appearance is predictable and can be anticipated, and thus, controlled. In a manner that is comparable to *Dark City*'s Schreber, however, after initially fulfilling her task ("she" suggested creating the Agent programs designed to protect the matrix and to find and control the rebels), the Oracle develops empathy for the humans and starts rejecting "her" (really, "its") purpose, to work toward establishing a more conciliatory relationship between humans and machines—one less fraught by power, domination, and exploitation.

For our purposes, what is interesting about the Schreber and Oracle characters is that, while not being able to engender qualitative change themselves, it is the combination of their empathy for the humans with a willingness to understand the systems of control they are part of as they actually work, rather than how they are supposed to be interpreted from the human perspective, which enables them to conceive of "a way out," a strategy oriented toward radical qualitative change which leaves humans to be better off, or at least setting the stage for the latter to be less alienated and exploited. Ironically, the fact that both Schreber and the Oracle are social theorists of sorts whose task it was to enable those in power (the Strangers and the machines, respectively) to maintain their control over humans and to use the latter for the Strangers'/machines' purposes, and to discard the humans when no longer useful or dangerous, is what puts both in the position to produce knowledge about the system of control they are part of. The strangers and the machines allow Schreber and the Oracle to "know the truth" of their world, in order to work with this knowledge to fulfill their instrumental purpose as it is consistent with the Strangers' and the machines' intent. Yet, it is precisely this knowledge that enables these "white saviors" (see Hughey, 2014) to go beyond their programming, and to relay the knowledge to one or several humans, who thus are being empowered to bring about revolutionary change, as a consequence of forming an intimate relationship with one other human that is not a function of the established system of social relations, but which transcends the realm of the alienation the latter truly is.

Conclusion: Critical Theory of Science Fiction
Qua Critique of Social Relations?

There is a growing sense—and mounting evidence supporting it—that the future is slipping away from us. This seemingly nonsensical and highly paradoxical observation appears to apply more strongly the further we move into the 21st century, especially in the United States. Logically, modern societies will not survive loss of the future—both future in general, and their own future, specifically. Indeed, the time-horizon of modern societies is oriented toward and built on the future, even though historically, empirically, and realistically speaking, modern societies—as embodied, personified, and represented by most of its members—remain suspended in a field of tensions between premodernity and modernity. As social systems, neither modern societies, nor most of their human components, are either willing to face this fact, or to consider what it might or would mean to embrace future, inevitable and inescapable as it is, or especially make determined and sustained efforts to escape this field of tensions between progress and regression, conceived in conventional terms. The observation of the future slipping away from us applies in many regards, disturbingly so, and there are few (and ever fewer) indications providing a basis for hoping that things will turn out well "in the end"—another paradoxical conceit. In fact, if there is a sentiment that characterizes the prevailing state of mind, heart, and soul in the early 21st century, it would have to be crisis of confidence, to put it mildly.

The foundation of modern *society* is alienation: the continuous reconfiguration of the relationship between individual, society, and nature in a manner that is conducive to the continuous pursuit of prosperity in its capitalist vein. By implication, this highly dynamic context presents a moving target not just for critique, but also for *analysis*. The concepts, categories, tools, methods, and theories that at one point were conducive to discerning more or less rigorously the social world, those tools emerged from the social context which they were intended to illuminate, but they are ever in danger not just of becoming outdated (and, in fact, likely to do so, sooner rather than later), but of fulfilling ideological purposes regarding the concealment of the constitutional logic of modern society as it is related to the logic of capital.

In *The Art of Loving* (1963) Fromm wrote,

If love is a capacity of the mature, productive character, it follows that the capacity to love in an individual living in any given culture depends on the influence this culture has on the character of the average person. If we speak about love in contemporary Western culture, we mean to ask whether the social structure of Western civilization and the spirit resulting from it are conducive to the development of love. *To raise the question is to answer it in the negative.* No objective observer of our Western life can doubt that love—brotherly love, motherly love, and erotic love—is a relatively rare phenomenon, and that it is taken by a number of forms of pseudo-love which are in reality so many forms of the disintegration of love. (p. 70; my emphasis)

How we love—in essence, just as any other practice—is as much a reflection of how we coexist with and relate to others as it is an expression of who we are, if not more so, especially as we continue to move further into the future. The self is tied into, and dependent on, social relationships we enter into and maintain, and the system of social relations we are part of. Yet, in modern capitalist societies, these social relations are profoundly counterintuitive, and for critical theory and especially sociology to be pertinent at all, a consistent effort is essential that is being directed at the fact that in our world, social practices and social relations are likely to be indicative of a process that is neither social in nature, nor expressive of our "human nature," nor nonproblematic. Quite the opposite applies: Those practices and relations provide an inkling of what sustains human civilization in the 21st century. A quarter of a century ago, in *Time, Labor and Social Domination* (1993), Moishe Postone provided a systematic effort to accept and develop further the kind of gaze on social life sociologists must maintain, conceptualizing

capitalism in terms of a historically specific form of social interdependence with an impersonal and seemingly objective character. This form of interdependence is affected by historically unique forms of social relations that are constituted by determinate forms of social practice and, yet, become quasi-independent of the people engaged in these practices. The result is a new, increasingly abstract form of social domination—one that subjects people to impersonal structural imperatives and constraints that cannot be adequately grasped in terms of concrete domination (e.g., personal or group domination), and that generates an ongoing historical dynamic. (pp. 3–4)

When viewed through the prism not of traditional Marxism (as is the target of Postone's reinterpretation of Marx), but of critical Marxism, the terminology of *social relations* suggests the need for and the possibility of a perspective (or set of perspectives) that is (or are) necessary for sociology, social theory, and critical theory in the 21st century, and which must go far beyond the work that has been done on this issue to date, which tends to be overly general, even though important steps are being taken in the direction encouraged here. At the same time, when viewed through the prism of critical (rather than traditional, or orthodox or dogmatic) Marx interpretations, this terminology not only takes on a critical veneer also, it provides a vantage point from which to reassess the import of sociology in the 21st century, and a basis from which to reconstruct its history, present and the future as a social science that requires a very specific kind of intellectual and normative discipline.

The social relations and forms of domination that characterize capitalism, in Marx's analysis, cannot be understood sufficiently in terms of class relations, rooted in property relations and mediated by the market. Rather, his analysis of the commodity and capital—that is, the quasi-objective forms of social mediation constituted by labor in capitalism—should be understood as an analysis of this society's fundamental social relations. These impersonal and abstract social forms do not simply *veil* what traditionally has been deemed the "real" social relations of capitalism, that is, class relations; they *are* the real relations of capitalist society, structuring its dynamic trajectory and its form of production.

Far from considering labor to be the principle of social constitution and the source of wealth in *all* societies, Marx's theory proposes that what uniquely characterizes capitalism is precisely that its basic social relations are constituted by labor and, hence, ultimately are of a fundamentally different sort than those that characterize noncapitalist societies. Though his critical analysis of capitalism does include a critique of exploitation, social inequality, and class domination, it goes beyond this: it seeks to elucidate the very fabric of social relations in modern society, and the abstract form of social domination intrinsic to them, by means of a theory that grounds their social constitution in determinate, structured forms of practice. (p. 6)

Postone's observations and related position regarding social relations and their entwinement deserve far closer and more careful consideration and elaboration than this opportunity provides for, especially as far as *real* possibilities for radical transformation are concerned, and how they are tied into how we relate to each other, especially in an essay that examined imaginary roads toward and prospects for such transformation. Evidently, there is a growing need to communicate ideas that pertain to conflation of purportedly *social* relations with the logic of *capital* much more effectively and constructively, and to far larger audiences than undergraduate classrooms and seminar rooms provide for. Science-fiction films appear to be as good a venue for making related efforts as any other, especially if the purpose is to educate, to "unplug," to provide tools that are conducive to types of self-critique which does not produce even more cognitive dissonance, and to encourage individuals to develop a stronger sense of self than the existing system of social relations allows for, without the former reflecting and reinforcing the latter. As Gandesha (2018) and others have pointed out, when Habermas (1983, 1987) began to retool critical theory in a fashion that jettisoned "subject philosophy" and "philosophy of consciousness," he may well have contributed to the increased and proliferating willingness among teachers and researchers to *believe* in the part of the ideology of modernity that suggests that there is less of a need to confront its dark side consistently and radically. What currently is unfolding around the planet—the intensifying rejection of enlightenment, modernity, and democracy—may have less to do with human fears, choices, and forms of regression, as with the logic of capital moving to the next level, without most of its objects—human beings—noticing, or even having the notion that there might be something worth noticing. It may be most appropriate to conclude this preliminary examination of the firm link that *should* exist between critical theory and sociology, on the one hand, and science fiction, on the other, with a taunt—a quote from a passage Adorno formulated more than seven decades ago, and which we may be well advised to take to heart, particularly if doing so has an unsettling effect:

Everywhere bourgeois society insists on the exertion of will; only love is supposed to be involuntary, pure immediacy of feeling. In its longing for this, which means the dispensation from work, the bourgeois idea of love transcends bourgeois society. But in erecting truth directly amid the general untruth, it perverts the former into the latter. It is not merely that pure feeling, so far as it is still possible within the determinate system of the economy, becomes precisely thereby society's alibi for the domination of interests and bears witness to a humanity that does not exist. . . . If love in society is to represent a better one, it cannot do so as a peaceful enclave, but only by conscious opposition. . . . Loving means not letting immediacy wither under the omnipresent weight of mediation and economics, and in such fidelity it becomes itself mediated, as a stubborn counterpressure. . . . The fidelity exacted by society is a means to unfreedom, but only through fidelity can freedom achieve insubordination to society's command. (Adorno, 1978, p. 172)

Notes

1. On the nexus between issues relating to individuals being "supposed" to adhere to certain norms and values and the imperatives of markets and social structures, see Dux (2004).

2. There are many obvious links and parallels between science fiction and religion, and both serve comparable functions for individuals, in many instances for individuals with very different outlooks and orientations, in other instances for individuals with very similar outlooks. See, e.g., Cowan (2010).

3. This is the theme of Cloud Atlas (2012), directed by the Wachowskis and Tom Tykwer.

4. Just as prejudice at least in equal measure should be subject to both psychological and sociological examination, since it is both a psychological and a social phenomenon, so should cognitive dissonance; see, e.g., Harmon-Jones & Mills (1999); Cooper (2007); Engdahl (2018).

5. Evidently, premodern societies were fraught with these characteristics also, though arguably to a lesser extent and, more importantly, in the absence of a notion of "society" that would have translated into standards according to which a significant segment of the population would have felt justified and dared to apply critical reflexivity to "facts and norms," for example, to the social structure in comparison to claims made by authorities about social and political

order, especially in relation to divine order. For present purposes and the sake of simplicity (as I have done elsewhere), I pinpoint the beginning of the modern age in 1776, the year when Adam Smith published *The Wealth of Nations*, and the year of the Declaration of Independence of the British colonies in North America from the Crown, both triggering the political and economic revolutions that precipitated the formation of modern society.

6. For all practical purposes, we still live in bourgeois society, as Marx identified it as the system of social relations that co-emerged with and is necessary for the continual spread of the capitalist mode of production. See Dahms (2006).

7. Although sociology has been relying on some aspects of the writings of Marx and identifying him as one of the founders of the discipline, sociologists would be well advised to keep in mind that he neither was a sociologist, nor did he regard sociology as an appropriate response to the transformations that produced and would sustain the social and economic structure of bourgeois society. There were good reasons for Marx to be critical of the beginnings of sociology.

8. In this regard, sociologists' widespread rejection since the 1970s of the contributions of Talcott Parsons that were dedicated to prepare a *lingua franca* for sociology, is symptomatic of the refusal to consider the possibility that collaboration would reveal modern societies to be less baffling than they are generally assumed to be. Regarding the problem of knowledge in the 21st century, see Crombez and Dahms (2015).

9. See Frankfurt Institute for Social Research (1972); and Adorno's contributions in Adorno et al. (1977).

10. This is true to differing degrees for individual members of the Institute for Social Research in the early-to-mid-1930s, e.g., Grossman (1992, 2017), but also to the more well-known representatives of critical theory; see Braunstein (2016) on Adorno's critique of political economy.

11. In this context, Adorno's lectures and his conversations with Becker about education are most instructive (Adorno, 2005, 1983; Adorno & Becker, 1982). See also Cho (2009), Stojanov (2012), and Robertson & Dale (2009).

12. See, e.g., Gandesha (2018) and Dahms (2017b).

13. E.g., Lowenthal and Guterman (1970), Fromm (1973)

14. Adorno (1997, p. 83). See Adorno (1967) for his most explicit engagement with science fiction. Adorno's attitude regarding film was not known to be particularly positive either—"Every visit to the cinema leaves me, against all my vigilance, stupider and worse" (Adorno, 1974, p. 25)—but it was not as one-dimensional as his thought, paradoxically, and contrary to all the evidence, has often been accused of having been. For a more differentiated assessment of Adorno's stance regarding film, see, e.g., Seel (2004).

15. Adorno (1973, p. 399). Note that Günther Anders—the third recipient of the City of Frankfurt's Adorno Prize (in 1983; after Norbert Elias and Jürgen Habermas), and author of *Die Antiquiertheit des Menschen* (The Obsoleteness of

Humankind; 2 vol.; 1992 and 1992), which still has been translated only in parts, and which concerns "The Soul in the Age of the Second Industrial Revolution" (vol. 1) and "The Destruction of Life in the Third Industrial Revolution (vol. 2)—published a book in 1970, only four years after Adorno's *Negative Dialectics*, and in response to the Soviet and U.S. American space programs, entitled *Der Blick vom Mond: Reflexionen über Weltraumflüge* (The View from the Moon: Reflection on Space Flights; 1994), which was not meant sarcastically, but which posited that "the decisive event of the space flights does not consist in reaching the distant regions of space or of the distant moonscape, but in Earth for the first time having the opportunity to see itself, to encounter itself in such a manner in which the reflecting human being could encounter himself in the mirror" (p. 12). See in a similar vein the more expansive, ambitious, and philosophical book by Blumenberg (1997). The reference in the Adorno quote is to the purportedly giant, 8-foot tall Maximinus of Thrace who became Emperor of Rome in AD 235. The poem by Stefan George, "*Entrückung*" (referred to above as "Rapture"), runs as follows (in Carl Engels's translation, which Schönberg preferred):

Transport

I feel the air of another planet./ The friendly faces that were turned toward me/ but lately, now are fading into darkness./ Trees and paths I knew and loved so well/ are barely visible, and you beloved/ and radiant specter—cause of all my anguish—/ You are wholly dimmed within a deeper glow,/ whence, now that strife and tumult cease, there/ comes the soothing tremor of sacred awe./ I am dissolved in swirling sound, am weaving/ unfathomed thanks and unnamed praise, and/ wishless I yield myself into the mighty breath./ A wild gust grips me suddenly, and I can/ hear the fervent cries and prayers of women/ prone in the dust and seized in pious rapture:/ And then I see the hazy vapors lifting/ above the sunlit, vast and clear expanse/ that stretches far below the mountain crags./ Beneath my feet a flooring soft and milky, or endless chasms that I cross with ease./ Carried aloft beyond the highest cloud,/I am afloat upon a sea of crystal splendor,/ I am only a sparkle of the holy fire,/ I am only a roaring of the holy voice.

16. Schetsche and Schmidt's (2015) collection provides an informative and in many ways telling set of analyses pertaining to the prevalence and ubiquity of *Fremdkontrolle*, loosely translated as "control by other," or "control by strangers," or "alien control," stressing the centrality and varieties of modes of control in and to modern social life that individuals are oblivious to or incapable to conceive of.

17. Lem's *Solaris* (1970), as well as the films with the same title by Tarkovsky (1972) and Steven Soderberg (2002), address the issue of how humans would act when encountering a truly alien intelligence. Lem was highly critical of humans obsessing about the search for alien life and intelligence, which really is a search for mirrors when venturing "out there," and constitutionally being unable to engage with life-forms that might threaten humankind's perception and description of itself, including especially humankind in its modern form. Tarkovsky's and Soderbergh's versions address this issue in ways that are slightly more "constructive," and which also—and more importantly—take the leap from studying the planet Solaris from a human perspective (effectively turning it into a function of human existence and meaning, which to Lem is inevitable)—to acknowledging, in Tarkovsky's version, that Solaris has the ability to perceive and to study the human visitors, in the effort to "make contact," after having existed for eons of solitude in space, and in Soderbergh's version, to go as far as to embrace Solaris as equal, if not superior to humans, thus inverting (without negating or denigrating) Lem's message. Christopher Grau's (2014) otherwise excellent essay on Soderbergh's version unfortunately misses this point, which would have made his analysis about "love, loss, and identity" even stronger.

18. Tarkovsky's œuvre included two major contributions to science fiction film—*Stalker* (1979) being the other one—whose compatibility and complementarity with Adorno's thought has been documented, esp. Mussell (2013) and Truskolaski (2017).

19. The most important exception are the writings of Carl Freedman, esp. *Critical Theory and Science Fiction* (2000); see also Fuhse (2003).

20. Two noteworthy recent examples in the American context for sociology of film are the collection edited by Sutherland and Feltey (2013) and the study by Hughey (2014). For examples from the early 1970s, when a kind of sociology of science fiction started emerging and then abruptly disappeared, see Ofshe (1970), McNelly & Stover (1972), Milstead, Greenberg, Olander & Warrick (1974) and Greenberg, Milstead, Olander & Warrick (1975). Also see British science-fiction writer Stableford's "sociological investigation of literature and its consumers" and "why people read, why they choose to read the things they do choose to read, and what effects their reading has on them" (Stableford, 1987, p. 5). Finally, see Prokop (1982) for the most rigorous and comprehensive attempt at establishing a sociology of film in German(y) that includes a political economy of the film industry with regard to both the production side of film and to audience behavior, and how market considerations shape developments in specific genres. Incidentally, Prokop studied with Adorno.

21. Reactionary stances are more common in the fantasy genre. See also Orson Scott Card's known racism, and Robert H. Heinlein's notorious conservatism. Still, these are the unavoidable exceptions that confirm the rule.

22. On Marx as an "aestheticist" of capitalism of sorts, see Gandesha and Hartle (2017).

23. On the project of an aesthetic of science fiction, see Russ (1975) and Stockwell (2014).

24. The first, 1944 typescript version of Horkheimer and Adorno's *Dialectic of Enlightenment* (2002) and the revised, published 1947 version is instructive in this regard, as the first version is more explicitly consistent with language employed to capture the logic of capital than the revised version; see van Reijen and Bransen (2002). Regarding the concept of logic of capital, see also Dux (2008), although—ironically—he framed his critique of neoliberalism with regard to "market society." Regarding my use of the concept, *logic of capital*, see Dahms (2015a, 2017a).

25. Prominent earlier attempts—such as those of Kautsky (1988) and Hilferding (1981), and especially Grossman (1992)—were efforts to update Marx's critique to later conditions, but the problem was that: (1) those efforts implicitly worked with static assumptions—Marx's theory applies the way he developed it, though superficially, circumstances changed; (2) before the rise of sociology, he did not recognize that the social itself had transformed in radical ways, including every aspect of it, especially with regard to forms of solidarity; (3) during the 1830s, the logic of capital inserted itself into pre-capitalist world; by the 1930s, this logic had assimilated the pre-capitalist world (which was not capable of understanding this) to its thrust; Georg Lukács sensed this, but did not (or refused to) grasp that forms of praxis that might have worked in the 19th century no longer stood a chance in the 20th century.

26. The most obvious connection between studying the link between critical theory and science fiction films is the chapter on the culture industry in Horkheimer and Adorno's *Dialectic of Enlightenment* (2002, pp. 94–136); however, since directly engaging with this chapter and the related literature would lead this chapter in a very different direction, I am refraining from addressing it directly. Suffice it to point out a paradoxical feature of the relevance of Horkheimer and Adorno's essay and the underlying argument about the link between "culture," enlightenment, and mass deception in the present context: Starting during the 1960s and especially the 1970s, film, and to a lesser extent, television (e.g., Rod Serling's *The Twilight Zone* series (1959–1964), began to play an important role as a form of implicit or explicit social and cultural commentary and critique that would have been difficult, and difficult to imagine, from the 1940s to the early 1960s, due to World War II and then the Cold War, and the limitations both imposed on artistic freedom and creativity in the area of mass entertainment. With efforts to engage in social and cultural critique through mass media and mass entertainment, especially in science fiction, growing creativity was required to tell stories that were not utterly obvious, but still conducive to heightened awareness and a kind of messaging. Evidently, other forms of creativity co-emerged alongside accelerating social change also. In certain regards, *film noir* took steps in the direction of social critique (e.g., Dimendberg, 2004, Naremore, 2008), and it is no accident that

a new kind of science fiction emerged during the 1980s that has come to be
referred to as *Tech-noir*, or, as we will see later on, and less commonly so, as
"ultra noir" (Freedman, 2009), both of which relied heavily one elements of
film noir (see Meehan, 2008; Auger, 2011).—As a sustained effort to "update"
the culture industry concept to conditions that emerged during the latter part
of the 20th century, see Prokop (2003); and Raupach (2017) for an examination of the link between culture industry and the "logic of commodities." See
also Hamenstädt's (2014) examination of theories of political economy in film,
especially Marx, Gramsci, Polanyi, Foucault, Poulantzas, and Hardt and Negri.

27. Also Dahms (2008).

28. When read against the grain, and especially with regard to his late
works, Luhmann's version of systems theory is an important reference point for
addressing related dilemmas and challenges. His retirement lecture (Luhmann,
1994) is intriguing in this context, particularly when his conclusions are being
appreciated, *and developed further*. See also his magnum opus, published in English
under the title, *Theory of Society* (2012 and 2013), and a growing literature
representing recent efforts to integrate systems theory with critical theory (e.g.,
Amstutz & Fischer-Lescano, 2013; Scherr, 2015; Möller & Siri, 2016).

29. The title of Lemert's (2007) textbook on the classics of social theory,
Thinking the Unthinkable, is peculiarly apt and fitting in this regard.

30. See the reference to the "camera obscura" in Marx/Engels (1998).
Evidently, the impetus behind Marx's critique of political economy was to
explicate how classical political economy in the late 18th and 19th century did
not (and by implication, neoclassical modern economics in the 20th century)
provide a suitable means to understand and theorize empirical economic processes, but how those processes are being framed in economics, with key issues,
such as the origin of private property or value, or rapidly increasing economic
inequality (see Piketty 2014; Smith & Langman, 2018; Dahms 2015a, 2015b),
not being addressed at all, which turns economics as a "social" science into
ideology. Regarding the "new Marx reading," see Backhaus (2011), Reichelt
(2013), Postone (1993), and Braunstein (2016).

31. Consider such recent developments as the reduction of the global
population of vertebrate animals by 52 percent between 1970 and 2010, or the
decimation of insect life in Germany since the fall of the wall, by 89 percent.

32. The difference between European and American critical theory is
important in this regard, and especially between philosophy and social science.

33. John Ralston Saul's *The Unconscious Civilization* (1997) remains an
intriguing reference point, in this regard.

34. We like to think that the developments after World War II were
indicative of humankind having reached a higher level of social awareness and
responsibility, but we must situate those developments in the context of the *logic
of capital*, too: Expanding markets and willingness around the world to adhere to

the requisite rules of the game required a degree of social and political stability and order that could not have been achieved without progressive public policies and social legislation, plus fear of another Great Depression, and competition with the other modernity, the Soviet Union. Without World War II, assuming that capitalism would have recovered from the Great Depression without the war and its myriad forms of destruction (economic, organizational, human and social and cultural), there would have been nowhere near as much of a need and occasion for progressive public policies and social legislation.

35. Mugambi Jouet's *Exceptional America* (2017) is instructive in this regard, inasmuch as the United States today represents two different populations and societies, with two different value systems and guiding ideas—progressive and conservative—and two different futures.

36. Hazelrigg (1989, p. 225); the latter quote is a phrase used by Gadamer (1977, p. 9).

37. Evidently, the reference "poetries of the future" is to Marx's famous passage in *The Eighteenth Brumaire of Louis Bonaparte* (1978, p. 597):

> The social revolution of the 19th century cannot draw its poetry from the past, but only from the future. It cannot begin with itself, before it has stripped off all superstition in regard to the past. Earlier revolutions required world-historical recollections in order to drug themselves concerning their own content. In order to arrive at its content, the revolution of the 19th century must let the dead bury their dead. There the phrase went beyond the content; here the content goes beyond the phrase. It appears that we are currently living through another revolution, one that tries to revive the dead.

38. Quote from Gadamer (1977, p. 59).

39. This last quote within the quote is from Alain Robbe-Grillet (1965, p. 160).

40. See Heller (2019) on planetary responsibility.

41. See Fukuyama (1992), even though more recently, he appears to have disavowed his earlier stance. See Harrison (2020).

42. See Horkheimer and Adorno (2002), Mignolo (2003, 2011), Alexander (2013), Jalata and Dahms (2015).

43. In this regard, the history of the modern age can be understood as a shift from the liberation of spirit (human intelligence) from its religious connotations (as described by Hegel, esp. *Phenomenology of Spirit*) to the conversion of spirit into capital (as described by Marx, as the narrowing of spirit to economic—or "instrumental"—reason) as the first form of "artificial intelligence" for whose emergence in the form of technology we are currently in the process of creating the necessary infrastructure.

44. Suvin (1979, p. 7). He also referenced Bloch (1972). Regarding Suvin's take on Brecht, see Suvin (1984).

45. Suvin (1979, pp. 4–5). See also Parrinder (2001) and Bould and Miéville (2009).

46. See also the special section ("dossier") on the question, "Can Love Save Us?" in the German *Philosophie Magazin* (2017), which includes an interview with Alain Badiou, an essay by the magazine's editor on Arendt and Heidegger, a typology of love by Wilhelm Schmid, who teaches philosophy at the University of Erfurt, and several other contributions (pp. 38–65). The issue also contains an interview with Yale historian Timothy Snyder on how to prevent tyranny (pp. 32–36) (his *On Tyranny* [2017] has been an academic bestseller of sorts) and another with Alexander Kluge on his trust in humans (pp. 71–75).

47. Rama-Kandra, in *The Matrix Reloaded*.

48. For instance, in Andrei Tarkovsky's *Solaris* (1972)—as well as Steven Soderbergh's 2002 version—the "connection the word [love] implies" is between a psychologist and his late wife, who committed suicide; in Richard Fleischer's *Soylent Green* (1973), between a detective and his much older colleague; in Ridley Scott's *Blade Runner* (1982)—depending on the interpretation—between a male human and a female replicant, or between a male and female replicant (presumably the latter); in James Cameron's *The Terminator* (1984) between a waitress (Sarah Connor; played by Linda Hamilton) from the present and the father (Kyle Reese; played by Michael Biehn) of her son (John Connor; to appear in the sequels), with Kyle also being the future comrade-in-arms of John, who in turn will be the leader of the human resistance against "the machines"; in Christopher Nolan's *Interstellar* (2014), between a father and his daughter; and in Denis Villeneuve's *Arrival* (2016), between a mother and her daughter. There are many more such examples.

49. There are numerous other examples which, for slightly different purposes, would serve well also, in addition to Nolan's *Interstellar* and Villeneuve's *Arrival*, such as the Wachowskis' *The Matrix* (1999), James Cameron's *Avatar* (2009), Joseph Kosinsky's *Oblivion* (2013), Doug Liman's *Edge of Tomorrow* (2014), and especially Ridley Scott's *Blade Runner* (1982), particularly in light of Villeneuve's sequel, *Blade Runner 2049* (2017), as well as less notable, but still noteworthy films, such as George Nolfi's *The Adjustment Bureau* (2011). With regard to the *Blade Runner* films, so much could be said that even to try to begin doing so here would be little more than a teaser, and probably misleading (see Hazelrigg, 2020).

50. As is not unusual for this kind of undertaking, it took years from initial conception to completion. Many individuals were involved in the process of producing a workable script. Veteran film maker Robert Wise was responsible for bringing the script to the screen. His science-fiction credentials reached

back to the early 1950s, when he directed the original version of *The Day the Earth Stood Still* (1951).

51. Numerous parallels can be drawn between the *Star Trek* franchise in general, *Star Trek: The Motion Picture*, and the second television series, *Star Trek: The Next Generation* (1987–1994), and Christian spirituality. See Maher (1999, esp. 166–169), as well as Porter and McLaren (1999).

References

Adorno, T. W. (1967 [1942]). Aldous Huxley and Utopia. In *Prisms*, Translated by S. Weber (pp. 97–117). Cambridge, MA: MIT Press.

Adorno, T. W. ([1951] 1974). *Minima Moralia: Reflections from Damaged Life*. Translated by E. F. N. Jephcott. London, UK: Verso.

Adorno, T. W. et al. ([1969] 1977). *The Positivist Dispute in German Sociology*. Translated by G. Adey & D. Frisby. London, UK: Heinemann.

Adorno, T. W. ([1966] 2005). Education after Auschwitz. In *Critical Models: Interventions and Catchwords* (pp. 191–204). Translated by H. W. Pickford. New York, NY: Columbia University Press.

Adorno, T. W., & Becker, H. (1982). *Erziehung zur Mündigkeit. Vorträge und Gespräche mit Hellmuth Becker 1959–1969* (8th ed.). G. Kadelback (Ed.). Frankfurt at Main, Germany: Suhrkamp.

Adorno, T. W. ([1969] 1983). Education for autonomy. *Telos, 56* (June 20), 103–110.

Adorno, T. W. ([1970] 1997). *Aesthetic Theory*. Edited by G. Adorno & R. Tiedemann. Translated by R. Hullot-Kentor. Minneapolis: University of Minnesota Press.

Adorno, T. W. ([1966] 1973). *Negative Dialectics*. Translated by E. B. Ashton. New York, NY: Continuum.

Alexander, J. (2013). *The Dark Side of Modernity*. Malden, MA: Polity.

Allen, A. (2015). Are we driven? Critical theory and psychoanalysis reconsidered. *Critical Horizons, 16*(4), 311–328.

Allen, A. (2016). *The End of Progress: Decolonizing the Normative Foundations of Critical Theory*. New York, NY: Columbia University Press.

Amstutz, M., & Fischer-Lescano, A. (Eds.). (2013). *Kritische Systemtheorie: Zur Evolution einer normativen Theorie*. Bielefeld, Germany: Transcript-Verlag.

Anders, G. ([1956] 1992). *Die Antiquiertheit des Menschen: Über die Seele im Zeitalter der zweiten industriellen Revolution* (vol. 1). Munich, Germany: C. H. Beck.

Anders, G. ([1980] 1992). *Die Antiquiertheit des Menschen: Über die Zerstörung des Lebens im Zeitalter der dritten industriellen Revolution* (vol. 2). Munich, Germany: C.H. Beck.

Auger, E. E. (2011). *Tech-Noir Film: A Theory of the Development of Popular Genres*. Chicago, IL: Intellect/University of Chicago Press.

Backhaus, H.-G. (2011). *Dialektik der Wertform: Untersuchungen zur marxschen Ökonomiekritik* (2nd ed.). Freiburg, Germany: Ça ira.

Badiou, A. ([2010] 2013). *Cinema*. Translated by S. Spitzer. Malden, MA: Polity.

Baudrillard, J. ([1981] 1994). *Simulacra and Simulation*. Translated by S. F. Glaser. Ann Arbor: University of Michigan Press.

Beller, J. (2006). *The Cinematic Mode of Production: Attention Economy and the Society of the Spectacle*. Hanover, NH: Dartmouth College Press.

Benhabib, S. (1986). *Critique, Norm, and Utopia: A Study of the Foundations of Critical Theory*. New York, NY: Columbia University Press.

Benjamin, J. (1988). *The Bonds of Love: Psychoanalysis, Feminism, and the Problem of Domination*. New York, NY: Pantheon.

Berger, P., & Luckmann, T. (1966). *The Social Construction of Reality*. Garden City, NY: Doubleday.

Bloch, E. ([1938–47] 1995). *The Principle of Hope* (3 vol.). Cambridge, MA: MIT Press

Bloch, E. (1972). Entfremdung, Verfremdung: Alienation, Estrangement. In E. Munk (ed.), *Brecht* (pp.7–11). New York, NY: Bantam.

Block, J. (2012). *The Crucible of Consent: American Child Rearing and the Forging of Liberal Society*. Cambridge, MA: Harvard University Press.

Blumenberg, H. (1997). *Die Vollzähligkeit der Sterne*. Frankfurt at Main, Germany: Suhrkamp.

Boltanski, L. ([1989] 2012). Agape: An introduction to the states of peace. In *Love and Justice as Competences: Three Essays on the Sociology of Action* (pp. 89–165). Translated by C. Porter. Malden, MA: Polity.

Booker, M. K. (2006). *Alternate Americas: Science Fiction Film and American Culture*. Westport, CT: Praeger.

Bould, M., & Miéville, C. (Eds.). (2009). *Red Planets: Marxism and Science Fiction*. Middletown, CT: Wesleyan University Press.

Braidotti, R. (2013). *The Posthuman*. Malden, MA: Polity.

Braunstein, D. (2016). *Adornos Kritik der politischen Ökonomie* (2nd ed.). Bielefeld, Germany: Transcript-Verlag.

Cho, D. (2009). Adorno on education or, can critical self-reflection prevent the next Auschwitz? *Historical Materialism, 17*(1), 74–97.

Constable, C. (2009). *Adapting Philosophy: Jean Baudrillard and The Matrix Trilogy*. Manchester, UK: Manchester University Press.

Cook, D. (2012). *Adorno, Habermas and the Search for a Rational Society*. London, UK: Routledge.

Cooper, J. (2007). *Cognitive Dissonance: 50 Years of a Classic Theory*. Thousand Oaks, CA: Sage.

Cowan, D. E. (2010). *Sacred Space: The Quest for Transcendence in Science Fiction Film and Television.* Waco, TX: Baylor University Press.

Crary, J. (2013). *24/7: Late Capitalism and the End of Sleep.* London, UK: Verso.

Crombez, J., & Dahms, H. F. (2015). Artificial intelligence and the problem of digital ontotheology: Toward a critical rethinking of science fiction as theory. *Bulletin of Science, Technology and Society, 35*(3–4), 104–113.

Couldry, N., Hepp, A. (2017). *The Mediated Construction of Reality.* Cambridge, UK: Polity.

Dahmer, H. (1994). *Pseudonatur und Kritik: Freud, Marx und die Gegenwart.* Frankfurt at Main, Germany: Suhrkamp.

Dahmer, H. (2001). *Soziologie nach einem barbarischen Jahrhundert.* Vienna, Austria: WUV Universitätsverlag.

Dahms, H. F. (1992). Die gesellschaftliche Rationalisierung der Ökonomie: Vom garantierten Mindesteinkommen als konstitutionellem Anrecht. *Soziale Welt, 43*(2), 141–167

Dahms, H. F. (1995). From creative action to the social rationalization of the economy: Joseph A. Schumpeter's social theory. *Sociological Theory, 13*(1), 1–13.

Dahms, H. F. (2005a). Globalization or hyper-alienation? Critiques of traditional Marxism as arguments for basic income. In J. M. Lehmann (ed.), *Social Theory as Politics in Knowledge (Current Perspectives in Social Theory, 23,* 205–276). Amsterdam, Netherlands: Elsevier. (Identical with ch. 4 in Dahms, 2011).

Dahms, H. F. (2005b). The *Matrix* trilogy as critical theory of alienation: Communicating a message of radical transformation. *Transdisciplinary Journal of Emergence, 3*(1), 108–24.

Dahms, H. F. (2006). Does alienation have a future? Recapturing the core of critical theory. In L. Langman & D. K. Fishman (eds.), *The Evolution of Alienation: Trauma, Promise, and the Millennium* (pp. 23–46). Lanham, MD: Rowman and Littlefield. (Identical to ch. 5 in Dahms, 2011)

Dahms, H. F. (2007). Confronting the dynamic nature of modern social life. *Soundings: An Interdisciplinary Journal 90* (3–4 Fall–Winter), 191–205.

Dahms, H. F. (2008). How social science is impossible without critical theory: The immersion of mainstream approaches in time and space. In H. F. Dahms (ed.), *No Social Science without Critical Theory (Current Perspectives in Social Theory, 26)* (pp. 3–61). Bingley, UK: Emerald. (Identical to ch. 6 in Dahms, 2011)

Dahms, H. F. (2009). Democracy. In H. Fagan & R. Munck (eds.), *Globalization and Security: An Encyclopedia* (vol. I) (pp. 42–60). Westport, CT: Praeger.

Dahms, H. F. (2011). *The Vitality of Critical Theory. Current Perspectives in Social Theory, 28.* Bingley, UK: Emerald.

Dahms, H. F. (2013). Decoding modern society: The *Matrix* trilogy and the realm of alienation. In J.-A. Sutherland & K. Feltey (eds.), *Cinematic Sociology. Social Life in Film* (2nd ed.) (pp. 42–54). Thousand Oaks, CA: Sage.

Dahms, H. F. (2015a). Which capital, Which Marx? Basic income between mainstream economics, critical theory, and the logic of capital. *Basic Income Studies*, *10*(1), 115–140.

Dahms, H. F. (2015b). Toward a critical theory of capital in the 21st century: Thomas Piketty between Adam Smith and the prospect of apocalypse. *Critical Sociology*, *41*(2), 359–374.

Dahms, H. F. (2017a). Critical theory in the twenty-first century: The logic of capital between classical social theory, the early Frankfurt School critique of political economy, and the prospect of artifice. In D. Krier & M. Worrell (eds.), *The Social Ontology of Capitalism* (pp. 47–74). New York, NY: Palgrave

Dahms, H. F. (2017b). Critical theory as radical comparative-historical research. In M. Thompson (ed.), *The Palgrave Handbook of Critical Theory* (pp. 165–184). Houndmills, UK: Palgrave.

Dahms, H. F. (2017c). Critical theory, Brexit, and the vicissitudes of political economy in the twenty-first century. In W. Outhwaite (ed.), *Brexit: Sociological Responses* (pp. 183–192). London, UK: Anthem Press.

Dahms, H. F. (2018). Critical theory, radical reform and planetary sociology: Between impossibility and inevitability. In D. A. Smith & L. Langman (eds.). *Piketty, Inequality and 21st Century Capitalism* (pp. 152–168). Leiden, UK: Brill.

Dahms, H. F. (Ed.). (2020). *The Challenge of Progress: Theory between Critique and Ideology*. (Current Perspectives in Social Theory, vol. 36). Bingley, UK: Emerald.

Dahms, H. F. (Ed.). (forthcoming). *Planetary Sociology: Beyond the Entanglement of Identity and Social Structure*. Bingley, UK: Emerald.

Dandaneau, S. P. (2001). *Taking It Big: Developing Sociological Consciousness in Postmodern Times*. Thousand Oaks, CA: Sage.

The Data Team (2018). Democracy continues its disturbing retreat. *The Economist* (January 31). www.economist.com/blogs/graphicdetail/2018/01/daily-chart-21

Diamond, L., & Plattner, M. F. (Eds.). (2015). *Democracy in Decline?* Baltimore, MD: Johns Hopkins University Press.

Diamond, L., Plattner, M. F., & Walker, C. (Eds.). (2016). *Authoritarianism Goes Global: The Challenge to Democracy*. Baltimore, MD: Johns Hopkins University Press.

Dimendberg, E. (2004). *Film Noir and the Spaces of Modernity*. Cambridge, MA: Harvard University Press.

Diocaretz, M., & Herbrechter, S. (Eds.). (2006). *The Matrix in Theory*. Amsterdam, The Netherlands: Rodopi BV.

Drescher, A., Esser, J., & Fach, W. (1986). *Die politische Ökonomie der Liebe: Ein Essay.* Frankfurt at Main, Germany: Suhrkamp.

Dux, G. (1994). *Geschlecht und Gesellschaft: Warum wir lieben. Die Liebe nach dem Verlust der Welt.* Frankfurt at Main, Germany: Suhrkamp.

Dux, G. ([2000] 2011). *Historico-Genetic Theory of Culture: On the Processual Logic of Cultural Change.* Bielefeld, Germany: Transcript-Verlag.

Dux, G. (2004). *Die Moral in der prozessualen Logik der Moderne: Warum wir sollen, was wir sollen.* Weilerswist, Germany: Velbrück Wissenschaft.

Dux, G. (2008). *Warum den Gerechtigkeit: Die Logik des Kapitals. Die Politik im Widerstreit mit der Ökonomie.* Weilerswist, Germany: Velbrück.

Ehrenberg, A. (2009). *The Weariness of the Self: Diagnosing the History of Depression in the Contemporary Age.* Montreal, Canada: McGill-Queens University Press.

Ehrenberg, A. (2010). *La société du malaise.* Paris, France: Editions Odile Jacob.

Engdahl, F. W. (2018). *Manifest Destiny: Democracy as Cognitive Dissonance.* Wiesbaden, Germany: mine.books.

Frankfurt Institute of Social Research ([1956] 1972). *Aspects of Sociology.* Translated by J. Viertel. Boston, MA: Beacon Press.

Freedman, C. (2000). *Critical Theory and Science Fiction.* Hanover, NH: Wesleyan University Press.

Freedman, C. (2009). Marxism, cinema and some dialectics of science fiction and film noir. In M. Bould & C. Miéville (eds.). *Red Planets: Marxism and Science Fiction.* Middletown, CT: Wesleyan University Press.

Fromm, E. (1955). *The Sane Society.* New York, NY: Rinehart.

Fromm, E. ([1956] 1963). *The Art of Loving.* New York, NY: Bantam Books.

Fromm, E. (1973). *The Anatomy of Human Destructiveness.* New York, NY: Holt, Rinehart, and Winston.

Fuhse, J.A. (2003). Das Andere der Gesellschaft—Science Fiction als Kritische Theorie. *Soziale Welt* 54: 223—240.

Fukuyama, F. (1992). *The End of History and the Last Man.* New York, NY: Free Press.

Gadamer, H.-G. ([1966] 1977). The Universality of the Hermeneutic Problem. In *Philosophical Hermeneutics* (pp. 3–17). Translated and edited by D. E. Linge. Berkeley: University of California Press.

Gandesha, S. (2018). The Neoliberal Personality. *Logos: A Journal of Modern Society and Culture.* Retrieved from logosjournal.com/2017/the-neoliberal-personality

Gandesha, S. & Hartle, J. F. (Eds.). (2017). *Aesthetic Marx.* London, UK: Bloomsbury.

Grau, C. (Ed.). (2005). *Philosophers Explore* The Matrix. Oxford, UK: Oxford University Press.

Grau, C. (2014). Love, loss and identity in *Solaris.* In S. Wolf & C. Grau (eds.), *Understanding Love: Philosophy, Film, and Fiction* (pp. 97–122). Oxford, UK: Oxford University Press.

Greenberg, M. H., Milstead, J. W., Olander, J. D., & Warrick, P. (Eds.). (1975). *Social Problems through Science Fiction*. New York, NY: St. Martin's Press.

Grossman, H. ([1929] 1992). *The Law of Accumulation and Breakdown of the Capitalist System*, Translated by J. Banaji. London, UK: Pluto Press.

Grossman, H. (2017). *Capitalism's Contradictions: Studies in Economic Theory before and after Marx*. Translated by I. Birchall, R. Kuhn & E. O'Callaghan. Edited by R. Kuhn. Chicago, IL: Haymarket.

Gunn, J., & Candelaria, M. (Eds.). (2005). *Speculations on Speculation: Theories of Science Fiction*. Lanham, MD: The Scarecrow Press.

Habermas, J. ([1981] 1983). *The Theory of Communicative Action* (vol. 1). Translated by T. McCarthy. Boston, MA: Beacon Press.

Habermas, J. ([1981] 1987). *The Theory of Communicative Action* (vol. II). Translated by T. McCarthy Boston, MA: Beacon Press.

Habermas, J. ([1985] 1989). The New Obscurity: The Crisis of the Welfare State and the Exhaustion of Utopian Energies. In *The New Conservatism: Cultural Criticism and the Historians' Debate* (pp. 71–99). Cambridge, MA: MIT Press.

Hamenstädt, U. (2014). *Theorien der politischen Ökonomie im Film*. Wiesbaden, Germany: Springer VS.

Harmon-Jones, E., & Mills, J. (Eds.). (1999). *Cognitive Dissonance: Progress on a Pivotal Theory in Social Psychology*. Washington, DC: American Psychological Association.

Harrison, D. M. (2020). Sociology at the end of history: Profession, vocation and critical practice. In H. F. Dahms (ed.), *The Challenge of Progress: Theory between Critique and Ideology* (pp. 133–155). Current Perspectives in Social Theory, vol. 36. Bingley, UK: Emerald.

Haskel, J., & Westlake, S. (2018). *Capitalism without Capital: The Rise of the Intangible Economy*. Princeton, NJ: Princeton University Press.

Hazelrigg, L. E. (1989). *Claims of Knowledge—On the Labor of Making Found Worlds* (Vol. 2 of *Social Science and the Challenge of Relativism*). Tallahassee: Florida State University Press.

Hazelrigg, L. E. (2020). "How Can We [Not] Know?" *Blade Runner* as cinematic landmark in critical thought. In H. F. Dahms (ed.), *The Challenge of Progress: Theory between Critique and Ideology* (pp. 111–132). Current Perspectives in Social Theory, vol. 36. Bingley, UK: Emerald.

Heilbroner, R. L. (1986). *The Nature and Logic of Capitalism*. New York, NY: W. W. Norton.

Heim, T. (2013). *Metamorphosen des Kapitals. Kapitalistische Vergesellschaftung und Perspektiven einer kritischen Sozialwissenschaft nach Marx, Foucault, und Bourdieu*. Bielefeld, Germany: Transcript-Verlag.

Heller, A. (2019). Freedom and security. European Forum Alpbach. www.alpbach.org/en/heller

Hemingway, A. (2017). *Landscape between Ideology and the Aesthetic: Marxist Essays on British Art and Art Theory, 1750–1850*. Chicago, IL: Haymarket Books.

Hilferding, R. ([1910]1981). *Finance Capital: A Study of the Latest Stage of Capitalist Development*. London, UK: Routledge and Kegan Paul.

Hochschild, A. R. (2016). *Strangers in Their Own Land: Anger and Mourning on the American Right*. New York, NY: The New Press.

Honneth, A. ([1994] 1995). *The Struggle for Recognition: The Moral Grammar of Social Conflicts*, Translated by J. Anderson. Malden, MA: Blackwell.

Horkheimer, M. ([1937] 1972). Traditional and Critical Theory. In *Critical Theory: Selected Writings* (pp. 188–243). Translated by M. J. O'Connell. New York, NY: The Seabury Press.

Horkheimer, M., & Adorno, T. W. ([1944] 2002). *Dialectic of Enlightenment: Philosophical Fragments*. Edited by G. Schmid Noerr. Translated by E. Jephcott. Stanford, CA: Stanford University Press.

Hughey, M. W. (2014). *The White Savior Film: Content, Critics, and Consumption*. Philadelphia, PA: Temple University Press.

Illouz, E. (1997). *Consuming the Romantic Utopia: Love and the Cultural Contradictions of Capitalism*. Berkeley: University of California Press.

Jalata, A., & Dahms, H. F. (2015). Theorizing modern society as an inverted reality: How critical theory and indigenous critiques of globalization must learn from each other. In H. F. Dahms (ed.), *Globalization, Critique, and Social Theory: Diagnoses and Challenges* (*Current Perspectives in Social Theory*, 33) (pp. 75–133). Bingley, UK: Emerald.

Jameson, F. (2005). *Archaeologies of the Future: The Desire Called Utopia and Other Science Fictions*. London, UK: Verso.

Jouet, M. (2017). *Exceptional America: What Divides Americans from the World and from Each Other*. Berkeley: University of California Press.

Kaplan, R. (1997, December). Was democracy just a moment? *The Atlantic Monthly*. www.theatlantic.com/magazine/archive/1997/12/was-democracy-just-a-moment/306022

Kautsky, K. ([1927]1988). *The Materialist Conception of History*. Edited by J. H. Kautsky. Translated by R. Meyer. New Haven, CT: Yale University Press.

Keen, S. (1997). *To Love and Be Loved*. New York, NY: Bantam.

Kepler, J. ([1608] 1634). *Somnium, seu opus posthumum De astronomia lunari*. Frankfurt, Germany.

Kracauer, S. ([1947] 2004). *From Caligari to Hitler: A Psychological History of the German Film*. Revised and expanded edition. Edited by L. Quaresima. Princeton, NJ: Princeton University Press.

Kracauer, S. (1960). *Theory of Film: The Redemption of Physical Reality*. Oxford, UK: Oxford University Press.

Kumar, K. (1987). *Utopia and Anti-Utopia in Modern Times*. Oxford, UK: Basil Blackwell.

Kurlantzick, J. (2013). *Democracy in Retreat: The Revolt of the Middle Class and the Worldwide Decline of Representative Government*. New Haven, CT: Yale University Press.

Leigh, M. K., & Durand, K. K. (Eds.). (2013). *Marxism and the Movies: Critical Essays on Class Struggle in Cinema*. London, UK: McFarland & Co.

Lem, S. ([1961] 1970). *Solaris*. Translated by J. Kilmartin. New York, NY: Walker.

Lemert, C. (2007). *Thinking the Unthinkable: The Riddles of Classical Social Theories*. Boulder, CO: Paradigm.

Lemert, C. (2011). *The Structural Lie: Small Clues to Global Things*. London, UK: Routledge.

Litch, M. M. (2002). *Philosophy through Film*. New York, NY: Routledge.

Lowenthal, L., & Guterman, N. ([1949] 1970). *Prophets of Deceit: A Study of the Techniques of the American Agitato* (2nd ed.). Palo Alto, CA: Pacific Books.

Luhmann, N. ([1969] 2008). *Liebe: Eine Übung*. Frankfurt at Main, Germany: Suhrkamp.

Luhmann, N. ([1982] 1986). *Love as Passion: The Codification of Intimacy*, Translated by J. Gaines & D. Jones. Cambridge, MA: Harvard University Press.

Luhmann, N. ([1993] 1994). "What is the case?" and "What lies behind it?" The two sociologies and the theory of society. Translated by S. Fuchs. *Sociological Theory* 12(2), 126–139.

Luhmann, N. ([1997] 2012). *Theory of Society* (vol. I). Translated by R. Barrett. Stanford, CA: Stanford University Press.

Luhmann, N. ([1997] 2013). *Theory of Society* (vol. II). Translated by R. Barrett. Stanford, CA: Stanford University Press.

Maher, I. (1999). The Outward Voyage and the Inward Search: *Star Trek* Motion Pictures and the Spiritual Quest. In J. Porter & D. McLaren (eds.). *Star Trek and Sacred Ground: Explorations of Star Trek, Religion, and American Culture*. Albany: State University of New York Press.

Marcuse, H. ([1955] 1974). *Eros and Civilization: A Philosophical Inquiry into Freud*. Boston, MA: Beacon Press.

Marx, K., Engels, F. ([1845–46] 1998). *The German Ideology*. Amherst, NY: Prometheus Books.

Marx, K. ([1852] 1978). *The Eighteenth Brumaire of Louis Bonaparte*. In K. C. Tucker (ed.), *The Marx-Engels Reader* (2nd ed.) (pp. 594–617). New York, NY: W. W. Norton.

Mazierska E., & Kristensen, L. (Eds.). (2014). *Marx at the Movies: Revisiting History, Theory, and Practice*. New York, NY: Palgrave Macmillan.

McNelly, W. E., & Stover, L. E. (Eds.). (1972). *Above the Human Landscape: An Anthology of Social Science Fiction*. Pacific Palisades, CA: Goodyear.

Meehan, P. (2008). *Tech-Noir: The Future of Science Fiction and Film Noir*. Jefferson, NC: McFarland.

Mignolo, W. (2003). *The Darker Side of the Renaissance: Literacy, Territoriality, and Colonization*, 2nd ed. Ann Arbor: University of Michigan Press.

Mignolo, W. (2011). *The Darker Side of Western Modernity: Global Futures, Decolonial Options*. Durham, NC: Duke University Press.

Milstead, J. W., Greenberg, M. H., Olander, J. O., & Warrick, P. (Eds.). (1974). *Sociology through Science Fiction*. New York, NY: St. Martin's Press.

Möller, K., Siri, J. (Eds.). (2016). *Systemtheorie und Gesellschaftskritik: Perspektiven der Kritischen Systemtheorie*. Bielefeld, Germany: Transcript-Verlag.

Mussell, S. (2013). Mimesis reconsidered: Adorno and Tarkovsky contra Habermas. *Film-Philosophy* 17(1). www.film-philosophy.com/index.php/f-p/article/viewFile/294/868

Naremore, J. (2008). *More than Night: Film Noir in Its Contexts*. Berkeley: University of California Press.

Ofshe, R. (Ed.). (1970). *The Sociology of the Possible*. Englewood Cliffs: Prentice-Hall.

Parrinder, P. (Ed.). (2001). *Learning from Other Worlds: Estrangement, Cognition, and the Politics of Science Fiction and Utopia*. Durham, NC: Duke University Press.

Philosophie Magazin (2017, June/July) 4(34).

Piketty, T. (2014). *Capital in the Twenty First Century*. Translated by A. Goldhammer. Cambridge, MA: Belknap Press (Harvard University Press).

Porter, J. E., & McLaren, D. L. (Eds.). (1999). *Star Trek and Sacred Ground: Explorations of Star Trek, Religion, and American Culture*. Albany: State University of New York Press.

Postone, M. (1993). *Time, Labor and Social Domination: A Reinterpretation of Marx's Critical Theory*. Cambridge, UK: Cambridge University Press.

Prokop, D. (1982). *Soziologie des Films* (expanded edition). Frankfurt at Main, Germany: Fischer.

Prokop, D. (2003). *Mit Adorno gegen Adorno: Negative Dialektik der Kulturindustrie*. Hamburg, Germany: VSA Verlag.

Raupach, T. (2017). *Die autopoietische Kulturindustrie: Moderne Massenmedien zwischen Selbsterzeugung und Warenlogik* (2nd ed.). Wiesbaden, Germany: Springer VS.

Reichelt, H. (2013). *Neue Marx-Lektüre: Zur Kritik sozialwissenschaftlicher Logik* (2nd ed.). Freiburg, Germany: Ça Ira Verlag.

Rosa, H. ([2005] 2015). *Social Acceleration: A New Theory of Modernity*. Translated by J. Trejo-Mathys. New York, NY: Columbia University Press.

Rosa, H. (2016). *Resonanz: Eine Soziologie der Weltbeziehung*. Berlin, Germany: Suhrkamp.

Russ, J. (1975). Towards an Aesthetic of Science Fiction. *Science Fiction Studies* #6, Vol. 2, pt. 2. Retrieved from https://wwwdepauw.edu/sfs/backissues/6/russ6art.htm

Robbe-Grillet, A. ([1963] 1965). *For a New Novel*. Translated by R. Howard. New York, NY: Grove Press.

Robertson, S. L., & Dale, R. (2009). The World Bank, the IMF, and the possibilities of critical education. In M. W. Apple, W. Au, & L. A. Gandin (eds.), *The Routledge International Handbook of Critical Education* (pp. 23–35). New York, NY: Routledge.

Sanders, S. M. (Ed.). (2008). *The Philosophy of Science Fiction Film*. Lexington: University of Kentucky Press.

Saul, J. R. (1997). *The Unconscious Civilization*. New York, NY: The Free Press.

Scherr, A. (Ed.). (2015). *Systemtheorie und Differenzierungtheorie als Kritik: Perspektiven im Anschluss and Niklas Luhmann*. Weinheim, Germany: Beltz.

Schetsche, M., Schmidt R.-B. (Eds.). (2015). *Fremdkontrolle: Ängste, Mythen, Praktiken*. Bielefeld, Germany: Springer VS.

Schluchter, W. (1996a). *Unversöhnte Moderne*. Frankfurt/M.: Suhrkamp.

Schluchter, W. (1996b). *Paradoxes of Modernity: Culture and Conduct in the Theory of Max Weber*. Stanford, CA: Stanford University Press.

Schneider, S. (Ed.). (2009). *Science Fiction and Philosophy: From Time Travel to Superintelligence*. Oxford, UK: Wiley-Blackwell.

Seel, M. (2004). Adornos Apologie des Films. In *Adornos Philosophie der Kontemplation* (pp. 77–95). Frankfurt/M.: Suhrkamp.

Seel, M. ([2013] 2018). *The Arts of Cinema*. Translated by K. S. Walker. Ithaca, NY: Cornell University Press.

Shelley, M. ([1818] 2007). *Frankenstein; or, The Modern Prometheus*. Edited by S. J. Wolfson. New York, NY: Pearson Longman.

Smith, D. A., & Langman, L. (Eds.). (2018). *Piketty, Inequality and 21st Century Capitalism*. Leiden, UK: Brill.

Snyder, T. (2017). *On Tyranny: Twenty Lessons from the Twentieth Century*. New York, NY: Penguin.

Stableford, B. (1987). *The Sociology of Science Fiction*. Long Beach, CA: Borgo Press.

Stojanov, K. (2012). Theodor W. Adorno—Education as Social Critique. In P. Siljander, A. Kivelä, & A. Sutined (eds.), *Theories of Bildung and Growth* (pp. 125–134). Boston, MA: Sense Publishers.

Stockwell, P. (2014). Aesthetics. In R. Latham (ed.), *The Oxford Handbook of Science Fiction* (pp. 35–46). New York, NY: Oxford University Press.

Sutherland, J.-A., & Feltey, K. (Eds.). (2013). *Cinematic Sociology: Social Life in Film* (2nd ed.). Thousand Oaks, CA: Sage.

Suvin, D. (1979). *Metamorphoses of Science Fiction: On the Poetics and History of a Literary Genre*. New Haven, CT: Yale University Press.

Suvin, D. (1984). *To Brecht and Beyond: Soundings in Modern Dramaturgy*. Bright, UK: The Harvester Press.

Suvin, D. (1988). *Positions and Presuppositions in Science Fiction*. Kent, OH: Kent State University Press.
Suvin, D. (2010). *Defined by a Hollow: Essays on Utopia, Science Fiction and Political Epistemology*. Bern, Switzerland: Peter Lang.
Truskolaski, S. (2017). Adorno's imageless materialism. *Studies in Social and Political Thought 23*, 14–23.
Van Reijen, W., & Bransen, J. (2002). The disappearance of class history in "Dialectic of Enlightenment": A commentary on the textual variants (1947 and 1944). In Horkheimer & Adorno, *Dialectic of Enlightenment: Philosophical Fragments* (pp. 248–252). Edited by G. Schmid Noerr. Translated by E. Jephcott. Stanford, CA: Stanford University Press.
Verhaeghe, P. (2014). Neoliberalism has brought out the worst in us. *The Economist* (29 September). Retrieved from www.guardian.com/commentisfree/2014/sep/29/neoliberalism-economic-system-ethics-personality-psychopathicsthic
Wartenberg, T. E. (1999). *Unlikely Couples: Movie Romance as Social Criticism*. Boulder, CO: Westview Press.
Whitebook, J. (1995). *Perversion and Utopia: A Study in Psychoanalysis and Critical Theory*. Cambridge, MA: MIT Press.
Wilde, L. (1989). *Marx and Contradiction*. Aldershot, UK: Gower Publishing.
Wolf, S., Grau, C. (Eds.). (2014). *Understanding Love: Philosophy, Film, and Fiction*. Oxford, UK: Oxford University Press.
Žižek, S. (2006). *The Parallax View*. Cambridge, MA: MIT Press.

Films

Cameron, J. (1984) *The Terminator*
Cameron, J. (2009) *Avatar*
Fleischer, R. (1973) *Soylent Green*
Frakes, J. (1996) *Star Trek: First Contact*
Kosinsky, J. (2013) *Oblivion*
Kubrick, S. (1956) *The Killing*
Kubrick, S. (1968) *2001: A Space Odyssey*
Lang, F. (1927) *Metropolis*
Liman, D. (2014) *Edge of Tomorrow*
Nolan, C. (2014) *Interstellar*
Nolfi, G. (2011) *The Adjustment Bureau*
Proyas, A. (1998) *Dark City*
Scott, R. (1979) *Alien*
Scott, R. (1982) *Blade Runner*
Soderbergh, S. (2002) *Solaris*

Tarkovsky, A. (1972) *Solaris*
Tarkovsky, A. (1979) *Stalker*
Villeneuve, D. (2016) *Arrival*
Villeneuve, D. (2017) *Blade Runner 2049*
Wachowski, L. & L. (1999) *The Matrix*
Wachowski, L. & L. (2003) *The Matrix Reloaded*
Wachowski, L. & L. (2003) *The Matrix Revolutions*
Wachowski, L. & L. (2003) *The Animatrix*
Wachowski, L. & L., and Tykwer, T. (2012) *Cloud Atlas*
Wilder, B. (1944) *Double Indemnity*
Wise, R. (1951) *The Day the Earth Stood Still*
Wise, R. (1979) *Star Trek: A Motion Picture*

Chapter 10

Magical Marx

Objective Method and Aesthetics

MARK P. WORRELL

The College de Sociologie offers an interesting response to social degeneracy: "Guided by their formulation of a sacred sociology, contributors to the College transgressed the confines of their bourgeois *habitus* to devise alternative modes of communication and understanding" (Richman, 2002, p. 209). Formulating a "sacred" sociology is tantamount to adopting a position of *authority* which runs against a 500-year project of liquidating the very principle of authority itself (Dewey, 1946. p. 93). The word "authority" seems to resonate on the same frequency as superstition, oppression, and tradition (Royce, 1969, p. 301). The suspicion, then, is that authority is synonymous with *authoritarianism* (Smith, 2016). But the result of negation that animates the critical spirit is the collapse of the normative order as a coherent totality, that is, the reduction of life to matter and mechanism, desires and dollars, monsters and prey. Marx's immoderate "deicide principle" (Wilson, 1967, p. 122) applies not only to gods but to Hegel's absolute, the Idea, as well as all "transcendent" facts of any kind, including "social facts" that constitute the subject matter of sociology.[1] The critical tradition in sociology almost always pursues an anti-fact line of attack with an eye on a utopia of radical autonomy as the payoff. People thirsting for novelty find little enjoyment in facts, ontic depth, or big anythings, especially when perverted structures and

301

dissolution provide copious titillation (Worrell & Krier, 2015). In such an environment we find paradoxical demands coming from the likes of, for example, Zizek who insists that what is needed today is a new universal order, yet, simultaneously rendering the notion of the social absolute (the veritable nucleus of that order) nothing more than a fiction. As Zizek has famously stated on numerous occasions: "There is no big Other." One cannot have a universal order (of understanding *and* rights—"you should") sans an absolute constellation (of reason and obligation—"you must") because it is the absolute that infuses representations with authority and energy. In a world where the absolute is a delusion, mere understanding passes for reason, mediating institutions are cynically waved off as hopelessly corrupt, and signifiers no longer adhere to signifieds. Today we are suffering from a world where authority no longer functions normally (although we find an overabundance of traditional and charismatic nonsense) and authoritarian monstrosities are rising up all around us. All we are left with is the hope for some new carrier class to answer history's call or some liberating Event (the eruption of charisma) or revelation to save us.[2] Critical sociology confronts the unusual but not unprecedented task of again formulating a sacred sociology against those that would reduce society to nothing more than a jumble of interests (anarchists, libertarians, etc.) as well as the spirit of fanatical negation that levels the world down to a flat ontic plane of biology, ego autonomy, and technological salvation (e.g., technocracy, automatocracy, and Robot Marxism, and so on). Here, I will not examine the ins and outs of the College de Sociologie in itself but conjure the notion of a "sacred sociology" as an embarkment to advocate for a renewed "absolute" project that connects Marx to the Durkheimian tradition as two sides (negative and positive) of the broader world of Hegelian speculative idealism and, in this, we are rubbing up against some of the same currents that the College drew inspiration from.[3] This resulting "Marxheimian" synthesis has been one of my projects over the last several years and, here, I want to focus on part of the methodological considerations involved in this endeavor, namely, dialectical analysis.

Negations: Sacred and Profane

Piketty is correct that mainstream economics tells us virtually nothing about anything (2014, p. 33), but his blockbuster is itself rife with a naive realism that hobbles his analysis of inequality. Notions such as the pure value of virgin land and stores of value, and the like, are more than 100 years behind us. As Hegel puts it, even the lower animals refute this kind of crude realism (1991, p. 76; see also Worrell, 2009a and 2009b). The ability to overcome the dead ends of reductionistic nominalism necessitates a return to the dialectical method as it was worked out by Hegel and redefined by neo-Marxism. Dialectics literally means split reasoning: driving through a thing in thought (analysis, dissection, division, etc.) and separating the logos (*spiritus*) from the material prop (*corpus*) as well as dividing logos itself up into kinds (e.g., pure and impure, holy and diabolical). We find a perfect example of dialectical analysis in Marx's exploration of the commodity in *Capital*.[4]

In the first chapter of *Capital* we find the commodity dissected to death (cf. Hegel, 1991, pp. 78)[5] into its use-value (utility), on the one hand, and exchange-value (value), on the other. The dialectical method that Marx uses accomplishes three important things from the standpoint of our current problem: first, it subverts the reified and alien nature of the commodity, revealing that the thing is, at bottom, created by humans; two, the dialectic moves the thing, discursively, into the arena of contested objects that have to legitimate their existence with reasons; finally, the dialectic weaves together a third, irreducible and objective concept from the sublation of its shuttling back and forth between the twin dead ends of materialism (the concrete) and idealism (the abstract). *Capital* is a masterpiece of analysis whereby the bourgeois sacred (money, commodities, and capital) is exposed via analytical inversion to be not holy but an *unholy* nightmare resting on the brutalization and exploitation of the true sacred, the laboring classes forced to sell labor power and perform surplus work due to a loss of their means of subsistence and the prevailing and legalized (valid) relations of production, consumption, accumulation, and the distribution of wealth. Marx "kills off" the new god of modernity and appears to restore labor to a place of honor (revaluation). However, a few things muddle this accomplishment. First, postcapitalist relations are nowhere in Marx's writings made coherent or even plausible—at best we find an "atopia" built on a set of presuppositions that leave it exposed to self-destruction. This line of thinking has been covered elsewhere (Worrell & Krier, 2015) and will not be rehashed at this point. Secondly, the sacred status of the worker that appears to be restored in the pages of *Capital* through analytical inversion is hobbled by a reduction of "The Worker" to, first, a myth,[6] and, secondly, to a profane status—this is tied to the preceding problem of the communist atopia. In other words, Marx is "magical" to the very end. We will have to sidestep this problem for now because it will entail a detailed examination of misleading translations of Marx's texts that obscure his theory of human *instincts* and move along to the pseudo-positive moment at the conclusion of *Capital* as we find it the text most students and scholars read today in the US and the UK.

The now-standard Fowkes translation of *Capital* includes the *Resultate* section as a pseudo-conclusion and the addition of this external document at the end of *Capital* leads us astray in at least two ways: on the one hand, it actually restores[7] the commodity to a place of power and ascendency (facticity) over and against proletarian consciousness[8] and, on the other, it suggests that Marx's dialectical method terminates in a positive synthesis when, in fact, as an act of restoration, it abandons the reader in a world of where diabolical spirits reign uncontested. Marx famously rejected Hegel's negation of the negation (1964, p. 172) but performs just this feat in *Capital* as we know it. Marx's true "positivity" resides over the horizon in the imagined world of the Revolution (the negation of the negation will come in class action, not in thought and analyses). However, the postrevolutionary world of communist association, with production humming along in the background, is one of individualism, profanity, and play. I would call this kind of hyper-negation a "magical" dialectics where the negationist takes a "professional pleasure" in inverting and reducing the sacred to nothing more than infraliminal matter (Durkheim, 1995, p. 40). The "magical" dialectician is engaged in what amounts to an "astrological" "conjunction" of a "third element" between two stars, delivering a revelation (Benjamin, 1999, p. 696); in the case of Marx, what is revealed through division, inversion, excavation, and so on, is the realization that the value of the commodity, the subject-substance of modernity, is our own external transfigured spirit in a monstrously coercive form (Marx, 1976, p. 1054). But for Marx, the program is not the administration of value but the elimination of value from the world entirely (draining the swamp in today's Trumpian jargon)—when exchange-value is driven from the world, presumably, the constellation of repressed and alienated human values (the capitalist leftovers) will refill the vacuum.[9] The problem with "magical" dialectics is that in delivering consciousness to a spiritless, infaliminal domain it leaves subjects paradoxically susceptible to a rebound mystification via disenchantment. Unbeknownst to positivism, there exist underground tunnels and trap doors that connect the phenomenal back to an eternal and inaccessible dimension. As Durkheim famously observed, opposites (e.g., mindless empiricism on the one hand, and transcendental rationalism on the other, amount to the same thing in the end, they are "more or less equivalent" in their effects (1995, p. 14; cf. Hegel, 1991, pp. 76–78).[10] As Goethe says, they "Mock themselves and don't realize it" (1961, p. 199; cf. Hegel, 1991, pp. 79, 315).

The "magical" moment of dialectics is necessary but insufficient on its own as a critical sociological method because, on one hand, it leads to total disenchantment and possibly diabolical reenchantment when pursued to the end and, on the other, it fails to realize that magical negation already presupposes a "positive" but conceptually irrational moment. Without a conscious and conceptually plausible counterdialectics that engages in an absolute reconstruction and, crucially, a synthetic reconstruction that does not function merely as a fatalistic restoration, the best we can hope for is social anarchy. Magical dialectics presupposes and is built upon a "religious" dialectics that it cannot neglect. In *Elementary Forms*, Durkheim engages in his own dialectical dissection, not of the commodity, but of the totem and his approach has much to offer critical sociology.

The totem is in simplistic terms the collective representation of the clan. Taking the form of a plant or animal species the group (a) worships itself in an external and transfigured form (the most sacred is the name and image of the clan, the totemic emblem) and (b) ritually generates impersonal moral energies, the real object of the cult in the final analysis. The totem, like the commodity in Marx's analysis, is separated into its concrete (prop or envelope) aspect and the abstract moment (the totemic principle: mana, wakan, orenda, etc.).[11] For Durkheim, the program of sociology is not one of destroying the absolute (reducing the world to a "happy go lucky" world of pragmatic fluidity and hyper-constructionism) but rendering the collective representation, the Big Other, luminous and non-terrifying where it was once an opaque Thing of awesome and uncanny powers. We can have the absolute, a Big Other, without it being a big, nasty Thing casting unbearably long shadows. Another way of thinking of this is that Durkheim, while engaged in de-reification and deftishizing the social fact is also not, as we find in relentless hyper-criticism, leaving people with nothing but disenchantment. There is a difference between the worship of society and the destruction of society—recall that the young Marx actually says that society is the enemy of humanity (1964, p. 136). In other words, he pines for the immediate unity of individuals (the unalienated) and the universal order. The project of de-reification is the reason the French Revolution was so decisive for Durkheim: for the first time a society worshiped itself in a non-alien form "without transfiguration of any kind." Society made itself into a god (Durkheim, 1995, pp. 215–216). We can pursue the devolution of 1789 into Terror at another time, but, in the final analysis, both commodities and totems are objectified manifestations of alienated collective human energies that appear to take on a life of their own. Where, for Marx, the key to surplus value can be traced back to relative and absolute quantities of surplus labor, for Durkheim, mana (the totemic principle) is grounded in what we might think of as surplus ritual conduct, hyper-praxis in which the group's moral surplus takes on a life of its own (becomes reified or hypostatic) through a complex process of signification and regulation. Where Marx envisions a world devoid of supernatural forces (humans living free and autonomously) Durkheim knows that human assemblage produces "special effects" (Durkheim, 1951, p. 310) and that that the sacred is always and unceasingly being created—it is inevitable and unavoidable because, and he is correct, consciousness is not simply a reflex of underlying material practices and relations but takes on a life of its own. It was for this reason that Durkheim waved off Marxism as infantile: the poetics of collective consciousness engenders its own novelties for no other reason than to enjoy its own creative powers that cannot be reduced to theories of ideology or false consciousness. Note, however, that this "qualified idealism" as Durkheim calls it is still, nonetheless, rooted in a kind of hyperpraxis or hypermaterialism; in short, unrestrained by instincts, humans in association will tend toward excess (or deficiency) in every sphere of life: too much labor, too much ritual, too much knowledge, too much everything and consciousness will not only track and reflect this excess praxis but will also generate its own excesses.[12]

The Sacred Pure and the Sacred Impure

The sacred, dialectics, syllogisms, and commodities may seem to be unconnected in any internally necessary way but I would like to hash this out briefly to demonstrate Durkheim's idea that all the world is a system of representations and that these representations are held together in discernible forms reflecting an underlying social organization. I will try to connect this premise with Hegel's presentation of the syllogism and Marx's analysis of the commodity.

The syllogism[13] appears to most of us to be something applicable only to formal logic games[14] or "an empty piece of book learning" (Hegel, 1991, p. 260) but the syllogism is *in the world*[15] and, as far as sociology goes, the syllogism relates to how ideas and collective representations are brought into relation with one another, how these ideas form sui generis hierarchies whereby ideas subsume and contain other ideas, or come to be subsumed and contained by others, and, finally, how these processes are regulated by social norms regarding what passes for rational and valid thinking. If one has it in their head that syllogisms are irrelevant to sociology consider this: if universals exist as anything more than empty signifiers, for example, Marx's "universal equivalent" then universals conform or deviate from one thing, syllogistic thinking. To comprehend the commodity (or the totem) one must grasp them as syllogistic moments.

When we seek a vocation for ourselves, affirm the best way to get ahead in life is to work hard, deliberate between two objects as the best qualified to satisfy our needs or desires, or feel that one is equally an "American" regardless of whether or not one is a Christian, or a Jew, or a Muslim, and so on, but not an atheist or similar, one is engaging in syllogistic reasoning. Syllogisms are, for us, not just formal deductions but the manner in which socially-generated ideas form unfolding chains or spirals of propositions and meanings as well as, and this is crucial, the way we are affected by authority and how social forces will motivate or take possession of individuals and push them to action. Depending upon one's "unit of analysis" we can generate an integrated system of facts, from the most aggregate (the "superior" or "higher orders") to the most infinitesimal.

Any number of syllogisms can be constructed according to the problem and the point of view from the religious, political, economic, technological, vocational, and cultural, and so on, and with different "units of analysis" such as world systems, international affairs, states, regional dynamics, urban life, and so on. Contemporary sociology has generally not concerned itself with the most aggregate nor the most granular (the grand abstraction of "humanity" as an undifferentiated whole nor the infinite vortex of the isolated psyche) but the sweeping "middle range" from civilizations to dyadic interactions is where we find our problems and explanations (Durkheim & Mauss, 2006, pp. 35–39). The result is not merely an arbitrary string of superficial syllogisms, as the above admittedly are, but a vast constellation of spiraling and interconnected concepts (each containing a syllogism of its own).

Social reality is rational or has a rationality about it and everything rational is by definition syllogistic (Hegel, 1969, pp. 664–665; see also Hegel, 1991, p. 256). Hegel even goes so far as to say that "Everything is a syllogism . . ." (1969, p. 669) so even the irrational or rationalizations fall under the syllogism. No good sociological explanation is possible without the "triangulation" and interpenetrations enabled by the concept, driven into syllogistic development. If we wish to raise our grasp of society and history to an objective level then it is through the syllogism (Hegel, 1991, p. 257). Tony Smith does a good job in showing that, deep down, Hegel's syllogisms are really about how our thoughts are regulated by principles and that we project our reasons into the principled (1993, pp. 7–21). In other words, there is a logic to social life whether or not we are consciously aware of it: "these conceptions of the general medium and process of social life are pushed home into the actual formative operation of the social mind and will. Society, we are told, may be compared not . . . to an organism, but rather to a mind; it is a co-operative mind, a syllogism, in which the principles held by one part are modified and applied by another" (Bosanquet, 1965, p. 41; see also Bouglé, 1970, pp. 255–256; Durkheim, 1973, p. 13; and Gangas, 2007).[16] According to Tarde, society inclines toward "great agglomerations, great centralizations, to the formation of majestic and perpetually growing systems where Social Logic marvels at itself, in pyramids of syllogisms higher and stronger than any tomb of the Pharaohs" (in Davis, 1906, p. 23). Each science that attempts to grasp nature or society is itself a syllogism (Durkheim, 2004, p. 197).[17] This sounds rather abstract and superfluous to everyday subjectivist concerns, however, if we wish to see consciousness raise itself out of mere existence and subjectivism where it is pushed around by uncomprehended external causes (a short-circuiting of reason where a collection of "becauses" and mindless compulsions dominate) and, instead, grasp the internal necessity of some—not all—facts (see Findlay, 1958, p. 240) by virtue of reflection ("speculation")[18] and conceptual thought, syllogisms are not only relevant but essential to sociology. As Durkheim put it in his philosophy lectures, an abyss stretches out between the individual and the universal, "an abyss that induction leaps across—but by means of what principle?" (2004, p. 201).

The principle is causality.[19] Causality, then, must mediate as a moment of particularity the relation between the individual and the universal. But once consciousness can reason on the basis of the concept (which includes within it syllogisms) genuine causes (social forces motivating conduct) can be separated from rationalizations and subjective confusions.[20] Hegel's syllogistic renovations were important: "Hegel hit on the idea of translating the elements of the Aristotelian logical mechanism back into genuine philosophical conceptualities. So successful was this operation indeed that Hegel is scarcely ever mentioned in the history of logic, as though he had somehow suppressed the method and the mechanics which made it "logic" in the first place" (Jameson, 2009, p. 76).[21] More than any other writer in the classical tradition, it was Durkheim who unknowingly carried forward the program of Hegel: society is a conceptual being first and foremost (Harms, 1981). Indeed, Durkheim's entire analysis of the totem and mana in *Elementary Forms* follows a precise and deliberate syllogistic form: universal totems, particular totems, and singular totems as well as the corresponding mana forms: universal, particular, and singular. However, Hegel's syllogistic innovations were also carried forward by Marx in transformed ways and it creeps in where one least expects it.

Explicit references in Marx to Hegel's syllogisms can be found, for example, in reference to the circulation of commodities (C-M-C) and the general formula for capital[22] but one of the most important deployments of Hegel's syllogistic reasoning is found in a footnote in the first chapter of *Capital* where Marx compares the commodity to the relationship between Peter and Paul: Peter (singularity) knows himself as a human being (universal) in the use-value form of Paul (the particular equivalent) who recognizes his claim to be a human—"Peter only relates to himself as a man through his relation to another man, Paul, in whom he recognizes his likeness" (1976, p. 144).[23] That one recognizes something in the alter ego such that the latter can function as a particular (an alienated or split/doubled singularity taking on a new social function) for the shining singularity means that we are not in the domain of mere understanding (*Verstehen*) but witnessing a moment in the odyssey of the Absolute in one of its shapes (see Hegel, 1991, p. 239). Lacking Paul, Peter will never bask in the reflected glory of the universal equivalent. But, of course, for the deluded Peter, he thinks he has an *immediate* relationship to the universal[24] and this will spell disaster for the dyad and the emerging symbolic order they have generated.[25]

The same logic obtains with regards to royalty. "For instance, one man is king only because other men stand in the relation of subjects to him. They, on the other hand, imagine that they are subjects because he is king" (Marx, 1976, p. 149). However, this is a weak spot in Marx's own thinking, he too, like the nominalists and Luther has it in for mediation.

In the *Grundrisse*, as a prime example, we see Marx quite brilliantly expounding upon a process of dialectical mediation:

> It is important to note that wealth as such, i.e., bourgeois wealth, is always expressed to the highest power as exchange value, where it is posited as *mediator*, as the mediation of the extremes of exchange value and use value themselves. This intermediary situation always appears as the *economic* relation in its completeness, because it comprises the opposed poles, and ultimately always appears as a one-sidedly higher power vis-a-vis the extremes themselves; because the movement, or the relation, which *originally* appears as mediatory between the extremes necessarily develops dialectically to where it appears as mediation with itself, as the subject for whom the extremes are merely its moments, whose autonomous presuppositions it suspends in order to posit itself, through their suspension, as that which alone is autonomous. Thus, in the religious sphere, Christ, the mediator between God and humanity—a mere instrument of circulation between the two—becomes their unity, God-man, and, as such, becomes more important than God; the saints more important than Christ; the popes more important than the saints. Where it is posited as middle link, exchange value is always the total economic expression, itself one-sided against the extremes; e.g. money in simple circulation. Within capital itself, one form of it in turn takes up the position of use value against the other as exchange value. (1973, pp. 331–332)

Marx carries this analysis forward until we find the ultimate apotheosis of capitalist civilization in the form of the *financier* (capital personified). Clearly, we are here in direct contact with Hegel's syllogistic logic where the universal middle term mediates two extremes, but it leads, according to Marx, to a dictatorship of the banker. In other words, what was sacred does not undergo a desublimation into the profane but a declination and transmogrification into the diabolical, the monstrosities of vampires, werewolves, and beasts that populate bourgeois civilization. Let's take this model and develop it a bit in order to disclose the emergence of the sacred, both pure and impure, within this unconsciously syllogistic relation between Peter and Paul.

In order to relate to one another and form an embryonic society or durable association, Peter and Paul, like all of us, will have to alienate themselves.[26] Let's take a look at it from the standpoint of the sacrifices that Paul will have to make as he transforms himself from just another individual into a particular equivalent and scaffolding that Peter will cross into the sphere of valid universality. Paul's self-alienation (sacrifices) results in a splitting or division of Paul into a sacred self (the pure and simple side that reflects his calling) and the enigmatic profane residue, his undividable (individual) leftover. In other words, we have here the production of a "surplus Paul." We have two moments of Being (the passing over) and Essence or the shining of consciousness into the other's reflective facet. Of course, here resides the great chasm between the *individual* (the unalienable) and authentic social *individuality*, the "excess." But now Paul the professional is prepared to associate with Peter qua singularity. The emergent normative order that, at first, only "comes and goes" (Marx, 1976, p. 183) will crystalize over time and develop itself from a set of contingent and fluid "accidental" interactions into a "general" form that enjoys fixed durability (a social fact, i.e., external and coercive). And let us not fall into Adorno's misconception about the negativity of dialectics (1973). We know from Nelson that what is good is simply "the evil we choose to ignore," that is, everything is always, already evil (1957, p. 90).[27] Hegel was already aware of this. As Gadamer says, "The good *is* the bad. One cannot take Hegel literally enough here" (1976, p. 51).[28] Negativity is positivity (1991, p. 93). This is not so bad; we cannot conceive of any kind of rational society (as Durkheim would have it, the positive hell of community) without sacrificial practices and voluntary self-alienations whereby we become other and objective to ourselves. If we cannot "other" ourselves then we will fail to raise ourselves from the base level of utility and the path to subject-object unity (the Idea) will be foreclosed. The real problem resides in our inabilities to manage the return of the repressed materials that are pushed out in the sacrifices and self-alienations (*dyspraxia*). Alienation now becomes compounded—alienation passes over into surplus alienation and others become monstrosities. As depicted in Figure 10.1,

$$
\text{U}
$$

```
                                              Paul'
            Peter (s) ————————————— (p)
                                              Paul
                  R
```

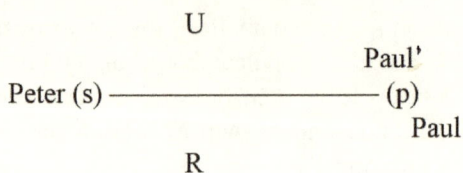

Figure 10.1. The dialectic of Peter and Paul.

purity acquires a double, impurity, and it tends to contaminate not only the particular$_i$ equivalent but also the Universal Equivalent that both Peter and Paul "stand under" in a relationship of universal identity (e.g., Human Beings).

Of central importance is that the Universal (U) possesses a double, the repressed (R). Like the mysterious disjunctive syllogism in Hegel's big logic, we have here a Universal dimension that doubles itself, however, unlike the successful bridge to objectivity we find in the *Logic*, this doubling is a failure—sacrifice does not absorb (sublate) the syllogism but marks the entrance of the diabolical that must be eradicated in order to purify the social order. The repressed (the sacred impure) colors Paul's social appearance as a particular equivalent (p) in relation to Peter's singularity (s) as well as the Big Other—it is marked with a sign of corruption, some kind of surplus negative-X (Paul plus delta Paul, or Paul') that impedes the totalization and the perfection (necessity) of the universal dimension, that is, its capacity to rule as an absolute is broken, and now, at best, we can only hope for "mutual understandings" and pragmatic consensus on the one hand, or, on the other, conflict and perhaps a death struggle between the saint and the sinner. For Peter to be pure, Paul must die and when Paul boards the train to the reeducation camp ("For the sake of consensus, comrade!") Peter will have disposed of the very ground of his own social becoming. The murder is coterminous with a suicide. Had our "Paul" been not just an individual with limited resources but a mega-institution (e.g., the bride of Christ, heaven on earth, etc.) that was capable of absorbing massive quantities of contradictions and sin, he might have destroyed himself at a more moderate rate. But, like a crusader in a time of undomesticated magic (see Riley–Smith, 2014) Peter could not punish himself (or Paul) enough.[29]

Magic and Religion

In 1947, a curious book, *Pattern for World Revolution* by an author named "Ypsilon" was published. The identity of Ypsilon is contested. It seems certain that it was the *nom de plume* of Julian Gumpertz in collaboration with at least one other person—variously attributed to "Karl Volk," Jules Humbert-Droz (Blanc 2016, p. 348), Georg Grosz, and "Johann Rindl."[30] Whoever the authors actually were, the interesting aspect for our purpose is the chapter on Lukacs as "The Sorcerer's Apprentice." Why was Lukacs merely an apprentice and not a full-blown sorcerer? Though he deftly navigated the myriad twists and turns of communist politics, Lukacs was unable to be in two places at once, that is, remaining true to his theoretical perspective while staying alive under the political regime. A "sorcerer" would have been able to pull off this trick of commanding the double.

Some objects, like money (dead people) for example, can be in two places at once. The magician, essentially, is one who can double himself and keep both aspects under control in carrying out a magical act. The generic structure of magic looks something like this: cult participants gather in a ritual setting with their implements to generate collective effervescence that is sustained and focused through mimetic enactments (verbal, gestural, etc.) designed to invoke (or evoke) a possession (the mounting of the body by the impersonal principle) and splitting or doubling of the magician into two beings: the magician and their deputy that is capable of carrying out a magical act or performance that satisfies the needs or desires of [31] a paying client (Mauss, 1972).

Possession and doubling, undergirded by the generation of group ekstasis, are the essential features. It must appear that in one version (let us call it the archaic) the magician and the deputy are two completely different beings, for example, the body of the magician and, say, a crow or a snake or, in another, (a modern variation) the magician has the capacity to be in two places simultaneously: "He was one man. He was in one place. He appeared in another" (Priest, 1995, p. 113). Possession is a modality of alienation and, here, the magician is able to alienate their being and bring the alter ego, the deputy, under external control. A perfect literary representation of the magician's powers can be found in Mann's *Mario and the Magician* (1931) or *The Prestige* (Priest, 1995). In Mann's book, the controlled double is the audience participant whereas in *The Prestige*, the double under control happens to be an identical twin. In both cases, though, the playing "client" is the large audience paying to be entertained. This is the difference between magic and "stage magic."

Where religion is altruistic and meets collective needs, the magician, through the manipulation of taboo forces, disrupts, suspends, or otherwise devalues the positive normative order (Durkheim, 1995, p. 40). Magic is egoistic and antisocial, carried out for a paying customer. As Durkheim tells us, there is no church of magic. However, both Mann's *Mario* and *The Prestige* demonstrate the "need" for magic in a society, its irrepressible aspect. Stage magic toys with taboo in such a way that it both conjures the realm of the impure while also domesticating it by rendering the demonic as a consumable product for entertainment. Normally magic is kept to the fringes of society and practitioners are figures of awe and fear (e.g., the image of the blacksmith in traditional societies) while religion and its personnel are central to the core of society.

A "magical" sociology, one dominated by the spirit of interminable negations and the reduction of all that is sacred down to the infraliminal dimension of life only makes sense as one side of a dialectical method that also positively synthesizes the transparent sacred. However, like the magician, a truly negative dialectics also results in the marginalization of praxis and this has been the fate of critical social theory and critical sociology: it has not, and probably cannot, infiltrate and subvert the capitalist order. But the moment of "magical" dialectics is also crucial. In the dialectic of freedom, reason and magic intersect in the theoretical constellation (Mann, 1948, pp. 193–194). A good theorist, like a good magician, has the capacity to be in two places at once and function as force operating from the bottom up against superior social forces. We return time and again to the classical masters such as Hegel, Marx, Weber, and Durkheim not only because they revealed the logic of impersonal social forces but are still to this day themselves irreducible intellectual forces. Thousands of talented thinkers have made their contributions to the sociological tradition but even the most noteworthy seem to fall short in decisive ways; shortcomings are not infrequently due to working one side of the street at the expense of the other. Marxism might be correct that capitalism cannot be regulated and Durkheim is undeniably correct that political Marxism is a dead end because the drive to eliminate the sacred blows up in the form of substitutionism and the totalitarian administrative state. With Hegel and Durkheim we have to contend with the "eternality" of the sacred and, as such, the relative permanence of religion[32] or, at best, the rational control of the secular sacred.

Sacred Sociology

In a dialectical sociology, concepts represent the unity of two contradictory points simultaneously. The poetic moment is the sublation of two conceptual poles into a sui generis third and the sacrifice of the prosaic for the sake of poetic power that leaps across time and space to comprehend the totality of human becoming. Sacred sociology is, if it is anything, a poetic sociology, that is, while it negates and revels in freedom it is also unified with its opposite, mediation and acceptance (Bataille, 1991, p. 158). We have for generations couched our work in terms of praxis (the unity of thought and action) or abstract theory but seldom has *poiesis* been thrust into the center of the sociological imagination. Poetic value, says Kierkegaard, comes when dialectical oppositions reflect off of one another (1954, p. 163). Sacred sociology at the level of methods amounts to the speculative reflection and interplay of both the impure and the pure, the negative and the positive, as they take possession of the profane. In isolation, neither can get the job done because interminable negation leads to *formless* ekstasis and "positivity" winds up in apologetics and one-sided (nondynamic) *resignation*. In terms of ontology and processes, sacred sociology[33] recognizes the essential and eternal aspects of social creativity and the crystallization (not necessarily reification) of these forces into sacred representations and these authorities are essential to social and therefore human life. Moving forward, sociology has to (again!) make a choice between a nominalistic framework and a socially realistic one. A sacred sociology takes society as its absolute and struggles to make this absolute transparent and to defend it against mystics, reductionists, and fanatics.

Notes

1. Social facts as sui generis realities are immanent but appear to consciousness as if they are eternal and transcendental, that is, they are reified.

2. See Gillespie (2008, p. 360) on the connections between Eventism, Zizek, and Heidegger.

3. Yes, Durkheim, the last box to be opened in the long history of synthesizing Marx with just about everything else available. This is made more plausible by the rehabilitation of Durkheim over the last 10 or 15 years.

4. Dialectics are traditionally opposed to structure and dualism (see Lichtman, 1982, p. 42) yet, in Marx, dialectics is first and foremost a method and this method is, at the outset, dualistic. It involves the crucial first step not of fetishstic splitting but analytic separation.

5. What Marx demonstrates is that the "goods" that result from production for exchange are undergirded by an underworld of brutalization and "the bad." Though individual commodities do their darndest to conceal the wrong contained in their being the repressed always returns in the forms of contradictions and class struggle.

6. During the second world war the Frankfurt School set out to locate and examine the revolutionary worker of Marxist ideology in the most advanced capitalist society in history and found exactly zero—not only was the radical worker a myth but the people most opposed to authoritarianism were also the people who were not attracted to communism (Worrell, 2008).

7. Marx makes clear in the first chapter that what is essential is wholly contained within the "mystery" of the accidental value form (1976, p. 139) whereas in the *Resultate* (which I think is an unwarranted addition) the commodity is restored to the total constellation of goods "as the mere depository of capital" (1976, p. 966) and rendered impenetrable.

8. The *Resultate* restores an excess of power that was negated in the preceding analysis, resulting in a document that amounts to a graveside eulogy for the revolution. This is the problem that Marxism cannot solve: how to negate the commodity and production for exchange while retaining the effervescence of social life above the scale of frivolity. Typically, Marxists just want to fight over commodities and capital (dragging millions into bureaucracy and gulags) while Marx's own writings on revolution and postrevolutionary society seem rather anomic and granular—lots of contingent dyadic relations unbound by any social division of labor or vocations (see Worrell & Krier, 2015; Krier & Worrell, 2017).

9. Actually, what Western Marxists have done a superb job in keeping repressed is Marx's notion that what will be restored in a postcapitalist society is humanity's *instincts* that were not relinquished due to evolutionary processes but stripped away by the powers of capital.

10. Empiricism does not know that it is also engaged in syllogistic reasoning, dialectical analysis, and sporting its own metaphysics—all these take place behind the backs, so to speak, of the naive empiricist; while empiricism believes that it is dabbling in the concrete it is actually transforming the concrete into the abstract (Hegel, 1991, pp. 76–78).

11. On the connections between value and mana see Durkheim (1995, p. 421) and especially Smith (1988).

12. The phrase "surplus value" is instructive: value is already a sui generis surplus or excess and a surplus of value is not merely more of the same but a superplus—*super* (in addition) and *plus* (more). On top of the utilizable body of the labor product is the super plus excess known as value. On the deep moral geometry of the commodity and a New General Formula for capital see Worrell (2017).

13. "Syllogism" comes from the Greek "*sullogizesthai*" which gives us "*logizesthai*" (to reason) which is itself rooted in the Greek *logos* (reason). The syllogism is the dance of Logos.

14. This would be the merely boring and "subjective form" of the syllogism (Hegel, 1969, p. 669).

15. "Like the judgment, the syllogism is also in the world (and not merely in our heads and our thought). Yet where the judgment is merely a thing in the outside world, it seems more appropriate to grasp the syllogism as an event. "The several forms of syllogism make themselves constantly felt in our cognition. If anyone, when awakening on a winter morning, hears the creaking of the carriages on the street, and is thus led to conclude that it has frozen hard in the night, he has gone through a syllogistic operation—an operation which is every day repeated under the greatest variety of conditions. . . . In reality, however, it is the very world of this early morning in Berlin so many years ago which has performed a syllogism" (Jameson, 2009, p. 97).

16. "Society acquires the status of a 'syllogism' characterized by cooperation and interdependence of parts. . . . Although Hegel ascribes to the state the status of a syllogism . . . clarifying within it moments of 'particularity,' 'singularity,' and 'universality,' Durkheim's modelling of organic solidarity can be reconstructed as a syllogism. In his classic work on religion, Durkheim comes very close to the conception of society as a syllogism, when he writes: 'If society is something *universal* in relation to the individual, it is none the less an *individuality* itself, which has its own personal physiognomy and idiosyncrasies; it is a *particular* subject and consequently *particularizes* whatever it thinks of . . . These 'moments' constitute the path through which the complex web of mediations leads to the idea of 'unity-in-difference.' Clearly, Durkheim lacks the systematic character of Hegel's exposition. Yet, organic solidarity may be reconstructed as the culmination of this logical configuration since it preserves unity (solidarity) and difference (the freedom of the individual in his or her right to a *particular* life and vocation)" (Gangas, 2007, p. 325).

17. The individual sciences are "an immense prosyllogism, and, unless the utility of these sciences is denied and it's asserted that there's nothing more in the most complex formulas they arrive at than there is in the definitions

that serve as their base, the utility of syllogistic reasoning must be recognized" (Durkheim, 2004, p. 197). A prosyllogism is "an argument composed to two syllogisms such that the conclusion of the former becomes the major premise of the latter. We could also have a prosyllogism composed of multiple syllogism such that the conclusion of each one of them becomes the major premise of the one following" (Durkheim, 2004, p. 196).

18. "For in Hegel the concept of speculation, removed from its terminological shell, means in turn none other than life forced to turn inward . . ." (Adorno, 1993, p. 91).

19. "At the core of the historical-materialist conception of social determination . . . is the idea, no matter how qualified, that social phenomena are *causally* related to one another. One of the primary challenges for explanation is thus to go beyond the mere description of how social forms are constructed to identification of the complex hierarchy of causal forces and principles" (Mohanty 1997: 51–52). Another point worth drawing out here is that explanation has to go beyond not only descriptions but beyond explanation itself. To explain something is to do no more than make things intelligible by spreading or flattening them out (the Latin *explānāre* = to spread out flat, flatten out, to make intelligible). Reason includes explanations but it goes beyond this in composing the right causal narrative; reason is the voice of the absolute made intelligible for itself.

20. It is the norm to find individuals fetishizing things like nations or parties, etc., whereby they arrive at "wrong" (Hegel) syllogistic structures whereby particularities ("America" or "Christian") assume the position of universals within a syllogism such that things like an international order or a brotherhood of humanity cease to exist as anything more than balderdash cooked up by talkers. For the cosmopolitan "talker" types, universality may mean anything up to the genus *Homo* whereas for the provincial "doer" civilization is synonymous with nation. "The conviction that what we call civilization is a national product has entered people's minds to the extent that it has become a foundation for territorial claims. It is almost comic to see some ill-known, ill-studied folkloric elements being invoked during the [Versailles] Peace Conference as evidence that such and such nation should extend here or there, on the grounds that we can still find there such or such shape of house or some bizarre custom" (Mauss, 2006, p. 43). Territorial disputes between nations is literally a dispute over the syllogistic middle term. "The same thing happens in diplomatic negotiations . . . for example, when various powers lay claim to one and the same piece of land. In this case, the right of inheritance, the geographic lie of the land, the descent and language of its inhabitants, or any other ground, can be brought up as a *medius terminus*" (Hegel, 1991, p. 261).

21. That Hegel reconstructed syllogistic reasoning and took it so seriously is a wonder considering the underlying basis of modern scientific thought is

nominalistic and hostile to the syllogism, rooted as it is in the hypothesis (see Gillespie, 2008, pp. 19–43).

22. See my embryonic attempt to reconstruct a "new" general formula (Worrell, 2017).

23. "In this conception, *the universal* is not metaphysically opposed to *the particular* and *the individual* as a mental abstraction to a sensually given fullness of phenomena . . ." (Ilyenkov, 1960, n.p.).

24. "That which is common to many individuals or returns constantly in the individual does not have to be more stable, eternal, or deeper than the particular. The scale of types is not identical to the scale of significance" (Horkheimer & Adorno, 1972, p. 220).

25. Paul's act of sacrifice, the self-alienation that constituted his particularity for Peter, is doubled (compound alienation). Once Peter identifies the gap in the symbolic order with Paul's defects he will love him to death.

26. They will, with Goethe, say "Ich erscheine mir selbst immer mehr und mehr geschichtlich" (in Dye, 2004, p. 169). When Goethe says that "I appear to myself more and more historically" (my translation) he is pointing to this transformation of the singular into an ego and alter-ego in a temporal process (it's not a once-and-for-all event) but an ongoing relation between ego, alter, other ego, and "transcendental" other.

27. If the good is ignored evil, evil, by contrast, is merely surplus good—what is viscousness but excess virtuousness? Evil is the good we can't get enough of. Good and evil are merely polarities of an "excess in two contrary directions" (Bataille, 1991, p. 78).

28. "And pious action we do sugar o'er / The devil himself" (Shakespeare, 2001, p. 64). "Present day psychology is increasingly turning back to Spinoza's idea that things are good because we like them, rather than that we like them because they are good. . . . An act is socially evil because it is rejected by society" (Durkheim, 1984, p. 40). "When all tend to debauchery none appears to do so. He who stops draws attention to the excess of others, like a fixed point" (Pascal, 1941, p. 124). "Irreligion is simply a word for other people's religion; immorality, a term for behavior different from our own" (Hook, 1934, n.p.).

29. "In the eleventh and twelfth centuries the ascetic temper underwent a revival which was like an intellectual storm . . . . It was connected with the demonism and fetishism which had taken possession of the Christian church in the ninth and tenth centuries" (Sumner, 1940, p. 514).

30. Schueller (1951) and Martin Jay (1996) indicate that the book was authored by Gumpertz and the artist Robert Rindl while Ulmen (1978) clarifies that "Karl Volk" and "Johann Rindl" were pseudonyms for Rindl. As you may recall, Gumpertz was an early member of the "Frankfurt School" and the one-time husband of Hede Massing, the famous communist spy. Gumpertz fell out with the communists and went on to a career in finance (Worrell 2006).

31. See Durkheim (1995) on the magician and how magic compares to religion.

32. In simple terms, religion is nothing other than the "administration of the sacred" (Caillois, 1959, p. 20).

33. The poet (*poeta*) was originally one who created, a maker, and in the Old Occitan language, *poeta* meant authority (Oxford English Dictionary).

References

Adorno, T. (1973). *Negative Dialectics*. Translated by E. B. Ashton. New York, NY: Continuum.

Adorno, T. (1993). *Hegel: Three studies*. Translated by Shierry Nicholsen. Cambridge, MA: MIT Press.

Bataille, G. ([1962] 1991). *The Impossible*. Translated by Robert Hurley. San Francisco, CA: City Lights.

Benjamin, W. (1999). *Selected Writings*, vol. 2, part 2. Translated by Rodney Livingstone. Cambridge, MA: Harvard University Press.

Blanc, P. (2016). *Lenin and the Revolutionary Party*. Chicago, IL: Haymarket.

Bosanquet, B. ([1923] 1965). *The Philosophical Theory of the State*. New York, NY: St Martin's.

Bouglé, C. ([1926] 1970). *The Evolution of Values*. New York, NY: Augustus M. Kelley.

Caillois, R. (1959). *Man and the Sacred*. Urbana, IL: University of Illinois Press.

Davis, M. (1906). Gabriel Tarde: An essay in sociological theory. Doctoral dissertation, Columbia University, New York, NY.

Dewey, J. (1946). *Problems of Men*. New York, NY: Philosophical Library.

Durkheim, E. ([1893] 1984). *The Division of Labor in Society*, Translated by W. D. Halls. New York, NY: The Free Press.

Durkheim, E. ([1912] 1995). *The Elementary Forms of Religious Life*. Translated by Karen E. Fields. New York, NY: Free Press.

Durkheim, E. (1973). *On Morality and Society*. Chicago, IL: The University of Chicago Press.

Durkheim, E. (2004). *Durkheim's Philosophy Lectures: Notes from the Lycée de Sens Course, 1883–1884*. Edited by N. Gross & R.A. Jones. Cambridge, UK: Cambridge University Press.

Durkheim, E., & Mauss, M. ([1903] 1963). *Primitive Classification*. Translated and edited by Rodney Needham. Chicago, IL: University of Chicago Press.

Durkheim, E., & Mauss, M. ([1913] 2006). Note on the concept of civilization. In N. Schlanger (ed.), *Marcel Mauss: Techniques, Technology and Civilization* (pp. 35–39). New York, NY: Durkheim Press/Berghahn.

Dye, E. (2004). *Love and Death in Goethe: "One and Double."* Rochester, NY: Camden House.

Findlay, J. (1958). *Hegel: A Re-examination.* New York, NY: Collier.

Gadamer, H. (1976). *Hegel's Dialectic.* New Haven, CT: Yale University Press.

Gangas, S. (2007). Social ethics and logic: Rethinking Durkheim through Hegel. *Journal of Classical Sociology,* 7(3): 315–338.

Gillespie, M. (2008). *The Theological Origins of Modernity.* Chicago, IL: University of Chicago Press.

Goethe, J. ([1808] 1961). *Faust.* Translated by Walter Kaufmann. New York, NY: Anchor Books.

Harms, J. (1981). "Reason and social change in Durkheim's thought." *Pacific Sociological Review* 24(4): 393–410.

Hegel, G. ([1812] 1969). *Science of Logic.* Translated by A. V. Miller. Atlantic Highlands, NJ: Humanities Press International.

Hegel, G. ([1830] 1991). *The Encyclopedia of Logic, Part I of the Encyclopedia of Philosophical Sciences with the Zusätze.* Translated by T. F. Geraets, W. A. Suchting, & H. S. Harris. Indianapolis, IN: Hackett Publishing.

Hegel, G. ([1821] 1991). *Elements of the Philosophy of Right.* Translated by H. B. Nisbet. Cambridge, UK: Cambridge University Press.

Hook, S. (1934). Karl Marx and Moses Hess. Retrieved from www.marxistsfr. org/history/etol/writers/hook/1934/12/hess-marx.htm

Horkheimer, M., & Adorno, T. ([1944] 1972). *Dialectic of Enlightenment.* Translated by John Cumming. New York, NY: Continuum.

Ilyenkov, E. (1960). *Dialectics of the Abstract and the Concrete in Marx's Capital.* Retrieved from www.marxists.org/archive/ilyenkov/works/abstract

Jameson, F. (2009). *Valences of the Dialectic.* London, UK: Verso.

Jay, M. ([1973] 1996). *The Dialectical Imagination.* Berkeley: University of California Press.

Kierkegaard, S. (1954). *Fear and Trembling* and *Sickness unto Death.* Translated by Walter Lowrie. Princeton, NJ: Princeton University Press.

Krier, D., & Worrell, M. (2017). The organic composition of the big mother. *Continental Thought and Theory,* 1(4), 636–652.

Lichtman, R. (1982). *The Production of Desire.* New York, NY: The Free Press.

Mann, T. (1931). *Mario and the Magician.* Translated by H. T. Lowe-Porter. New York, NY: Knopf.

Mann, T. (1948). *Doctor Faustus,* Translated by H. T. Lowe-Porter. New York, NY: Knopf.

Marx, K. ([1857] 1973). *Grundrisse.* Translated by Martin Nicolaus. New York, NY: Penguin.

Marx, K. ([1867] 1976). *Capital: A Critique of Political Economy, Vol. 1.* Translated by Ben Fowkes. New York, NY: Penguin.

Mauss, M. (1972). A General Theory of Magic. New York, NY: Norton.

Mohanty, S. (1997). Literary Theory and the Claims of History. Ithaca, NY: Cornell University Press.

Nelson, L. ([1917] 1957). Critique of Practical Reason. Frankfurt, Germany: Verlag.

Pascal, B. (1941). Pensées. Translated by W. F. Trotter. New York, NY: Modern Library.

Piketty, T. (2014). Capital in the Twenty-First Century. Cambridge, MA: Belknap/Harvard.

Priest, C. (1995). The Prestige. New York, NY: Valancourt.

Richman, M. (2002). Sacred Revolutions. Minneapolis: University of Minnesota Press.

Riley–Smith, J. (2014). The Crusades. London and New York, NY: Bloomsbury.

Royce, J. (1969). The Basic Writings of Josiah Royce, vol. 1. Edited by J. J. McDermott. Chicago, IL: The University of Chicago Press.

Schueller, G. (1951). The Politburo. Stanford, CA: Stanford University Press.

Shakespeare, W. (2001). Hamlet. New York, NY: Penguin.

Smith, D. (1988). Authorities, deities, and commodities: Classical sociology and the problem of domination. PhD dissertation, University of Wisconsin–Madison.

Smith, D. (2016). Capitalism's future: Self-alienation, self-emancipation and the remaking of critical theory. In D. Krier & M. P. Worrell (eds.), Capitalism's Future (pp. 11–62). Leiden, UK: Brill.

Smith, T. (1993). Dialectical Social Theory and Its Critics. Albany, NY: SUNY Press.

Sumner, W. ([1906] 1940). Folkways. New York, NY: Mentor.

Wilson, E. ([1940] 1967). To the Finland Station. New York, NY: New York Review of Books.

Worrell, M. (2006). The other Frankfurt school. Fast Capitalism, 2(1). Retrieved at www.uta.edu/huma/agger/fastcapitalism/2_1/worrell.html

Worrell, M. (2009a). A faint rattling: A research note on Marx's theory of value. Critical Sociology, 35(6): 887–892.

Worrell, M. (2009b). The cult of exchange value. Fast Capitalism, 5(2). Retrieved at www.uta.edu/huma/agger/fastcapitalism/5_2/Worrell5_2.html

Worrell, M. (2017). The sacred and the profane in the general formula for capital: The octagonal structure of the commodity and saving Marx's sociological realism from professional marxology. In D. Krier & M. P. Worrell (eds.), The Social Ontology of Capitalism (pp. 75–119). New York, NY: Palgrave Macmillan.

Worrell, M., & Krier, D (2015). Atopia awaits! A critical sociological analysis of Marx's political imaginary. Critical Sociology, 44(2), 213–239. Retrieved at doi.org/10.1177/0896920515620476

Ypsilon (1947). Pattern for World Revolution. Chicago, IL: Ziff-Davis.

Contributors

James Block is a professor of political science at DePaul University, Chicago. He has taught in the political science department and honors program at DePaul University (USA) for three decades and has written for journals of opinion and the *New York Times*. His books include *A Nation of Agents: The American Path to a Modern Self and Society* (2002) and *The Crucible of Consent: American Child Rearing and the Forging of Liberal Society* (2012). Jim writes on American national formation, contemporary political culture, and the crisis of the republic for *Huffington Post*. He currently leads workshops throughout the world with youth and social activists on the dynamic of social change.

Harry F. Dahms is professor of sociology, director of the Center for the Study of Social Justice, and co-chair of the Committee on Social Theory at the University of Tennessee-Knoxville. He is editor of *Current Perspectives in Social Theory* and director of the International Social Theory Consortium. He is the author of *The Vitality of Critical Theory* and has published in *Sociological Theory*, *Current Perspectives in Social Theory*, *Comparative Sociology*, *Critical Sociology*, *Basic Income Studies*, and other journals, along with chapters in encyclopedias and handbooks. Currently, he is finishing a book, *Modern Society as Artifice: Critical Theory, the Dynamics of Alienation, Anomie, the Protestant Ethic, and the Logic of Capital*.

Dan Krier is professor of sociology at Iowa State University. He writes on political economy, critical theory, and comparative-historical sociology. Books include *Speculative Management: Stock Market Power and Corporate Change* (2005), *NASCAR, Sturgis and the New Economy of Spectacle* (with Bill Swart, 2016), *Capitalism's Future: Alienation, Emancipation, and*

Critique (co-edited with Mark P. Worrell, 2016), *and The Social Ontology of Capitalism* (co-edited with Mark P. Worrell, 2017). Krier has published articles in *American Journal of Economics and Sociology, Current Perspectives in Social Theory, Critical Sociology, Fast Capitalism*. He is the organizer of *Symposia for New Directions in Critical Social Theory* and was co-organizer of the 2016 International Social Theory Consortium.

Christian Lotz is a professor of philosophy at Michigan State University. His main research area is post-Kantian European philosophy. Recent book publications include *The Art of Gerhard Richter: Hermeneutics, Images, Meaning* (2015); *The Capitalist Schema: Time, Money, and the Culture of Abstraction* (2014); *Christian Lotz zu Karl Marx: Das Maschinenfragment* (2014); *Ding und Verdinglichung: Technik- und Sozialphilosophie nach Heidegger und der Kritischen Theorie* (editor, 2012); and *From Affectivity to Subjectivity: Revisiting Edmund Husserl's Phenomenology* (2008). Lotz has published numerous articles in critical Marxist thought, aesthetics, and continental philosophy. His current research interests are in Marx, aesthetical realism, and contemporary European political philosophy.

Patrick Murray is professor of philosophy and the John C. Kenefick Faculty Chair in the Humanities at Creighton University. He is author of *Marx's Theory of Scientific Knowledge* (1988) and editor of *Reflections on Commercial Life* (1997). A collection of his essays on Marx, *The Mismeasure of Wealth: Essays on Marx and Social Form*, was published in 2016 in the book series of the journal *Historical Materialism*. He is working on a book on Marxian social theory under the title *Capital's Reach: How Capital Shapes and Subsumes*. His research interests center on the relation between capitalism and modern philosophy and include the British empiricists, Hegel, Marx, and the Frankfurt School. With Jeanne Schuler, he is completing a book of essays entitled *False Moves: Basic Problems with Philosophy*; it is a study of the ways in which dualisms between the subjective and the objective breed skepticism.

Jeanne Schuler is associate professor of philosophy at Creighton University. She has published in the history of philosophy and critical theory, including articles on Hume, Kant, Hegel, Marx, Arendt, Iris Murdoch, and Habermas. She has written on philosophy and film, including essays on Stanley Kubrick and Woody Allen. Schuler is a former co-coordinator of the Radical Philosophy Association. She has begun publishing a series of articles on Hegel's criticisms of modern philosophers, including Locke, Hume, the French Enlightenment thinkers, and Spinoza. With Patrick Murray, she is completing a book of essays entitled *False Moves: Basic Problems with Philosophy*, a study of the ways in which dualisms between the subjective and the objective promote skepticism.

Tony Smith is professor of philosophy at Iowa State University. He has published widely in Marxist philosophy and political economy. His books include *Beyond Liberal Egalitarianism: Marxism and Normative Social Theory in the Twenty-First Century* (2018), *Globalisation: A Systematic Marxian Account* (2005), *Technology and Capital in the Age of Lean Production: A Marxian Critique of the "New Economy"* (2000), *Dialectical Social Theory and Its Critics: From Hegel to Analytical Marxism and Postmodernism* (1993), *The Role of Ethics in Social Theory: Essays from a Habermasian Perspective* (1991), and *The Logic of Marx's Capital: Replies to Hegelian Criticisms* (1990). He recently co-edited *Hegel's Logic and Marx's Capital: A Reexamination* (with Fred Moseley, 2015).

Michael J. Thompson is Professor of Political Theory in the Department of Political Science at William Paterson University (USA). His books include *The Politics of Inequality* (Columbia University Press, 2007), *The Domestication of Critical Theory* (Rowman and Littlefield, 2016), *The Specter of Babel: A Reconstruction of Political Judgment* (SUNY Press, 2020) as well as the forthcoming, *Twilight of the Self: Cybernetic Society and the Eclipse of Autonomy* (Stanford University Press).

Mark P. Worrell is associate editor of the journal *Critical Sociology*. Mark's work has appeared in *Telos*, *Critical Sociology*, *Fast Capitalism*, *Current Perspectives in Social Theory*, *Logos*, *Rethinking Marxism*, and elsewhere. His most recent books include *The Sociogony*, *Terror*, and a co-edited volume (*Capitalism's Future*) along with Dan Krier. Mark is currently working on a large-scale synthesis of the classical and critical traditions of sociological theory. The second volume of this project, *Disintegration: Suicide and the Moral Geometry of Collective Consciousness* is forthcoming in the Studies in Critical Social Sciences series at Brill.

Index

absolute, 223, 302, 309

abundance, 215

Adorno, Theodor W., 2, 64, 66, 68, 70, 77, 130, 187, 194

aesthetics, 3–5; in Brecht, 65; and contradiction, 81–82; critical, 63, 79; Marxist, 65, 72; realist, 65, 66, 71, 81; *see* alienation effect; *see* mimesis; *see* photographs; *see* visibility

Agamben, Giorgio, 4

alienation, 225, 311

alienation effect, 79; and distance between work and audience, 72, 79, 80–82; and irony, shock, surprise 81; poetic, 81

Amidon, Kevin, 1

Angerer, Kathrin, 86

Arendt, Hannah, 79, 221

Arnold, Matthew, 195

art and philosophy, 93–95

art, and emotions, 71–72, 84; as critical self-consciousness of society, 70–71; as praxis, 66; and rationality, 71–72, 84; and sympathy, 79; *see* aesthetics; *see* Brecht; *see* mimesis; *see* montage; *see* society

Arthur, C., 89, 105, 118n.36, 119

Atwood, Margaret, 214

Austen, Jane, 3, 19, 90, 112n.1, 214

authoritarianism, 301, 302

authority, 301, 302

Autobiography of John Stuart Mill, 114n.17

Bakhtin, Mikhail, 2

Balzac, Honore, 3, 19, 90, 214

Barthes, Roland, 64, 66

Bataille, George, 117n.32, 119

beauty, 186–195, 202–207

Becker, George, 109, 117n.32, 120

Becker, Howard, 221

Bellamy, Edward, 214

Benjamin, Walter, 2, 64, 68, 71, 77; Arcades Project, 68

Bentham, Jeremy, 97, 99, 102, 114n.19, 121

Berlau, Ruth, 83, 84

Beuys, Joseph, 66

Billy Budd, 214

Bitzer, 96, 102–104, 113n.7, 114n.13, 117n.31

Blackpool, S., 95, 103, 106–108

Block, James, 11–12

Bounderby, J., 92–93, 95–96, 101, 104, 107, 114n.15, 117n.33, 118n.35

Brecht, Bertolt, 6–7, 67–83; and GDR, 76–77; *Mother Courage*, 82;